ROBERT BURNS AND TRANSATLANTIC CULTURE

Ashgate Series in Nineteenth-Century Transatlantic Studies

Series Editors: Kevin Hutchings and Julia M. Wright

Focusing on the long nineteenth century (ca. 1750–1900), this series offers a forum for the publication of scholarly work investigating the literary, historical, artistic, and philosophical foundations of transatlantic culture. A new and burgeoning field of interdisciplinary investigation, transatlantic scholarship contextualizes its objects of study in relation to exchanges, interactions, and negotiations that occurred between and among authors and other artists hailing from both sides of the Atlantic. As a result, transatlantic research calls into question established disciplinary boundaries that have long functioned to segregate various national or cultural literatures and art forms, challenging as well the traditional academic emphasis upon periodization and canonization. By examining representations dealing with such topics as travel and exploration, migration and diaspora, slavery, aboriginal culture, revolution, colonialism and anti-colonial resistance, the series will offer new insights into the hybrid or intercultural basis of transatlantic identity, politics, and aesthetics.

The editors invite English language studies focusing on any area of the long nineteenth century, including (but not limited to) innovative works spanning transatlantic Romantic and Victorian contexts. Manuscripts focusing on European, African, US American, Canadian, Caribbean, Central and South American, and Indigenous literature, art, and culture are welcome. We will consider proposals for monographs, collaborative books, and edited collections.

Robert Burns and Transatlantic Culture

SHARON ALKER
Whitman College, USA

LEITH DAVIS
Simon Fraser University, Canada

and

HOLLY FAITH NELSON
Trinity Western University, Canada

Routledge
Taylor & Francis Group

LONDON AND NEW YORK

First published 2012 by Ashgate Publishing

Published 2016 by Routledge
2 Park Square, Milton Park, Abingdon, Oxon OX14 4RN
711 Third Avenue, New York, NY 10017, USA

First issued in paperback 2017

Routledge is an imprint of the Taylor & Francis Group, an informa business

British Library Cataloguing in Publication Data
Robert Burns and transatlantic culture. – (Ashgate series in nineteenth-century transatlantic studies)
   1. Burns, Robert, 1759–1796 – Appreciation – North America. 2. Burns, Robert, 1759–1796 – Appreciation – South America. 3. Burns, Robert, 1759–1796 – Political and social views. 4. Collective memory and literature – North America. 5. Collective memory and literature – South America.
   I. Series II. Alker, Sharon-Ruth. III. Davis, Leith, 1960–. IV. Nelson, Holly Faith, 1966–
   821.6-dc23

Library of Congress Cataloging-in-Publication Data
Robert Burns and transatlantic culture / edited by Sharon Alker, Leith Davis, and Holly Faith Nelson.
     p. cm. — (Ashgate series in nineteenth-century transatlantic studies)
   Includes bibliographical references and index.
   ISBN 978-1-4094-0576-4 (hardcover: alk. paper)
   1. Burns, Robert, 1759–1796—Criticism and interpretation. I. Alker, Sharon. II. Davis, Leith, 1960–. III. Nelson, Holly Faith, 1966–.
   PR4338.R553 2012
   821'.6—dc22

                                                                     2011040918

ISBN 13: 978-1-138-10781-6 (pbk)
ISBN 13: 978-1-4094-0576-4 (hbk)

To our transatlantic mothers and grandmother:

Nancy (Lintott) Davis
Marion Paterson Wilson (Dunn) Henderson
and
Agnes Fleming (MacDonald) Dunn

Contents

List of Figures

List of Tables

Notes on Contributors

Sharon Alker, Associate Professor of English at Whitman College, has published articles in *The European Romantic Review, Lumen, Eighteenth-Century Scotland, Eighteenth-Century Fiction*, and *Studies in English Literature* and has contributed to several book collections on the literature of the long eighteenth century. With Holly Faith Nelson, she has published an article on Shakespeare's treatment of the Scot in *Macbeth*, three articles on the life and works of James Hogg, and co-edited *James Hogg and the Literary Marketplace: Scottish Romanticism and the Working-Class Author* (2009).

Fiona A. Black, former Associate Dean of the Faculty of Management and a professor in the School of Information Management at Dalhousie University, was a co-editor of the major three-volume project funded by SSHRC, *History of the Book in Canada*, issued in both French and English. Her research in print culture and digital humanities has been published in such journals as *Papers of the Bibliographical Society of Canada, Paradigm*, and the award-winning *Book History* (1998). Her latest SSHRC-funded research investigates international migrations of print workers and their ensuing contributions to colonial print cultures.

Rhona Brown has been a lecturer in Scottish Literature at the University of Glasgow since 2006. Her research focuses on eighteenth-century Scottish literature, with particular emphasis on the work of Robert Fergusson and the eighteenth-century periodical press. She is currently preparing a monograph on Fergusson's corpus in the context of Edinburgh's periodical culture, which explores the poet's literary relationship with his "patron" journal, Walter Ruddiman's *Weekly Magazine, or Edinburgh Amusement*. In addition to her work on Fergusson, she has published work on Robert Burns, Laurence Sterne, and James Hogg.

Gerard Carruthers is General Editor of the new multi-volume Oxford University Press edition of the works of Robert Burns (to be published from 2012). He is the author of *Robert Burns* (2006), editor of the *Edinburgh Companion to Robert Burns* (2009), and co-editor, with Johnny Rodger, of *Fickle Man: Robert Burns in the 21st Century* (2009). He is Professor of Scottish Literature since 1700 at the University of Glasgow, where he is also Co-Director of the Centre for Robert Burns Studies and Principal Investigator of the AHRC funded major project, "Editing Robert Burns for the 21st Century."

Robert Crawford is Professor of Modern Scottish Literature at the University of St Andrews. His most recent collection of poems, *Full Volume* (2008), was shortlisted for the T.S. Eliot Prize. His *The Bard: Robert Burns, A Biography*

(2009) won the Saltire Society Scottish Book of the Year Award. His other books include a history of Scottish literature, *Scotland's Books* (2007, 2009), and he has edited with Christopher MacLachlan *The Best Laid Schemes: Selected Poetry and Prose of Robert Burns* (2009).

Leith Davis is a professor in the Department of English and Director of the Centre for Scottish Studies at Simon Fraser University. She is the author of *Acts of Union: Scotland and the Literary Negotiation of the British Nation, 1707–1830* (1998) and *Music, Postcolonialism and Gender: The Construction of Irish National Identity, 1724–1874* (2005); and she is co-editor (with Ian Duncan and Janet Sorensen) of *Scotland and the Borders of Romanticism* (2004).

Carole Gerson is a professor in the Department of English at Simon Fraser University and a Fellow of the Royal Society of Canada. She has published extensively on Canadian literary history and was a co-editor of the major three-volume project, *History of the Book in Canada*, issued in both French and English. Her ongoing research on early Canadian women writers has resulted in two books on Pauline Johnson and various publications about many other authors, including Susanna Moodie, Marshall Saunders, and L.M. Montgomery. Her latest book, *Canadian Women in Print, 1750–1918* (2010), unites her interests in book history and women's writing.

Nigel Leask is Regius Professor of English Language and Literature and Head of the School of Critical Studies at Glasgow University. His most recent book is *Robert Burns and Pastoral: Poetry and Improvement in Late-Eighteenth Century Scotland* (2010), joint winner of the Saltire Research Book of the Year prize for 2010. He is currently editing the *Collected Prose of Robert Burns* for the new AHRC-funded Oxford *Collected Works of Robert Burns* (general editor Gerard Carruthers). He is also the author of numerous books and articles on Romantic literature, including *The Politics of Imagination in Coleridge's Critical Thought* (1988), *British Romantic Writers and the East: Anxieties of Empire* (1992), *Curiosity and the Aesthetics of Travel Writing, 1770–1840: "From an Antique Land"* (2002); the editor of *S.T. Coleridge's Biographia Literaria* (1997) and *Romantic Period Travel Narratives of Spanish America and the Caribbean*, the fourth volume of *Travels, Explorations and Empires: Writings from the Era of Imperial Expansion 1770–1835* (2001). He is co-editor of *Land, Nation and Culture, 1740–1840: Thinking the Republic of Taste* (2004) and *Romanticism and Popular Culture in Britain and Ireland* (2009).

Susan Manning is Grierson Professor of English Literature and Director of the Institute for Advanced Studies in the Humanities at the University of Edinburgh. She works on the Scottish Enlightenment and Romantic periods, and on Scottish-American literary relations, the topic of her comparative studies *The Puritan-Provincial Vision* (1990) and *Fragments of Union* (2001). She is one of the editors of *The Edinburgh History of Scottish Literature*, 3 vols (2006), and has co-edited the first *Transatlantic Literary Studies Reader* (2007). She convenes the STAR (Scotland's Transatlantic Relations) Project (www.star.ac.uk) and is currently completing a book on transatlantic character; it contains two chapters on Burns.

Kirsteen McCue is Head of Scottish Literature and Co-Director of the Centre for Robert Burns Studies at the University of Glasgow. She has published widely on Romantic song culture. She is currently completing an edition of James Hogg's *Songs by the Ettrick Shepherd* and a companion volume of Hogg's *Contributions to Musical Collections and Miscellaneous Songs* for the Stirling/South Carolina Research Edition of *The Collected Works of James Hogg.* She will then edit Robert Burns's songs for George Thomson for the new Oxford University Press edition of the *Collected Works of Robert Burns*.

Carol McGuirk teaches English at Florida Atlantic University and (in a non-Burnsian vein) is an editor of the journal *Science Fiction Studies*. She has published numerous articles on Scottish poetry as well as *Robert Burns and the Sentimental Era* (1985; rpt 1997), *Critical Essays on Robert Burns* (1998), and *Selected Poems of Burns* (1993). Her book near completion, *Poet Burns*, considers literary and cultural contexts for his early self-fashioning as a poet as well as Burns's impact on later song-writers (Lady Nairne, Stephen Foster) and poets (Wordsworth, Byron, Clare, and Hugh MacDiarmid).

Holly Faith Nelson, Professor of English and Co-Director of the Gender Studies Institute at Trinity Western University, has co-edited five volumes, including *James Hogg and the Literary Marketplace: Scottish Romanticism and the Working-Class Author* (2009). She has published widely on Scottish, Welsh, and English writers of the seventeenth and long eighteenth centuries. With Katherine Ellison, of Illinois State University, she co-founded and co-edits *Digital Defoe: Studies in Defoe & His Contemporaries* (http://english.illinoisstate.edu/digitaldefoe/).

Andrew Noble is a graduate of Aberdeen and Sussex Universities. He was also a Junior Research Fellow at Peterhouse, Cambridge. His teaching career was entirely at Strathclyde University, where he was for a time Head of the English Literature Section. He specialized in teaching American Literature and Romanticism. Before his retirement, he was the Convener of the Scottish/Irish Initiative. His published research is mainly in Scottish literature and film. His extensive writings on Burns culminated in the publication of his joint-edition with Patrick Scott Hogg of *The Canongate Burns* (2001–2003). He has recently been appointed Honorary Visiting Senior Lecturer in the School of English, Queen's University, Belfast.

Murray Pittock is Bradley Professor of English Literature and Head of College and Vice-Principal (Arts) at the University of Glasgow; he has previously held senior positions at the universities of Manchester, Edinburgh and Strathclyde. His books on redefining the writing, culture, politics, and society of the long eighteenth century in the British Isles are cited and set worldwide: most recently *Scottish and*

Irish Romanticism (2008). During the last five years, he has won five grants to work on redefining national Romanticisms, including three from the UK Arts and Humanities Research Council: currently he is Principal Investigator of the AHRC Beyond Text programme grant, Robert Burns: Inventing Tradition and Securing Memory, and is associate general editor of the Oxford Collected Burns. In 2006, he co-organized the Scottish Romanticism in World Literatures conference at the University of California, Berkeley, which marked a watershed in the recognition of a distinct Scottish Romanticism and its global encounters.

Michael E. Vance is Professor of History at Saint Mary's University, Halifax, Nova Scotia. His research focuses primarily on early nineteenth-century Scottish emigration and settlement, but he also has an interest in the nature of Scottish overseas identity. In 1990 he co-edited, with Marjory Harper, *Myth, Migration and the Making of Memory: Scotia and Nova Scotia*. His most recent publication, undertaken with co-editor Scott McLean and published by Dundurn Press, is an annotated edition of the unpublished memoir of Rev. William Wye Smith, a nineteenth-century Scottish-Canadian poet, newspaperman, and congregational clergyman.

Susan Wilson, a Canadian scholar of Scottish and Irish ancestry, holds a PhD in Scottish Poetry. Her fascination with Gaelic language, culture, and traditions was first nurtured by her maternal grandfather, a native *Gàidhlig* speaker born in Inverness, Scotland. She holds a BA Hons in Celtic Studies through the University of Toronto. Her MA thesis compared the portrayal of Gaelic culture in the work of Máirtín Ó Cadhain and John Synge. Edinburgh University Press recently published her first book: *The Correspondence Between Hugh MacDiarmid and Sorley MacLean: An Annotated Edition* (2010).

Acknowledgements

A number of agencies and individuals played a critical role in supporting the production of *Robert Burns and Transatlantic Culture*. We would like to thank the Social Sciences and Humanities Research Council of Canada for its financial contribution to the project. The Centre for Scottish Studies at Simon Fraser University, the Vancouver Burns Club, Scotland Development International, the English Departments of Simon Fraser University and Trinity Western University, the Dean of the Faculty of Arts and Social Sciences and the Vice-President Academic of Simon Fraser University, the Dean of the Faculty of Humanities and Social Sciences of Trinity Western University, and the Provost of Whitman College also provided financial support to allow contributors of this volume to meet in Vancouver in 2009 to engage in meaningful scholarly conversions on Robert Burns in a transatlantic context before undertaking to publish the volume. SFU's Rapid Response Publication Fund contributed toward the copyediting and indexing of this volume.

We are indebted to our graduate and undergraduate students Laura E. Ralph, Emma Pink, Cameron Glen Fediuk, Ingerlise van der Eyk, and Aakanksha Veenapani, our exceptional research assistants on this project; and we greatly appreciate the Abshire Research Scholar award administered by Whitman College that allowed us to fund one of these assistants. Our thanks are also due to the librarians at Whitman College, Simon Fraser University, and Trinity Western University for their professionalism and patience, in particular Sharon Vose and Shirley Lee at Trinity Western University's Norma Marion Alloway Library and Dalia Corkrum, Jen Johnson, and Roger Stelk at Whitman College's Penrose Library. We would also like to thank Michael Paulus, in particular, for his generous assistance in collating the archival material used in our cover image, and Penrose Library for permission to use the material.

We would also like to acknowledge the influence of the late Professor Douglas S. Mack, whose passion for Scottish literature, and generosity of spirit as a scholar, was a constant inspiration. We are also most grateful to Alan Alker, Crystal and Amethyst Lo, Rob McGregor and Ciaran, Devin, and Nia Davis-McGregor, and Russell, Caleb, and Faith Nelson for their unremitting encouragement and support.

Introduction

"Ae ['Electric'] Spark o' Nature's Fire": Reading Burns Across the Atlantic

Leith Davis, Holly Faith Nelson, and Sharon Alker

The January 1870 edition of *Stewart's Literary Quarterly*, one of a number of periodicals devoted to art and culture that sprung up in the years after 1867 to educate the citizens of the new Dominion of Canada, featured an article on "Burns's Natal Day" for the 111th anniversary of the birth of the Scottish poet.[1] The writer, a Reverend M. Harvey from the colony of Newfoundland, writes of Burns, "In his poetry he has embodied whatever is greatest, strongest, most distinctive and most ennobling in the Scottish genius and character, and interpreted the national heart as it has never been interpreted before."[2] Harvey suggests, however, that "it would be a mistake to suppose that love and admiration of Burns are confined to the Scottish land and race."[3] On the contrary, "His fame is every year deepening and extending, and rapidly becoming world-wide."[4] America, in particular, Harvey notes, which "has given a home to so many Scotchmen, has taken their national bard to her heart, and cherishes his memory as one of the most precious inheritances bequeathed to her by one of the Old Land."[5] Harvey's paean to Burns rises to a crescendo as he effuses: "The poetry and songs of Burns link together nationalities and bind together human hearts, [like] the electric spark that flashes along the Atlantic cable, through 'the dark unfathomed caves of ocean,' and unites the Old World with the New."[6]

The "Atlantic cable" to which Harvey refers, a 2,000-mile telegraph line between Valentia Island in Ireland and Heart's Content in his own Newfoundland, had become operational in July 1866. Hailed as the "umbilical cord with which

---

[1]   Rev. M. Harvey, "Burns's Natal Day," *Stewart's Literary Quarterly*, 3/4 (January 1870): 425–42 (428–9). *Stewart's Literary Quarterly* (1868–1872) was published by George Stewart, Jr., in Saint John, New Brunswick; see Micheline Cambron and Carole Gerson, "Authors and Literary Culture," in Yvan Lamonde, Patricia Lockhart Fleming, and Fiona A. Black (eds), *History of the Book in Canada, Volume Two: 1840–1914* (Toronto, 2005), pp. 119–34 (p. 127).

[2]   Harvey, "Burns's Natal Day," p. 425.

[3]   Ibid., p. 426.

[4]   Ibid., p. 427.

[5]   Ibid., p. 428. Harvey later observes that "the sale of his [Burns's] works is, at present, double that of Byron's and forty times as great as the poetry of Scott" (p. 440).

[6]   Ibid., pp. 428–9.

the old world is reunited to its transatlantic offspring,"[7] it became one of the Victorians' major contributions to the "time-space compression" associated with "the condition of postmodernity."[8] For Reverend M. Harvey, the work of Burns is equally as efficacious as the transoceanic cable in eliminating spatial distance in this newly mobile world. In Harvey's commentary, Burns's "spark o' Nature's fire" transmutes into an "electric spark" of dots and dashes traveling the course of the Atlantic, ensuring continuity between communities separated by the wide ocean. Burns may have been born into "dark unfathomed" origins, but by 1870 he was a well-known modern technology sparking off an electronic version of Humean sympathy between the nations on either side of the Atlantic Ocean.[9]

Harvey's comments in *Stewart's Literary Quarterly* provide a valuable entry point into the concerns of this collection. First and foremost, Harvey's observations focus attention on a different kind of Burns than has been previously examined, a Burns who is centered not in Ayrshire, but in the interchange of ideas on the Atlantic periphery. Harvey's comments also suggest both the malleability and continuity of Burns as a cultural phenomenon; his fame develops teleologically, "deepening and extending" in a "world-wide" context. Moreover, Harvey intimates that the "electric spark" of Robert Burns, like the Atlantic cable to which he is likened, travels in both directions. Burns may be an "inheritance" from "the Old World to the New," but he also sends a message back the other way. The essays in this volume follow a similar trajectory. Detailing the ways in which Burns and his writing were reconfigured and invested with new meaning in transatlantic contexts, they also revise critical perceptions of Burns's work, connecting it not only to local and national concerns, but also to the transatlantic circulation of ideas. They indicate that though Burns's *oeuvre* has remained relatively fixed over the last 250 years, barring a few new discoveries and debates over particular poems, his meaning as a social signifier has been extremely unstable, as he has been conscripted to serve numerous perspectives and ideologies—conservative and radical, popular and academic. At the same time, they gesture toward the way that transatlantic perceptions of Burns also doubled back to influence the construction of the Burns phenomenon in Great Britain. In mapping these various processes, *Robert Burns and Transatlantic Culture* has a double focus. It aims to shift Burns—and Scottish Studies in general—beyond the purview of a national framework. Simultaneously, it suggests the ways that transatlantic studies can benefit from a consideration of the example of Robert Burns.

As Murray Pittock points out in *Scottish and Irish Romanticism*, academic study of Burns plummeted after 1945.[10] It is only in relatively recent years

---

    [7]   John Bigelow (U.S. Minister to France) to William H. Seward (U.S. Secretary of State), qtd. in Andrew Herod, *Geographies of Globalization: A Critical Introduction* (Malden, 2009), p. 40.

    [8]   See David Harvey, *The Condition of Postmodernity* (Oxford, 1990), especially Part III: "The Experience of Time and Space."

    [9]   For more on Burns as a globalizing force, see Ann Rigney, "Embodied Communities: Commemorating Robert Burns, 1859," *Representations*, 115/1 (2011): 71–101.

    [10]   Murray Pittock, *Scottish and Irish Romanticism* (Oxford, 2008), p. 6.

that Burns has been considered a fit object for academic inquiry. In this newly revivified form, he has been customarily represented as a working-class writer who imagined a Scottish identity in an era of British Romantic nationalism.[11] While this perspective has yielded much fruitful commentary on Burns, it has also placed geographical and theoretical limitations on the way his work is understood. While the 250th anniversary of his birth saw an upsurge of attention, as demonstrated by new biographies and collections of essays,[12] only two critical works examine Burns beyond his national borders: Murray Pittock's *Robert Burns in Global Culture* and Frank Ferguson and Andrew R. Holmes's *Revising Robert Burns and Ulster*.[13] Strangely missing from this renewal of critical energy is a study that considers Burns from a transatlantic perspective, despite his considerable impact in the Americas and his suitability as a subject for the rapidly expanding field of transatlantic studies.[14]

As the essays in this volume suggest, Burns is a particularly useful figure for this field of study because transatlantic impulses in his work take multiple and

---

[11]   See, for example, Fiona Stafford, *Starting Lines in Scottish, Irish, and English Poetry: From Burns to Heaney* (Oxford, 2000); Fiona Stafford, "Scottish Poetry and Regional Literary Expression," in John Richetti (ed.), *The Cambridge History of English Literature, 1660–1780* (Cambridge, 2005), 340–362; Hamish Mathison, "Robert Burns and National Song," in David Duff and Catherine Jones (eds), *Scotland, Ireland, and the Romantic Aesthetic* (Lewisburg, PA, 2007), pp. 77–92.

[12]   Gerard Carruthers (ed.), *The Edinburgh Companion to Robert Burns* (Edinburgh, 2009); Robert Crawford, *The Bard: Robert Burns, A Biography* (London and Princeton, 2009); Patrick Scott Hogg, *Robert Burns: The Patriot Bard* (Edinburgh, 2009); Nigel Leask, *Robert Burns and Pastoral: Poetry and Improvement in Late Eighteenth-Century Scotland* (Oxford, 2010).

[13]   Murray Pittock (ed.), *Robert Burns in Global Culture* (Lewisburg, 2011); Frank Ferguson and Andrew R. Holmes (eds), *Revising Robert Burns and Ulster: Literature, Religion and Politics, c. 1770–1920* (Dublin, 2009).

[14]   Looking back over the recent history of transatlantic studies, Laura M. Stevens observes, "Few terms have spread across the academic landscape with the speed and thoroughness of *transatlantic*" ("Transatlanticism Now," *American Literary History*, 16/1 [Spring 2004]: 93–102 [93]). In his introduction to a special edition of *Romantic Circles' Praxis Series*, entitled *Sullen Fires Across the Atlantic: Essays in Transatlantic Romanticism*, Lance Newman documents the evolution of the field, noting that scholarship on transatlanticism has developed from early concerns regarding an "anxiety of influence" on the part of writers from the Americas to a more balanced sense of "the diversity of literary expression in English along the Atlantic Rim" and the "multiple episodes and vectors of ideological exchange" (Newman, "Introduction: A History of Transatlantic Romanticism," http://www.rc.umd.edu/praxis/sullenfires/intro/intro.html). Susan Manning and Andrew Taylor discuss some of the critical paradigms that are particularly germane to the field in their anthology *Transatlantic Literary Studies: A Reader* (Edinburgh and Baltimore, 2007). Joel Pace's extensive "Towards a Taxonomy of Transatlantic Romanticism(s)" (*Literature Compass*, 5/2 [2008]: 228–91), works to classify "existing research as well as outlines categories for future scholarship, based on where knowledge of the field runs threadbare and where there is the most pressing need for scholarly study" (p. 228).

complex forms. First, Burns himself expressed interest in transatlantic dealings, both personally and poetically. His comments in poems and letters suggest that he was well aware of, and responsive to, global affairs and the ways in which transatlantic matters intersected with local and national concerns. Writing to James Burness on 21 June 1783, for example, Burns connects the high price of food and the decrease in the industries of "Silk, Lawn & Carpet Weaving" as well as the destruction of the "trade in the Shoe w[ay]" to "the unfortunate beginning of this American war, & its … unfortunate conclusion."[15] In the "Address of Beelzebub," he speculates that it is the oppressive policies of Highland landlords that encourage their tenants to emigrate "to the wilds of CANADA, in search of that fantastic thing—LIBERTY,"[16] while in "The Twa Dogs," the dog with the most intimate knowledge of the corruptions of the Scottish class system, Caesar, is a transatlantic émigré, having been brought to Kyle from the shores of Newfoundland, the land of codfishing. A transatlantic awareness permeates Burns's poetic and political understanding from its very beginning.

Of particular interest in Burns's own transatlantic considerations, of course, is his relationship with and attitude toward the darker side of global commerce: what Paul Gilroy describes as the trade in "sugar, slaves and capital" that was being placed in the public eye even as Burns first started writing.[17] Burns's comments on the prospect of going to Jamaica are disturbingly sketchy. In June 1786, he wrote a number of letters informing his friends and acquaintances that he was preparing to depart his "native soil" for a more promising situation "among the mountains of Jamaica."[18] As he wrote to the shoemaker David Brice, "the Ship is on her way home that is to take me out to Jamaica; and then, farewel [*sic*] dear old Scotland, and farewel [*sic*] dear, ungrateful Jean, for never, never will I see you more!"[19] In his autobiographical letter to Moore, he reflects back on his motivations for heading to "the torrid zone" just at the time when he put his poetry into print: "it was a delicious idea that I should be called a clever fellow, even though it should never reach my ears—a poor negro-driver—or, perhaps, a victim to that

---

[15]   *The Letters of Robert Burns*, J. De Lancey Ferguson (ed.), 2nd edn, G. Ross Roy (ed.) (2 vols, Oxford, 1985), vol. 1, p. 19. He also notes that the "great trade of smuggling carried [on] along our coasts" has alleviated some of the distress for some individuals, but that it is "destructive to the [in]terests of the kingdom at large" and is carried out "at the expence of [ou]r Morals" (vol. 1, p. 19).

[16]   *The Poems and Songs of Robert Burns*, James Kinsley (ed.) (3 vols, Oxford, 1968), vol. 1, p. 255.

[17]   Paul Gilroy, *There Ain't No Black in the Union Jack: The Cultural Politics of Race and Nation* (London and New York, 1987), p. 157.

[18]   Burns, *Letters*, Ross Roy (ed.), vol. 1, p. 37.

[19]   Ibid., vol. 1, p. 39. He continues, "You will have heard that I going [*sic*] to commence Poet in print; and tomorrow, my works go to the press.—I expect it will be a Volume about two hundred pages.—It [is ju]st the last foolish action I in[tend] to do; and then turn a wise man as fast as possible" (vol. 1, p. 39).

inhospitable clime, and gone to the world of spirits."[20] In "On A Scotch Bard Gone
to the West Indies," he projects this blend of love, composition, and leaving onto
a third-person *"rhyme-composing billie"* as he rails against the circumstances that
have prompted the poet to seek his fortune abroad.[21] Such cavalier comments on
the part of Burns have enlisted much criticism. Gerard Carruthers has proposed
that the slave trade is a "humanitarian blind-spot" for Burns, for example.[22] In this
volume, Murray Pittock suggests a productive way of moving beyond the question
of whether or not Burns condoned slavery in the British colonies by investigating
the varying understandings of the idea of slavery in Burns's time.[23]

Whether or not Burns supported emancipation, his transatlantic writings did
participate in other strands of what Felicity Nussbaum calls "the connective tissues
of resistance" operating in Europe during his lifetime.[24] Burns's anonymously
published poem, "A Man's a Man for a' that," is the best known example of his
radical notions. Less well known are the international connections of what is seen
as his most nationalist poem, "Robert Bruce's March To Bannockburn," which was
written in response to the Treason Trials of 1793.[25] Such poems suggest Burns's
alignment with the transnational circulation of radical ideas popularized by the
Friends of the People and late eighteenth-century corresponding societies. But
Burns's first connection with radical thought was a transatlantic one as he engaged
with the events and consequences of the American Revolution. Burns's first political
poem, as Robert Crawford points out, was "When Guilford Guid," which makes
direct reference to central events in and elements of the War of Independence,
including the Boston Tea Party and the Declaration of Independence.[26] Burns's
"Ode for General Washington's Birthday" also reiterates the hope that Scotland
can reinvigorate its sense of identity and agency by looking across the Atlantic to
American vigor and energy.

This collection does not reject the importance of considering Burns's writings
in terms of national boundaries, for as Akira Iriye argues, "To speak of movements
across national boundaries is to continue to recognize the saliency of nations,

---

[20] Ibid., p. 145.

[21] *The Poems and Songs of Robert Burns*, Kinsley (ed.), vol. 1, p. 239.

[22] Gerard Carruthers, qtd. in Andy McSmith, "Robert Burns: Socialist Hero or Just
a Scottish Social Climber?" *The Independent UK*, 24 January 2008; see also Gerard
Carruthers, "Robert Burns and Slavery," *Drouth*, 26 (Winter 2008): 21–6.

[23] More work needs to be done in reading Burns in the context of global flows and
the routes of diaspora, while acknowledging Scotland's complex relationship to the Black
Atlantic. For a useful resource on this subject, see Ian Whyte, *Scotland and the Abolition of
Black Slavery, 1756–1838* (Edinburgh, 2006).

[24] Felicity A. Nussbaum, editorial introduction to *The Global Eighteenth Century*
(Baltimore, 2003), p. 10.

[25] See Nancy Moore Goslee, "Contesting Liberty: The Figure of William Wallace in
Poems by Hemans, Hogg, and Baillie," *Keats-Shelley Journal*, 50 (2001): 35–63 (36).

[26] See Robert Crawford's essay in this volume.

whether or not their frontiers are being broached by individuals or cultures."[27] The continued assertion of nation in Burns's own corpus and in the way the poet and his canon has been configured in other nations to refine national identity elsewhere, would make such a posture counter-productive. Rather, the collection seeks to situate the "mythic" pull of the nation as the location of individual and collective identity within a larger context, and it reads Burns's concern with local and national affairs in the context of what Lance Newman calls "the transatlantic circulation of literary nationalism."[28] A transatlantic focus in Burns studies can work to encourage a reconceptualization of Burns—and of the Scotland of his time—within the wider processes of globalization that were being renegotiated in the wake of the Seven Years' War, the American Revolution, and the forging of the Second British Empire.

As well as offering a new perspective on the impact of "oceanic interculture" on Burns and his nation, this collection also provides a fuller perspective on the creation and transatlantic circulation of Burns as a figure of cultural memory both in terms of the dissemination and reception of his works and in terms of his own reconfiguration in the Americas. Burns and his corpus are a particularly useful means by which transatlantic scholars can trace the detailed dissemination of culture as it crosses and recrosses the Atlantic, finding fruitful soil elsewhere. Édouard Glissant describes the rhizome, a concept developed by Gilles Deleuze and Félix Guattari and increasingly used to explain transatlantic relations, as "an enmeshed root system, a network spreading either on the ground or in the air, with no predatory rootstock taking over permanently."[29] Deleuze and Guattari promote mapping as a means to engage with the rhizome, discarding in the process earlier genealogical concepts of tracing that privilege descent.[30] As they suggest,

> [t]he map … fosters connections between fields, the removal of blockages on bodies without organs, the maximum opening of bodies without organs onto a place of consistency. It is itself a part of the rhizome. The map is open and connectable in all of its dimensions; it is detachable, reversible, susceptible to constant modification. It can be torn, reversed, adapted to any kind of mounting, reworked by an individual, group, or social formation. It can be drawn on a wall, conceived of as a work of art, constructed as a political action or as a mediation.

---

[27]   Akira Iriye, "Internationalizing International History," in Thomas Bender (ed.), *Rethinking American History in a Global Age* (Berkeley, 2002), 51.

[28]   Newman, "Introduction: A History of Transatlantic Romanticism."

[29]   Édouard Glissant, *Poetics of Relation*, Betsy Wing (trans.) (Ann Arbor, 1997), p. 11. For an example of how the rhizomatic works in practice, see Susan Manning's essay in this volume, particularly page 158.

[30]   Foucault, of course, would argue that genealogies are far less cohesive than Deleuze and Guattari's description suggests. He writes that "we should not be deceived into thinking that this heritage is an acquisition, a possession that grows and solidifies; rather it is an unstable assemblage of faults, fissures, and heterogeneous layers …" (qtd. in Joel Pace and Matthew Scott [eds], *Wordsworth in American Literary Culture* [New York, 2005], p. 5).

Perhaps one of the most important characteristics of the rhizome is that it always has multiple entryways.[31]

Burns's cultural work and refashioned concepts of Burns himself, as this collection demonstrates, are reworked by a wide variety of communities and individuals, emptied of earlier geographic connotations, invested with new local and regional meanings, and then dispersed in various directions to ultimately regenerate in a new form.

As cultural objects traverse the Atlantic and map onto North American culture through multiple points of entry, they are reassembled anew. As the rhizome model suggests, this is not a tidy process. Paul Giles has expressed concern with the rhizomorphic model used by Paul Gilroy, noting that "it is at times curiously reminiscent of the writings of Enlightenment *philosophes*, with its vision of how a seamless cosmopolitan world of exchange might gradually supersede 'overintegrated conceptions of pure and homogeneous culture'."[32] Our intention in this collection is to foreground the fragmentation and dissonance of the numerous remediated shoots that emerge in the Americas, recognizing Giles's emphasis on the importance of "[a] critical transnationalism [that] can probe the significance of cultural jagged edges, structural paradoxes, or other forms of apparent incoherence."[33] Thus Burns, the man and his work, will be reformulated as radical or conservative, idealistic or pragmatic, Canadian or American in ways that are relevant to specific contexts in the Americas, each new formulation fruitfully creating the potential for new roots and shoots.

There is growing recognition that a keen focus on the dissemination and re-creation of the work of an individual artist can be reconfigured beyond issues of influence to engage at a deeper level with the nodes of connection themselves. Joel Pace and Matthew Scott's edited collection *Wordsworth in American Literary Culture* takes such an approach, seeking to transform an understanding of cultural migration by paying close attention to the way the corpus of a single writer enters a new geographic space. Such approaches to the rhizomatic spread of a single artist may gesture towards what Deleuze and Guattari call a Nomadology, a history that focuses on a nomadic form of geographic movement rather than emerging from a "sedentary point of view."[34] While still centered on one poet, the focus of study is not merely the work itself, but the manner in which it crosses borders and oceans, changing its identity as it feeds on different nutrients in new soil. Burns's

---

[31]   Gilles Deleuze and Félix Guattari "Introduction: Rhizome," in Manning and Taylor (eds), *Transatlantic Literary Studies: A Reader*, pp. 226–31 (p. 230).

[32]   Paul Giles, *Transatlantic Insurrections: British Culture and the Formation of American Literature, 1730–1860* (Philadelphia, 2001), p. 9; the inset quotation is from Paul Gilroy's *The Black Atlantic: Modernity and Double Consciousness* (1993; London, 2002), p. 31.

[33]   Paul Giles, "Transnationalism and Classic American Literature," in Manning and Taylor (eds), *Transatlantic Literary Studies: A Reader*, pp. 44–52 (p. 47).

[34]   Deleuze and Guattari, "Introduction: Rhizome," p. 230.

popularity and thus the rapid and broad spread and transmutation of his songs, poetry, and even poetic identity to multiple regions in North America make him a particularly fertile locus for such a study, as it allows us to explore in detail many points in which culture regenerates. The "spark o' Nature's fire" is, more accurately, multiple sparks that traverse space in different ways, a poem in textual form, a song brought over in the memory of a migrant, an aphorism taken from a poem, a concept of the poet inherited from a biography or artistic rendition, each of which forms different connections once it arrives in Canada, the United States or Latin America.

Thus, as the essays collectively suggest, the image of Burns as a poet of "universal truth" was not merely initiated in Scotland and then transported to America.[35] Rather, it developed as a consequence of the fact that he found currency not just in Scotland and Great Britain but also abroad, particularly in the United States, which was a growing site of print publication and dissemination. By focusing on one figure, this collection offers to transatlantic studies a specific case study of the circuits of exchange between Great Britain and the Americas during the late eighteenth and early nineteenth centuries and beyond. It charts the development and differentiation of Burns's global reputation as it traces the specific routes that Burns's works took in the transatlantic circuit. This refashioning of Burns, as recorded here, significantly impacted the development of the national literatures of the Americas. Universal themes in Burns's work, such of those of loss, liberty, and nostalgia, were reinvigorated in innovative and sometimes surprising ways in the emergent cultures of the New World. Moreover, this book will extend transatlanticism to explore the importance of "Atlantic double-crossing," as it is to a great extent Burns's reputation in the New World that has assured his continuing currency as a global commodity in the Old World.[36]

Robert Burns and Transatlantic Culture consists of five roughly chronological sections, each of which focuses on a different aspect of Burns in the Americas. Part 1 begins by drawing attention to Burns's own awareness and discussion of transatlantic concerns in his work. Part 2 addresses the material aspects of Burns's early publication in America and Canada, discussing the contexts in which readers first encountered the Scottish bard and the dissemination of his works in the New World print networks. Part 3 shifts the focus to the question of Burns's reception in the Americas. As the essays in this section suggest, Burns came to serve as a signifier whose meaning shifted according to the particular sign system in which he appeared. Thus, he became a convenient symbol for both radical and conservative impulses in Canada and the United States. Part 4 attends to the afterlives of Burns in cultural memory, focusing on his refashioning in individual emigrants' lives and transatlantic national cultures. The essays in the final section of the book consider

---

[35]   James Ballantine (ed.), *The Chronicle of the Hundredth Birthday of Robert Burns*, (Edinburgh and London, 1859), p. 232.

[36]   See Robert Weisbuch, *Atlantic Double-Cross: American Literature and British Influence in the Age of Emerson* (Chicago, 1986).

the non-literary ways in which Burns was represented in a transatlantic context, focusing on his memorialization in statues, music, and new technologies.

In Part 1, Murray Pittock's and Andrew Noble's essays highlight the ways in which Burns's work reflects the crossing and double-crossing of ideas, thus revising critical understandings of him as primarily a Scottish poet. In "Slavery as a Political Metaphor in Scotland and Ireland in the Age of Burns," Pittock situates Burns's sometimes competing references to slavery in the contemporary debates taking place in Europe and the Americas on abolition, voluntary and involuntary servitude, and tyranny and republicanism. Pittock pays particular attention to the application of the trope of slavery to Irish and Scottish Catholics, who then appropriate the literary figure for their own political ends. For Pittock, Burns is, in many respects, a man of his age on these subjects, inasmuch as his writings envision slavery both as a form of "voluntary moral inferiority" and as a state of "unconditional victimhood" (30). In "Burns, Scotland, and the American Revolution," Noble also reads the poetry and epistolary prose of Burns in light of its engagement with contemporary ideological debates in a transatlantic context. Noble establishes the varied influence of the American Revolution on politically radical and conservative Scots near the end of the eighteenth century to provide a backdrop against which to interpret Burns's conviction that Scotland's future political character and prospects were utterly dependent on that revolution. Though Noble envisions Burns as a political idealist, he affirms that Burns eventually came to recognize that the British had failed to adopt what in his view was the ideal political formation operating in the American Republic.

In Part 2, the transatlantic approach to Burns adopted by this volume is directed at determining how Burns himself became a transatlantic commodity both during his lifetime and after his death. Crucial to this project is the obtaining of data regarding the circulation of his works in a transatlantic context. In "Tracing the Transatlantic Bard's Availability," Fiona Black provides a book history perspective on Burns in Canada. Black details the roles played by publishers, printers, booksellers, general merchants, wholesalers, and libraries in advertising and making available volumes of Burns's songs and poems in both urban and rural locations in the British colonies in North America (which became the new nation of Canada in 1867) from the late eighteenth to the early nineteenth centuries. She finds that the importation patterns of other Scottish Enlightenment works and select pre-1820 volumes of British poetry to British North America shed significant light on the ready availability of Burns's writings in "hundreds of … Canadian towns and villages" in this period (69).

Without an accurate picture of what was transported to American shores, we cannot begin to understand how Burns was consumed and reframed across the Atlantic Ocean. In "'Guid black prent': Robert Burns and the Contemporary Scottish and American Periodical Press," Rhona Brown maintains that despite the political nature of a number of his poems, especially those on America, the works of Burns printed and reprinted in periodicals in Edinburgh and Philadelphia during his lifetime are chiefly those that spoke to common human experiences. The Burns that thereby emerges in these periodicals is the divinely inspired Ayrshire Bard who speaks to the emotional and spiritual needs of his fellow creatures rather than a political apologist intent on defending a democratic or republican ideal.

In turning to the subject of Burns's reception in the Americas, we need to be sensitive to the fact that poetry, unlike sugar or china tea sets, carries with it a particular affect and is interpreted in distinct ways by those consuming it on foreign shores. Burns's inflection by particular readers is addressed in the four essays that make up Part 3 of this collection. While in agreement with Rhona Brown's assessment of the less than radical Burns transported to America in the late eighteenth century, Gerard Carruthers explores in "Burns's Political Reputation in North America" the evolution of political readings of his works in America and Canada in the nineteenth century. Carruthers first considers why Scottish and Irish radicals contemporary with Burns who left their homeland and reinvented themselves on American soil failed to write in a "Burnsian idiom" (97). He then explores the American impulse to read Burns in more radical political terms from the 1830s onwards, while acknowledging that a more conservative Romantic engagement with Burns as "the bard of nature and of feeling" remained entrenched even in the works of the "American Burns" John Greenleaf Whittier (92). Carruthers concludes by comparing the nineteenth-century reception of Burns in America with that in English Canada, only to find that the "version of Burns" that often manifests in the works of Canadian poets, especially Alexander McLachlan, is "stripped of both formal and ideological nuance" to make it "palatable to the identity of empire" (97).

In "America's Bard," Robert Crawford argues that Burns's appeal to American readers was inevitable, given the Bard's advocacy of democracy, equality, and independence in his verse and, in certain works, "Pro-revolutionary sympathies" (101). Burns's Scottish dialect did not temper his charm for American readers, and Crawford maintains, in fact, that Burns's politics of language deeply resonated with American politicians and poets in the nineteenth century, notably Thomas Jefferson, Abraham Lincoln, Frederick Douglass, and Walt Whitman. This is not to say that all Americans "translated" Burns in the same way. As Crawford notes, for Whitman, Burns was a middle-class democrat whom he engaged in an intensely embodied way, while for Longfellow, Burns had a "misty ephemerality" (110). Regardless of the distinct version of Burns that appears in their work, suggests Crawford, American writers from the nineteenth century onward are invigorated by the energy of Burns's vernacular voice. Crawford concludes with the hope that all American readers of this century will attend and attune themselves to Burns's "fellow critturly, democratic accent" in defense of the "social union" of Nature that humans in Burns's time and ours have bitterly "broken" (116).

In "The Presence of Robert Burns in Victorian and Edwardian Canada," Carole Gerson and Susan Wilson examine the Canadian inflections of Burns, noting that his popularity in nineteenth-century Canada is attributable to the nostalgia for the homeland felt by many Scottish immigrants, the desire of middle-class Scottish-Canadians to establish a firm ethnic identity, and the appeal of Burns to Canadian social reformers across class lines. Adopting an interdisciplinary approach, Gerson and Wilson explain the lasting social, political, and cultural legacy of Burns in Canada, attending closely to his presence in nineteenth-century Canadian literature, the treatment of his works in Canadian schoolbooks, and the role played by his words and ideas in social and political communities in Canada. In their essay, we see the multiple and often contradictory positions that Burns came to occupy in transatlantic locations even within the same national boundaries.

This study of transatlantic Burns is necessarily skewed toward the northern hemisphere. Nigel Leask's essay, "Robert Burns and Latin America," attempts to understand what is at stake in this imbalance by examining Burns's lack of popularity in South America. Leask begins with the notable facts that no Castilian or Portuguese translations of Burns's poems were published until the twentieth century and that no Latin American press has ever published a volume of only Burns's works. Yet Spanish translations of two of Walter Scott's novels, for example, were shipped to and circulated in Latin America in the 1820s. Leask suspects that Burnsian Scots dialect delayed the production and publication of Spanish and Portuguese translations of his poems, which would also explain why existing translations often paraphrase or interpret rather than directly translate Burns's poems. Although he recognizes that Burns's verse "had zero, or at least minimal, influence on nineteenth-century Latin American poetry and literary criticism" (132), Leask opens up four new avenues for reading Burns in a South American context when he reflects on Burns's knowledge of, and occasional references to, South America; considers the cultural role played by Burns among Scottish emigrants to (and their descendants in) Latin America; probes connections between Burns and the embryonic "cause of Latin American independence" (136); and reads rural Burns poems alongside those composed by Latin American poets about the same time. Leask also opens up a space to investigate transatlantic disconnections and their aftermath. In their account of the rhizome, Deleuze and Guattari note that "a rhizome may be broken, shattered at a given spot, but it will start up again on one of its old lines or on new lines. You can never get rid of ants because they form an animal rhizome that can rebound time and again after most of it has been destroyed."[37] Here it is evident that Burns's choice of linguistic register may have had a stunting effect that caused a temporary disruption in the spread of culture, but also that a broken root system can regenerate given the right conditions.

Together, the essays in Part 3 suggest ways in which the study of Burns in a transatlantic context can encourage a fine-tuning of the geographic scope of transatlantic studies, as it acknowledges the fact that Burns was received differently in each of the nations (and the various regions within them) that constitute the transatlantic. As the work of Robert Crawford and Murray Pittock suggests, Burns has already figured importantly in the reconception of English literature, helping to devolve a focus on writing emerging from a London-based hegemony

---

[37] Deleuze and Guattari, "Introduction: Rhizome," pp. 227–8.

into a study of the literature of "Four Nations" with distinct political and cultural histories.[38] By taking into account the different situations in Canada, the United States, and the South American nations, Burns studies can help steer transatlantic studies away from the fate of becoming American studies in new clothes.

The essays in Part 4 of the collection, "Robert Burns and Transatlantic Cultural Memory," examine the multiple ways in which Burns was remembered in a North American context. In her article "Plenitude, Scarcity and the Circulation of Cultural Memory," Ann Rigney argues for "the need to conceptualize cultural memory, not as merely derivative of individual psychology, but in terms of a 'working memory' ... that is constructed and reconstructed in public acts of remembrance and [that] evolves according to distinctly cultural mechanisms."[39] She grants a special place to "artistic media in crossing and helping to re-define the borders of imagined memory communities" by virtue of the fact that they are more "mobile" and "exportable" than other forms of representation: "Certain stories travel and, increasingly within the modern world, they do so beyond the boundaries of the immediate community and beyond national boundaries. As such they may be instruments par excellence in the 'transfer' of memories from one community to another, and hence as mediators between memory communities."[40] The essays in this section suggest that Robert Burns came to serve as a key "mediator between memory communities" in Scotland and in North America.[41] By considering Burns from a transatlantic perspective, however, they read him not just as an "instrument" that effected the "transfer" of memories from Scotland to the Americas but as a fluid entity whose various translations have flowed both ways to feed new creative energies and encourage membership in new kinds of memory communities.

In "Robert Burns's Transatlantic Afterlives" and "Burns and Aphorism; or, Poetry into Proverb: His Persistence in Cultural Memory Beyond Scotland," Susan Manning and Carol McGuirk respectively theorize the role played by "memory and imagination" in Burns's transatlantic afterlives (151). Manning reads the figure of Burns in America through the filter of Colin McArthur's notion of the "Scottish discursive unconscious" and Toni Morrison's conception of "rememory" to chart Burns's "transposed or dis-located" American afterlife. She emphasizes the need to attend to the "rhythms, echoes, voices and images" of Burns that surface in America in ways "beyond the reach of documentary trace" (151). In Burns's self-fashioning, she suggests, we find the germ of the politically and socially inflected figure(s) of the Bard carried by many Scottish emigrants to the New World. McGuirk draws on Jacques Derrida's theory of aphoristic transmission in her account of Burns's voiceprint in American culture. She envisions Burns as

---

[38]   See Robert Crawford, *Devolving English Literature*, 2nd edn (Edinburgh, 2000), pp. 88–110; and Pittock, *Scottish and Irish Romanticism*, Ch. 6.

[39]   Ann Rigney, "Plenitude, Scarcity and the Circulation of Cultural Memory," *Journal of European Studies* 35/1 (2005): 11–28 (11).

[40]   Ibid. p. 26.

[41]   Ibid.

both mediating and mediated, exploring the absorption of Scottish folk aphorisms in his poetry and examining the aphoristic circulation of portions of his poems in American print and oral culture, from the fiction of Laura Ingalls Wilder to the lyrics of Sting. For McGuirk, Burns is reconstituted in America—where bits and pieces of his texts are routinely recycled—as an archive of folk wisdom, an identity Burns encouraged but also complicated (174).

In "The Robert Burns 1859 Centenary: Mapping Transatlantic (Dis)location," Leith Davis suggests that the sense of connectedness between Burns enthusiasts, so celebrated in the 250th anniversary celebrations, has its conceptual origins in the 100th anniversary celebration of Burns's birth. While Burns was viewed before 1859 as a link between different locations abroad to which Scots had traveled or emigrated, it was the centenary that consolidated Burns as a global modern phenomenon, encouraging links among centers around the world. Davis draws attention, however, to the various ways in which that reverence was inflected in different geopolitical sites. The commemorations of Burns effected very different sorts of national and political affiliations depending on which side of the Atlantic they took place.

The essays in Part 5 of the volume, "Remediating Burns in Transatlantic Culture," suggest that a transatlantic approach to Burns invites a particular focus on the issue of mediation. As recent studies by Maureen McLane and Steve Newman have shown, the rise of new media is making us examine the presence of other media within the story of the rise and naturalization of print over the last 300 years.[42] The case of Burns stands out in this process of rethinking media in the Romantic age, as his career was built from several kinds of media and multi-medial convergences. His early poems were written out and sent to friends, an indication of the importance of manuscript culture even toward the end of the eighteenth century. His phenomenal popularity among the gentry, if we are to believe early commentators, was as much due to his conversation at their houses as to the publication of his poems. His rise to fame corresponded with increasingly inexpensive book production and mass-marketing techniques as well as an increasing readership, phenomena which William St Clair has recently discussed.[43] Finally, Burns's turn to song culture in the later years of his life marks a challenge to our idea of the primacy of print in the Romantic era. The three essays in the final section, therefore, take account of the various mediations of Burns's work and his life story as it traveled across the ocean. Print culture obviously has played an important part in the transatlantic mediation of Burns. But so have other media. Attending to the mediations of Burns leads us beyond a focus on Burns as an author with a fixed *oeuvre* to a consideration of the way in which

---

[42]   Maureen McLane, *Balladeering, Minstrelsy, and the Making of British Romantic Poetry* (Cambridge, 2008); and Steve Newman, *Ballad Collection, Lyric and the Canon: The Call of the Popular from the Restoration to the New Criticism* (Philadelphia, 2007).

[43]   William St Clair, *The Reading Nation in the Romantic Period* (Cambridge, 2004).

his works and the much-revised and re-interpreted story of his life were circulated in communications networks.[44]

In "Burns in the Park: A Tale of Three Monuments," Michael Vance addresses the significance of the Burns monuments erected in three Canadian cities— Toronto, Halifax, and Vancouver—in the first two decades of the twentieth century. He presents a thorough history of the groups that promoted and provided funding for these monuments, details the physical locales in which they were erected, evaluates their iconography, and describes the societal context and transatlantic nature of the ceremonies in which they were unveiled. While he recognizes that the statues shed light on the reception of an "egalitarian" Burns in Canada, Vance reminds us that they are also part of a "collective colonial legacy" which "not only speaks to the influence of British imperialism, but more specifically to the dispossession of indigenous peoples" (232).

In "'Magnetic Attraction': The Transatlantic Songs of Robert Burns and Serge Hovey," Kirsteen McCue examines the transatlantic Burns project undertaken by the twentieth-century American composer Serge Hovey in the 1950s, a project he continued to work on until his death in 1989. Hovey's work, including the unpublished manuscript "The Retrieval and Performance of the Songs of Robert Burns," serves for McCue as a remarkable case study of a modern American composer's intellectual and artistic engagement with the Scottish musical tradition out of which Burns's songs emerged. The transatlantic nature of this enterprise is further complicated, McCue shows, when Hovey works alongside Jean Redpath, a "traditional Scottish folk singer" who learns only by ear, to produce musical recordings of Hovey's settings for Burns songs (242). McCue's chapter is an eloquent comment on the way in which the construction of Burns has often taken place within collaborative transatlantic networks.

The final essay in the collection, Sharon Alker and Holly Faith Nelson's "Transatlanticism and Beyond: Robert Burns and the World Wide Web," considers the current digital mediation of Burns in cyberspace, discussing a number of Burns websites that originate in Britain and North America and involve transatlantic exchange. Paul Giles has noted in relation to virtual geography that "[i]n this digital age, telesthesia's repositioning of a discrete object of analysis in terms of 'relationality and mobility' threatens to introduce instability into what have traditionally been self-enclosed systems."[45] Thus, if the rhizomatic growth of Burnsian culture has already been disturbed by its cartographic maneuvers, as this collection demonstrates, it is now doubly so as it moves into this new medium. As they map the "afterlife of Burns in the Digital Age," Alker and Nelson work

---

[44]   It also leads to a consideration of the precariousness of communication, of which readers in 1870 would be only too aware. The translation of any message depends very much on the two parties understanding the same code; it also depends on the reliability of the service and the mechanics of the medium.

[45]   Paul Giles, *Virtual Americas: Transnational Fictions and the Transatlantic Imaginary* (Durham, NC, 2002), pp. 19–20.

within and move beyond transatlantic boundaries in an effort to determine how academics in the humanities can create multi-sensory scholarly depth online in Burns studies, despite the Internet's association with superficial information and inadequate methods of knowledge acquisition (248). In the process, they reflect on ways that Burns scholars can guide web users through a series of online encounters with Burns in a fashion that "deepen[s] in imaginative and innovative ways the knowledge and understanding" of his life, writings, and evolving reception (260).

Reverend Harvey's image of Burns as the "electric spark that flashes along the Atlantic cable" uniting "the Old World with the New" received an "imaginative and innovative" technological update during the 250th anniversary of Burns's birth. On 25 January 2009, at 1:00 pm Pacific Standard Time, Burns lovers from Sydney, Australia, to Vancouver, Canada, to Ayrshire, Scotland, linked themselves not by telegraph but by Internet, sending "reply all" messages from blackberries, iPhones, and computers. "Sparks" were replaced by binary code as greetings were bounced off satellites to land on the other side of the world. More germanely for this collection, the image of the wire through which Burns's essence travels unidirectionally across the Atlantic was replaced by a multiplicity of connections, a rhizomatic map of contacts.[46] It is our hope that *Robert Burns and Transatlantic Culture* will achieve for the academic study of Burns what that virtual celebration did for the popular enjoyment of Burns: to suggest "multiple entryways" into Burns and his work and to use Burns to reflect on the particularities of transnational exchange. At the very least, if this collection encourages further consideration of the "Scotch bard" from a perspective that moves him "owre the sea," it will have achieved its purpose.[47]

---

[46] The virtual greetings were organized by the Centre for Scottish Studies at Simon Fraser University Ironically, the idea for such a virtual celebration came not from Ayrshire, nor from Scotland, nor even from Britain, but from a transatlantic location that also doubles as a gateway to the Pacific: Vancouver, Canada. That evening, Vancouverites also gathered at one of the most colorful local inflections of Burns Day anywhere, the Gung Haggis Fat Choy Festival invented by Todd Wong, a fifth-generation Chinese-Canadian. Participants ate haggis wontons, listened to pipa music, and enjoyed the spectacle of the dragon dance to the music of Highland bagpipes.

[47] "On A Scotch Bard, Gone to the West Indies," *The Poems and Songs of Robert Burns*, Kinsley (ed.), vol. 1, p. 239.

PART 1
Burns's Transatlantic Concerns

Chapter 1
Slavery as a Political Metaphor in Scotland and Ireland in the Age of Burns

Murray Pittock

As well as a dreadful reality and source of extensive policy debate, slavery was also a major literary, political, religious, and social metaphor in the age of Burns. Burns's age was the age of the abolition movement and its deployment of, in Nigel Leask's words, a "full rhetoric of sensibility" in support of its cause.[1] In 1787, the year of the Edinburgh edition of Burns's *Poems*, Josiah Wedgwood produced his famous "Am I not a man and a brother?" seal, with its image of a suppliant (rather than defiant) African. This badge of sensibility was adopted by the Quaker-led Society for Effecting the Abolition of the Slave Trade. In 1788, a number of these badges were shipped to Philadelphia, and in the same year, the image appeared on the cover of a pamphlet about Guinea. Within a few years, many thousands of copies of Wedgwood's design had been produced, and it soon became a cultural icon. Between 1788 and 1792, between 600 and 700 abolitionist petitions reached Parliament, signed by an estimated 400,000 people.[2] Abolition in the age of Burns was not a minority liberal taste.

Nonetheless, the language used to describe slavery as a condition remained slippery and problematic, because it was inherited from an earlier language unconcerned with black slavery, but seeing the condition as one brought about by tyranny and voluntary subjection to it. One of the problems with the rhetoric of slavery was that one of its most prominent roles, with regard to the slave-like condition of Catholics, embedded the assumption that it was a voluntary condition, and that continued acquiescence in it was the mark of personal inadequacy, a "mind-forged manacle." The long-established mantra of "Popery and Slavery" was arguably one element in the source of a damaging metaphorical confusion between the voluntary and involuntary status of slavery, for in compressed form the use of the term in political rhetoric had long implied that it was in part a willful surrender of liberty, rather than its theft. It was no surprise that from the 1780s the new United States, as the home of republican virtue, was far from the forefront of abolition: for part of the rhetoric of that virtue was itself symbiotically linked to the idea that to be a freeman and not a slave was in some sense a *moral*

---

[1]   Nigel Leask, "Burns and the Poetics of Abolition," in Gerard Carruthers (ed.), *The Edinburgh Companion to Robert Burns* (Edinburgh, 2009), pp. 47–60 (p. 50).

[2]   See www.bodley.ox.ac.uk/dept/scwmss/projects/abolition for further details.

choice, the choice of a Protestant not a Catholic, a republican not a monarchist. Even Wedgwood's anti-slavery medal drew on the imagery of conversion, as the supplicant slave is in a praying posture.

Slavery had also long been used to describe the nature and condition of the politically disaffected. Sir John Temple's 1646 account of the 1641 Ulster Rising portrayed the native Irish as savages with "beastly manners and customs," unfit for the civility of English law. In 1652, when the English Commonwealth held sway over an earlier—and forced—union of the Britannic polities, "Scotsmen, Negroes and Indians" were bound together in a single class in the Massachusetts Bay regulations governing the formation and recruitment of militia; in 1705 in Virginia, "Catholics, Indians and negro slaves" were forbidden from appearing as witnesses.[3] In works of the long eighteenth century it is easy to find the use of a terminology of slavery to characterize both Catholics and Jacobites, usually Scottish and Irish Jacobites, and the association of fitness for slavery with assumptions of racial inferiority long before the period of "simianization" identified by Perry Curtis in *Apes and Angels*.[4] For example, the Cameronian William Cleland had described Highland Scots as monkeys as early as the late 1670s or early 1680s, a term no doubt intended to conflate their alleged primitivism and Catholicism: "At this Discourse their tails all bobed ... They threw there faces like Babowns."[5] A Native American terminology was also heavily deployed to describe actually or potentially disaffected Scots or Irish. This had somewhat different, though connected, implications for their status as subjects possessed by, but not participating in, the British state's rhetoric of liberty, itself increasingly tied to the quasi-racist position of Germanicity from the 1730s on, where the identity of English and Lowland Scots as "Teutons" was used to align Protestant liberty with ethnicity. Celts were prey to absolutism; Teutons loved liberty.[6]

However, this racial position (which can be found not only in the eighteenth, but also in the nineteenth century) could be veiled in its ethnic discrimination by the Catholicism of Ireland, and the posited Catholicism of northern Scotland, in

---

[3]   Joseph Richardson, "Political Anglicanism in Ireland 1691–1801: From the Language of Liberty to the Language of Union," in Michael Brown, Patrick M. Geoghegan, and James Kelly (eds), *The Irish Act of Union, 1800: Bicentennial Essays* (Dublin, 2003), pp. 58–67 (pp. 61–2); David Dobson, *Scottish Emigration to Colonial America, 1607–1785* (Athens, GA, 1994), p. 36; Giovanni Covi et al., *Caribbean-Scottish Relations: Colonial and Contemporary Inscriptions in History, Language and Literature* (London, 2007), p. 164.

[4]   Perry Curtis, *Apes and Angels: The Irishman in Victorian Caricature*, 2nd edn (Washington, DC, 1997).

[5]   William Cleland, "A Mock Poem Upon the Expedition of the Highland Host," *A Collection of Several Poems and Verses, Composed upon Various Occasions* (1697), p. 31. Cleland was killed at the battle of Dunblane in 1689.

[6]   Paul Hopkins, *Glencoe and the End of the Highland War* (1986; Edinburgh, 1998), p. 185; Murray Pittock, "Historiography," in Alexander Broadie (ed.), *The Cambridge Companion to the Scottish Enlightenment* (Cambridge, 2003), pp. 258–79.

fact more fictional than real, as a distrust not of race, but of religion. Catholicism was the free choice of Irish and Scots Highlanders: in choosing it, they chose Romish slavery over British liberty, and in volunteering for slavery, were to an extent morally culpable for their own "inferiority." In 1689, the publication of *The Muses' Farewell to Popery and Slavery* was only one of the markers of a new generation of English liberties made possible by the "free parliament" which in The Bill of Rights had done away with the tyranny of popish government that, in the more extreme language of its detractors, sought to make all souls slaves to the pope and all bodies slaves to France. For the next fifty-five years, England was to be repeatedly saved from invasion by what was termed the "Protestant wind," the defining presence of which was most memorably celebrated in "Rule Britannia," where the implicit equation is that ruling the waves frees Britain from Continental influences and hence Catholicism, which *is* slavery: "Rule Britannia, Britannia rules the waves / Britons never never never shall be slaves." Catholicism not only enslaved souls: it devoured bodies by fire or fraud. When Catholic Emancipation was advanced in 1829, many of the most enthusiastic British petitioners against slavery, from towns and guilds, petitioned against Catholic Emancipation also.[7]

These views were still strong in the middle of the nineteenth century: M.H. Seymour's *Nature of Romanism* (1849) called Catholicism "the slave-master of the human mind," while a classic like Alexander Hislop's *The Two Babylons* (1853) strongly reaffirmed Catholicism's identification with Babylon the Great, "Mother of harlots and abominations of the earth," the feminized, lascivious, decayed, immoral orient.[8] Catholicism was the indispensable ingredient in the dehumanization of the white other and their presentation as slaves. In this context, the continued association of Irish Catholics with primitivism, blackness, and even primates is well documented, and was itself interrogated by contemporary liberal opinion. The wily Milesian face of Pius IX trying to enslave John Bull while asleep in an 1850 *Punch* was only one indicator that subject races and subject religions belonged together. In the United States, the 1876 *Harper's Weekly* illustration "The Ignorant Vote" shows Irish Catholics in the North in perfect balance with emancipated slaves in the South, as equals—by implication, equals in inadequacy—under the skin.[9]

In the above context, it comes as little surprise that after the future James VII and II's initial conversion to Catholicism in 1669, as Ros Ballaster points out, he is frequently portrayed not only in the guise of a French Catholic absolutist monarch but also as an Islamic tyrant: the orientalizing of the king preceded his exile. As Linda Colley has observed, the orientalism of the seventeenth and early

---

7   Michael Wheeler, *The Old Enemies: Catholic and Protestant in Nineteenth-Century English Culture* (Cambridge, 2006), p. 99; Iain Whyte, *Scotland and the Abolition of Black Slavery, 1756–1838* (Edinburgh, 2006), p. 208.

8   Qtd. in Wheeler, *Old Enemies*, pp. 9, 11, 18.

9   Wheeler, *Old Enemies*, p. 18; Curtis, *Apes and Angels*, p. 60.

eighteenth centuries was not that of the nineteenth century addressed by Said,[10] but nonetheless, oriental absolutism was feared: the siege of Vienna in 1683 by the Ottomans was as much a marker for the age as the ambitions of Louis XIV. In such circumstances, the orientalizing of Catholicism and the national groups to which it was linked were important components of a political discourse that could metaphorically combine the sultan with the Catholic imperialists of France and Spain. There were other possible comparators: intriguingly, the eighteenth-century comparisons between Gustavus Vasa and the Jacobite leadership as fellow absolutists may be reflected in the naming of Olaudah Equiano (*c*. 1745—*c*. 1797) as "Gustavus Vasa." "Gustavus" as a name for black slaves dated to 1721.[11] The relationship of servility to absolutism was symbiotic: it entailed guilt on both parties, base slaves as well as brutal tyrants. Hence, its use in the labelling of those enslaved involuntarily chillingly confused the central issue: the moral culpability of a system in which the slave did not acquiesce and had no control.

The imputation of Catholicism thus strengthened any taint of slavishness towards arbitrary power immeasurably, although the two were often interlinked in any case. Slavery in the form of Catholicism, though a matter of moral culpability, was also seen as a position of suffering and unhappiness, although, as Homi Bhabha points out, Locke's *Second Treatise* uses a double definition of slavery, the first being a "legitimate form of ownership," the second "an intolerable, illegitimate exercise of Power," without dwelling much on the similarity of the slave's experience in both these contexts.[12] In 1745, William Henry presented the Jacobites as those who suffer under "the Misery of submitting to Slavery or a false Religion … it unmans, dissolves, and dissipates the soul."[13] As late as the propaganda attending the restoration of the Catholic hierarchy in England and Wales in 1850, *Punch* (both the most anti-Catholic and anti-Irish of mainstream periodicals) made the ludicrous assertion that a Stuart restoration was an inevitable outcome of Cardinal Wiseman's move. The papacy was routinely described as a "slave-master": the "yoke" of "Romish bondage" it exercised sought (through Jesuitry) to convert freemen to slaves, a trafficking in souls, who were not altogether to be pitied, because their slavery was a sign of their weakness and

[10]   Ros Ballaster, *Fabulous Orients: Fictions of the East in England 1660–1785* (Oxford, 2005), p. 84; Linda Colley, *Captives: The Story of Britain's Pursuit of Empire and How Its Soldiers and Civilians Were Held Captive by the Dream of Global Supremacy* (New York, 2002).

[11]   See also Niall Mackenzie, "Some British Writers and Gustavus Vasa," *Studia Neophilologica*, 78 (2006): 63–80 (73–4); and Whyte, *Scotland and the Abolition of Black Slavery*, p. 15.

[12]   Homi Bhabha, "Of Mimicry and Man: The Ambivalence of Colonial Discourse," in Gaurar Desai and Supriya Nair (eds), *Postcolonialisms: An Anthology of Cultural Theory and Criticism* (Oxford, 2005), pp. 265–73 (p. 266).

[13]   William Henry, *A Philippic Oration, against the Pretender's Son, and his Adherents. Addressed to the Protestants of the North of Ireland* (Dublin, 1745), p. 23. I am indebted to Carolyn Williams for this reference.

their unfitness for liberty. Catholicism, "eunuch-like, dirty and Oriental," as one Irish Protestant called it, bred slaves for arbitrary power: such slaves deserved the treatment they received from freemen.[14] As Bishop John MacDonald, one of the first to make the comparison explicit, said in 1772, "No people on earth, not even the Negro slaves excepted, suffer so much oppression and misery of every kind" as did the Catholics of Scotland. In such circumstances it was not surprising that, as Nicholas Hudson points out, "Jacobitism is a revealing source of antislavery sentiment."[15]

This equation lends an interesting insight into the defensive self-identification as orientals found in Irish writing of the Romantic era in the work of Burke, Sheridan, Owenson, Moore, and many others, and discussed by modern critics such as Joseph Lennon, Fintan O'Toole, and Julia Wright.[16] In this defensive orientalism, the eastern-ness of the alienated self is acknowledged, but is located in the position of struggling for freedom against imperial power, not enslaved and resisting the freedom proffered by that power. So it was that Charles Vallancey's cumbrous etymologies of Irish Phoenician/Carthaginian origins ("several colonies from Africa settled in Ireland") were adopted in patriot rhetoric: Clare O'Halloran traces in particular the link between Vallancey and Henry Flood. Vallancey's alignment of Ireland with Carthage gained an obvious resonance in patriot eyes ("delenda est Hibernia"), and the genocidal tendencies of the classical West were also alluded to in William Drennan's *Letters of Orellana, an Irish Helot* (1785), in a metaphor which was carried through to de Vere's 1849 comment that "Famine makes lean the Helots' helpless land."[17]

In 1788, Hugh Mulligan's *Poems Chiefly on Slavery and Oppression* connected "Irish oppression, British imperialism, and the enslavement of Africa." Ostensibly a set of straightforward anti-slavery poems dedicated to William Wilberforce, Mulligan's collection began with "The Slave, An American Eclogue," continuing through "The Virgins, An Asiatic Eclogue" and "The Herdsman, a European Eclogue" (the Eclogue being a genre of political dispossession dating back to

---

[14]   George Moore, qtd. in Wheeler, *The Old Enemies*, pp. 9, 11, 17, 290.

[15]   John, Bishop MacDonald, qtd. in Clotilde Prunier, *Anti–Catholic Strategies in Eighteenth-Century Scotland* (Frankfurt, 2004), p. 86; Nicholas Hudson, "'Britons Never Will be Slaves': National Myth, Conservatism and the Beginnings of British Antislavery," *Eighteenth Century Studies*, 34/4 (2001): 559–76 (565).

[16]   Joseph Lennon, *Irish Orientalism: A Literary and Intellectual History* (Syracuse, 2004); Fintan O'Toole, *A Traitor's Kiss: The Life of Richard Brinsley Sheridan, 1751–1816* (New York, 1998); Julia M. Wright, *Ireland, India, and Nationalism in Nineteenth-Century Literature* (Cambridge, 2007).

[17]   Charles Vallancey, *An Essay on the Antiquity of the Irish Language*, 3rd edn (London, 1818), p. 12; Clare O'Halloran, *Golden Ages and Barbarous Nations: Antiquarian Debate and Cultural Politics in Ireland, c. 1750–1800* (Cork, 2004), p. 55; Mary Helen Thuente, *The Harp Re–strung: The United Irishmen and the Rise of Irish Literary Nationalism* (New York, 1994), p. 45; Aubrey Thomas de Vere, "Irish Colonization," in Seamus Deane (gen. ed.), *The Field Day Anthology of Irish Writing* (3 vols, Derry, 1991), vol. 2, p. 56.

Vergil) to "The Lovers, An African Eclogue." "The Herdsman" clearly identifies European slavery with Ireland, portraying a land of bards, minstrels and rural decay. British tyranny is attacked.[18] One of the questions that Mulligan's collection touches on is the extent to which American revolutionary rhetoric was qualified in its acceptance in Irish radical circles precisely because of the continued presence of slavery in the American republic. Leading United Irish figures such as Thomas Russell expressed their distaste for slavery by boycotting its products. In 1792, the *Northern Star* proclaimed that "Equal Rights and Equal Laws" would end "*slavery*,"[19] a reference apparently made to both the position of Catholics and blacks; the oppression of Catholics is key here, not their voluntary surrender to absolutism. The phrase "equal rights and equal laws"—of course it was one typical of the time—reappears in line 79 of the later "Tree of Liberty," a poem probably by Burns.

Even among more moderate figures, the effect of Irish orientalism was marked. Burke in particular, clearly made the equation between the orient and Ireland in reverse, where the "servile patience" of the Indian and Irishman alike is the response that renders them victims, not of absolutism and Catholicism, but of the tyranny of a Protestant state. Both Burke and Sheridan also, of course, opposed slavery itself.[20] In 1799, Sheridan spoke on the impending Union as accomplishing "for ever the subjugation of Ireland and the slavery of its inhabitants." Category reversal continued to abound in his speech:

> We are told in England, that the unhappy Africans were insensible to the ordinary feelings of humanity, and to the custom of the slave-trade. On similar motives, the character of the Irish peasantry has been foully misrepresented by some men, both in this country and in Ireland also ... [W]hen you thus pledge yourselves to inquire as to the property of the West India planters, is it too much to propose a pledge that you will take into consideration ... the Irish ...?[21]

It may be, opines Sheridan, because "England had adopted a more ignorant and barbarous system of management with respect to Ireland, than ever one nation ... had adopted with respect to another," that it cares more for planters than Irish subjects. The metaphor is reversed: England enslaves the free, Jamaicans or Irish,

---

[18]   Hugh Mulligan, *Poems Chiefly on Slavery and Oppression* (London, 1788), pp. 1, 8, 16, 18, 23, 34, 72ff; Stuart Curran, *Poetic Form and British Romanticism* (Oxford, 1987), p. 97.

[19]   *Northern Star*, 58 (18–21 July 1792): 3.

[20]   Conor Cruise O'Brien, *The Great Melody: A Thematic Biography and Commented Anthology of Edmund Burke* (1992; London, 1993), pp. 91–2, 459; Edmund Burke to Lord Fitzwilliam, 10 February 1795, qtd. in Luke Gibbons, *Edmund Burke and Ireland: Aesthetics, Politics and the Colonial Sublime* (Cambridge, 2003), p. 99; see also p. 167.

[21]   *The Speeches of the Right Honourable Richard Brinsley Sheridan* (1842), Edited by A Constitutional Friend (3 vols, New York, 1969), vol. 3, pp. 52, 272, 277, 534, 539; O'Toole, *A Traitor's Kiss*, p. 429.

whom it re-categorizes as "slaves" because of their interior inadequacy, not their external oppression. The comparison between absenteeism in the West Indies and Ireland was revisited after Sheridan's speech by a number of writers, including Maria Edgeworth in *The Absentee* and Sydney Owenson in *The Wild Irish Girl*.

The convergence of Irish orientalism and the abolitionist reversal of categories of what constituted slavery and freedom is clearly evident in many places in the 1790s, and I can only touch on some of them here. The first number of *The Northern Star* printed "The Negroe's Complaint," and followed it up on 14 January 1792 with "The Dying Negro." In 1796, an "anti-slavery coin was used as a token of recognition by United Irishmen in County Derry"; in February 1797, rack rents and tithes in Ireland were explicitly connected to black slavery, for they "made a free people become Negroes," a theme returned to by Edgeworth. In the same year Mary Anne McCracken wrote to her brother Henry Joy with "an incisive analysis, linking slavery in America, political slavery in Ireland, and the slavery of women in general," while the United Irishmen defined slavery as "that state in which men are governed without their consent," with a strong implication once again of the Catholic position.[22] In 1798, William Cobbett commented that there was a belief in Virginia and the Carolinas that "some of the free negroes have already been admitted into the conspiracy of the United Irishmen."[23] The linkage between slave emancipation and Catholic emancipation is clear: it has been identified by Kevin Whelan among others, and is a key part in the discourse of Irish blackness so established in some areas of postcolonially oriented Irish studies. The adoption of the rhetoric used to abuse Catholics to defend their position is a striking development of the 1780 to 1830 era. Thomas Moore compared Emancipation to the orientalist image of Cleopatra's banquet in *Captain Rock* and of course used *Lalla Rookh* to defend Iran (Erin), the home of oriental absolutism from Herodotus to the 2007 film *300* as a people fighting for liberty against religious tyranny, rather than being its willing slaves: Moore's Zoroastrians defend their altars and liberties against the chains and bigots of what is fairly transparently Protestant oppression.[24]

The increasing use of chains as an iconographic symbol of enslavement may have had something to do with the importance of depicting slavery as an externally

---

[22]   Thuente, *The Harp Re–strung*, p. 45; Nancy J. Curtin, *The United Irishmen: Popular Politics in Ulster and Dublin, 1791–1798* (Oxford, 1994), pp. 121, 250; Thomas Bartlett, Kevin Dawson and Dáire Keogh, *The 1798 Rebellion: An Illustrated History* (Boulder, 1998), pp. 31, 35; Kevin Whelan, *Fellowship of Freedom: The United Irishmen and the 1798 Rebellion* (Cork, 1998), pp. 25, 36.

[23]   William Cobbett, qtd. in Peter Linebaugh and Marcus Rediker, *The Many-Headed Hydra: Sailors, Slaves, Commoners, and the Hidden History of the Revolutionary Atlantic* (London, 2000), p. 279; see William Cobbett, *Detection of a Conspiracy Formed by the United Irishmen* (Philadelphia, 1798), pp. 28ff.

[24]   Thomas Moore, *Memoirs of Captain Rock* (London, 1824), pp. 364–5; see also Jeffery Vail, "Thomas Moore in Ireland and America: The Growth of a Poet's Mind," *Romanticism*, 10/1 (2004): 41–62 (56).

imposed, not inwardly accepted state. In Moore's poetry, the chain recurs as an image of Irish Catholic oppression in many poems, among them "Dear Harp of My Country," "The Minstrel Boy," and *Lalla Rookh*. Likewise, the "fetters rent in twain" of Thomas Davis's "A Nation Once Again" is just one in a whole catalogue of uses of this trope; while in the teeth of the Famine crisis, when Davis's Young Ireland colleagues planned armed insurrection, the relationship of Irish landlord to tenant was described as that of "slave holders with white slaves." In "Celts and Saxons," Davis compared Ireland to Egypt and Phoenicia; despite their differences, for his part O'Connell, perhaps aware of the paradox inherent in his reference, had described the Irish as "too religious to be slaves" in a June 1845 meeting in Cork, while his monster meetings of the 1840s frequently used chains and black slavery as props in a pageantry of comparison between the condition of Ireland and that of the West Indies. In 1848, Charles Gavan Duffy used the same metaphor, which can be found in multiple other locations in prose and verse. As Marjorie Howes has argued, "for Young Ireland a slave was both a physical spectacle and a state of mind": the two parts of slave discourse, ideological and physical enslavement, were united in O'Connellite theatre.[25]

The context of abolition was a potent one: and yet, as has been often observed, Burns almost never addresses the subject directly. Poets such as Mulligan, Hannah More, Helen Maria Williams, or Ann Yearsley might produce explicitly abolitionist poetry, but Burns's approach to one of the great issues of his day was notoriously more oblique. Nigel Leask has argued that the reference to "honest poverty" in Williams's "The Slave Trade," and Burns's 1789 letter commenting on it illuminates a complimentary commentary by Williams on Burns's decision not to go to Jamaica in 1786.[26] This is a powerful, intriguing, and persuasive suggestion: but Williams's perception of Burns's motives may nonetheless have been more benign than the uncomfortable reality.

For it seems that Burns wavered in his use of the lexis of slavery between its history as a metaphor for voluntary inadequacy and its acknowledgement of an external and inescapably oppressive reality, an "accursed trade." It is clear that despite his strong interest in the politics and practice of sympathy, and the central presence of Adam Smith's *Theory of Moral Sentiments* and the writing of Henry Mackenzie in his work and thought, Burns's use of the term "slavery" utilizes both the voluntarist and victim models, sometimes in the same poem. In this way, his much-vaunted independency of mind and the appeal of his sturdy individualism to

---

[25] O'Connell, qtd. in Robert Kee, *The Most Distressful Country* (London, 1972), pp. 197, 238, 264; Cecil Woodham-Smith, *The Great Hunger: Ireland 1845–1849* (1962; London, 1991), p. 297; Davis, qtd. in *Field Day*, Deane (ed.), vol. 2, p. 54. The image may also be present in Burns's "The rank is but the guinea's stamp," as Nigel Leask has suggested. Marjorie Howes, plenary address ("The Irish in Nineteenth-Century Atlantic Culture"), *Global Nations? Irish and Scottish Expansion Since the 16th Century*, University of Aberdeen, 31 October 2009.

[26] Leask, "Burns and the Poetics of Abolition," pp. 50–54.

the classical republican tradition in the United States was a two-edged sword. The Presbyterian and nonconformist Protestant tradition (had not Cromwell's soldiers been "Independents" in religion?) valued personal liberty, but also identified slavery to absolutism (whether papal or crown) as a condition which anyone would free themselves from if only they were prepared to defend their own interests. Inevitably, this made those who endured slavery inferior in courage (Burns's "coward slave" in "Is there for honest Poverty"), ability, and will: this view made it easier for Protestants to own slaves while holding strong concepts of personal liberty. Lucy Snowe, the heroine of Charlotte Bronte's *Villette* (1853), a novel which is about, among other things, the restored Catholic hierarchy, manifests this outlook very markedly in her contempt for what she sees as the slave mentality of Continental Catholicism: its dirt, evasion, deceit, and cowardice.

Yet "Is there for honest Poverty" became a universal marker of Burns's internationalism, radicalism, and erosion of class difference. The lines "come it may … It's comin yet for a' that / That Man to Man, the warld o'er / Shall brothers be for a' that,"[27] just possibly refer to the "Am I not a Man and a Brother?" medal (a likelihood increased by the phrase "guinea stamp," which may be a reference to the 1788 Guinea pamphlet), and may contain possible allusions to the universal republican ideal of Revolutionary France; or indeed (as Robert Crawford has suggested) Freemasonry. It may be wrong to pass "[t]he coward-slave" by: he too must be liberated, as a victim rather than a voluntary slave. Yet, he remains a "coward": there is no suggestion in Burns's poem that this word is inappropriate.

Just as "Is there for honest Poverty" acquired a contemporary life in a radical context, so too did "Scots Wha Hae," sung by the mixed-race William Davidson on his arrest for his part in the Cato Street Conspiracy as he was "led away."[28] "Scots Wha Hae" was—as has been well observed by William Donaldson in *The Jacobite Song* (1988) among others—a song with deliberately contemporary and radical reference in Burns's own terms. Interestingly, it combines both the voluntary and the involuntary models of the slavery metaphor. On the one hand, "proud EDWARD" offers "Chains and Slaverie" to the Scots if he defeats them, the instruments of oppression; on the other hand, slavery is again equated with moral cowardice: "Wha sae base as be a Slave?" (vol. 2, p. 708). If "FREE-MAN stand, or FREE-MAN fa'," then death is a real alternative which preserves liberty when freely chosen, just as Moore's Minstrel Boy averts the "foeman's chain" pulling down his soul, because he freely breaks the harp, a national self-immolation which saves him from slavery (vol. 2, p. 708). On the other hand in Burns, the "Sons in servile

---

27   *The Poems and Songs of Robert Burns*, James Kinsley (ed.) (3 vols, Oxford, 1968), vol. 2, pp. 762–3; subsequent quotations from Burns's poetry are from this edition and will be cited in the text by volume and page number; Leask, "Burns and the Poetics of Abolition," p. 56; Robert Crawford, *The Bard: Robert Burns, A Biography* (London and Princeton, 2009), p. 112.

28   Covi et al., *Caribbean–Scottish Relations*, p. 176. Leask was the first to point out the possibility that "guinea stamp" in Burns's poem referred to the "accursed trade."

chains" are worth draining "our dearest veins" for, advancing once more the idea of slavery as compulsion from which the individual deserves to be freed (vol. 2, p. 708). The song sits finely balanced between the two: the moral superiority of those who die if they cannot do is advanced, but slavery is also a condition of no moral opprobrium, which it is worth fighting against to free others.

The "independent wish" is balanced against the condition of being the "lordling's slave" by design in "Man Was Made to Mourn": here the "will and pow'r" of the lord suggests that only the enslaver is truly free, while the freedom of the other is a "wish" merely (vol. 1, p. 118). Slavery is moral victimhood, here, and the death which releases one from it is not that freely chosen by the valiant Scots at Bannockburn, but is rather the inevitable deliverance offered by "the poor man's dearest friend" (vol. 1, p. 119). The suffering of enslaved man in this poem is like the sufferings of the nature over whom "Tyrannic man's dominion" imposes cruelty and domination (vol. 1, p. 5). Similarly, in "The Tree of Liberty," "Gallia's slaves" are taken pity on by "the chiel … Wha … staw a branch, spite o' the deil, / Frae yont the western waves, man" (vol. 2, p. 911). Here the similarity with Blake's Orc, the reversal of the categories of divine order and hierarchy and so on are very marked: but there is also the sneaking sense that the "slaves" cannot free themselves. If the fruit of "Liberty" "raises man aboon the brute" and is "worth a' Afric's wealth" (vol. 2, p. 911), then it both constitutes what is truly human and can be weighed in the balance with the commodities—including human commodities of course—of Africa. Liberty, Burns may be saying, is worth any number of slaves.

For Burns can provide us with poems that treat dominance with respect. In "To a Louse," the speaker's vision of the "thick plantations" and the "kindred, jumping cattle" who inhabit them (with the implied reference to the West Indies, where "cattle" was the plantocracy's term for slaves) is one where the lice swarm on the beggars, the meal they are designed by nature to enjoy (vol. 1, p. 193). Entering a competition to dine on the poor is a fit outcome for the lowest of the low; but the louse's sturdy independency resists the fate imagined for him by the jealous onlooker, whose desire for the woman and inability to take his eyes off her makes him more like the "weary slave frae sun to sun" who desires the notice of "Mary Morison" than the louse whom he imagines as a slave violating his lowly social role (vol. 1, p. 42), but who in fact in his cheerful independency possesses the woman as the voyeur never can. This point is reinforced by the fact that the "red smeddum" the speaker wishes to thrash the louse with is a mercury compound, and mercury was the treatment for syphilitic infection (vol. 1, p. 194).[29] The louse sexually possesses the lady as well as feeding off of her, contrasting his freedom to act with the speaker's, whose closing Smithian imprecation, "O wad some Pow'r the giftie gie us," ironically reflects on himself (vol. 1, p. 194). The "[d]evotion" from which one might be free if one had that "giftie" is prima facie a theological one, but is also of course his own "[d]evotion" (vol. 1, p. 194). To be "devoted" is

---

[29]   I am indebted to Sir Kenneth Calman for this point.

to be given up for sacrifice: the condition of the victim or the slave. Here slavery is voluntary, just as elsewhere in Burns the "slave" who indulges his "sneer" against the Covenanters displays his moral worthlessness by doing so (vol. 2, p. 803).

Nor is "To a Louse" the only reference in Burns to slaves as cattle, as the "Epistle to John Rankine" makes clear:

> As soon's the *clockin-time* is by,
> An' the *wee powts* begun to cry,
> L-d, I'se hae sportin by an' by,
> For my *gowd guinea;*
> Tho' I should herd the *buckskin* kye
> For't, in Virginia! (vol. 1, p. 63)

The image of the "guinea" returns: the "*buckskin* kye" of Virginia are plantation slaves. Burns's tone here is not encouraging to those who wish to see him at the forefront of radical causes.[30]

"The Slave's Lament"—depending on how much of it Burns wrote—posits the condition of victimhood for the slave. Yet even here Burns can never quite avoid resorting to the imputation that slavery may be in a number of circumstances a voluntary condition, and that the "independant mind" is a superior condition to which the slave may not attain without the intervention of those more fortunate souls who possess it already (vol. 2, p. 763). This was the ambivalence at the heart of the metaphor of slavery in his own age; nor did he escape it himself. As a result, it is at least arguable that Burns's poetry resembles his abortive career move to Jamaica more than it contradicts it; for the "driver" which Burns imagined himself as there is the one who exerts "dominion": tyrannic perhaps, but also quite close to the "independency" Burns praises elsewhere.[31]

"Driving" is the means by which a man possesses a woman as well as an owner a slave in Burns's writing: some forms of domination are allowed, indeed demonstrate independent mindedness, and here we are close to an uncomfortable truth about the poet, who in later life especially acted rather like a "gentleman" of an established exploitative type in his relations with women. Is it of interest in this context that his only explicit poem or song about slavery is "The Slave's Lament," which is associated with two broadsides, "The Trapann'd Maid," which is noted by Kinsley,[32] and "The Virginian Maid's Lament," which is not. In both cases, a woman has been betrayed who is (presumably) white. In "The Virginian Maid's Lament," she is associated with the kidnapping of Scots in the North East (as in

---

[30]   This identification is clear at Kinsley (ed.), vol. 3, p. 1038. I am grateful to Clark McGinn for bringing this to my attention.

[31]   Robert Burns to Dr Moore, 2 August 1787, in *Letters of Robert Burns*, J. De Lancey Ferguson (ed.), 2nd edn, G. Ross Roy (ed.) (2 vols, Oxford, 1985), vol. 1, pp. 133–46 (p. 144).

[32]   *Roxburghe Ballads*, W. Chappell and J.W. Ebsworth (eds) (9 vols, Hertford, 1871–1899), vol. 7, p. 513.

the case of "Indian Peter," one of hundreds abducted in this way) and the "selling them for slaves to the planters," which was rife in the 1730s and 40s. Burns may inject "Senegal" into the equation (vol. 2, p. 647), but his original sources suggest that this is no black slave: if she is a victim, she is a victim of an exploitative system Burns knew much better than the "accursed trade": the exploitation of poor whites by rich ones, an abuse the man of independent mind should resist and not permit. Moreover, the Senegal trade to Virginia "was not part of the British slave trade after 1776," so Burns may just be quoting a lost earlier broadside, while if these are his own words they do not refer to the contemporary trade. "The Slave's Lament" appeared in the 1792 *Scots Musical Museum*, "the year of the great Abolitionist petition campaign spearheaded by William Dickson in Scotland": if this was the case, its references were not nearly so contemporary, whether by accident or design.[33] We should not perhaps pass by the "coward slave," but in this conjunction Burns exhibits the concept of slavery as a voluntary moral inferiority, one which stalks the idea of it as unconditional victimhood throughout his work as throughout the history of his time, and—in the argument presented here— serves to muffle in his poetry the sound of moral indignation gathering force in contemporary British society.

---

[33]   Peter Buchan, *Ancient Ballads and Songs of the North of Scotland* (2 vols, Edinburgh, 1878), vol. 2, pp. 215, 333n; Ian Adams and Meredyth Somerville, *Cargoes of Despair and Hope: Scottish Emigration to North America, 1603–1803* (Edinburgh, 1993), p. 23; Eric J. Graham, *Burns and the Sugar Plantocracy of Ayrshire*, Ayrshire Monographs 36 (Ayr, 2009), p. 96.

Chapter 2
Burns, Scotland, and the American Revolution

Andrew Noble

… I fell in love with the Atlantic Ocean, imagining I saw it as somehow suspending very wonderful promises about freedom and democracy.[1]

It is relatively recently, significant of our deeply retarded sense of Burns's not only democratic but republican impulses, that the American Revolution has been granted its proper status in his poetry. Marilyn Butler's excellent, precursive 1997 essay, "Burns and Politics," marks this sea-change by defining "poems which praise America as a land of freedom" as one of five principal categories into which Burns's political poetry can be subdivided.[2] This, of course, is a primary indicator of Burns as a child of the westward-orientated radical Enlightenment. As Susan Neiman has recently remarked, "America set out to be Enlightenment made tangible!—a land not determined by the traditions you draw from the past, but the visions you have for the future."[3] This is the America celebrated in Burns's poetry. America for him is also the seminal site from where democracy is to be exported eastwards. Thus in "The Tree of Liberty," noted here for the first time as modelled on Thomas Paine's similarly inclined "Liberty's Tree," he writes:

My blessings aye attend the chiel
   Wha pities Gallia's slaves, man,
And staw a branch, spite o' the Deil,
   Frae yont the western waves, man.
Fair Virtue water'd it wi' care
   And now she sees wi' pride, man,
How weel it buds and blossoms there
   Its branches spreading wide, man.[4]

---

[1]   Andrew O'Hagan, *The Atlantic Ocean: Essays on Britain and America* (London, 2008), p. 1.

[2]   Marilyn Butler, "Burns and Politics," in Robert Crawford (ed.), *Robert Burns and Cultural Authority* (Iowa City, 1997), pp. 86–112 (p. 87).

[3]   Qtd. by Jane O'Grady in her review of *Moral Clarity: A Guide for Grown-up Idealists*, by Susan Neiman, *Guardian Review* (25 July 2009): 7.

[4]   Andrew Noble and Patrick Scott Hogg (eds), *The Canongate Burns* (Edinburgh, 2001 and 2003), p. 845; as well as the commentaries provided on this and the other main American poems dealt with in this essay ("When Guilford Good or Ballad on the

While, as we shall see, Burns's ultimate vision was a tragic one in that such American salvation had not taken root in Scotland, in this earlier poem, despite a prevaricating England, he believed that it had. America, thus, is a consistent focus of his political idealism. It is also the site in which the Hanoverian monarchy, which he loathed, another quality he shared with the equally America-devoted Paine, received a brutal military comeuppance.

What, then, is startling about Burns's American poetry is not its content but the fact there is in volume so little of it. There are only *three* poems and some significant elusive fragments which deal with America. This entails that these poems, to bear the burden of our pro-American argument, must be not only formally, linguistically excellent but of profound political importance.

The first step in asserting their importance is to note the fact that of the three American poems ("When Guilford Good," "The Address of Beelzebub," and "Ode on General Washington's Birthday") only the first, after significant hesitancy, was published in Burns's lifetime. To so withhold two such linguistically and formally disparate but equally extraordinary poems, Burns must have deeply feared their personally endangering explosive impact on an increasingly apprehensive establishment's consciousness. Our retarded ability to perceive this also entails a chronic weakness in Scottish historiography of the 1790s cogently defined no little time ago by the American academic Arthur Sheps: "American influences have not been noticed in the reform activities of the 1790s while those of France have been abundantly and perhaps exaggeratedly chronicled."[5] As a necessary prelude to the recontextualization of the American poems in terms of both their genesis and genre, it is essential to examine their proper historical context. Happily, the scholarship of Bruce P. Lenman provides a singular, splendid antidote to what Sheps then defined as an acute deficiency in our understanding of the importance of America to Scotland in the 1790s.[6]

Lenman's erudite, forensic account of Scottish responses, intellectual, political, and physical, to America in the late eighteenth century reveals, notwithstanding the ongoing "braveheart"-inspired popular mythology on the subject, how heavily the dice were loaded against those small minority of Scots sympathetic to the incipient republic's aspirations. Of the forty-five Scottish MPs at Westminster, at best a government-conforming rump, only one, George Dempster, MP for

---

American War," pp. 220–227; "Address of Beelzebub," pp. 613–18; and "Ode for General Washington's Birthday," pp. 814–20), the introduction deals specifically with America (pp. xxvii–xxix). Thomas Paine, "Liberty Tree," in Michael Foot and Isaac Kramnick (eds), *The Thomas Paine Reader* (London, 1987), pp. 63–4.

[5]   Arthur Sheps, "The Edinburgh Reform Convention of 1793 and the American Revolution," *Scottish Tradition*, 5 (1975): 23–37 (23).

[6]   This essay is deeply indebted to Bruce P. Lenman's essay "Aristocratic 'Country' Whiggery in Scotland and the American Revolution," in Richard B. Sher and Jeffrey R. Smitten (eds), *Scotland and America in the Age of Enlightenment* (Edinburgh, 1990), pp. 180–192, and to his chapter "Scotland and the American Revolution 1775–1784," in his *Enlightenment and Change: Scotland 1746–1832* (Edinburgh, 2009).

Perth Burghs from 1761 to 1790, supported the American cause. Revealingly, Dempster's eloquence and integrity are thrice praised in Burns's poetry, albeit not in an American context. A fringe majority of Scottish aristocrats highly partisan to the American cause, such as the Earl of Lauderdale (who astonishingly fought a duel with apostate American Benedict Arnold), the Earl of Selkirk and his son, Lord Daer, and, most importantly for Burns's Washington poem, the Earl of Buchan, were seen by the other Scottish peers not as men of civic virtue but as eccentric mavericks acting against their own class interests. Probably, however, the principal reason that the American Revolution did not have the galvanic impact on Scotland that it had on Welsh national consciousness and Irish colonial militancy was that from early in the eighteenth century, post-Union Scotland, especially its establishment, had been far too integrated into the enormously profitable activities of the British Empire to brook thoughts of supporting a burgeoning rival. Furthermore, Scotland's dominant social, intellectual, political, and, indeed, theological group in the late eighteenth century, the so-called Moderates, were British hyper-patriots. Lenman's cogent description of this Moderate culture acutely reveals the hostile terrain in which Burns's American enthusiasms and its consequent poetry had to operate.

The Scottish Enlightenment was never part of Peter Gay's international conspiracy of liberal anticlericals. The majority of its secular scholars were as conservative as the society they lived in, and its single most important structure was a national network of conservative, if urbanely cosmopolitan, Presbyterian clergymen known as the Moderates. In the great antipathy between court and country, the Scottish Whig establishment was undoubtedly an extreme example of that ultraconservative court Whiggery, with its exaltation of the executive and minimalist views of the Glorious Revolution, which H.T. Dickinson has taught us to see as the normal political stance of the eighteenth-century British establishment. Scotland is also, arguably, an extreme example of the proposition that there never was the slightest possibility of serious social revolution in early modern British society.[7]

The consequence of Lenman's argument is that for him the only significant Scottish support for America derived from a small group of distant Scottish aristocrats who, along with the Founding Fathers of the American Revolution, spoke, although slightly differently accented, the language of the British country Whigs which had evolved as an antidote to an over-centralized, highly militarized, fiscally corrupt metropolitan state. Lenman describes the situation thus:

> The Lords Lauderdale, Selkirk and Buchan, who were contemporary with and admirers of the American Revolution, were gentlemen of the Enlightenment rather than nineteenth-century rabble-rousers. So were George Dempster, James Boswell and John Maclaurin … It is doubtful if he and his Scots political allies would have had much time for the wilder demagogues of the American Whig tradition, but they closely resembled the Virginia gentlemen George Washington

---

[7] Lenman, "Aristocratic 'Country' Whiggery," pp. 180–181.

and Thomas Jefferson, whose achievements they admired and, like them, they deserve to be remembered with pride by their fellow countrymen.[8]

While he himself seems not to be aware of it, Lenman's thesis is overwhelmingly confirmed by an exchange of letters between Buchan and Thomas Jefferson in 1803. This correspondence with Jefferson is significantly more revealing than Buchan's earlier correspondence with George Washington, though, as we shall see, the earlier correspondence seems absolutely crucial to understanding Burns's "Ode to General Washington." Here is Buchan's note about the Jefferson letter followed by Jefferson's response:

> (Considering the state of Great Britain and of Europe, and what I believed to be the principles and character of Mr. Jefferson, I sent to him, with a short expressive inscription, a copy of my Essay on the life and writings of Fletcher of Salton [sic], and James Thomson, author of the Castle of Indolence, the Seasons, etc.; my intention was to defeat, as far as my opinion could, the prejudices conceived against Mr. Jefferson on both sides of the Atlantic.)

> Thomas Jefferson, President of the United States of America, to the Earl of Buchan.

> Washington, July 10. 1803.

> My Lord,

> I received, through the hands of Mr. Lennox, on his return to the U.S. the valuable volume you were so good as to send me on the life and writings of Fletcher of Salton.

> The political principles of that Patriot were worthy of the purest periods of the British constitution. They are those which were in vigour at the epoch of the American emigration. Our ancestors brought them here, and they needed little strengthening to make us what we are; but, in the weakened condition of English Whiggism, at this day, it requires more firmness, to publish and advocate them, than it did then to act upon them. This merit is peculiarly your Lordship's, and no one honours it more than myself; freely admitting, at the same time, the right of a nation to change its political principles and constitution at will, and the impropriety of any but its own citizens censuring that charge. I expect your Lordship has been disappointed, as I acknowledge I have been in the issue of the convulsions on the other side of the channel. This has certainly lessened the interest which the philanthropist warmly felt in those struggles. Without befriending human liberty, a gigantic force has risen up, which seems to threaten the world; but it hangs on the thread of opinion, which may break from one day to another.[9]

----

8   Ibid., p. 190.

9   David Stewart Erskine, Earl of Buchan, *Address to the Americans at Edinburgh, on Washington's birth-day, February 22nd, 1811* (Edinburgh, 1811), Glasgow University Library, Special Collections, d.9.8.

The gigantic intrusive force was, of course, Napoleonic France. While Jefferson loathed Napoleon as the iconic perverter of the Revolution's humanistic initial impulses into covert bureaucratic control at home and predatory imperialism abroad, this loathing was not sufficient to drive America into a European war. In his vastly erudite, deeply stimulating study of that most crucial and intransigent problem, leadership in a modern democratically constituted society, *Voltaire's Bastards: The Dictatorship of Reason in the West*, John Ralston Saul pays homage to Jefferson as the sole post-Enlightenment republican leader to avoid by common sense and compassion a politics based on violent, indeed homicidal, abstraction.[10]

If Saul is correct in his absolute discrimination between Jefferson and Napoleon, this would entail that probably the nature and certainly the consequences of the French Revolution were utterly different from its American predecessor. As we shall see in this detailed textual study of "Ode on General Washington's Birthday," this comparative question, albeit for wholly different reasons, obsessed both radicals and loyalists in the crucial years 1793 and 1794. As Sheps has argued, these conventions were dominated both by American personalities and arguments in favor of the theories and practices of the American Revolution.[11] For a deeply anxious British government, its intention was immediate translation of this inherited Anglophone speech into the terrifying, alien diction emanating from Paris.

It is also to be said, of course, that while Jefferson believed that at some point America had to deal with slavery, he, at least in his public role, could do nothing. It is also the case that revolutionary France was arguably not alone in pursuing a foreign policy of exploitative violence in the name of universal democratic and fraternal liberation. In reviewing Robert Kagan's *Dangerous Nation: America and the World, 1600–1898*, Martin Jacques has remarked that America saw its natural dominion as stretching from Canada to Mexico with Cuba and Puerto Rico thrown in. In response to Kagan's claim that "colonial America was characterised not by isolation and utopianism, not by cities upon hills and covenants with God, but by aggressive expansionism, acquisitive materialism, and an overarching ideologist civilization that encouraged and justified both,"[12] Jacques observes,

> It bred both a particularly abhorrent form of racialism and a new kind of capitalism. With a seemingly limitless supply of land, every white male settler could ultimately fulfill their dream of becoming a landowner: colonial America, in Kagan's words, was like an "expansionist pressure cooker."[13]

---

[10] John Ralston Saul, *Voltaire's Bastards: The Dictatorship of Reason in the West* (New York, 1993).

[11] Sheps, "The Edinburgh Reform Convention," pp. 27–9.

[12] Qtd. in Martin Jacques, review of *Dangerous Nation: America and the World, 1600–1898*, by Robert Kagan, *Guardian Review* (17 October, 2009): 8.

[13] Jacques, review of *Dangerous Nation*, 20.

Loyalist Britain had no belief in America as Arcadia, whereas the British and European dissenters supporting America, particularly the French, tended to see it as an innately rural society safe from commercial and industrial development.[14] Quite avoiding their own often murderous imperial practices in the East, the British government operated a propaganda campaign against America. In his excellent *The Persistence of Empire: British Political Culture in the Age of the American Revolution*, Elija H. Gould lucidly demonstrates how the Scottish Literati, recruited and paid by London, were frequently in the van of the pamphlet war waged against the incipient republic.[15] The principal focus of this propaganda war was Dr Richard Price, the Welshman who was the chief advocate of a post-Lockean, contractual republic the evolution of which, for Price, marked not only a political but also a spiritual quantum leap in human affairs. As D.O. Thomas has remarked, "Price thought that after the foundation of Christianity the American Revolution was the most important event in the history of mankind."[16] Despite his millennial idealism, Price also believed that both the practice of slavery and the propensity for debt profoundly endangered this project. Dr Price had significant connections not only with Anglo-Scottish radicals but also inside Scotland itself. As we shall see when dealing with "When Guilford Good," Burns may have read a letter of his in *The Scots Magazine*. Also in January 1791, he ordered "Dr. Price's dissertations on Providence, prayer, Death & Miracles" from his Edinburgh bookseller friend, Peter Hill. Whether or not Burns actually read Price's last, most inflammatory (for the Literati) pro-American piece, *A Discourse on the Love of Our Country* (1789), its theme and tone are profoundly compatible with Burns's American poetry. Price has a similar sense of aspiration and consequence:

> Behold Kingdoms, admonished by you, starting from sleep, breaking their fetters, and claiming justice from their oppressors! Behold the light you have struck out, after setting America free, reflected to France and there kindled into a blaze that lays despotism in ashes and warms and illuminates Europe.[17]

Tragically, of course, Burns's last American poem on Washington records that such a transfer for Scotland had not taken place. Famously or notoriously, Dr Price provoked Edmund Burke's *Reflections on the Revolution in France*.

---

[14]   For a related highly ironic and sceptical account of such idealized, pastoral projections of European Romanticism on America see Adam Zamoyski's chapter "The American Parable" in his *Holy Madness: Romantics, Patriots and Revolutionaries* (New York, 2000).

[15]   In *The Persistence of Empire: British Political Culture in the Age of the American Revolution* (Chapel Hill, 2000), Eliga H. Gould cites the propagandist hard-line pamphleteering of such loyalist Scots as Adam Ferguson, James MacPherson, Allan Ramsay, Alexander Carlyle, Joseph Cawthorne, and John Stevenson.

[16]   D.O. Thomas, editorial introduction to *Richard Price: Political Writings*, D.O. Thomas (ed.) (Cambridge, 1991), pp. vii–xxii (p. xxi).

[17]   Richard Price, "A Discourse on the Love of Our Country," in *Richard Price: Political Writings*, Thomas (ed.), pp. 195–6.

Less well known is that earlier he had also provoked a near sub-genre in the Edinburgh Literati's sermonizing and pamphleteering against his American writings. Alexander Carlyle and John Stevenson wrote to repudiate him. James MacPherson, of Ossianic fame, was hired by the British government to undermine Price's personality and principles. Adam Ferguson was similarly involved in 1796. What is perhaps as yet underestimated is the degree to which Enlightenment Scotland's vastly improved academic performance provided educated Scots with very considerable administrative and military opportunities within the British Empire. Thus, for example, in 1778 Adam Ferguson formed part of the Carlisle Commission sent to America to attempt to conclude the war. The tone of his report back to his fellow Scot Alexander Carlyle was hardly placatory:

> We have 1200 Miles of Territory in Length occupied by about 3,000,000 People of which there are about 1,5000,000 with Johny Witherspoons at their head against us And the rest for us. I am not sure that the proper measures were taken but we should reduce Johny Witherspoons to the small Support of Franklin Adams & two or three more of the most Abandoned Villains in the world but I tremble at the thought of their Cunning & determination opposed to us.[18]

Ironically, John Witherspoon was a Scotsman from the evangelical side of the Scottish church. He and Ferguson had earlier tangled over the question of theatrical performance in Scotland. Ferguson's liberalism in that case seems not to have been matched by any sympathy for American democracy. The Literati's sentimental aesthetics always seem to contradict their petrified politics. What we also gather is that even at this stage, Ferguson's "proper measures" suggest that military action might save the day. Instead, Ferguson seems implicated in the Commission's final report "that self-preservation justified England's destruction of the colonies; that Franco-American alliance made the contest a world struggle."[19] Both in his personal contacts and his avid reading of the press, Burns must have been wholly aware of Edinburgh as an overwhelmingly anti-American city. Two years after Burns came to Edinburgh, William Drennan, an Irish medical student, later to become a prominent American-inspired United Irishman, described the city thus:

> Nothing is going on here at present but raising regiments, to be devoted to destruction in America. Every order of men from the highest to the lowest are emptying their pockets (and what more could be asked from Scotchmen?) in the support of the war.[20]

---

[18] See "The American Crisis" in the Biographical Introduction, written by Jane B. Fagg, to Vincenzo Merolle's splendid edition of *The Correspondence of Adam Ferguson* (2 vols, London 1995), vol. 3, p. xlviii.

[19] Ibid., p. liii.

[20] Letter from William Drennan to Mrs M. McTier at North Street, Belfast, 20 January 1778, qtd. in E.W. McFarland's seminal *Ireland and Scotland in The Age of Revolution: Planting the Green Bough* (Edinburgh, 1994), p. 51. This letter is currently in the holdings of the Public Record Office of Northern Ireland (T.765, Drennan Letters, no. 20).

Stimulated by the Rev. Alexander Carlyle's memoirs, studies of the Edinburgh Literati have stressed, with its dinners, concerts, and balls, a world of fraternal *bonhomie*. In actual fact, as Michael Brown has shown in a remarkable essay on Carlyle, while the Literati were amiability unto themselves, they lived in an unstable world from the Jacobite Rebellion through the American War to the French Revolution, and thus were in a state of deep anxiety, even dread, about the intrusion of alien violence causing the upset of their restrictively hierarchical, hence hyper-loyal, social status. Edinburgh was no more a city of brotherly love than Philadelphia. As Brown remarks: "The Scottish Enlightenment was forged in violence, shaped by it and ultimately destroyed by it."[21] Scottish imperial careers were founded on the violence of Hanoverian triumphalism. To comprehend "Ode for General Washington's Birthday," the poem must be understood not only in this general context but, as we shall see, in the particular provocation of that most imperially inclined and anti-American of Scots, Allan Ramsay, the younger.

Burns's American Poems

Burns's first brief but pointed reference to American affairs come in the Kilmarnock edition in his "Epistle to John Ranken." Like almost all of these early Ayrshire epistles, it is preoccupied with the poet's own reputation or, more often, his lack of it. The corollary of these simultaneously comical and fraught musings, equally pervasive in so many of his letters, is Burns's rehearsal of various alternative selves, occasionally comic but frequently self-loathing. These alternative selves are predicated on his inability to achieve his true vocation as poet. His favorite poet, Oliver Goldsmith, in this crucial matter and, indeed, as we shall see in so many others, precisely located for Burns their common crucial lifelong dilemma. As Goldsmith wrote of his muse: "Thou source of all my bliss and all my woe / Who found'st me poor at first, and keep'st me so."[22]

The specific occasion of the Ranken epistle was Burns's impregnation of Betty Paton and the consequent clerical fury directed against him. This fateful coital act is described in terms of a seemingly somewhat transparent extended metaphor of a poacher who slightly wounds a partridge. The clerical fire and fury directed against him caused in Burns a partly comic sense of self-denigration which finds expression in two American-derived identities. These identities are in no way commensurate with an America whose essential libertarian promise to all men was that they would be granted personal visibility as an expression of their true needs and natures for the first time in history. Thus in stanza six we find this:

---

[21]   Michael Brown, "Alexander Carlyle and the Shadows of the Enlightenment," in Bob Harris (ed.), *Scotland in the Age of the French Revolution* (Edinburgh, 2005), pp. 226–46 (p. 234).

[22]   Oliver Goldsmith, "The Deserted Village," *Poems and Plays* (Dublin, 1785), pp. 43–56 (p. 56).

> Tho' faith, sma' heart hae I to sing:
> My Muse dow scarcely spread her wing:
> I've play'd mysel a bonie *spring*
>   An' *danc'd* my fill!
> I'd better gaen an sair't the King
>   At Bunker's Hill.[23]

In the last two lines, Burns brilliantly combines his self-image as one of the humiliated redcoats, a thousand of their comrades dead, with that of the king whose reputation in this climactic defeat is even more lost.

Stanza eleven is perhaps more complex and certainly more troubling:

> And soon's the *clockin-time* is by,
> An' the *wee pouts* begun to cry,
> Lord, I'se hae sportin by an' by
>   For my *gowd guinea*;
> Tho' I should herd the *buckskin* kye
>   For't, in Virginia![24]

This allusion to Southern slavery seems deeply problematic. It is also analogous to another of Burns's fantasized transatlantic emigrations. This is his protracted anxiety about leaving the repressive penury of Ayrshire to go to Jamaica to become a "poor Negro driver."[25] What I would suggest, however, is that Burns is in neither case belittling the slaves but seeing in the mirror a hellish image of what these positions would reduce him to and, by implication, the reality of the institution of slavery. This, after all, is the same man who in desperately seeking economic security for his family as a Customs Officer felt he had prostituted himself. Economically, Burns lived his whole life with his back to the wall. To be so often thwarted provoked in Burns an understandably perverse self-directed sadomasochism. Perhaps what Burns really felt about slavery is expressed in "The Slave's Lament," praised by Maya Angelou because of its grasp not only of the substance but the very rhythm of African American experience.[26]

Hugh Blair, one of the Literati's foremost critical theorists, on reading this epistle did not initially comprehend its sexual implications. When it did dawn on him, he was outraged and demanded that the poem be withdrawn from the second Edinburgh edition. Quite bizarrely, the poem's political allusions seem to have wholly escaped him. "When Guilford Good or Ballad on the American War" appeared in the Edinburgh edition of 1787, even Blair could not miss such

---

[23]   *Canongate Burns*, p. 149.

[24]   Ibid., p. 150.

[25]   Robert Burns to Dr Moore, 2 August 1787, in *Letters of Robert Burns*, J. De Lancey Ferguson (ed.), 2nd edn, G. Ross Roy (ed.) (2 vols, Oxford, 1985), vol. 1, pp. 133–46 (p. 144).

[26]   For a reading of this poem and its relation to the Scottish anti-slavery movement, see *The Canongate Burns*, pp. 397–8.

an overt assault. Without allegorical or Aesopian formal disguise, this poem is a full frontal assault on the failure of British arms in America and the resultant chaos in Parliament. Of this poem, Blair condescendingly remarked: "Burns's politics always smelt of the smithy."[27] The Literati must have realized, however, that with this poem a poet of real politically dissenting menace had slipped under their radar. This is not the work of a self-alleged, naively ahistorical pastoral peasant. This poem bristles with a language whose hybrid strength stems from a carnivalesque erotically and politically charged traditional vernacular combined with a vocabulary and imagery saturated in the language and caricatures of the contemporary popular press. It also reveals Burns's incredible power of compressed narrative. If Byron subjects history to louche meandering, Burns has an astonishing capacity to concentrate it. Thus, he deals with the course of the American War in four stanzas and its political fall-out in five. He himself thought the poem might be a step too far and sought the advice of Henry Erskine, Lord Buchan's younger brother. Burns had met Henry Erskine through Ayrshire Freemasonry and was to become his rhetorical and literal sparring partner in an Edinburgh club, the Crochallan Fencibles, tellingly so named as a parody on the many fencible regiments being raised in Scotland for the American War. We can only presume that the conversation inside this, the most beloved of Burns's clubs, was replete with dissenting politics and pro-American politics. As we shall see, Burns had an admiration for Henry Erskine's legal rhetoric, which may also have extended to his emigration poem. Henry was also a much more sympathetic spirit for Burns than his brother, Lord Buchan.

Since 1818, "Address to Beelzebub," Burns's second American poem has, until the last decade, led a peripheral life in the Burns canon. Carol McGuirk's perception that it was Burns's most dramatic underrated monologue happily preceded a highly contrary response.[28] Edwin Morgan, in a newspaper opinion poll, has declared it his favorite Burns poem. Marilyn Butler and Susan Manning have also endorsed the satirical greatness of its ironic monologue.[29] Burns thus sets the scene:

> To the Right Honorable, The Earl of Breadalbane, President of the Right Honorable the Highland Society, which met on the 23rd of May last, at the Shakespeare, Covent Garden, to concert ways and means to frustrate the designs of five hundred Highlanders who, as the Society was informed by Mr. M'Kenzie of Applecross, were so audacious as to attempt an escape from their lawful lords and masters whose property they were, by emigrating from the lands of Mr. Macdonald of Glengary to the wilds of Canada, in search of that fantastic thing—LIBERTY.

---

[27]   Ibid., p. 224.

[28]   See Carol McGuirk's notes in her excellent Penguin Classics *Robert Burns: Selected Poems* (London, 1993), pp. 238–9.

[29]   Butler, "Burns and Politics," p. 91; Susan Manning, "Burns and God," in *Robert Burns and Cultural Authority*, pp. 113–35 (p. 116).

What follows is the devil's address to this London/Highland audience. The address is of a Swiftian irony embodied in a manic, near-hypnotic, vernacular energy. By provoking his aristocratic audience to take the most brutalising, repressive action against their recalcitrant clansmen, he baits a trap which will lead them for their sins to hell. As Susan Manning has eloquently written:

> It is the flyting voice of earlier Scots poetry re-released against the established powers of late-eighteenth century Britain. Adopting the very voice of Evil itself, as he does in this "Address of Beelzebub," Burns pits an older Scottish cultural authority against the new order: Satan in person (or im-personated) embodies a vigour and vindictive skill which invokes the enormous historical presence assumed by the Devil in Scotland's living out of the Augustinian, Manichean dimension of Calvinist theology.[30]

It is a poem which seethes with contending violences. The degenerate aristocracy brutally repressed Atlantic emigration, hence exposing Highland men and women to both the legal and physical cruelties and enslaving work, including prostitution, of the socially deprived life in the South. The crux of the poem, a sort of double irony, lies in the Devil's envisagement of a scenario where the American forces which demolished the British are not only resurrected on behalf of the deracinated Highlanders but the losing British generals also appear allegedly to defeat the Highlanders.

Recent performed readings of this poem, by no means exclusive to Highland audiences, have proved electrifying. There is, of course, the problem of whether its recently resurrected emotive power is compatible with the nature and volume of Highland post-Culloden emigration. The most current research on the matter, however, provides substantial evidence for Burns's case. It is calculated that between 15,000 and 20,000 Highlanders emigrated in the period 1760 to 1775:

> Migration was a response to the profound changes that swept the region following the Battle of Culloden in 1746, which transformed traditional society and released forces that were to have far-reaching consequences. Recent writers have emphasized the social impact of agrarian improvement and rent inflation after 1760 ... Many landowners systematically "subordinated their estates to the pursuit of profit," and in so doing brought about a fundamental realignment in the laird-tenant relationship, from one based on a finely graded system of reciprocal duties and loyalties to one founded on money and market rates.[31]

The fundamental obligation of the feudal Highlander was martial duty to his chief. Burns's poetry, even more his songs, is not only replete with the sufferings of the post-Culloden Jacobites, the dead and maimed men and keening women,

---

[30] Manning, "Burns and God," p. 116.

[31] James Horn, "British Diaspora: Emigration from Britain, 1680–1815," in P.J. Marshall (ed.), *The Oxford History of the British Empire: The Eighteenth Century* (Oxford, 1998), pp. 28–52 (p. 43).

but also with the same sufferings now endured in the context of service in the British Imperial Armies. Culloden and its Jacobite Catholic victims sat heavily on him. We now know that, astonishingly, "by 1810 one third of the entire Catholic population had left the Highlands and Islands for America."[32] Specific to "The Address of Beelzebub," he may have known the 1786 report that "Last year upwards of three hundred souls left Glengarry and its neighbourhood almost all Roman Catholics and settled in Canada above Mont-Real, where were already settled eight hundred Highlanders."[33] Some prosperous Highlanders with their retainers went to America to advance themselves. Some of them went to what were envisaged as conservative, ideal communities. This is particularly true of Burns's admired friend Lord Daer's younger brother, the Earl of Selkirk:

> Some were attracted to sponsored projects, such as those of the Earl of Selkirk at Baldoon, near Detroit, in 1804, and Red River, near Lake Winnipeg, which were intended to preserve Gaelic-speaking enclaves from the sort of pernicious commercial influences undermining traditional ways of life at home. For many Highlanders, emigration was not motivated primarily by considerations of material gain but was reluctantly perceived as a necessary, if painful, means "to preserve in the New World that which was being destroyed in the Old."[34]

These conservative, idealized projects are a Highland variant on a plethora of similar European schemes, all of which fragmented on impact with American realities. In Gaelic poetry itself, there is evidence that the emigrants' woods were dark, deep, but also deadly. There is also some evidence to support Burns's hatreds and aspirations. As one poet writes,

> But if ever you go
> Over the sea
> Bring my greetings to my friends
> Urge them without delay
> To flee the rents
> And come out as soon as opportune for them.
> If they could find a time
> And means to come over
> They would not be beholden to MacDonald
> They would get land
> In which to sow crops,
> And potatoes and barley would grow very well.
>
> This is the isle of contentment
> Where we are now.
> Our seed is fruitful here;
> Oats grow

---

[32] Ibid., p. 45.

[33] Ibid.

[34] Ibid., p. 46.

And wheat, in full bloom,
Turnip, cabbage, and peas.
Sugar from trees
May be had free here;
We have it in large chunks
There is fresh red rum
In every dwelling and shop.[35]

This sense of material well-being has nothing to do with Highland radical aspirations as the Burns poem suggests it should. The post-Culloden Highlands were too traumatized to politically defy the British state. For example, plans made in London by the celebrated Anglo-Scottish radical Thomas Hardy for a Gaelic translation of Paine's *Rights of Man* appear to have been aborted. Even if this text had been available, it would have fallen on dead and stony ground. There is no evidence in Scottish Gaelic poetry of sympathy for the American cause. Irish Gaelic poetry, however, as Vincent Morley has pointed out, is replete with American allusions, as is evident in Morley's prose translation of a "drinking song" by Tomás Ó Míocháin:

> It's a joy and a pleasure to me that Howe and the English, are spent and destroyed for ever, and stalwart Washington, supporting, courageous, is at the helm and in command of his realm; behold the mercenaries screaming without a refuge or city, without troops, without ships on the sea, and by Halloween it's certain that the British boors, will be trapped and in the custody of Louis [XVII].[36]

There is indeed a seething violence here comparable to "The Address of Beelzebub." It is, however, a violence at the center of an essentially reactionary politics. Washington is here merely as a means to a resurrectionary Jacobite end. As Morley has remarked: "The sympathy of lower-class Catholics for the American rebels was superficial and rested on nothing more profound than the pragmatic calculation that 'my enemy's enemy is my friend'."[37]

If, however, Irish Gaelic poetry offers little sustenance to Burns's democratic politics, one Anglo-Irish poem is of deep generic significance to "The Address of Beelzebub" in particular and radical British emigration to America poetry in general. John Barrell has recently pointed out that by the 1790s, Oliver Goldsmith's seminal emigrant poem "The Deserted Village" had metamorphosed from a conservative poem that envisaged a paradise of lost communal equality to a poetry that projected this equality across the Atlantic. Thus, Barrell writes of a poem by John Towell Rutt, "The Prospect of Emigration":

---

[35]   This poem is by Calum Ban Mac Mhannian (1758–1829), "Imrich nan Eileanach/ Emigration of the Islanders," in *The Emigrant Experience: Songs of the Highland Emigrants in North America*, Margaret MacDonell (ed.) (Toronto, 1982), pp. 105–13 (pp. 111–3).

[36]   Vincent Morley, *Irish Opinion and the American Revolution, 1760–1783* (Cambridge, 2002), p. 111.

[37]   Ibid., p. 112.

The poem lamented the oppression and corruption of Britain, and the violent justice that had sentenced Muir and Palmer to transportation, and imagined an escape from what he called "Europe's servile coast" to the land "beyond the western wave." There, as once in Auburn, they would be under the protection of God, and in the shadow of no great house:

Nor o'er those meads shall frown th'embattled dome,
     Rear'd by some haughty Tyrant of the soil,
But Independence glad the peasant's home,
     And Plenty recompense his willing toil.

There all the children of one bounteous Sire,
     In friendship join, on Nature's equal plan,
To virtue's true nobility aspire,
     And boast alike the *dignity of Man*.[38]

Two things can be suggested from this. First, that Burns similarly inverts the politics of "The Deserted Village." His Highlanders enter a landscape commensurate with their political desires and are not savagely consumed in an alien jungle. Second, though formally and linguistically different and arguably superior, Burns's themes and tropes are largely indistinguishable from those prevailing in English radical poetry in the 1780s and 90s.

It is also the case that other Scottish responses to Goldsmith's poem retain their political bias of conservative loss into the 1790s. Thus, written in 1796, we have Alexander Wilson's "The Tears of Britain." We also have another fine poem, Henry Erskine's "The Emigrant," written originally in 1773 and republished by Brash and Reid in 1797. As noted above, Burns was a great admirer of Erskine's rhetorical court performances and, even more germane, Erskine was one of his intimates in the Crochallan Fencibles. It seems likely, therefore, that he knew the Erskine emigrant poem, given Brash and Reid's acknowledgement of its extended publication history:

The following very beautiful and pathetic Poem, the production of the Honorable Henry Erskine, was written upon occasion of the frequent Emigrations from Scotland, more especially from the Highlands....

     Copies of it appeared, some time ago, in a mutilated form; the present is printed from that done with permission of the amiable and distinguished author, and it will afford the Reader more pleasure, when he is assured that it is entire.[39]

---

[38]   John Barrell, "*Rus in Urbe*," in Philip Connell and Nigel Leask (eds), *Romanticism and Popular Culture in Britain and Ireland* (Cambridge, 2009), pp. 109–27 (p. 114).

[39]   Henry Erskine, "The Emigrant," published by Brash and Reid in their four volume *Poetry; Original and Selected* (Glasgow, 1796–1798), largely an anodyne, random selection of mainly English verse apparently partly designed for the American market.

The poem is in the form of an elegiac monologue by an ancient Highlander about to embark to America. If sentimental, it is hardly Ossianically so. Burns would certainly have concurred with Erskine's detailed analysis of what had gone wrong. Indeed, all his own elements of Highland suffering are present in Erskine's poem:

> Thou, dear companion of my happier life,
> Now to the grave gone down, my virtuous wife,
> 'Twas here you rear'd with fond maternal pride,
> Five comely sons: three for their country died!
> Two still remain, sad remnant of the wars,
> Without one mark of honour but their scars;
> They live to see their sire denied a grave,
> In lands his much lov'd children died to save:
> Yet still in peace and safety did we live,
> In peace and safety more than wealth can give.
> My two remaining boys with sturdy hands,
> Rear'd the scant produce of our niggard lands:
> Scant as it was, no more our hearts desir'd,
> No more from us our gen'rous lord requir'd.
>
> But ah, sad change! those blessed days are o'er,
> And peace, content, and safety charm no more,
> Another lord now rules those wide domains,
> The avaricious tyrant of the plains,
> Far far from hence he revels life away,
> In guilty pleasures, our poor means must pay.
> The mossy plains, the mountains' barren brow,
> Must now be tortur'd by the tearing plough,
> And, spite of nature, crops he taught to rise,
> Which to these northern climes wise Heav'n denies,
> In vain, with sweating brow and weary hands,
> We strive to earn the gold our lord demands,
> While cold and hunger, and the dungeon's gloom,
> Await our failure as its certain doom.[40]

While "Address of Beelzebub" is unmistakably Burns in both its rhythmical form and its virile vernacular energy, Burns's third American poem, "Ode on General Washington's Birthday," is composed in an inflated standard English, a vocabulary he occasionally used to varied effect. Formally, it is utterly different from anything else in his poetry. This ode remains a source of some mystery with regard to both its genesis and its formal nature. What I now have to say about these issues is of a significantly speculative nature. What follows is necessarily a rehearsal of questions rather than a definitive critical evaluation.

---

[40] Erskine, "The Emigrant," in Brash and Reid, *Poetry; Original and Selected*, vol. 1, pp. 4–5.

For example, if we consider the poem formally, it is possible to suggest that Burns brilliantly adapts, indeed usurps, the earlier Pindaric ode form employed to celebrate monarchs in the seventeenth century in order to celebrate Washington who was, especially for upper-class radical Scots, the consummate American democratic hero. If this is the case, it does not contradict the fact that Burns may have chosen both the poem's form and language to disguise his authorship. As we have seen, the only admission he ever made of writing this poem was in a letter to Mrs Dunlop. If disguise was his purpose, this is little to be wondered at given both his absolute condemnation of the degeneration of England in the poem from its alleged roots in Alfred's Anglo-Saxon democracy combined with his utter pessimism about the state of Scotland. All the defiance present in 1792 and 1793, as in "Scots Wha Hae," has evaporated. The poem's last stanza is the darkest and bleakest that Burns, nearing the end of his life, ever wrote about Scotland:

> Thee, Caledonia, thy wild heaths among,
> Fam'd for the martial deed, the heaven-taught song,
>   To thee, I turn with swimming eyes. —
>   Where is that soul of Freedom fled?
>   Immingled with the mighty Dead!
> Beneath that hallow'd turf where WALLACE lies!
> Hear it not, Wallace, in thy bed of death!
>   Ye babbling winds in silence sweep;
>   Disturb not ye the hero's sleep,
>   Nor give the coward secret breath. —
> Is the ancient Caledonian form,
> Firm as her rock, resistless as her storm?
> Shew me that eye which shot immortal hate,
>   Blasting the Despot's proudest bearing:
> Shew me that arm which, nerved with thundering fate,
>   Braved Usurpation's boldest daring!
>   Dark-quenched as yonder sinking star,
>   No more that glance lightens afar;
> That palsied arm no more whirls on the waste of war. —[41]

Before we deal with the pressure of immediate historical events that caused such negation of all Scottish hopes in Burns, we have to deal with the positive vision of the ode, which is that of Washington's America. In fact, Burns's eulogization of Washington was no singular act but emerged from an extensive body of Scottish opinion. The primary evidence for this is an anonymous English poem, sub-Miltonic in tone, which was also published in Glasgow in 1797 by Brash and Reid.[42] Here is the poem:

---

[41] *Canongate Burns*, pp. 815–6.

[42] Brash and Reid, *Poetry; Original and Selected*, vol. 3, sec. 13, pp. 7–8. The choice of this poem may have been partly due to Brash and Reid's transatlantic export market. All efforts to identify the author of this poem or its place of earlier publication have so far proved fruitless.

Verses
on
General Washington

Oh for a spark of fire from that bright source,
Which beam'd on Milton, while he struck the lyre
To sing our first great parents' blissful state;
Then might the humble Muse record that praise
Of honest modest worth in language meet;
Might sing of one who more substantial good
To his dear country wrought more solid joys
Than fell Ambition ever yet achiev'd;
Of one who Nature's sacred dictates priz'd,
And firmly cherish'd in his social breast;
Who, without crafty wiles and tricks, could find
The means to govern men by their own wills.

  Great Washington alone, of all who live
In Plutarch's page, or elsewhere yet survive,
Of best esteem, from calumny is free;
His counsels sweet, like those divine behests
Bestow'd on Israel's sons from Sinai's mount,
Must cheer the mind that is not callous grown,
To deeds of great emprize, howe'er it dreads
Lest wicked men defeat the great design.

  Nor pride of riches, nor the lust of rule,
Came near his heart; his privilege to feel
And own the law of universal love.
This his vast power. The world might thus be sway'd,
Could Nature's kind pre-eminence avail;
City with city then might vie; each seek its fame
In Philadelphia's * mild and unassuming claim.

*Brotherly love

This poem, probably unknown to Burns, is, however, very close in its eulogization to the first Washington-inspired stanza of his own ode. Was Burns's poem written and this poem published to mark the near total disparity between the American Revolution and the chaos prevailing in France by the mid-1790s? Were they meant to reassure radical opinion that Washington was exemplary of a leader who could wholly beneficially integrate, rather than exploit, the people's will with his own? What is not in doubt is that these idealized versions of Washington were held by many Scottish radicals. In only one case, however, did this come through any degree of personal contact. Norman MacLeod, MP for Inverness, celebrated by Burns for his radical activities, became a prisoner of war in America. This proximity to Washington was sufficient to make him appreciate the American's greatness.[43] MacLeod's singular experience was to reappear, somewhat dubiously, in Thomas Muir's memorandum to Talleyrand regarding what Muir estimated as the vast pro-French revolt that would break out in Scotland on the landing of French troops:

> The Real Scotch soldiers are deeply tinctured with revolutionary principles. In combating liberty in America they caught its spirit. They have reared … their children in its principles & the tyranny of England now forces them to wage war against France. They only want the moment when Insurrection may present a rational hope of success.[44]

Mutilated, disorientated in Paris toward the end of his life as Muir was at this point, this statement represents a quite unrealistic but unhappily characteristic assessment of the Scottish situation. Hector MacMillan reveals that at key moments in Muir's desperately troubled political career both he and, indeed, his father sought by letter Washington's intercession. There is no evidence of reciprocation on Washington's part.[45]

Sadly for the Earl of Buchan, his correspondence with Washington was marked not by silence but by a characteristic caution on the American's part. This, however, is not immediately evident in Buchan's retrospective commentary on his relationship with Washington, which was published by Buchan in 1811 under the title *The Earl of Buchan's Address to the Americans at Edinburgh on Washington's Birthday February 22nd, 1811*. Somewhat pompous in tone, occasionally eccentrically prophetic, this could equally be entitled *Some Extraordinary People I Have Corresponded With*, since only the first few pages can be considered as an address to an audience. The rest is made up of exchanges of letters not only with Washington himself but also, as we have seen, with Jefferson and Pitt the Elder, along with occasional supporting material of Buchan's often eccentric contriving. Buchan begins his address with a prophetic account of world history that is beyond the present writer's comprehension: "It is my intention, in the following lines to show, that a new situation has occurred in the arrangement of human affairs and how it may be improved in coincidence with superintending Providence." The traces of astronomical observation in India are said to agree with a period of fifty-two centuries; and with the Newtonian and received theory of gravitation, and consequent diminution of the inclination of the planetary axis to the plane of their orbits.[46]

---

[43]   I am indebted to Hector MacMillan's *Handful of Rogues: Thomas Muir's Enemies of the People* (Glendaruel, 2005) for this information on both MacLeod and Thomas Muir.

[44]   Thomas Muir, "Letter & Memorandum—Muir to Talleyrand," Appendix C in MacMillan, *Handful of Rogues*, p. 259.

[45]   As well as revealing the varied epistolary evidence of both father's and son's faith in Washington as political savior, MacMillan also reveals that the rescue of Muir off the Australian coast by the American ship *Otter* was almost certainly a random event and not, as has been alleged, arranged by Washington.

[46]   Washington did have Scottish correspondents: James Anderson, editor of *The Bee*, Sir John Sinclair and, most persistently, the Earl of Buchan. Matters of revolution and

Leaving this obscurity aside, Buchan's main message, although less cogent, is very similar to Richard Price's. America does represent for both spiritual and socio-economic reasons a quantum leap that will not be subject to imperial decline:

> The colonists from Great Britain, settling in America, have furnished the example of what constitutes the cement for erecting the true and lasting edifice of government, *knowledge mixt with virtue building upon the platform of real prosperity, and agricultural industry and simplicity of manners.*[47]

Buchan concludes this opening section with an account of his first letter to Washington:

> Impressed with the view of the advantages likely to ensue from the wise administration of the Infant States of America, and reflecting on the great part which it has pleased the Almighty Governor of the Universe to enable Mr. Washington to perform in the New World, I was desirous of contributing my mite to the exaltation of his character, as a medium of legitimate power founded in the opinion of the people. I sent to him a letter expressive of my esteem, and of my wishes for the prosperity of the States, which I inclosed in a box made of oak that afforded shelter to our great Wallace after the battle of Falkirk; and I afterwards expressed my hope that the States would cultivate peace, friendship, and correspondence with my country, and shun every occasion of mingling in the unhappy contentions of Europe.[48]

While Buchan attempts to integrate Wallace with the American spirit in 1792, it is relevant to recall that a mere two years later, Burns describes the spirit of that national hero as irretrievably dead in Scotland itself. In his reply, Washington, while promising Buchan a portrait of himself, also announced that he was returning the box, a matter to which we will return.

What is immediately relevant is the fact that, in the last few pages of his address entitled *On Omens by Albanicus* (Buchan's pen-name), Buchan's belief in his own prophetic soul turns from light to dark in his analysis of British guilt toward America: "these are instances of what we call, in Scotland, readings of sins in punishments."[49] Two of the chief revelatory British punishments for him are the unprecedented surrenders of Burgoyne and Cornwallis to British arms. It is even more significant for our argument, however, that Buchan sees Scotland's conduct toward America as even more nefarious than Britain's :

---

global politics are not, however, to be discovered in the correspondence. Washington's sole preoccupation was with acquiring highly professional Scottish gardeners for his American estate. See vol. 7, *George Washington: First in Peace*, by Mary Wells Ashworth and John Alexander Carroll [Completing the Biography of Douglas Southall Freeman], of *George Washington: A Biography* (7 vols, London, 1948–1957).

[47] Buchan, *Address to the Americans*, p. 7
[48] Ibid., p. 8.
[49] Ibid., p. 35.

Scotland was the great abettor of the unjust war with the American colonies, and on St Andrew's Day the Parliament of England passed the resolution to reduce America to obedience by force. On the same anniversary, did the whole power of Britain, by its representative at Paris, sign the preliminary articles, by which America was acknowledged to be a sovereign and independent nation; and the great Franklin signed the definitive treaty, on the 23rd of January in the same dress he had been insulted in the House of Lords, that day being also the anniversary of the motion of Lord Chatham to withdraw the fleets and armies from North America.[50]

Buchan starts his address with a vision of Scottish and American symbiotic democratic growth. He ends it with a damning vision, however tendentious his evidence, of Scotland as the chief American enemy. This is even darker than anything in Burns's poem, though there are obvious parallels between them. Arguably, these parallels are of a tangible nature. While Burns was fifteen years dead by 1811, he seems to have been so much in Buchan's mind. The text of Buchan's address also contains in several places comments in his own handwriting. On his letter to Washington of 28 June 1791 promising the oak box, we find this piece of marginalia:

This Box was recommitted to me by the will of the General & delivered into my hands at Mill Grove near Gogar by Mr. Liston the British Envoy on his return from America. I afterwards sent it to America by the hand of Dr. Chapman to contain Prize Medals of the Bust of Washington to be presented to the most learned and Virtuous Student in the University founded by the General. On Dr. Chapman's journey to Philadelphia it was Stolen and is now probably in the possession of some future BURNS.[51]

If Buchan foresaw an American Burns as the necessary poet-creator of the republic, it has to be said that his earlier attempts to enlist the original Burns in such democratic Scottish campaigning was not always harmonious. His desire to involve Burns in the commemoration of James Thomson went largely awry. Perhaps Buchan's patronage entailed mere cashless exhortation. However, on 12 January 1794, Burns wrote to Buchan enclosing "Scots Wha Hae," his remarks appropriate to the poem's defiant, upbeat aspirations. The triumph over English oppression in this poem is, it will be noted, the very reverse of the Anglo-Scottish relations described in the stanza of the Washington ode to Mrs Dunlop on 25 June 1794. The first part of 1794, then, saw a precipitate collapse in Burns's anticipations. Revealingly, it also saw three letters from Buchan in what appears to be a renewal of their correspondence. Sadly, only summarized fragments of these letters exists. The key letter is from Dryburgh Abbey, 3 February 1794: "Plans a poem for Burns on Ramsay's American Revolution."[52]

---

50   Ibid., p. 35.
51   Ibid., p. 15.
52   Burns, *Letters*, Ross Roy (ed.), vol. 2, p. 426.

While this seems to prove that there is a tangible connection between Buchan and the Washington ode, it also seems likely that the Ramsay in question is the often-admirable painter and arch-conservative polemicist Allan Ramsay, who wrote prolifically and passionately against the American cause. If he is, indeed, the Ramsay in question, it is most probable that Buchan is referring to the last and most bitter of Ramsay's anti-American writings. In this book, *A Succinct Review of the American Contest, Addressed to Those Whom it May Concern. By Zero*, Ramsay advocates that the British should not fight the Americans on their strategic and territorial grounds but use the mobility of British sea power as a form of brutal guerrilla tactics.[53] Bruce Lenman has also identified Ramsay as the most extreme Scottish opponent of American independence: "he preached a systematic devastation of property and, if necessary, life in the revolting colonies in order to bring them back to appropriate subjection to the Crown."[54] Ironically, it is possibly the poet Allan Ramsay's son who becomes Robert Burns's political antithesis.[55]

---

[53] Allan Ramsay, *A Succinct Review of the American Contest, Addressed to Those Whom it May Concern. By Zero* (London, 1782).

[54] Lenman, *Enlightenment and Change*, p. 92.

[55] The polar opposition between the two men, not only over America, can be seen in Ramsay's devotion to the House of Hanover and its imperial ambitions and the fact that Ramsay perceived the good society as a petrified hierarchy where the mass of men owed complete obedience to their aristocratic protectors. Thus for Ramsay, American aspirations must have seemed to be those of The Great Satan. From what we have seen, Ramsay is not really distinguishable from the Moderate Literati. Is then this late eighteenth-century Scottish culture in any way definable as a product of Enlightenment values? Should it not be better defined as a highly advanced precursor of Victorian Imperialism?

PART 2
Burns and New World
Print Networks

Chapter 3
Tracing the Transatlantic Bard's Availability

Fiona A. Black

On 18 June 1789, the following notice appeared in the *Quebec Gazette*:

> Charlottetown, May 4, 1789. Proposals for printing by subscription, the Poems of that celebrated Scots ploughman Robert Burns. To be printed in one neat pocket volume, three to four hundred pages, on fine writing paper and a good type. Price to Subscribers, six shillings ... Subscriptions are received by Mr. James Robertson (the Publisher) at his Printing Office in the Island of St John and at the Printing Office ... Quebec. The fame of this author is spreading rapidly and the merit of his works is acknowledged by all who have had an opportunity of seeing them. The Demand is so great that the first edition (published last May) is already exhausted and a second edition is now being printed in London. Price 6 Shillings in boards.[1]

While there is no evidence that this proposed edition was ever published, the very fact of a subscription notice suggests an early, if cautious, economic interest in the poetry of Burns by printers in British North America (see Figure 3.1). This economic interest was indisputably allied to cultural interest, as James Robertson was one of many Scots who were instrumental in establishing the printing and allied trades in what was to become Canada.[2] During the following 150 years, this interest focused primarily on the wholesaling and retailing of imported rather than local editions—a less risky business venture than local publication. Book exporters and importers were critical players in ensuring that volumes of Burns played out their geographically unbounded role, defined by Innis and later theorists, as "important carriers of cultural value."[3] Innis's views that societal development is integrally

---

[1] *Quebec Gazette*, 18 June 1789, qtd. in Marie Tremaine, *A Bibliography of Canadian Imprints, 1751–1800* (1952; Toronto, 1999), Entry 584. The lack of evidence of printing is further confirmed, following exhaustive research, in Patricia Lockhart Fleming and Sandra Alston, *Early Canadian Printing* (Toronto, 1999), Entry 584.

[2] Fiona A. Black, "Searching for the 'Vanguard of an Army of Scots' in the Early Canadian Book Trade," *Papers of the Bibliographical Society of Canada*, 38/2 (2000): 65–100; Warren McDougall, "James Robertson," in Patricia Lockhart Fleming, Gilles Gallichan, and Yvan Lamonde (eds), *History of the Book in Canada, Volume I: Beginnings to 1840* (Toronto, 2004), pp. 69–70.

[3] Harold Innis, *Empire and Communications* (Toronto, 1950).

Fig. 3.1   John Pinkerton. "British possessions in North America," in *A Modern Atlas, from the latest and best authorities, exhibiting the various divisions of the world, with its chief empires, kingdoms and states, in sixty maps, carefully reduced from the largest and most authentic sources* (London: T. Cadell and W. Davies; and Longman, Hurst, Rees, Orme, and Brown, 1815). © David Rumsey Map Collection, www.davidrumsey.com. Reproduced with permission.

tied to communications media are implicitly embedded in several models of book history and print culture. Robert Darnton's model of the "Communications Circuit" in book history particularly emphasizes the role of communication and the importance of "agents of the press" in cultural development.[4]

In this way, knowledge of the mechanisms of the book trade, especially those factors that influenced the international movement of books, contributes to a nuanced understanding of the literary history of any region. How readers acquired access to Burns's poems and songs informed the context in which they read or listened. The constraints faced by the publishing industry, due to transportation costs, legislative frameworks, and lack of trading networks, directly contributed

---

[4]   Robert Darnton, "What is the History of Books?" *Daedalus*, 111 (Summer 1982): 65–83.

to book availability in Canadian towns and villages.[5] Furthermore, business historians can help us to question our assumptions about geographical distance and its effects on such book availability. For example, some Scottish publications were available in Nova Scotia before they were accessible in Elgin, Scotland. The 3,000 miles of ocean were thus sometimes less of a hindrance than might be expected, due to existing trading networks and proactive local merchants and booksellers. Early urban and rural Canadian readers were much better served than some provincial areas of Britain.[6]

The research presented here indicates a generalized availability in Georgian Canada of printed copies of Burns's poems and songs, whether in codex or single-sheet format. Burns might be considered a quintessentially appropriate writer for the varied psyches of colonists and settlers. His work "blends English with Scots, sentiment with satire, literary with local references."[7] From Highland emigrants to lowland teachers, soldiers, and merchants, Burns's works had the potential to strike an emotional or intellectual chord. Perhaps especially for those who left Scotland against their will, Burns's view of his country as "an imagination of freedom" would have held a special resonance.[8]

Those who sold Burns's works in Canadian towns were savvy business people, often familiar with the content of reviewing journals as soon as they were offloaded at the local wharf. Many would have read the glowing report by James Sibbald (of Edinburgh circulating library fame) in his *Edinburgh Magazine* in October 1786.[9] In addition, they would have seen the *Monthly Review* in December of that year, in which the reviewer commented on the Kilmarnock edition in many favorable ways, though also including the following caution:

> We much regret that these poems are written in some measure in an unknown tongue, which must deprive most of our Readers of the pleasure they would otherwise naturally create; being composed in the Scottish dialect, which

---

5   Before Confederation in 1867, the geographic area that would become Canada was a collection of British colonies, corporate-owned fur-trading areas, French settlements, and contested fishing grounds. For the sake of convenience, this chapter refers to all of these regions collectively as Canada or Georgian Canada, the latter specifically for the period 1750 to 1820.

6   Fiona A. Black, "Book Distribution to the Scottish and Canadian Provinces, 1750–1820: Examples of Methods and Availability," in Peter Isaac and Barry McKay (eds), *The Reach of Print: Making, Selling and Using Books* (Winchester and New Castle, DE, 1998), pp. 103–20.

7   Carol McGuirk, "Writing Scotland: Robert Burns," in Susan Manning, Ian Brown, Thomas Owen Clancy, and Murray Pittock (eds), *The Edinburgh History of Scottish Literature Volume Two: Enlightenment, Britain and Empire, 1707–1918* (Edinburgh, 2007), pp. 169–77 (p. 169).

8   McGuirk, "Writing Scotland: Robert Burns," p. 176.

9   Richard B. Sher, *The Enlightenment and the Book: Scottish Authors and Their Publishers in Eighteenth-Century Britain, Ireland and America* (Chicago and London, 2006), pp. 113–4.

contains many words that are altogether unknown to an English reader: beside, they abound with allusions to modes of life, opinions and ideas, of the people in a remote corner of the country, which would render many passages obscure, and consequently uninteresting, to those who perceive not the forcible accuracy of the picture of the objects to which they allude.[10]

This issue of dialect was apparently of little concern to Canadian readers and listeners, based on the evidence of Burns's works being imported to Halifax, Saint John (New Brunswick), York/Toronto, Kingston, Quebec, and Montreal by specialized booksellers, local printers, and general merchants. Published editions of Burns's poems arrived in these ports and were thereafter distributed to other towns and villages within weeks of coming off the presses in Scotland, England and, to a lesser extent, America. Indeed the wholesaling networks of urban booksellers and general merchants were crucial elements in a supply chain that reached into villages and hamlets in most areas of Canada. Over the ensuing decades, knowledge of Burns spread through oral and literate mechanisms so that Canadian novelists in the nineteenth century, such as Amelia Barr, referred to him with an assurance that their readers would understand the allusion.[11]

The availability of editions of Burns was advertised initially in local newspapers and gradually, as Canada's print culture developed, in book trade and literary magazines and other periodicals. The imported volumes were sold by printers, booksellers, and general merchants and made available for loan in commercial circulating and private subscription libraries. Within two years of John Wilson's printing of the Kilmarnock edition,[12] printers J. and A. McLean in New York and publishers Peter Stewart and George Hyde in Philadelphia were competing with British editions, by distributing their own in several parts of North America. Nevertheless, by far the majority of editions of poetry broadsides and collections of Burns were published in Edinburgh or London and exported either directly from printers/publishers to colonial booksellers or, more commonly in the period to 1820, through the intermediary of general merchants and wholesaling warehouses.[13] Books tended not to move across the Atlantic through trade unless there was confidence on the supply and demand sides that the volumes would sell. Returning unsold stock, whilst not unknown, was a lengthy and risky procedure, highly unpopular with London and Scottish publishers.[14]

---

[10]   *The Monthly Review*, 85 (December 1786): 439–48 (440).

[11]   Amelia E. Barr, *A Daughter of Fife* (Toronto, Montreal, and Halifax, 1886), p. 168.

[12]   John Wilson was both printer and bookseller in Kilmarnock from 1782 to 1790 (Scottish Book Trade Index, www.nls.uk/catalogues/resources/sbti/).

[13]   Fiona A. Black, "Book Availability in Canada, 1752–1820, and the Scottish Contribution" (PhD dissertation, Loughborough University, 1999), Ch. 4.

[14]   Warren McDougall, "Scottish Books for America in the Mid-18th Century," in Robin Myers and Michael Harris (eds), *Spreading the Word: The Distribution Networks of Print, 1550–1850* (Winchester and Detroit, 1990), pp. 21–46; Black, "Book Distribution to the Scottish and Canadian Provinces, 1750–1820."

Book buyers and borrowers were not the only colonists and settlers who had access to Burns, of course, as newspapers reprinted individual poems, singers spread both words and tunes, and songsheets appeared in cottages and inns. In addition, individuals brought copies of Burns's poetry with them when they sailed into ports both large and small. Thus, there was the potential for multi-layered access to Burns's works in any given location. Multiple means of dissemination, through oral means and a variety of printed vehicles, likely resulted in an awareness and knowledge of Burns that transcended any single cultural or socio-economic group. Transatlantic trading networks contributed strongly to this availability.

Burns and the Book Trade

Susan Manning and Francis D. Cogliano assert that "there was no Enlightenment without the Atlantic."[15] Richard Sher's research dovetails with this assertion and delineates Scottish authors' relations with publishers in Britain, Ireland, and America and points out that Burns "interacted extensively" with many Enlightenment figures when he visited Edinburgh in 1786 to 1787.[16] His works may be considered, from a transatlantic book trade perspective, alongside those of Hugh Blair, Henry Mackenzie, William Robertson, Adam Ferguson, David Hume, Adam Smith, and others. Both Sher and Warren McDougall have amply demonstrated the business acumen of Enlightenment and earlier Scottish authors, whose works were either published solely in London, or by partnerships between Edinburgh and London, due to the imperative of using London's distributive networks to enhance profits, especially in relation to overseas trade.[17] Burns demonstrated his own awareness of the book trade when his Kilmarnock edition was published in order to help fund his proposed emigration to Jamaica, and his unexpected financial success led to his remaining in Scotland.[18]

Book trade practices in Scotland had, since the early eighteenth century, cautiously accommodated transatlantic business interests, frequently via London. There was remarkable stability in such trade practices well into the nineteenth century primarily because the technologies of communication, including those of transportation, did not change until the advent of steam-driven engines and presses.[19] Whilst there were very few technological innovations in the book trade in this period, the Union of 1707 and subsequent expansions of trading

---

[15]   Susan Manning and Francis D. Cogliano, editorial introduction to *The Atlantic Enlightenment* (Aldershot, 2008), pp. 1–18 (p. 1).

[16]   Sher, *The Enlightenment and the Book*, pp. 113–4.

[17]   McDougall, "Scottish Books for America in the Mid-18th Century"; Sher, *The Enlightenment and the Book.*

[18]   Magnus Magnusson (ed.), *Chambers Biographical Dictionary* (Edinburgh, 1990).

[19]   Bryan Dewalt, "Printing Technology," in Yvan Lamonde, Patricia Lockhart Fleming, and Fiona A. Black (eds), *History of the Book in Canada, Volume II, 1840–1918* (Toronto, 2005), pp. 89–101.

and related financial opportunities encouraged entrepreneurial activities amongst printers, publishers, and booksellers, including those who saw North America as a golden opportunity. Though Canada was considered to be on the periphery when compared to the trading hubs of Philadelphia, Boston, and New York, there is yet clear evidence in advertisements placed in weekly newspapers and in early library and auction catalogues of the presence of Burns's works for sale in Canadian towns. Table 3.1 illustrates examples of these.

Table 3.1   Selected Canadian Newspaper Advertisements and Catalogue Entries for "Burns's Poems," 1796 to 1818

Date	Canadian town	Newspaper/ Catalogue	Importing merchant or bookseller	Geographic origin of shipment	Format and price
1796, June 16th	Halifax	*Halifax Journal*	James Kidston	London	
1796, Nov. 2nd	Niagara	*Upper Canada Gazette and American Oracle*	Gideon Tiffany	New York[?]	
1797	Montreal	Catalogue of English and French Books in the Montreal Library			12mo, 2 vols
1799, May 2nd	Halifax	*Halifax Journal*	James Kidston	Glasgow/ Liverpool	2 vols New edition
1800	Quebec	Catalogue of English, French and Latin Books	John Neilson	London	8vo, 4 vols
1811	Quebec	Catalogue of Books	John Neilson	London	8vo; 3s 9d, 4s 6d
1818	York/ Toronto	Catalogue of Books in the York Circulating Library	George Dawson		18mo; 7s 6d

Testifying to the trade perception, by booksellers and merchants on both sides of the Atlantic, that it would be a steady seller, "Burns's Poems" was one of nine Enlightenment titles for which there is evidence of import from all three locations: Scotland, London, and America. The titles, in descending order of number of shipments up to 1820, discovered to date, with a known port of export are provided in Table 3.2. Whilst care is required in interpreting this sample evidence, it is striking that Burns's work is the only example of poetry to be imported from all three locations. It is especially notable, given that poetry is the sixth-ranked subject of Scottish Enlightenment first editions after history, medicine, philosophy, science (including mathematics), and fiction.[20] Exporters in a range of locations from the central hub of London and the ports along the Clyde, to large and small towns in America, felt assured that Burns's poems would sell arguably better than other poets' works which were also imported, but apparently not from all three countries.

Table 3.2   Scottish Enlightenment Works Imported to Canada from Scotland, London, and America up to 1820

Author	Short Title
Tobias Smollett	*Peregrine Pickle*
William Robertson	*Charles V*
William Robertson	*History of Scotland*
William Buchan	*Domestic Medicine*
Hugh Blair	*Lectures on Rhetoric and Belles Lettres*
Hugh Blair	*Sermons*
William Guthrie	*Geographical Grammar*
Robert Burns	*Poems*
William Smellie, translator	*Buffon's Natural History*

Those advertising these volumes in Canadian towns include specialist printer/ booksellers such as John Neilson of Quebec, Robert Fletcher of Halifax, and Gideon Tiffany of Niagara and Kingston, and general merchants such as James, Richard and William Kidston of Halifax, and Colin Campbell of Saint John (New Brunswick).

These nine Enlightenment titles are amongst the overall imported "bestsellers" in Canada up to 1820, and they were published, in several editions, in Edinburgh, London, and America. However, the evidence from newspaper advertisements is not sufficient to ascertain which edition was imported from which place.[21] Thus, we may only speculate about the precise editions advertised in weekly newspapers in Quebec, Halifax, Montreal, York, Kingston, and Saint John by 1800, as they may have been the Irish editions of 1787, the Edinburgh (and latterly Edinburgh and London) editions printed by William Creech in the same year, or the Philadelphia or New York editions of 1788.[22]

The Georgian period in Canada witnessed steady imports of Enlightenment works in addition to the nine titles highlighted here. Of equal importance for placing

---

[20]   Sher, *The Enlightenment and the Book*, p. 700, Table 3, "Subjects and Formats of First British Editions of Scottish Enlightenment Books."

[21]   Black, "Book Availability in Canada, 1752–1820, and the Scottish Contribution."

[22]   Complete bibliographic information is available in the *English Short Title Catalogue* online.

Burns's works in transatlantic book trade context is an examination of the imports of other poets' works. Whilst members of the Kidston family certainly imported Burns's poetry, sometimes they imported numerous other poets to the exclusion of the Bard himself. An example is Richard Kidston's advertisement in the *Royal Gazette and Nova Scotia Advertiser* of 23 June 1789. This issue advertised the fresh availability of James Thomson's *Works* and Thomson's *Seasons* as well as Allan Ramsay's *Poems*. This evidence suggests that Burns shared shelf space in the Kidston's general store with other noted Scots poets.

Ten years later, Richard Kidston's kinsman James advertised the recent arrival of many works of poetry in addition to Burns.[23] Table 3.3 illustrates the range of these. Milton and Pope appear here, and both were in evidence in considerably more pre-1820 Canadian newspaper advertisements than was Burns.

Table 3.3   Poetry Titles Advertised by James Kidston in the *Halifax Journal*, 2 May 1799

Author	Short Title
Robert Burns	*Poems*
William Cowper	*Poems*
William Cowper	*Elegant Extracts, Verse*
William Falconer	*Shipwreck*
Oliver Goldsmith	*Poetical Works*
John Milton	*Paradise Lost, with Newton's notes*
John Milton	*Paradise Lost*
John Milton	*Paradise Regained*
James MacPherson	*Ossian's Poems*
Edward Young	*Night Thoughts*
Alexander Pope	*Works*
Samuel Butler	*Hudibras*
Pomfret	*Poems*
John Denham	*Poetical Works*
Salomon Gessner	*Death of Abel*

These works of poetry vary widely in their cultural and political contexts. Samuel Butler's *Hudibras*, a satire on Cromwell first published in 1663, remained popular until the early nineteenth century. Butler's style was Chaucerian couplets, and Hudibras, his anti-hero, was greedy and stupid. To appreciate the work at a deeper level, the reader needed to understand British history. Reader response is notoriously challenging to confirm without recourse to extensive collections of contemporary diaries. However, it is reasonable to suppose that a proportion of early Canadian readers would be knowledgeable about seventeenth-century

---

[23]   *Halifax Journal* (2 May 1799).

history, and it is equally likely that they would understand the political and religious allusions within Burns's poems. MacPherson's *Ossian*, whilst presenting an arguably spurious historical vision of Scotland at odds with Burns's grounded view, would sit comfortably on the same general merchant's shelf with Burns's volumes in part because of the latter's own enthusiasm for the former and contemporary statements that likened Burns as bard to Ossian as bard.[24] Whether there are literary links among the works imported is of much lesser importance, however, than whether the exporting and importing wholesalers and retailers thought they would sell. Kidston was unusual in importing relatively large numbers of Scottish Enlightenment authors, and possibly he was declaring his Scottishness by so doing. Nevertheless, he was first and foremost a successful businessman, and he would not incur the expense of importing works that would languish unsold on his shelves.

By 1818 George Dawson, who claimed to have been in business in Edinburgh prior to his move to York (Toronto), was advertising the recent arrival of Burns's poems along with those of James Hogg, Walter Scott, Allan Ramsay, Robert Southey, Thomas Campbell, Keats, Byron, and others. As a point of comparison, the poetry of Ramsay is not much in evidence in Canadian book advertisements, although Scottish lumber and general merchants Campbell and Stewart promoted the availability of *The Gentle Shepherd* in their store in Saint John in the *Royal Gazette and New Brunswick Advertiser* on 17 October 1786, and George Dawson imported the same work for his library in York (*Upper Canada Gazette*, 26 February 1818).

While Canada's best-known early printer and bookseller, John Neilson of Quebec City, was a well-educated contributor to the cosmopolitan networks of the North Atlantic, he travelled to America, London, and Paris for book-buying trips and, notably, never to Scotland. He typified those effective businessmen with a "shrewd eye for market demand" whose bookstocks indicated a "relative indifference to the 'Scottishness' of their lists as they saw themselves as" proprietors of "cosmopolitan businesses within an expanding world economy."[25] Amongst works in English, French, and Latin, Neilson's first separately printed catalogue includes Burns's *Works* in four volumes, octavo, with illustrative plates. This bibliographic evidence tells us that Neilson was importing James Currie's *The Works of Robert Burns*. The catalogue, printed in November 1800, makes clear the predominant trading source for these books: "The greatest part of the Books in this Catalogue have been imported from London within these late years,

[24]   Robert Crawford, *The Bard: Robert Burns, A Biography* (London, 2009), pp. 154–5 and 265–6.

[25]   Bill Bell, "The Scottish Book Trade at Home and Abroad, 1707–1918," in Manning, Brown, Clancy, and Pittock (eds), *The Edinburgh History of Scottish Literature*, vol. 2, pp. 221–7 (p. 223).

and many of them are entirely new works imported this fall in the Brickwood."[26] The reference to London is meaningful, as it was not only the center of English-language book production; it also was the financial and trading hub of transatlantic book distribution. In terms of number of titles and editions, evidence from the English Short-Title Catalogue provided in Table 3.4 quantifies London's supremacy in publishing during Burns's lifetime. Also of relevance for studies of Burns is the fact that Edinburgh was the second-ranked center of printing and overwhelmingly the primary location of print culture in Scotland during Burns's lifetime. Books were exported from Scotland to Canada via the Clyde ports, but most of the volumes were published in Edinburgh rather than in Glasgow.[27]

Table 3.4   Number of Publications by Place, 1701–1800, drawn from the English Short Title Catalogue

Years	Place	Number of Titles/Editions
1701–1800	Scotland	23,580
	Edinburgh	17,686
	London	168,891
1750–1800	Scotland	15,381
	Edinburgh	10,371
	London	101,488

Which editions of Burns sat on which bookshop, library, or general store shelves is hinted at through newspaper and library catalogue evidence. James Kidston's general store in Halifax, which received several shipments from the Clyde ports and from London during the 1790s, may have held, for example, the Kilmarnock edition or the 1787 edition co-published by Creech in Edinburgh and Strahan and Cadell in London, with the latter edition being more likely. By contrast, the printer and bookseller Gideon Tiffany in Niagara imported books from America on consignment, and his shelves would be stocked with the New York or Philadelphia editions of 1788.[28] Using import and shipping information from newspapers, it is thus possible to speculate about particular editions. Library catalogues' edition information is often equally sparse. Thus, the copy or copies of Burns available for loan from the Montreal Library in 1797 may have been any of the editions from Burns's lifetime. Whilst we do not know which edition was imported by John Neilson in Quebec City in 1811, we do know from the evidence of his printed

---

[26] Sandra Alston, "Canada's First Bookseller's Catalogue," *Papers of the Bibliographical Society of Canada*, 30/1 (1992): 7–26 (13).

[27] Fiona A. Black, "'Advent'rous Merchants and Atlantic Waves': A Preliminary Study of the Scottish Contribution to Book Availability in Halifax, 1752–1810," in Marjorie Harper and Michael E. Vance (eds), *Myth, Migration and the Making of Memory: Scotia and Nova Scotia c.1700–1990* (Halifax and Edinburgh, 1999), pp. 157–88. Data are from Table 2, "Publication Data Drawn from ESTC and NSTC."

[28] *Upper Canada Gazette and American Oracle* (2 November 1796): 1.

catalogue that it was octavo in format and available for four shillings and sixpence or three shillings and ninepence, probably due to differing bindings. By 1818 in York, George Dawson was advertising an 18 mo edition for seven shillings and sixpence, which had likely come from an Edinburgh publisher.

The challenge of being precise about editions is compounded by the related challenge of identifying which intellectual product is being referred to in newspaper advertisements or catalogues. Some of the volumes imported and sold in Canadian towns would have been collections of Burns's poems, letters, and songs, supplemented by critical commentaries and biographical information. One such was the 1808 octavo, single-volume edition of the *Reliques of Robert Burns, Consisting in Letters, Poems and Critic on Scottish Songs* collected by R.H. Cromek. This volume was available for loan from the Quebec Library and advertised in that institution's catalogue printed in June 1810. Thus, Burns's works would be mediated for some Canadian readers, especially those who were members of subscription libraries, through third party biographical and textual commentaries.

Early shipments of Burns were ordered and arrived across the Atlantic bi-annually in line with colonial trade patterns.[29] While Burns's county town of Ayr was a busy port in its own right, and whilst small transatlantic book shipments may have originated there, the majority of such shipments came from Clyde ports, Liverpool and, notably, London. Books followed trade, as the profit margin and quantities of sales were never sufficient for them to be the primary cargo. Books therefore went where worsted stockings, rum, raisins, and other staples were shipped, especially within the triangular trading routes of Great Britain, the Caribbean islands, and British North America. Ships supplying manufactured goods to colonial towns and hinterlands arrived each spring and, depending on the weather, sometimes also in the autumn. A proportion of their cargoes included small collections of books, carefully wrapped in oilcloths and packed in cases: "On board wooden sailing ships, such cases were sometimes deck cargo, but by the age of the swifter steamships, most cargo travelled in the hold and was less likely to suffer water damage, as steamships were less leaky."[30] Freight charges and insurance costs, particularly during those frequent times of war so familiar to Burns himself, meant that colonists making local purchases were paying more than they would in British towns. In addition, the majority of books imported to Canada were ready bound, whereas purchasers in Britain could choose to buy their volumes of Burns in sheets, and then choose their own binding.

More frequent imports could be had by ordering from American booksellers, and two editions of Burns were published in 1788 in Albany and Philadelphia

---

[29]   Black, "'Advent'rous Merchants and Atlantic Waves'," pp. 157–88.
[30]   Fiona A. Black, "Supplying the Retail Trade," in Lamonde, Fleming, and Black (eds), *History of the Book in Canada, Volume II, 1840–1918*, pp. 197–208 (p. 198).

by Scottish expatriate printers, J. McLean and Stewart and Hyde respectively.[31] However, "the tense political relationship with both Great Britain and the northern colonies did not encourage" much formal trade in books from America in the later eighteenth century.[32] This is borne out by newspaper evidence for the port of Halifax, for which an analysis of 48 imported shipments of books indicates that 73 percent came from London, 18 percent from the Clyde ports in Scotland or from Liverpool, and only 4 percent from Philadelphia and Boston.[33]

There are several necessary caveats to any examination of the early transatlantic book trade. Newspaper advertisements, central to such an examination because they are extant when most business records are not, are notoriously lacking in detail. Thus, "Burns's Works" and "Burns's Poems," whilst likely to mean the volume or volumes of collected poems, cannot be guaranteed to be so. By the 1790s there were numerous separate publications of one or two individual poems such as *The Soldier's Return* printed for, and sold by, Brash and Reid in Glasgow. This was an eight-page booklet of the type that was very commonly sold by wholesaling stationers to both Scottish general merchants and, significantly for this discussion, to exporting merchants. The importance of general merchants for the transatlantic movement of books in the Georgian period meant that colonial residents had access to bound volumes by Burns as well as pamphlets containing recent poems and song and music sheets. These latter were imported and sold by music teachers and piano and fiddle sellers as well as by general merchants. In addition to pamphlets and volumes exclusively devoted to Burns, James Johnson's *Scots Musical Museum* regularly appeared in eighteenth-century newspaper advertisements, providing another means for colonists to learn and share Burns's and others' songs.

Using the example of Halifax in the period 1752 to 1810, it is possible to quantify the critical role played by general merchants in the availability of Burns's poetry. Of forty-four firms that advertised books in this period, 56 percent were general merchants and 18 percent were printers or booksellers, the remainder being auctioneers, hardware merchants, ship chandlers, and the like.[34] Of the general merchants who regularly advertised books for sale in Halifax, by far the steadiest importers were the Kidston family, whose members imported from both London and the Clyde from 1789 to about 1809.[35] Burns's poetry sat on the shelves in their general stores down near the Halifax wharves, and from there was sold by retail as

---

[31]   Anna M. Painter, "American Editions of the Poems of Burns Before 1800," *The Library*, 4/12 (1932): 434–56.

[32]   Black, "'Advent'rous Merchants and Atlantic Waves'," p. 168.

[33]   Ibid. Analysis based on Table 1, "Geographic Origins of Book Shipments to Halifax, 1752–1810."

[34]   Ibid. Analysis taken from Table 3, "Firms Advertising Books for Sale or Loan in Halifax, 1752–1810."

[35]   Black, "Book Distribution to the Scottish and Canadian Provinces, 1750–1820," pp. 103–20.

well as wholesaled to country merchants who received their book and stationery supplies when the Kidstons, whose main business was lumber, plied the coastal routes of Nova Scotia and beyond. In 1796, James Kidston imported books on the *Enterprize* from London and on the Neptune from Glasgow. In that year, Burns's *Poems* were included in the London shipment along with novels, music books, children's books, and others.[36] Three years later, Kidston advertised dozens of titles which he had imported, along with other goods, on the *Hunter* from Glasgow and the Rebecca from Liverpool. In this case, over half the advertised bookstock were by Scottish authors including Willy Buchan's indispensible and pragmatic *Domestic Medicine*, Burns's poetry and more challenging works such as Blair's lectures on rhetoric and Smith's *The Wealth of Nations*.[37] The Kidstons' customers included fellow members of the active North British Society in Halifax, of which Richard Kidston junior became President in 1815. This Society was akin to "a Scottish mercantile brotherhood."[38] The members discussed papers on "learned subjects" and will also have celebrated St Andrew's Day and Burns Night.[39]

The dominance of British book imports to Canada from British towns during Burns's lifetime can be explained by the political and legislative frameworks which governed trade. The Navigation Act of 1696 was familiar to all merchants as it "reinforced an earlier act stipulating that all goods shipped to the colonies had to be transported in British ... ships" with the clear intent of promoting the sale of manufactured goods from the home country.[40]

By 1865, the frequency of book imports from Britain to Canadian towns had markedly improved, and Rollo and Adam, wholesaling booksellers in Toronto, were able to advertise to the trade the Riverside Press Edition of Burns's poetry (complete edition, five volumes at $5.00), adding that they had a "constant influx and reflux of stock ... avail[ing] themselves of daily communication with the publishing houses of the States, and of weekly with those of Great Britain."[41] In December 1867, Adam, Stevenson and Company were offering luxury editions of Burns's complete works "with Life and Variorum Notes," bound as "full Roxburgh Turkey" for $11.00 in addition to a solid, but more modest crown octavo edition with gilt edges for $5.00.[42] These editions were available to the

---

[36] Black, "Searching for the 'Vanguard of an Army of Scots'," 76–7.

[37] Fiona A. Black, "Newspapers as Primary Sources in Canadian-Scottish Book Trade History: The Example of Halifax, Nova Scotia, 1752–1820," *Épilogue*, 10/1 and 2 (1995): 43–51 (46).

[38] J.B. Cahill, "Brymer, Alexander," in *Dictionary of Canadian Biography Online* (www.biographi.ca), accessed 9 February 2010.

[39] Nova Scotia Archives, MG 100, Vol. 172, No. 5d, "Kidston Family—Genealogy," Family Tree with Notes.

[40] Fiona A. Black, "Importation and Book Availability," in Fleming, Gallichan, and Lamonde (eds), *History of the Book in Canada, Volume I*, pp. 115–6.

[41] *Canada Bookseller* (March 1865): 8.

[42] *Canada Bookseller* (December 1867): 2.

retail market alongside separately printed songsheets, catering to multiple markets and audiences.

The availability of Burns's poetry and songs in library collections is evidenced in a variety of early printed catalogues. One scholar has speculated that, when Burns was *not* represented in the catalogue of a Mechanics Institute Library, this might be due to members' personal ownership of his work.[43] Analysis of private libraries through notices of sale, estate valuations, and other means indicates Burns's presence in such collections and helps us map the passage of individually owned copies of Burns. Sometimes, the library owner's Scottish roots are clearly evident, as with the library of Alexander David Ferrier, referred to in his entry in *The Canadian Biographical Dictionary and Portrait Gallery of Eminent and Self-Made Men*. Ferrier had inherited his volume of Burns from his mother, whose own father was Alexander Monro, famed Professor of Anatomy at the University of Edinburgh. Ferrier's copy of Burns, published in 1787, crossed the Atlantic when the Ferriers moved to Quebec in 1830.

Knowledge of Burns's songs, through the social life of towns and villages, complemented knowledge of the availability of his published works for sale or loan. Reviews, commentaries, and imitations soon swelled a cultural awareness of Burns's work. Within a few years of the Kilmarnock edition, his work began to influence contributions to indigenous literary publishing. Thereafter, numerous imitations of Burns and natal day odes to him contributed to the local content of the book and periodical publishing businesses in Canada. Examples such as Alexander McLachlan's oft reprinted "Hail to thee, King of Scottish song!" and W.M. MacKeracher's ode "To a Copy of Burns' Poems (Found in the house of an Ontario farmer)" appeared in volumes published by well-established Toronto businesses. Robert Nicoll's natal day ode appeared within an essay on Burns by the Reverend M. Harvey in *Stewart's Literary Quarterly Magazine* of Saint John, New Brunswick.[44]

Conclusion

Discussing the Scottishness and Britishness of Canada, J.M. Bumsted posits that "much of the Scottish identity that at least Lowland Scots took with them into Canada during the nineteenth century had been forged by Burns and Scott."[45] This

---

[43]   Heather Murray, "Readers and Society," in Fleming, Gallichan, and Lamonde (eds), *History of the Book in Canada, Volume I*, pp. 172– 82 (p. 178).

[44]   Alexander McLachlan, *Poems and Songs* (Toronto, 1874); *Selections from Scottish Canadian Poets, Being a Collection of the Best Poetry Written by Scotsmen and their Descendants in the Dominion of Canada*, Published under the Auspices of The Caledonian Society of Toronto (Toronto, 1900), p. 242; M. Harvey, "Burns's Natal Day," *Stewart's Literary Quarterly Magazine*, 3/4 (January 1870): 425–42 (425).

[45]   J.M. Bumsted, "Scottishness and Britishness in Canada, 1790–1914," in Harper and Vance (eds), *Myth, Migration and the Making of Memory*, pp. 89–104 (p. 92).

foray into the mechanisms whereby Canadians might acquire the works of Burns complements broader discussions of the availability of Scottish authors' works in North America.[46] These business mechanisms were driven, first, by a motive for profit, complemented often by a cultural interest amongst Scottish printers and general merchants. From the 1780s to the early twentieth century, Burns's name appeared in catalogues of recently acquired bookstocks.

In *Taylor's 1904 Calendar Cookbook*, published in Portage La Prairie, Manitoba, the historical events section for July includes, amongst widely resonant events such as the destruction of the Spanish Armada in 1588, the concise statement, "Robert Burns died, 1796." This phrase, even for readers in and around a non-Scottish prairie settlement more than a century after his death, may have had more resonance than sixteenth-century plans for invasion. Bell and other scholars have argued that Scots' inner lives were informed just as much by non-Scottish writers as they were by Burns or Scott and that there is little to support the view that Scots in Canada were "particularly patriotic in their reading."[47] What is certain, based on the evidence presented here, is that residents of Portage La Prairie and hundreds of other Canadian towns and villages had access to the poems and songs of Burns as readily as did urban dwellers, and these poems helped to forge both the oral and print culture of a developing nation.

---

[46]   Fiona A. Black, "North America," in Bill Bell (ed.), *The Edinburgh History of the Book in Scotland, Volume 3, Ambition and Industry, 1800–1880* (Edinburgh, 2007), pp. 442–53.

[47]   Bell, "The Scottish Book Trade at Home and Abroad, 1707–1918," p. 226.

Chapter 4
"Guid black prent":
Robert Burns and the Contemporary
Scottish and American Periodical Press

Rhona Brown

North America's relationship with Robert Burns in the nineteenth century has attracted much critical attention. While commentators celebrate the advent of the Burns Club in the United States in the 1800s, others argue that the esteem of American icons such as Walt Whitman and Ralph Waldo Emerson helped make Burns an idol of both cultural and literary proportions for the nineteenth-century American reading public. Similarly, Robert Burns's own portrayals of and attitudes towards eighteenth-century American politics have drawn critical notice: his statements on the American War of Independence and the Revolution have allowed critics to promulgate constructions of Burns's political radicalism in Scotland. Less is known, however, about the contemporary response to Robert Burns and his poetry both in Scotland and in the United States. An analysis of the appearance of Burns's works in eighteenth-century Scottish and American periodicals helps to address this critical deficiency and demonstrates that there is yet more to be excavated in the constant renewal of Burns criticism.[1]

In an article entitled "How Robert Burns Captured America," James Montgomery states, in his opening sentence, that, "Before America discovered Robert Burns, Robert Burns discovered America."[2] Montgomery continues by outlining the poet's considerable awareness of recent developments in political history:

> This self-described ploughman poet knew well the surge of freedom which dominated much of Europe and North America in the waning days of the eighteenth century. Burns understood the spirit and the politics of the fledgling United States. He studied the battles of both ideas and infantry.[3]

---

[1] I am grateful to the British Academy for their support in the preparation of this article, the foundation of which was initially presented as a paper to the "Scottish Romanticism and World Literatures" conference held in September 2006 at the University of California at Berkeley.
[2] James M. Montgomery, "How Robert Burns Captured America," in *Studies in Scottish Literature*, 30 (1998): 235–48 (235).
[3] Ibid.

Montgomery offers a version of the poet that is familiar to a twenty-first century audience: here, Burns is a voracious and informed reader, an ardent political commentator; he is, above all, a knowledgeable gentleman of the age of Enlightenment. Montgomery goes on to identify Burns's chief literary comments on American politics, analyzing the song "When Guilford good" alongside the poems "Address of Beelzebub" and "Ode for General Washington's Birthday." Each of these works, Montgomery argues, has something positive to say about America: "When Guilford good," which Thomas Crawford describes as "the earliest and by far the most daring"[4] of Burns's political pieces, was first printed in the 1787 Edinburgh edition of Burns's poems and follows the history of the American Revolution from, according to Montgomery, "the Boston Tea Party, through the Colonists' invasion of Canada, the siege of Boston, the stalemated occupation of Philadelphia and New York, the battle of Saratoga, the southern campaign and Clinton's failure to support Cornwallis at Yorktown."[5] Montgomery's triumvirate of Burnsian Americana continues with the vicious, raw, and enduringly astounding "Address of Beelzebub," in which Burns's narrator, a chief devil, congratulates the Earl of Breadalbane on his success in preventing Highland emigration to North America, thereby allowing the nobility to, as Beelzebub states, "keep the highlan hounds in sight."[6] Burns's anger on behalf of the oppressed tenants is plain in the devastating satire and heavy irony of the poem's central section, in which his devilish narrator contemplates what might have occurred had the Highlanders been allowed their freedom to cross the Atlantic:

> Then up amang thae lakes an' seas
> They'll mak what rules an' laws they please.
>
> Some daring Hancocke, or a Frankline,
> May set their HIGHLAN bluid a ranklin;
> Some Washington again may head them,
> Or some MONTGOMERY, fearless, lead them;
> Till, God knows what may be effected,
> When by such HEADS an' HEARTS directed:
> Poor, dunghill sons of dirt an' mire,
> May to PATRICIAN RIGHTS ASPIRE; (vol. 1, p. 254)

Here, as elsewhere, Burns portrays North America as the personification of democracy; as a distant yet accessible land where subjugated Highlanders "May to PATRICIAN RIGHTS ASPIRE." If the Highlanders are allowed to emigrate, the devil's horror is plain in his ironically fierce condemnation: "They'll mak what rules

---

⁴   Thomas Crawford, *Burns: A Study of the Poems and Songs* (1960; Edinburgh, 1965), p. 147.

⁵   Montgomery, "How Robert Burns Captured America," p. 235.

⁶   *The Poems and Songs of Robert Burns*, James Kinsley (ed.) (3 vols, Oxford, 1968), vol. 1, p. 254; subsequent quotations from Burns's poetry are from this edition and will be cited in the text by volume and page number.

and laws they please." In his conflation of Canada and the United States, Burns portrays North America as a sister state to Scotland: according to the "Address of Beelzebub," "HIGHLAN bluid" is entirely responsive to and sympathetic with those blood-"ranklin" words of "Some daring Hancocke, or a Frankline." The devil's vicious disgust at the poor man's emigrating enterprise is a prime example of Burns's favorite device of ironic self-revelation; Beelzebub is comparable to another of Burns's grandiloquent protagonists, Holy Willie, in his attempt to portray solid pride and poise, while in fact illustrating acute insecurity.[7] Accordingly, in the "Address of Beelzebub," while Burns's direct familiarity with the predicament of the tenant farmer allows him to display an Enlightened sympathy with the Highlanders' plight, the seemingly self-assured Beelzebub betrays a very real fear of the loss of tenants to "thae lakes an' seas" of North America. By damning American politics and "PATRICIAN" aspirations, Beelzebub unwittingly demonstrates their fearsome power.

The third poem to which Montgomery makes reference is Burns's "Ode for General Washington's Birthday." This poem, like the "Address of Beelzebub," follows, according to Crawford, Thomas Paine's strictures in his *Rights of Man* (1791) and presents America as a place where "Man's godlike form" has defeated the tyrant and celebrates "a People freed" (vol. 2, p. 732).[8] According to Gerard Carruthers, the "Ode" is the most "cogent" of Burns's American pieces which, having been written around 1794, is "armed with the political vocabulary of the French Revolution" and is "rousing in its rhetoric as it hymns Washington's America and its constitution."[9]

From his earliest pieces to his late democratic works, then, Burns is attentive to American history and politics, often presenting them as didactic models for Britain's and Scotland's instruction. Nevertheless, although Burns had discovered and known America at a very early stage in his poetic career—"When Guilford good," for example, was reportedly written in 1784[10]—it seems at first glance that America was slower to value Burns.

Many critical works on the poet, notably Donald A. Low's indispensable *Robert Burns: The Critical Heritage* (1974), cite such figures of the American tradition as Abraham Lincoln, Ralph Waldo Emerson, Walt Whitman, Mark Twain, and John Greenleaf Whittier as avid admirers of Burns, suggesting that American interest in Burns did not ignite until the late 1800s, while the diversity of these Burns devotees appears to demonstrate the poet's import in varying aspects of nineteenth-century American life. The interest of figures such as Emerson, Whitman, and

---

[7]   For the original discussion of the eighteenth-century technique of "ironic self-revelation," see Kenneth Simpson, *The Protean Scot: The Crisis of Identity in Eighteenth Century Scottish Literature* (Aberdeen, 1988), pp. 2, 31–2.

[8]   For a full discussion of parallels between Burns's and Paine's work, and of Burns as "poet of democracy," see Crawford, *Burns: A Study of the Poems and Songs*, pp. 236–56.

[9]   Gerard Carruthers, *Robert Burns* (Tavistock, 2006), p. 55.

[10]   Crawford, *Burns: A Study of the Poems and Songs*, p. 147.

Twain demonstrate the poet's literary authority, whereas the praise of Lincoln, the American President partly responsible for the abolition of slavery in 1865, establishes a sense of kinship which links the poet's literary ideals to Lincoln's democratic political principles. Similarly, Whittier is remembered primarily as a vigorous campaigner for abolition and as a poet whose works were often set as hymns. Whittier's literary affinity with Burns arguably demonstrates a poetic link that is both political and religious; Burns's literary elegance, his intense yet hesitant religious belief, and his democratic and collectivist stance make him a natural icon for these nineteenth-century American authors. In addition to Burns's literary significance, Low's *Critical Heritage* demonstrates that these prominent American idols had a crucial role to play in the development of the Burns Club in America, a cultural pursuit that reached the heights of its popularity during the 1800s. In the literary epoch of Emerson and Whitman, Burns appears to have been an icon for American writers just as he was for nineteenth-century British authors such as Thomas Carlyle.

Having said this, the Burns that we find in the pages of the Scottish and American periodical press of the 1780s is very different than the Burns of the "Address of Beelzebub" and "Ode for General Washington's Birthday." As is well documented, the publication of Burns's *Poems Chiefly in the Scottish Dialect* in Kilmarnock in 1786 catapulted the poet into bright fame in Ayrshire, but it was not until his visit to Edinburgh and the publication of the second edition of his work in 1787 that Burns came to wider literary celebrity. Notwithstanding the literati's lack of knowledge of Burns before 1786, the poet had a profound awareness of Edinburgh's cultural life, as filtered through his reading of the city's daily press and periodicals—we know, for example, that he subscribed to Robert Anderson's *The Bee, or Literary Intelligencer*[11]—familiarizing him with Edinburgh's personalities and procedures long before he arrived in the city himself. Figures, accounts, and anecdotes appearing in Edinburgh's newspapers demonstrate that Burns would come to be involved in the highest echelons of the capital's culture after his feted appearance in 1786. The pages of the *Edinburgh Evening Courant* in the last few decades of the eighteenth century read as a "who's who" of Burns poetry and criticism: glances at the newspaper reveal reports of Vincenzo Lunardi's aerial excursions in his hot-air balloons to which Burns alludes in "To a Louse," advertisements by the poet's future musical collaborator Pietro Urbani offering musical tuition to the capital's bourgeois inhabitants, and announcements of the Caledonian Hunt led by Burns patron the Earl of Glencairn. Edinburgh newspapers were, in the 1700s, repositories for diverse and miscellaneous information. In their pages appear notifications, often of newly arrived ship produce, anecdotes, theatrical billboards and reviews, news from Scotland, Europe, America, and beyond, and treatises on the latest fashions from Paris.

It is in the *Edinburgh Advertiser*, however, that we see a very early reference to Robert Burns. The announcement of the Edinburgh edition of Burns's *Poems,*

---

[11]   Liam McIlvanney, *Burns the Radical: Poetry and Politics in Late Eighteenth-Century Scotland* (East Linton, 2002), pp. 62–3.

Chiefly in the Scottish Dialect appears in the *Edinburgh Advertiser* dated 13–17 April 1787. Despite its conventionality, small details of the note reveal much about the contemporary response to Burns in Edinburgh:

> This day is published By WILLIAM CREECH,
>
> Handsomely printed in one vol. 8vo., and embellished with the Head of the Author, elegantly engraved by Beugo.
>
> Poems, Chiefly In The Scottish Dialect, By Robert Burns
>
> N.B.—As the book is published for the sole benefit of the Author, it is requested that subscribers will send for their copies, and none will be delivered without money.[12]

This first advertisement for the Edinburgh edition is an historic one. Appearances demonstrate that Creech had taken great care in the preparation of an elegant volume with a competent Head of the Author by a diligently selected engraver. Appearances also illustrate that Creech thought Burns to be stretched by poverty, and indeed in the small details of this advertisement, Creech corroborates Henry Mackenzie's portrayal of Burns as a stricken but nevertheless inspired "Heaven-taught ploughman": Creech announces that the book is published "for the sole benefit of the Author," and to facilitate his income, "none will be delivered without money." Despite these appearances, however, Burns's private references to the Edinburgh edition's progression confirm that the poet's attitude did not match that of his publisher. In a celebrated letter to John Ballantine from Edinburgh on 24 February 1787, Burns writes:

> I will soon be with you now *in guid black prent*; in a week or ten days at farthest … I am getting my Phiz done by an eminent Engraver; and if it can be ready in time, I will appear in my book looking, like other fools, to my title page.[13]

This self-effacing proclamation is a prime example of the Burnsian modesty topos—alongside the poet's characteristic self-deprecating humour there is a quiet but patent pride in appearing once again *"in guid black prent."* It should also be added that Burns's estimate of "a week to ten days" for the Edinburgh edition's publication at the end of February 1787 was amiss: as the date of the first announcement placed by Creech reveals, the collection was not ready to be advertised until mid-April, finally making its appearance on 21 April.

Burns's own ambivalence towards his reception in Edinburgh is well documented, and in another celebrated letter to Mrs Frances Dunlop from Edinburgh on 22 March 1787, Burns confesses to his critic and correspondent,

---

[12]   *Edinburgh Advertiser*, 13–17 April 1787.

[13]   Robert Burns to John Ballantine, 24 February 1787, in *The Letters of Robert Burns*, J. De Lancey Ferguson (ed.), 2nd edn, G. Ross Roy (ed.) (2 vols, Oxford, 1985), vol. 1, p. 96.

"I have the advice of some very judicious friends among the Literati here, but with them I sometimes find it necessary to claim the priviledge of thinking for myself."[14] His tentativeness regarding the social and literary whirl of Edinburgh and the role that he was forced—by himself and by others—to fit is clear in his comments to Mrs Dunlop. But Burns's private comments on William Creech are less courteous. In a letter from Ellisland to Dr John Moore, dated 4 January 1789, Burns writes:

> I cannot boast of M[r] Creech's ingenuous fair-dealing to me. —He kept me hanging on about Edin[r] from the 7th Aug. 1787, until the 13th April 1788, before he would condescend to give me a Statement of affairs; nor had I got it even then, but for an angry letter I wrote him which irritated his pride.[15]

Donald Low argues that Creech was ruthless in his dealings with Burns, and used the poet's celebrity for his own ends:

> Apart from his doubtful action in selling the "third" London edition of 1787 apparently without informing Burns of its existence, his delaying tactics and inability to see beyond considerations of profit stand against him. Moreover, by his later conduct Creech was probably responsible for reducing Burns's interest in further publication.[16]

Despite Creech's "conduct," Burns's final word on his Edinburgh publisher is forgiving. In his next letter to Moore from Ellisland, dated 23 March 1789, the poet states, "I was at Edin[r] lately, and settled finally with M[r] Creech; and I must retract some illnatured surmises in my last letter, and own that at last, he has been amicable and fair with me."[17] Burns's strained prose suggests that business had been taken care of as well as possible, but that relations with Creech remained difficult.

The *Edinburgh Advertiser*'s support of the poet is, however, steadier and more apparent. In the issue subsequent to Creech's advertisement, the following announcement appears on the front page of the newspaper dated 17–20 April 1787:

> EXTRACTS from BURNS'S POEMS.
>
> The work of the AYRSHIRE PLOUGHMAN, having attracted the attention of the *Literati*, both in this and our neighbouring country, we lay before our readers some extracts, written in a very different style, by this Heaven-taught Bard.[18]

---

[14]   Burns to Mrs Frances Dunlop, 22 March 1787, in *Letters*, Ross Roy (ed.), vol. 1, p. 100.

[15]   Burns to Dr John Moore, 4 January 1789, in *Letters*, Ross Roy (ed.), vol. 1, p. 351.

[16]   Donald A. Low, editorial introduction to *Robert Burns: The Critical Heritage* (London and Boston, 1974), pp. 1–57 (p. 11).

[17]   Burns to Dr John Moore, 23 March 1789, in *Letters*, Ross Roy (ed.), vol. 1, p. 386.

[18]   *Edinburgh Advertiser*, 17–20 April 1787.

The *Edinburgh Advertiser*'s journalists obviously saw the celebrity which Burns had accrued in the capital, and predictably, their extracts portray an untutored Bard, at once uneducated and brilliant: they portray Henry Mackenzie's "Heaven-taught ploughman." The poems that the newspaper prints are noteworthy, considering that this is the newspaper's first introduction to its readers of a poet who was already proving to be a literary phenomenon and cultural curiosity. On this front page, the editors print "Man was made to Mourn" in its entirety alongside "When Guilford good." They also print extracts from "A Dream," informing their readers, "We have left out several stanzas of the last poem for want of room, and refer those who wish to be better acquainted with this original genius, to the new edition of his Poems, just published."[19] From the start, Burns is referred to as "Bard," as "Heaven-taught," and most importantly, as an "original genius."

Despite Burns's own misgivings about his period in Edinburgh, his extended stay in the capital was fundamental to the development of his persona, both as poet and icon, at home and abroad. For the Edinburgh literati, and, as we shall see, for the readers of the American periodical press, Burns's "authenticity" was central to his appeal, long after Mackenzie's branding of the poet as merely "Heaven-taught." Burns's treatment by the capital's literary intelligentsia is explored by Carol McGuirk:

> When Burns came to Edinburgh in 1786 he became an urban phenomenon. It was impossible for the public to champion rustic obscurity in the way that Mackenzie and the other early reviewers had suggested. Almost unanimously, the literati worked out a new approach: praise for Burns's authenticity of manner combined with a warning about the danger of being ruined by the blandishments of civilized life. As though he were a country cheese, they talked about "spoilage."[20]

For McGuirk, Mackenzie's theorizing in his *Lounger* review of the Kilmarnock edition became reality when the poet arrived in Edinburgh. His "authenticity" was to be preserved at all costs, and his place as an example of inspired "rustic obscurity" to be presented as didactic. Burns was to be gazed at but also learnt from.

The literati's celebration of "rustic obscurity" and Burns's attempts to shape his own image continue throughout the pages of the *Edinburgh Advertiser*, and is clearly illustrated in Burns's first literary appearance therein. Of the poems printed in the newspaper dated 17–20 April 1787, "Man was made to Mourn" concerns religious despair and personal melancholy; "When Guilford good," as we have seen, deals with American history and politics. That the paper publishes "A Dream" is of added importance. Treating British affairs of state and the royal family in much the same manner as "When Guilford good" deals with America,

---

[19]   Ibid.

[20]   Carol McGuirk, *Robert Burns and the Sentimental Era* (1985; East Linton, 1997), p. 70.

Burns sets his poem against the poet laureate Thomas Warton's official "Ode XVII for His Majesty's Birthday, 4 June 1786" while simultaneously replicating the pose of Robert Fergusson, Burns's influential forerunner, in "The King's Birth-Day in Edinburgh," which was written in response to William Whitehead's birthday ode for George III fourteen years earlier in 1772. Burns's warm admiration for Fergusson is acknowledged in criticism of both poets' works, and in Burns's own poetic and epistolary comments on his meteoric Edinburgh predecessor. However, this issue of the *Edinburgh Advertiser* demonstrates that Burns may have been both directly and indirectly responsible for a reawakening of interest in Fergusson's poetry, just as he had fired the intelligentsia's enthusiasm for his own poetic achievements. It is known that Burns went to considerable expense in erecting a headstone adorned with elegant verses in memory of Fergusson in Edinburgh's Canongate Kirkyard, but it is not widely known that, in the same issue of the *Edinburgh Advertiser* which publishes initial extracts of Burns's poems, another advertisement appears:

This day is published

In one volume 12mo. price only 2s 6d sewed

POEMS, CHIEFLY IN THE SCOTTISH DIALECT By the late ROBERT FERGUSON Of Facetious Memory

Printed for C. Elliot, Edinburgh; C. Elliot, Strand, London.[21]

The very title given to this new London edition of Fergusson's works establishes the literati's concrete association of Fergusson and Burns. Significantly, Fergusson's *Poems*, published in 1773, has become, by 1787, *Poems, Chiefly in the Scottish Dialect*. Further into the same edition of the newspaper, we find another Burns poem: "Prologue Spoken by Mr. Woods on his Benefit Night, April 16, Composed by Mr. Burns." Burns's fame in Edinburgh was, by this time, assured.

Having seen Edinburgh's response to Burns, one might reasonably expect that his poems may have taken some months to make their way across the Atlantic. However, as Andrew Hook has argued, the cultural bonds which linked Scotland and America were strong, particularly those between Edinburgh and Philadelphia, Pennsylvania. According to Hook, Philadelphia was "part of the close-knit network of Scottish trading activities stretching from New York down the entire seaboard of the mid-Atlantic colonies."[22] Accordingly, as early as July 1787, only three months after the publication of the Edinburgh edition, Burns makes an appearance in the Philadelphian dailies. The *Pennsylvania Packet* of 24 July 1787 jubilantly ushers Burns in with the first of many selections from his poetry, and readers

---

[21]   *Edinburgh Advertiser*, 17–20 April 1787.
[22]   Andrew Hook, "Philadelphia, Edinburgh and the Scottish Enlightenment," in Richard B. Sher and Jeffrey R. Smitten (eds), *Scotland and America in the Age of Enlightenment* (Edinburgh, 1990), p. 229.

are offered "The Rigs o' Barley," by "Robert Burns, the Celebrated Ayrshire Ploughman."[23] A simple introduction to Burns, this song demonstrates a delight in the countryside and in female company, two clear icons of Burns's poetic corpus. The description of Burns as "the Celebrated Ayrshire Ploughman" proves that the poet had gained some renown in America before this publication. Links between the Scottish and Philadelphian descriptions of the poet illustrate that, for his early North American audience, Burns's rustic legitimacy was just as important as in the Scottish capital. In her study of transatlantic literary connections, Susan Manning echoes McGuirk's description of the poet's experience in Edinburgh. Burns's place as a song writer and song collector made him a social chameleon; his songs, according to Manning, "exercised … a uniting function, offering free passage across the threshold between high and low, traditional and classicising realms."[24] Therefore, despite his own cultural discomfiture in Edinburgh, Burns's position as "Heaven-taught ploughman" allowed a social facility traditionally unavailable to his class. For Manning, as for McGuirk, "'Authenticity' is, as it had been with Ossian, the crux."[25]

Burns continues to be published in the *Pennsylvania Packet* at the rate of a poem every three or four days. Throughout the month of November 1787, for example, the paper's editor presents "Man was made to Mourn" and "Banks of Ayr"; December offers "Despondency: An Ode" alongside "Behind yon hills where Stinchar flows." At this point, the audience's principal interest in Burns appears to be in his songs and in his deeply personal, melancholic effusions. But in the *Pennsylvania Packet* of Friday, 14 March 1788, the editors publish what they call "A Fragment," which bears the first line, "When Guilford good our pilot stood." This publication of Burns's ballad on the American War is timely for American readers: only five months earlier, the *Pennsylvania Packet* had sacrificed its news and poetry section altogether in order to publish the American Constitution in its entirety, and in the issue of Thursday, 10 January 1788, it had printed "Our Liberty Tree: A Federal Song" which finishes with the stanza:

> Then from East to the West let our Patriots convene,
>   Determin'd their Country to free;
> Our Constitution confirm—it firmly shall fix
>   Its idol—our Liberty Tree.[26]

With this political tenor clear throughout the newspaper's pages, the *Pennsylvania Packet* presents Burns as a friend to American ideology in "When Guilford good." From this point on, the poet's works are ubiquitous in the pages of the Philadelphian press. And as well as actual publications in the newspaper, Burns's

---

[23] *Pennsylvania Packet*, 24 July 1787.

[24] Susan Manning, *Fragments of Union: Making Connections in Scottish and American Writing* (Basingstoke, 2002), p. 162.

[25] Ibid.

[26] *Pennsylvania Packet*, 10 January 1788.

poetic influence appears to have infected its literary readership. In the issue of the *Pennsylvania Packet* dated Monday, 8 October 1787, we find a poem entitled "The Farmer and the Sparrows." This poem is the antithesis of Burns's famously empathetic "To a Mouse," a contemporary favorite: it tells the story of a farmer's killing of a nest of sparrows in his cornfield. Later in the paper, we find portrait poems which could be sequels to Burns's most popular poem of the period: "The Pretty Cottager: A New Song," from its title alone, is deeply influenced by "The Cotter's Saturday Night." All of this shows that Burns was part of an American enthusiasm for simple, country life, and sometimes more specifically, a nostalgic construction of the "home country." The pages of the newspaper contain the germ in which Romanticism would find its full flower.

Throughout the next few months, *Pennsylvania Packet* readers are offered "Scotch Drink," "A Prayer, in the Prospect of Death," "Address to the Unco Guid," "Green Grow the Rashes," "To a Louse," and a full transcription of the Edinburgh edition's celebrated preface, the "Dedication to the Noblemen and Gentlemen of the Caledonian Hunt." The Pennsylvania audience, however, seems to have had a substantial appetite for Burns's poems which describe great religious despair. Alongside the "Prayer, in the Prospect of Death," we find "A Prayer Under the Pressure of Violent Anguish," in which the poet pleads with God that he can "bear" his fate and "not repine," as well as "Stanzas Written in the Prospect of Death," in which Burns imagines "an angry GOD" with "sin-avenging rod" and frets about his inability to keep to "fair Virtue's way": this pious Burns is one version of the poet that was extremely popular in America (vol. 1, p. 23, p. 21). In May 1788, the *Pennsylvania Packet* publishes the tortured "To Ruin" as well as "The First Six Verses of the Ninetieth Psalm," poems which are rarely read in the twenty-first century and that offer a very different portrait of the poet than the one to which today's readers are accustomed. In these poems, the poet is God-fearing and repentant, despairing at his inability to be good, and quivering under the Calvinistic God's angry shadow.

As well as his poetic meditations on religious experience, Burns's portrayals of family life are also popular with the Philadelphian newspaper readership. In May 1788, the paper publishes "Lying at a Reverend's House one Night, the Author left the following VERSES in his Room where he slept." This piece, which is also largely neglected by twenty-first century readers of Burns's works, paints an idyllic and sentimental portrait of the eponymous Reverend and his family. The poem's final stanza is representative of the mood and tone of the piece as a whole:

> When soon or late they reach that coast,
> O'er life's rough ocean driven,
> May they rejoice, no wanderer lost,
> A Family in Heaven! (vol. 1, p. 307)

This is the Burns of "The Cotter's Saturday Night," so prized in the eighteenth and nineteenth centuries and so often rejected in the twentieth and twenty-first centuries. The paper's editorial choices demonstrate a very real contemporary appetite for the sentimental, pious Heaven-taught ploughman. Indeed, in the *Pennsylvania Packet* of Saturday, 14 June 1788, "The Cotter's Saturday Night" is printed in its entirety—no small sacrifice for the paper, considering the poem's length.

In the *Pennsylvania Packet* of Wednesday, 16 July 1788, an advertisement for the first American edition appears:

> POEMS, Chiefly in the Scottish Dialect
>
> By ROBERT BURNS, the celebrated *Ayrshire ploughman*. The peculiar merit of this work is sufficiently evinced by the very numerous list of subscribers prefixed to the Edinburgh edition (there being not less than sixteen hundred) among whom appears many of the Nobility and Gentry of Scotland.
>
> A number of the Pieces have been presented to the notice of the Public through the channel of Newspapers in this and some other states: viz. *Man was made to Mourn. The Cotter's Saturday Night. Invocation to Ruin. Despondency, an Ode*, &c, &c, which have been universally admired.[27]

The publisher then goes on to quote at length from Robert Anderson's piece on the poet and his works, which had been published in London's *Monthly Review* in December 1786:

> These Poems are chiefly in the comic strain. Some are of a descriptive cast, particularly *Hallowe'en*, which contains a lively picture of the magical tricks that are still practiced in the country at that season. Sometimes they are in the elegiac strain, among which class the Reader will find much of nature in the lines to a mouse ... and those to a mountain daisy ... His simple strains, artless and unadorned, seem to flow without effort, from the native feelings of the heart. They are always nervous, sometimes inelegant, often natural, simple and sublime; yet his verses are sometimes struck off with a delicacy, and artless simplicity, that charms like the bewitching though irregular touches of a Shakespear.[28]

It is significant that the publisher should choose to print this particular review of Burns's work. Anderson echoes many watch-words of early Burns criticism: "comic"; "lively"; "country"; "nature"; "simple"; "artless"; "unadorned"; "native"; "simplicity." Burns is, again, the untutored poet of nature, and a precursor of the Romantic approach to literature which would be described in William Wordsworth's Preface to the *Lyrical Ballads*: Burns's poetry "flows without effort," and is both "simple and sublime," just as Wordsworth's ideal poet utilizes "the language really

---

27 *Pennsylvania Packet*, 16 July 1788.

28 Ibid.

used by men" in a "spontaneous overflow of powerful feelings."[29] Anderson's review also echoes a constant concern, which is to be found particularly in London reviews of Burns: the comparison with Shakespeare. Contemporary critics share the same difficulties in reviewing Burns as Augustan critics of Shakespeare, and Anderson encapsulates the problem here in describing both as having "bewitching though irregular touches." It is not until 1798, according to Murray Pittock, that Wordsworth is equipped to "defend the low style" as "natural" in a new, Romantic sense.[30] The advertisement for the first American edition, however, is evidence of Burns's fame on both sides of the Atlantic, and particularly his popularity with the "Nobility and Gentry of Scotland."

Further evidence of Burns's American poetic presence can be found in another Philadelphian newspaper, entitled the *Freeman's Journal or, The North American Intelligencer*. This newspaper, which is greatly concerned with examining and debating the slave trade and other humanitarian issues such as the conditions of penitentiaries in the United States, proudly advertises the second American edition, printed in New York, on Wednesday, 23 July 1788:

> Now in the press, and speedily will be published, Poems, by ROBERT BURNS, The Ayrshire Ploughman. This American edition of Burns's Poems will be ornamented with a HEAD of the Author, neatly engraved by Mr. SCOTT, of Philadelphia, and, to render the work more worthy of public patronage, will be added, without any additional Expence, a number of POEMS selected from the Works of the celebrated R. FERGUSON.[31]

The link between Burns and Fergusson is once again plainly made, and the New York publishers make full use of the audience that this advertisement implies existed for Scots vernacular poetry in America. In fact, in this first New York edition, Fergusson's poems are presented as an incentive to buy Burns's poems; as an added extra in an already beautifully prepared edition: an ironic reversal of twentieth-century treatments of both poets. Subsequent to this first advertisement, the *Freeman's Journal* continues to publish a good many Burns poems, often those that have already appeared in the *Pennsylvania Packet*. Here we find "From thee, Eliza, I must go," "John Barleycorn," "Stanzas" and "Prayer in the Prospect of Death," the ubiquitous "When Guilford good" and "The Cotter's Saturday Night," as well as "Man was made to Mourn." Burns is certainly a fixture of the Philadelphian newspapers in his own lifetime.

The reviews, advertisements, and publications of early Scottish and American newspapers present a privileged vista of immediate, contemporary critical response to writers who have become giants of their literary traditions. The *Edinburgh Advertiser*, the *Pennsylvania Packet*, and the *Freeman's Journal* demonstrate that

---

[29]   William Wordsworth, "Preface to *Lyrical Ballads, with Pastoral and Other Poems* (1802)," in Stephen Gill (ed.), *William Wordsworth* (Oxford, 1984), pp. 597–8.

[30]   Murray Pittock, *Scottish and Irish Romanticism* (Oxford, 2008), p. 150.

[31]   *Freeman's Journal, or the North American Intelligencer*, 23 July 1788.

Burns's celebrity went ahead of him to his own capital city, but also much further, to the United States of America. John G. Dow's essay in J.D. Ross's *Burnsiana* (1897) delineates the sentimental and nostalgic but nevertheless legitimate reasons for Burns's popularity in America, particularly among expatriate Scots:

> In America, when the ubiquitous Scot leaves his native country, his patriotism grows, if anything, stronger and more sensitive. Amid strange scenes, strange faces, and alien tongues, memories of the Old Country grow warm in his heart, and the old familiar accent becomes very dear to him. Then it is that Burns's poetry, and more especially his songs, offer a rallying ground for troops of affectionate reminiscences and vague emotions that arise from instincts of the blood ... This was a voice straight from the democracy, speaking for the democracy with an unexampled directness and dignity ... In this Burns is more in sympathy with American than with Scottish life. The principle of individual worth and the spirit of independence which are to us in this country commonplaces of our daily lives are not so familiar in Scotland of to-day, and in the days of Burns they were startling in their novelty ... Therein lies the great ethic of his work, therein lies his just claim to sit among the great and beneficent spirits of the human race.[32]

Robert Burns discovered American history and politics very early in his poetic career. However, contrary to the traditional portrayal of the Burns story, America "discovered" Burns before many of his nearer neighbors did. And while the construction of Burns in eighteenth-century Philadelphia is very different than that of the twenty-first century bard, the contemporary response to Burns in the Scottish and American newspapers demonstrates the poet's versatility and universality. While twenty-first century criticism binds Burns to America with the ties of politics, the earliest reactions to Burns in the Scottish and American periodicals demonstrate that his appeal may have been simply human.

---

[32] John G. Dow, "Burns in America," in vol. 6 of J.D. Ross (comp.), *Burnsiana* (1897), in Low (ed.), *Robert Burns: The Critical Heritage*, pp. 439–40.

PART 3
Reading Burns in the Americas

Chapter 5
Burns's Political Reputation in North America

Gerard Carruthers

How has Robert Burns been received politically in North America? If it can be argued that the poet's legacy of revolutionary thinking was only very gradually appreciated in the British Isles, is it the same in the case of the American Republic and Canada? How do Burns's "republicanism," strong sense of "independence," and his famously humble background play out on the other side of the Atlantic?[1] This essay seeks to address these questions by evaluating transatlantic critical and creative responses to Burns's work.

For a start, we might be aware of a certain amount of latter-day reconstruction of Burns the political agitator in North America. According to Marie Tremaine, writing in 1999 in her excellent *A Bibliography of Canadian Imprints 1751–1800*, a poem found in a broadside published in Quebec in 1794 provides strong evidence of Burns's voice being associated with a "democratic theme." "Verses of the Printer's Boy Who Carries the Quebec Gazette to the Customers" features an ironic *de haute en bas* narrative voice which lashes the lower-class reformist thinker:

> Since you no Horace are, 'tis clear,
> 'Tis fit you in your shape appear:
> And to the world, behave as civil,
> As can do a poor printer's devil.
> Is it for you, you scurvy knave,
> With a *sous* your soul to save,
> The great or rich to dare attack,
> And bring them all upon your back?
> You! you poor dog, have an opinion!
> As soon they judge you a civilian.
> You who, on foot, like pedlars stroll
> Nor once, at ease, in carriage roll.

[1]   For a bringing together of some of these issues, generally, see G. Ross Roy (ed.), *Robert Burns and America: A Symposium* (Columbia, SC, and Kircaldy, 2001); for a highly nuanced and very modern account of Burns's relationship with North America through his work which suggests an entirely new critical paradigm, see Leith Davis, "Burns and Transnational Culture," in Gerard Carruthers (ed.), *The Edinburgh Companion to Robert Burns* (Edinburgh, 2009), pp. 150–163.

You're nobody—to no one known,
To you what favour can be shewn?
Where's your credentials, from below?
…
Or where did you the right receive,
By reason or by rhime to live?
Plead you the right of hands and head?
Poor fool, they stand you in little stead.[2]

However, it is difficult to see what might be particularly Burnsian in the lines above. By 1794, Burns's explicit comments in favor of the revolutionary ferment of the 1790s were to be found in his "Ode [For General Washington's Birthday]," but this remained unpublished until 1808 and even then not fully until 1873.[3] "Robert Bruce's March to Bannockburn" ["Scots wha hae"] (1793) appeared in the London *Morning Chronicle* for 8 May 1794, and though this signalled Burns's reformist sympathies in codified form, these remained less than widely appreciated until after Burns's death in 1796. "Is there for honest Poverty" ["A Man's a Man"], which Marie Tremaine most likely seems to be thinking of in the general resemblance of its thought to the lines just quoted, was not published until well into 1795, and even then not very widely.

Another retrospective North American construction of Burns the revolutionary is to be found in the exhibition of material by the poet at the Rosenbach Museum, Philadelphia, in 1995.[4] A striking narrative within the exhibition seeks to chart an essentially smooth and continuous political Burns from 1789 to 1795 onwards under the rubric, "'Tis liberty's bold note I swell." The Rosenbach displayed its autograph manuscript copy of Burns's short essay, "Address to the Right Honorable William Pitt," a work which was published pseudonymously under "John Barleycorn" in the *Edinburgh Evening Courant* in February 1789, a text complaining against London parliamentary taxes imposed on Scotch whisky. In the same section of the exhibition we find also the autograph manuscripts of "Ode [For General Washington's Birthday]" and "Is there for honest Poverty," the latter item being one which Burns had presented to his wealthy young friend Maria Riddell at some point in 1794. Another item displayed which the poet had given to Maria was a privately printed broadside. Like "Is there for honest poverty," this text also carries the refrain of "For a' that, and a' that," though the broadside is the First Heron Election Ballad.

However, the Rosenbach curators make a common error here with their assumption, based on the refrain and also on a surface reading of its "Whig" political allegiances, that the First Heron Election Ballad is straightforwardly part

---

[2]   Marie Tremaine, *A Bibliography of Canadian Imprints 1751–1800* (1952; Toronto, 1999), p. 432 (see pp. 432–3).

[3]   In a first pirated printing in the *Scottish American Journal* on 9 October 1873.

[4]   See the Rosenbach Museum and Library catalogue to the exhibition, *Robert Burns: The Poet's Progress* (Philadelphia, 1995).

of the sounding by Burns of "liberty's bold note." Patrick Heron, in support of whom Burns writes his four broadside election ballads in 1795 in the contest for the Stewartry of Kirkcudbright commons parliamentary seat, is nominally a Whig. However, this label has wrong-footed a number of commentators, since Heron was, in fact, no liberal reformer as some Whigs of the time were, but the Pitt-Dundas government candidate who voted against the abolition of slavery within weeks of taking his seat in parliament.[5] Modern commentators in the know regarding Heron's true political stamp have been rather perplexed by Burns's support for this politician. Did the poet know whom he was supporting? Might it be that the Rosenbach collocation of the two "For a' that's" sent to Maria Riddell actually highlights Burns's support for Heron as an attempt to curry favor with Maria? The Riddell family seem to have been amused onlookers to Burns's strongly expressed dislike of the Duke of Queensberry, against whose interest Heron was standing in the 1795 election. There is even a little internal evidence, to add to the external gift of it, that Maria might be the audience for the first Heron ballad, as Burns talks of "wit and worth in either sex," a "rights of women" stance he sometimes adopts when writing to, or about, Maria.[6] So, highly local 1790s Dumfriesshire county-set politics, arguably, are rather more highlighted, albeit implicitly, in the Rosenbach exhibition than anything larger.[7]

One potentially interesting source of information regarding Burns's early, indeed precisely portable, political reputation for North America is the work of others fleeing repression in the British Isles of the 1790s. These are Michael Durey's "transatlantic radicals," individuals who made new lives and careers in Philadelphia and Washington, especially.[8] Not only does there seem to be no real sense of Burns as being politically one of them among Scottish and Ulster émigrés of this sort, but when we look at the significant quotient of poets among their number, the Burnsian idiom seems not to be seen as very amenable to the expression of their ideals. This is shown to be the case in two of Burns's most significant Scottish literary contemporaries who were put to the horn in Edinburgh during 1793 and who took refuge across the Atlantic. The first of these, James Thomson Callender (1758–1803), had a steady output of republican poetry in the first half of the 1790s written in standard English and otherwise also seemingly

---

[5] See Norman R. Paton, *Song O' Liberty: The Politics of Robert Burns* (Fareham, 1994), p. 120.

[6] *The Poems and Songs of Robert Burns*, James Kinsley (ed.) (3 vols, Oxford, 1968), vol. 2, p. 775.

[7] It is interesting also that the Rosenbach exhibition does not include the poet's letter to Helen Maria Williams which it possesses and which shows Burns in rather less than heroic light a propos the abolitionist issue. See *Robert Burns 1759–1796: A Collection of Original Manuscripts, Autograph Letters, First Editions and Association Copies* (Philadelphia and New York, 1948), p. 36. See also Nigel Leask, "Burns and the Poetics of Abolition" in Carruthers (ed.), *The Edinburgh Companion to Robert Burns*, pp. 47–60.

[8] Michael Durey, *Transatlantic Radicals and the Early American Republic* (Lawrence, KS, 1997).

devoid of any influence from Burns. Callender fled Scotland just before being tried for sedition, going first to Dublin from where, carrying letters of recommendation from United Irishmen comrades, he travelled to Philadelphia and obtained employment with the radical émigré Irish publisher, Mathew Carey. Carey, editor of the widely ranging *American Museum* from 1787 to 1792, had a very large publishing and journalistic output encompassing much hard-hitting political and cultural commentary on both North America and Europe. According to Michael Durey he published "more than a thousand titles" between 1785 and 1821, from which Robert Burns is largely absent.[9] A second radical Scottish poet outlawed was James "Balloon" Tytler (1745–1804), who may have known Burns personally in Edinburgh. As with Callender, his own radical poetic output, including "The Rising of the Sun in the West" (1795), which he composed en route across the Atlantic, draws nothing from the Scottish bard. The puzzle here, of why the Scots idiom would seem to have been not all that amenable so far as Scottish reformist poets were concerned, warrants some further work. However, three ideas might be tentatively ventured. It may be the case rightly or wrongly, and as was certainly true in Ulster that pro-revolutionary activists believed that Burns, in publishing "The Dumfries Volunteers" ["Does haughty Gaul invasion threat"] (1795), to say nothing of the poet joining his local loyalist militia, was no longer on their side.[10] More widely, the 1790s saw something of a culture war between left and right attending on the political issues. One of Burns's would-be mentors, the highly radical Earl of Buchan (David Steuart Erskine), hoped that Burns, generally, might increasingly phrase his efforts in English. Writers like Callender and Tytler may well have regarded English as the appropriately progressive, civilized medium (as opposed to Scots with its long eighteenth-century associations with antiquarianism and also Tory ideals), with which to win political hearts and minds. It is noteworthy that the one radical poet of the 1790s who produced a consistent body of reformist work in Scots, the London-based Alexander Geddes, had also earlier produced a treatise that argued that Scots *was* a forward-looking language of expanding rather than contracting expressive possibilities. Finally, Scots was strongly associated, if anything, with loyalist political expression found in a wide culture of Scots songs and in the work of Hector Macneill, a writer whose work for a time from the 1790s and well into the period of the Napoleonic Wars was close in popularity to that of Burns.

---

[9]   Durey, *Transatlantic Radicals*, p. 204.

[10]   For a sophisticated discussion of this situation, see Liam McIlvanney, *Burns the Radical: Poetry and Politics in Late Eighteenth-Century Scotland* (East Linton, 2002), pp. 235–40; see also John Gray, "Burns and his Visitors from Ulster: From Adulation to Disaccord," *Studies in Scottish Literature*, 33–34 (2004): 320–334; and Jennifer Orr, "1798, Before, and Beyond: Samuel Thomson and the Poetics of Ulster–Scots Identity," in Frank Ferguson and Andrew R. Holmes (eds), *Revising Robert Burns and Ulster: Literature, Religion and Politics, c.1770–1920* (Dublin, 2009), pp. 106–26 (pp. 116–7).

As in the case of the British Isles, in fact, it seems to be that it was only really from the 1830s that a "revolutionary" Burns emerged for North America. This general situation is explicable in terms of the fact that it was not only posthumously but also very slowly that anything like Burns's entire poetic corpus emerged, taking fully the first seven decades of the nineteenth century. The editor James Currie was cautious with the poet's political profusions in the first attempted collection of Burns's "Works" in 1800, and it took the labors of many in the first part of the nineteenth century before the Burns corpus was disinterred amidst a confusing welter of bowdlerized, suppressed, and wrongly attributed material. One of the most significant North American collected editions in this regard is the two-volume version published by William Pearson in New York in 1832. A review of this edition in the American periodical *The Knickerbocker* for August of 1832 rightly makes much of the fact that the Pearson edition is more comprehensive than any ever before published in North America, making the proudly demotic claim also that it is cheaper than any previous Burns "Works" sold on either side of the Atlantic. With this edition we find part of a clear and common pattern to Burns Studies that only really exists from the 1830s: that Burns can be disinterred fully and explicitly in his reformist political predilections. It is also interesting that the Pearson edition predates that of Robert Chambers, perhaps even inspires Chambers, the man who does most in this regard on the British side of the Atlantic with his edition of 1838. The anonymous reviewer in *The Knickerbocker* is striking in being perhaps the most politically angry anywhere in the four decades following Burns's death, as he reports on a notorious meeting between one of the poet's sons and the British king:

> Did bold uncowering independence ever burst forth in more elevated strains, than in those glowing lines, "A man's a man for a' that"? That they were highly esteemed by the poet himself, may be ascertained from the fact that, these were the lines selected by the eldest of Burns's sons to repeat for George the Fourth, when introduced to that royal presence.
>
> And how did the heartless despot treat the orphan boy of the immortal bard, who left these manly lines as a precious deposit, not only to his family, but to all posterity? Dismissed him from his presence![11]

Such anti-monarchical outspokenness in the 1830s is found nowhere in British commentary on Burns. We find here, perhaps, a particularly American disregard for royalty.

A most interesting convergence between Burns's revolutionary sensibility and North America occurs with his poem "Ode [For General Washington's Birthday]," composed in 1794. Burns forbore from publishing this piece himself and was cautious with what he did reveal of the text, even in private. In a letter to Frances Anna Dunlop of 25 June 1794, he sent only the last nineteen of sixty-two lines of

---

[11]   *The Knickerbocker*, 2 (August 1833): 148–9 (148).

the complete poem. This is how it appeared in all subsequent printings until 1873, a year after an American bookseller, Robert Clarke, had purchased it from a sale in London and had it transported to Ohio.[12] Before this, the text in its bowdlerized form had been transformed, rather lamely, into a piece discussing only the Scottish Wars of Independence of the fourteenth century shorn of the more awkward nuances of the revolutionary 1770s to 1790s, such as are to be found in the complete four stanzas of the ode for Washington. Burns himself was partly responsible for the long delay in publication. At the time of its composition, he was a government employee in the Excise service and so understandably did not want to broadcast his views, evident in the text, of British tyranny in America of recent memory nor of his government's suppression of traditional British liberties of political expression during the 1790s. It remains somewhat mysterious, however, why it took so long for Burns's ode to be published and why this should occur across the Atlantic (leaving aside the obvious appeal to America of the subject matter). Prior to the London sale of the manuscript in 1872, it had gone on sale in the English capital in 1861, but the publicity of this event seems to have done nothing to spur any British editor of Burns into action to acquire the text for publication.[13]

In both the United States and the British colonies in North America, the nineteenth century found a number of writers particularly inspired by Burns, though principally, even after the change in Burns scholarship of the 1830s, without the revolutionary element. Here we come to a situation that is paralleled on both sides of the Atlantic, where Burns's Romantic status as a primitive bard sees him, by and large, not as a poet of radical political dynamic but of conservative, natural, unchanging essence, or as a "lowly" innocent. Perhaps most famously, John Greenleaf Whittier (1807–1892) was referred to as "the American Burns." His poem, "Burns. On receiving a sprig of heather in blossom" (1854), still determinedly sees the Scottish poet as the bard of nature and of feeling, a poet whose cultural value is precisely conservative. On reading Burns, Whittier's narrator "with clearer eyes":

>   saw the worth,
>   Of life among the lowly;
> The Bible at his Cotter's hearth
>   Had made my own more holy.[14]

---

[12]   Published first in Robert Burns, "Ode [For General Washington's Birthday]," in *Reliques of Robert Burns*, R.H. Cromek (ed.) (London, 1803), pp. 156–8; see *The Letters of Robert Burns*, J. De Lancey Ferguson (ed.), 2nd edn, G. Ross Roy (ed.) (2 vols, Oxford, 1985), vol. 2, pp. 297–8.

[13]   See "First Day's Sale," *Sales Catalogue for Puttock and Simpson*, May 1861, p. 24.

[14]   John Greenleaf Whittier, "Burns. On receiving a sprig of heather in blossom," *The Complete Poetical Works of John Greenleaf Whittier*, H.E. Scudder (ed.) (Boston, 1894), in *Robert Burns: The Critical Heritage*, Donald A. Low (ed.) (London and Boston, 1974), pp. 432–3 (p. 433).

In a maneuver that has worked its way through a number of iterations from Burns's own life until modern times, Burns is de-canonized by Whittier as the American poet defines him against two of the greatest of European vernacular poets, Dante and Milton:

> Not his the song whose thunderous chime
>> Eternal echoes render;
> The mournful Tuscan's haunted rhyme,
>> And Milton's starry splendour!

Whittier may be strictly correct in identifying Burns as unlike the two great European poets of epic religious writing. And the Scottish poet's "The Cotter's Saturday Night" does indeed depict the worship with which Burns was familiar as, in some senses, a rather humble affair. However, the patriarch in Burns's poem is a life-force sublime (and also, ironically, not unlike Milton himself, in his profound personal engagement with Scripture). More generally across his oeuvre, Burns is not so theologically unreflective a poet as Whittier's comparison with Dante and Milton suggests. Whittier ostensibly, and sincerely, praising Burns nonetheless reduces him in his literary amplitude. Burns the naïf suits a nineteenth-century version of Romanticism that prioritizes simple nature in a way that, if anything, becomes evasively anti-intellectual. Whittier, however, performs a rather dichotomous reception of Burns. If the figure of Burns walks the American poet's mind as a less engaged figure than he might be, elsewhere in his poetry, Whittier finds Burns an altogether more actively political influence. Amid Whittier's voluminous anti-slavery writings, we find "To W.L.G" (1833), addressed to the outspoken abolitionist, William Lloyd Garrison:

> Champion of those who groan beneath
>> Oppression's iron hand:
> In view of penury, hate, and death,
>> I see thee fearless stand.
> Still bearing up thy lofty brow,
>> In the steadfast strength of truth,
> In manhood sealing well the vow
>> And promise of thy youth.
>
> Go on, — for thou hast chosen well;
>> On in the strength of God!
> Long as one human heart shall swell
>> Beneath the tyrant's rod.
> Speak in a slumbering nation's ear,
>> As thou hast ever spoken,
> Until the dead in sin shall hear, —
>> The fetter's link be broken![15]

---

[15] *The Poetical Works of John Greenleaf Whittier* (London, 1874), p. 63.

Here, fairly clearly, the sentiment of outraged universal and national sensibility owes much to the Burns of "Robert Bruce's March to Bannockburn" and "Is there for honest poverty."

If in nineteenth-century Britain ideas become increasingly problematic leading to crises in political and religious confidence, in the United States there is a similar turning away from troublingly rational intellect. If the Victorians were to become increasingly angst-ridden in the face of troubling developments in natural and political science, the response to the same in the United States often took the form of a transcendental individualism which was often rapturous. Ralph Waldo Emerson proffers a rhapsody on Burns that is often admired in expressing the bigness of the poet, but which actually in effect disconnects Burns from history:

> His muse and teaching was common sense, joyful aggressive, irresistible. Not Latimer, nor Luther struck more telling blows against false theology than did this brave singer. The Confession of Augsburg, the Declaration of Independence, the French Rights of Man, and the "Marseillaise," are not more weighty documents in the history of freedom than the songs of Burns.[16]

Truly, one might suggest, Burns's lyricism is part of the "history of freedom," but it was inspired and enabled by the American and French revolutions, and was schooled, too, in theological controversy. Burns's expression did not run alongside these things borne out of pure "common sense"; it was *part* of history. Emerson exemplifies something that happens in the United States a propos Burns where his kinship with that country is increasingly identified in naked individualism that becomes little short of platitudinous.

We see this quite starkly by the end of the nineteenth century with the expatriate Scot, John G. Dow, writing from Wisconsin:

> The literary, like the political revolution of the 18th century, consisted chiefly in the assertion and establishment of the dignity of individual man; it lay also in a return to the healing powers of nature, and in both of these respects the Napoleon of this revolution was Robert Burns. Nature was his high priestess in song; and when equality and fraternity were being branded with blood and fire on the face of Europe, Burns gathered as into a burning focus the whole human sentiment of the revolution in "A man's a man for a' that." This was a voice straight from the democracy, speaking for the democracy with an unexampled directness and dignity — the voice of one who stood on the rock of his own independence, and esteeming every man at his mere intrinsic worth, proclaimed the new creed and gospel of humanity.
>
> In this Burns is more in sympathy with American than with Scottish life. The principle of individual worth and the spirit of independence which are to us in this country commonplaces of our daily lives are not so familiar in Scotland of

---

to-day, and in the days of Burns they were startling in their novelty. It is true that Burns seemed to have failed miserably, that he was silently crushed out and down by the allied respectabilities of social caste, whose extinction he so proudly heralded. But despite his apparent failure there is in the life and poetry of this herald of the dawn an immortal record of the true majesty of manhood. Therein lies the great ethic of his work, therein lies his just claim to sit among the great and beneficent spirits of the human race.[17]

Revolutionary political history may be mentioned here, but Dow's emphasis upon the historic birth of modern "democracy" soon gives way to non-political ideas of "independence" and the "individual" which in their divorce from any kind of communitarian context are vapid, even solipsistic. We can easily see here the disjunction in the cultural reception of Burns, whereby, simultaneously the poet came to be seen as exemplary in the capitalist USA and in Russia, which equally created a non-historical Burns in projecting him in early twentieth-century Soviet iteration as a proletarian peasant. In the United States, there has been something of a fascination in yoking Burns with presidents. There is the case of George Washington, which we shall come to in a moment. More prominently, Burns is mentioned (accurately) as a favorite writer of Abraham Lincoln.[18] However, the parallel between Burns and Lincoln is largely coincidental, having more to do with cultural status rather than with direct influence. As Ferenc Morton Szasz has commented, both Burns and Lincoln "had evolved into semi-sacred national icons shortly after their deaths."[19] Both men stand for myths of "liberty," expressed in rather one-dimensional fashion and ignoring on the one hand Lincoln's racist attitudes and on the other hand Burns's own less than clarion-clear politics while he was alive.

Much excellent Burns scholarship has issued from North America in the twentieth and twenty-first centuries. The same is true for the United Kingdom. However, in both places Burns's reputation continues to proceed alongside this scholarship in various shadow forms. On both sides of the Atlantic, one of these shadows concerns Burns's status as a freemason. In 2009 appeared the handsomely produced volume *A Bibliography of the William R. Smith Collection*, which describes the Burns materials held in Washington by those Freemasons of Accepted Scottish Rite, Southern Jurisdiction, USA.[20] The introduction "Brother

---

[17]   John Dow, *Selections from the Poems of Robert Burns* (Boston, 1898), in Low (ed.), *Robert Burns: The Critical Heritage*, p. 440.

[18]   At the time of Barack Obama's inauguration as U.S. president in January 2009, the present writer was telephoned by more than one journalist asking if Burns's influence could be heard in Obama's speeches since the new president had mentioned his own indebtedness to Lincoln.

[19]   Ferenc Morton Szasz, *Abraham Lincoln and Robert Burns: Connected Lives and Legends* (Carbondale, 2008), p. 140.

[20]   Larissa P. Watkins (ed.), *Burnsiana: A Bibliography of the William R. Smith Collection in the Library of the Supreme Council ...* (New Castle, DE, 2008).

Robert Burns" by Robert Cooper, Curator at the Grand Lodge of Scotland, makes much of two items, "Is there for honest poverty" and "Ode [For General Washington's Birthday]." Without doubting the presence of freemasonry in Burns's life and work, we might see here a partial over-emphasis. The former text's concluding hope that "Man to man the warld o'er, / Shall brothers be" might well be inspired by the language of freemasonry, but this is ultimately incidental to a democratic political inspiration specifically propelled by the circumstances of the 1790s.[21] Equally, Washington's freemasonry has very little to do with Burns's hymning of the American president in the second text. There is no other poet whose large-scale political utterances, across these two poems encompassing American and French revolutions, are so readily corralled within a much smaller context. This freemasonic deflation of Burns joins the nineteenth-century inflation of Burns, already mentioned, as a poet of "individualism" and "nature." Where Burns in the latter view becomes all too detached from history, the freemasonic deflation represents a too close attachment to one particular aspect of (Burns's) history. Commonly, on both sides of the Atlantic such over-generalizations and over-particularizations have bedeviled the proper appreciation of Burns.

In Canada, as in Scotland, Burns is sometimes implicated in a reading of native literary tradition that emphasizes its own inferiority. This note in Canadian criticism is largely at odds with Burns's reception in the criticism of the United States, where Burns's supposed primitivism, not as we have seen unproblematic, is nonetheless not a matter of anxiety. Elizabeth Waterston speaks for a number of unimpressed Canadian scholars when she says:

> Burns's stance suited the early Canadian taste too well perhaps. The ironic downrightness of "a man's a man for a' that" permeated the working-class, spreading from the nucleus of Scottish artisans into the whole early Canadian community. Its acceptance curtailed the desire for subtlety and elegance, and made laughable the finer social forms and conventions.[22]

And again: "Burns suited Canadian needs too well. Loving his work, finding it applicable, Canadian poets settled for his range, and sent out few feelers into the realms of experience more complicated than his."[23] As Waterston has rightly commented, "the climax of the Burns tradition in Canada is the work of Alexander McLachlan, a poor boy who came from Glasgow in 1840."[24] McLachlan (1818–1896) actually hailed from Johnstone in Renfrewshire and exemplified not so much a continuation of Burns the Scottish poet as a different nineteenth-century version of the bard, Burns the British poet. His "Britannia" precisely inhabits the cadences of "Scots wha hae," with a hymn to his nation, "Great mother of the

---

[21]   *The Poems and Songs of Robert Burns*, Kinsley (ed.), vol. 2, p. 763.

[22]   Elizabeth Waterston, "The Lowland Tradition in Canadian Literature," in W. Stanford Reid (ed.), *The Scottish Tradition in Canada* (Toronto, 1976), p. 208.

[23]   Ibid., p. 211.

[24]   Ibid., p. 208.

Mighty Dead," for which "Sir Walter sang, and Nelson bled." McLachlan's work is soaked in the Burnsian idiom as we see clearly, for instance, in "Young Canada or Jack's as Good as His Master" (1874):

> Our aristocracy of toil
> Have made us what you see —
> The nobles of the forge and soil,
> With ne'er a pedigree!
> It makes one feel himself a man,
> His very blood leaps faster,
> Where wit or worth's preferred to birth,
> And Jack's as good's his master![25]

In another poem from the same year, "The Anglo-Saxon," McLachlan's identity is clearly shown to make sense in the context of a celebrated British imperialism, where the common colonial British adventurer derives a moral superiority through dedication to hard work:

> He runs his plough in every land,
> He sails on every sea,
> All prospers where he has a hand,
> For king of men is he.
> He plants himself on Afric's sand,
> And 'mong Spitzbergen's snows,
> For he takes root in any land,
> And blossoms like the rose.[26]

This ordinary man is couched in Burnsian terms as the "king of men" (and where the plough, too, recalls the poet). It is interesting also that here we are more than a decade before a renascent "Celtic" identity gives racial color to the Scottish identity, and that "Anglo-Saxon" genes are simply part of the Scottish makeup (in a way that would not have been the case for the non-Anglophone Scottish-Canadian culture in the east). What we see in that strain of Canadian poetry which receives Burns and inhabits something of his idiom is, as Elizabeth Waterston identifies, an arguably partial outlook. However, we should be careful not to blame Burns *per se* for those Canadian poetasters who follow him. The overwhelming cause of Burns's less than happy influence is not their following of his poetic craft itself with its manifold subtleties, but a version of the poet that is stripped of both formal and ideological nuance. It is a version of Burns, the "heaven-taught ploughman," palatable to the identity of empire and almost completely insensitive to any version of class politics. It pertains long and in stubborn fashion as the

---

[25] Carole Gerson and Gwendolyn Davies (eds), *Canadian Poetry: From the Beginnings Through the First World War* (Toronto, 1994), p. 95.

[26] Ibid., p. 93.

instance of Marie Joussaye (1864?–1949) shows. Her "Two Poets" sees Burns's life and work in a way that seemingly "transcends" politics:

> There lived and died a poet, years ago—
>   A hardy, humble ploughman of the soil
> Who sang his heartfelt songs in simplest words
>   And earned his daily bread by humble toil.
> His songs brought gladness unto many hearts
>   And soothed men's sorrows with magic spell.
> His name was known in palace and in cot,
>   For king and peasant loved the poet well.
> And why? Because he sang of human faith,
>   Of human love, of human joy and pain,
> The grandest thoughts couched in the simplest words,
>   The lowliest mind could grasp the meaning plain.
> O poet ploughman! thine the laurel wreath,
>   Whose songs found answer in the hearts of men,
> Thy name shall live on Fame's immortal scroll
>   After his name has passed from mortal ken,
> Thine the true poet soul and master mind
>   Whose lyrics touched the heart of all mankind.[27]

As in the case of the United States of America, then, Canadian iterations of Robert Burns have sometimes "universalized" what he represents to the extent of becoming emptily platitudinous. That said, we should perhaps be careful not to be entirely scathing of poets who are operating, to some extent at least, within a "new world" blank canvas where the politics of the "old world" lack the urgency that they possess on their own side of the Atlantic. Both Whittier's heartfelt poetic abolitionism and McLachlan's intensely sincere attempt to comprehend a new world landscape of overwhelming natural resources can be said to draw upon an affective legacy from Burns that is suitably emotionally expansive. This Burnsian affectivity perhaps even helps pave the way towards the new American continental vision, eventually so brilliantly expressed by Walt Whitman, where nature and instinct reassume a necessarily equal place alongside rationality. The primitivist side of Burns has lain at the root of his trouble in being accepted in his full literary plenitude across the world, though it has also perhaps meant that his influence has endured in many places and through many literary movements where nature and feeling are powerful motors.

---

[27] Ibid., p. 321.

Chapter 6
America's Bard[1]

Robert Crawford

The first months of 2009 brought three events celebrated around the world: the inauguration of President Barack Obama, the 250th anniversary of Robert Burns's birth, and the bicentenary of the birth of Abraham Lincoln. In Washington on 24 February in the Thomas Jefferson Building of the Library of Congress, downstairs from the recently opened Abraham Lincoln Bicentennial Exhibition, a group of Senators and Congressmen pledged their loyalty to a Scottish Caucus on the evening which ended the first day of the Library's "Robert Burns at 250" celebrations; immediately afterwards, across the road in the Capitol building, President Obama addressed for the first time a joint meeting of both houses. On the other side of the Atlantic, not long after President Obama's inauguration, the Burns editor Christopher MacLachlan had read on 20 January alongside several poets at the Scottish Poetry Library in Edinburgh, close to the Scottish Parliament. A few days later, on Burns Night, the literary editor of a Scottish broadsheet described MacLachlan's as "the best of all" those readings.[2] Invoking President Obama and American traditions of liberty, MacLachlan had reminded his audience that Burns in his "Ode" composed in the mid-1790s for George Washington's birthday calls America "Columbia." This was, as one of MacLachlan's textual notes to the poem indicates, a name "favoured by those anxious to assert American independence from Britain," and it survives most obviously in the designation of the United States capital as "Washington, District of Columbia." MacLachlan's audience was struck by how resolutely angry Burns's Washington poem sounded when read aloud:

> No Spartan tube, no Attic shell,
>   No lyre Eolian I awake;
> 'Tis Liberty's bold note I swell,
>   Thy harp, Columbia, let me take.
> See gathering thousands, while I sing,

---

[1]   This chapter was developed from lectures delivered at the University of California, Berkeley, in 2007 and at the Library of Congress in 2009. Thanks are due to those institutions and especially to Ian Duncan (Berkeley) and Nancy Groce (Library of Congress) for their support; also to the Scottish Government, who co-sponsored the Library of Congress Burns celebration.
[2]   Stuart Kelly, "The Browser," *Scotland on Sunday*, 25 January 2009, review section, p. 12.

A broken chain, exulting, bring,
And dash it in a tyrant's face!
And dare him to his very beard,
And tell him, he no more is feared,
    No more the Despot of Columbia's race.
A tyrant's proudest insults braved,
They shout, a People freed! They hail an Empire saved.

    Where is Man's godlike form?
Where is that brow erect & bold,
That eye that can, unmoved, behold
The wildest rage, the loudest storm,
That e'er created fury dared to raise?
Avaunt! thou caitiff, servile, base,
That tremblest at a Despot's nod,
Yet, crouching under th'iron rod,
Canst laud the arm that struck th'insulting blow!
Art thou of man's imperial line?
Dost boast that countenance divine?
Each sculking feature answers, NO!
But come, ye sons of Liberty,
Columbia's offspring, brave as free,
In danger's hour still flaming in the van:
Ye know, & dare maintain, The Royalty of Man.[3]

One of the strengths of MacLachlan's textual work is that when (as here) the poem was not published by Burns, MacLachlan goes to a manuscript—in this instance in the Rosenbach Museum and Library, Philadelphia—and so catches more accurately than other Burns editors the capitalized, emphatic "NO!" of the poem, letting us hear just how rhetorically impassioned its voice sounds. We can mis-hear Burns today. We can be distracted, for instance, by that phrase "countenance divine," familiar to us now from William Blake's later "Jerusalem" poem, and so not realize that most probably both Burns and Blake have taken it from Mark Akenside's *Pleasures of the Imagination*, or possibly from John Glover's once popular *Leonidas*, a source appropriately Spartan and heroic for Burns's ode which begins with mention of "Spartan tube" and "Attic shell." MacLachlan's reading and MacLachlan's text alert us to the resolute anger of Burns's words; but we would need to be truly tin-eared not to hear the determined siding with America which this poem articulates, or to respond to that fine phrase which exalts not the British monarchy but the proudly independent "Royalty of Man."

It may seem strange that an eighteenth-century Scottish poet who almost went to work as an assistant overseer on a Jamaican slave plantation became a favorite

---

[3] *The Best Laid Schemes: Selected Poetry and Prose of Robert Burns*, Robert Crawford and Christopher MacLachlan (eds) (Edinburgh and Princeton, 2009), p. 152; unless otherwise noted, subsequent quotations from Burns's writings are from this edition and will be cited in the text by page number.

poet of Abraham Lincoln, let alone an inspiration to contemporary figures as different as Maya Angelou and Kofi Annan, but Burns is America's bard first and foremost because he made himself so in his own poetry. This is very evident in the 1794 ode that Burns told his friend Frances Dunlop he had composed for General Washington's birthday, but it is also apparent elsewhere. As I have pointed out in *The Bard*, my 2009 biography of Burns, "*America*," not Scotland, is the first nation named in Burns's poetry, which mentions "*Boston-ha*," "*Philadelphia*" and "*New-York*" some considerable time before it mentions Edinburgh.[4] Burns's relatively early song beginning "When *Guilford* good," displays a very detailed knowledge of the campaigning and political repercussions of what Burns called the American War—what we now term the American War of Independence. Probably Burns got this knowledge from conversation and periodicals. A keen reader of newspapers, he seems to have picked up that habit when still young. Recalling the summer of 1773 when Burns was fourteen, his tutor John Murdoch remembered telling the boy,

> I should like to teach him something of French pronunciation, that when he should meet with the name of a French town, ship, officer, or the like, in the newspapers, he might be able to pronounce it something like a French word. Robert was glad to hear this proposal, and immediately we attacked the French with great courage.[5]

This implies Murdoch was alert to the teenage Burns's interest in the reporting of international news. For any teenager in the mid-1770s, especially on the west coast of a Lowland Scotland harried by John Paul Jones and other raiders, the most interesting newspaper reports concerned the revolt of the American colonies. None of Burns's correspondence from this period survives, but we do know he and his community took a close interest in American affairs.

With just over 200 voters, Burns's Ayrshire was hardly democratic in the ancient, the modern, or the American sense. We should not take it for granted that it was natural for Burns to support democratic revolution in America or elsewhere. Like the inclinations of Glasgow's Professor John Millar, who "was constantly attacked in the newspapers" for his radical views which included backing the American rebels, Burns's pro-Revolutionary sympathies went against the orthodox current of political opinion about democracy. Locally, his community and friends were at times victims of the rebel colonies.[6] Ayrshire was economically damaged by the American War. Yet as a newspaper reader aged seventeen in 1776, Burns must have been keenly aware of the rebels' ideals, and he went on to become the first major poet to respond to them with excitement.

---

4   Robert Crawford, *The Bard: Robert Burns, A Biography* (London and Princeton, 2009), p. 77.

5   John Murdoch, qtd. in Crawford, *The Bard*, p. 57.

6   Christina Bewley, *Muir of Huntershill* (Oxford, 1981), p. 5.

During August 1776, in Burns's seventeenth year, the American Declaration of Independence was widely published in the British Press, appearing in such papers as the *Morning Chronicle*, the *British Chronicle*, the *St James's Chronicle*, the *General Evening Post*, and the *Caledonian Mercury*. American independence was at once discussed in the *Scots Magazine* and absorbed the intense attention of such intellectual luminaries as Adam Smith and the historian William Robertson as well as many less renowned readers of newspapers.[7] Did Burns read the Declaration of Independence? The answer, surely, is yes, and the best evidence is a poem. The substantial song fragment beginning "When *Guilford* good" dates from around 1784 and is roughly contemporary with Burns's "Epistle to Davie, A Brother Poet." When Burns writes at the start of his song fragment about how "Ae night, at tea, began a plea, / Within America, man," he is clearly referring to the 1773 Boston Tea Party. Equally clearly, when he moves beyond the pouring of that tea "in the sea," to say of the Americans that they "did nae less, in full Congress, / Than quite refuse our law, man" (p. 13), he is surely echoing the words of the Declaration of Independence which begins with the words "In CONGRESS" and repeats several times the words "refused" and "Laws."[8] If such phrases stuck in the mind of the young Burns so intently that they feature in a poem written several years after the publication of the Declaration in British newspapers, clearly the Declaration impressed him and helped shape his own declarations of independence.

The most ringing sentence of the American Declaration remains the best known: "We hold these truths to be self-evident, that all men are created equal, that they are endowed by their Creator with certain unalienable Rights, that among these are Life, Liberty and the pursuit of Happiness." A stress on liberty and the essential pursuit of happiness is articulated in Burns's "Epistle to Davie, A Brother Poet." Linked in their assumed fraternity, that poem's two young poets "wander out" like "Commoners of air." This last phrase surely signals a life of absolute shared liberty—it declares independence—though it may also pun on the town of "Ayr," the capital of Burns's Ayrshire, whose name might be spelled several ways in the eighteenth century. Still, Burns does not capitalize the word "air"; instead, he capitalizes in his first book the word "Commoners," exalting it to a status it might not usually be thought to enjoy. If "Commoners" is a word that seems raised up in this poem which celebrates life and liberty, then there is also a lowering and a democratic impulse in the stanza that follows with its emphasis on happiness:

> It's no in titles nor in rank;
> It's no in wealth like *Lon'on Bank*,
>   To purchase peace and rest;
> It's no in makin muckle, *mair:*
> It's no in books; it's no in Lear,

---

[7]   See David Armitage, *The Declaration of Independence: A Global History* (Harvard, 2007), pp. 70, 77, 263–4.

[8]   "The Declaration of Independence" in *The Debate on the Constitution: Federalist and Antifederalist Speeches, Articles, and Letters During the Struggle over Ratification, Part One: September 1787 to February 1788*, Bernard Bailyn (ed.) (New York, 1993), pp. 949–53 (p. 949).

To make us truly blest:
If Happiness hae not her seat
And center in the breast,
We may be *wise*, or *rich*, or *great*,
But never can be *blest*:
Nae treasures, nor pleasures
Could make us happy lang;
The *heart* ay's the part ay,
That makes us right or wrang.

Think ye, that sic as *you* and *I*,
Wha drudge and drive thro' wet and dry,
Wi' never-ceasing toil;
Think ye, are we less blest than they,
Wha scarcely tent us in their way,
As hardly worth their while?
Alas! How aft, in haughty mood,
GOD's creatures they oppress!
Or else, neglecting a'that's guid,
They riot in excess!
Baith careless, and fearless,
Of either Heaven or Hell;
Esteeming, and deeming,
It a' an idle tale! (pp. 22–3)

Emphasizing the centrality of "Happiness," these stanzas are attuned to the Declaration of Independence, but they are too an egalitarian challenge to "titles" and "rank" that foreshadow Burns's most celebrated song on universal brotherhood which hymns "The man of independant [*sic*] mind" rather than the titled person's "ribband, star, & a' that" (p. 158). These stanzas also anticipate the vehement championing of egalitarianism elsewhere in Burns's work, not least in the ode for Washington's birthday. So it was Burns himself who made Burns America's bard. He stands not just as the first of the great Romantic poets but also the one most attuned to that American Declaration of Independence which caused such a stir in his youth.

Burns maintained a long, sympathetic interest in American democracy. In the "Address of Beelzebub" he writes of Highlanders emigrating "to the wilds of CANADA, in search of that fantastic thing—LIBERTY—." Burns's Devil imagines what might happen if American Revolutionary heroes led these would-be Canadians:

Some daring HANCOCKE, or a FRANKLINE,
May set their HIGHLAN bluid a ranklin;
Some Washington again may head them,
Or some MONTGOMERY, fearless, lead them;
Till, God knows what may be effected,
When by such HEADS an' HEARTS directed:
Poor dunghill sons of dirt an' mire,
May to PATRICIAN rights ASPIRE; (p. 94)

Written in 1786, but first published in 1818, this powerful and politically radical poem is Burns's most explicit hymning of American Revolutionary values in the aftermath of the American War and before the upheavals of the French Revolution. Burns's explicitly American passages are revealing and important. A good deal can be—and has been—made of their politics.[9] In the present book, Rhona Brown shows that "When *Guilford* Good" was a poem often reprinted in early American newspapers, but that it was not always Burns's radical or vigorous Scots works which attracted early American readers. However, at least some of Burns's first American admirers belonged to Scottish networks with a clear taste for the Scots vernacular. Operating from the patriotically named Franklin's Head at number 41 Hanover Square in New York, the printers of the 1788 New York edition of Burns's *Poems, Chiefly in the Scottish Dialect* were Glasgow-born J. and A. McLean, the former a man with Burnsian Masonic interests who had also printed the 1785 *Rules for the St Andrew's Society of the State of New York*, and the latter a member of that Society. The edition appended to Burns's oeuvre "Scotch Poems, selected from the works of Robert Ferguson" [*sic*], the poet whom Burns had called "my elder brother in Misfortune, / By far my elder Brother in the muse" (p. 116). There then followed a glossary, almost identical to that in the 1787 Edinburgh edition, though it added on page 293 of the New York printing an explanation (unnecessary in Edinburgh) that "*Haggis*" was "*a kind of pudding boiled in the stomach of a cow or sheep.*"

If some of his words required glossing, this does not seem to have impeded the appeal of Burns's verse to the Americans he admired. There may be no mention of the poet Burns in George Washington's papers in the Library of Congress, but it is recorded that the McLeans' haggis-glossed New York edition of Burns's *Poems* was part of Washington's library.[10] Indeed, what made Burns loved by early and by later American audiences was, among other things, precisely his attitude to language. For leading thinkers among the Americans were very conscious that language itself had a politics and that as the English language came to terms with American circumstances it was bound to shift its ground. In 1813, before the publication of "Address of Beelzebub" or the Washington birthday ode, Thomas Jefferson wrote to John Waldo a letter worth quoting at length:

> I am no friend, therefore, to what is called *Purism*, but a zealous one to *Neology* which has introduced these two words without the authority of any dictionary. I consider the one as destroying the nerve and beauty of language, while the other improves both, and adds to its copiousness. I have been not a little disappointed, and made suspicious of my own judgment, on seeing the Edinburgh Reviews, the

---

9   See Roger J. Fechner, "Burns and American Liberty" in Kenneth Simpson (ed.), *Love and Liberty: Robert Burns, A Bicentenary Celebration* (East Linton, 1997), pp. 274–88; and James M. Montgomery, "How Robert Burns Captured America," *Studies in Scottish Literature*, 30 (1998): 235–48.

10   See, for example, Ferenc Morton Szasz, *Abraham Lincoln and Robert Burns: Connected Lives and Legends* (Carbondale, 2008), p. 29.

ablest critics of the age, set their faces against the introduction of new words into the English language; they are particularly apprehensive that the writers of the United States will adulterate it. Certainly so great growing a population, spread over such an extent of country, with such a variety of climates, of productions, of arts, must enlarge their language, to make it answer its purpose of expressing all ideas, the new as well as the old. The new circumstances under which we are placed, call for new words, new phrases, and for the transfer of old words to new objects. An American dialect will therefore be formed; so will a West-Indian and Asiatic, as a Scotch and an Irish are already formed. But whether will these adulterate or enrich the English language? Has the beautiful poetry of Burns, or his Scottish dialect, disfigured it? Did the Athenians consider the Doric, the Ionian, the Aeolic and other dialects, as disfiguring or as beautifying their language? Did they fastidiously disavow Herodotus, Pindar, Theocritus, Sappho, Alcaeus, or Grecian writers? On the contrary, they were so sensible that the variety of dialects, still infinitely varied by poetical license, constituted the riches of their language, and made the Grecian Homer the first of poets, as he must ever remain, until a language equally ductile and copious shall again be spoken.[11]

Strikingly, Burns is the only modern writer Jefferson mentions in what is in effect his manifesto for American language. Educated by Scots, and having been a former student of William Small's lectures on Rhetoric and Belles Lettres at Virginia's College of William and Mary, Jefferson has moved beyond the linguistic purism which that subject encouraged, but has kept its comparativist breadth. Burns himself had mentioned Theocritus in his preface to the first Kilmarnock edition of his *Poems*, and Jefferson is able to see Burns and Classical poets in an interesting relationship to each other. Seeking a new dialect, and dreaming of a global English language which, through its regional variations, will become as "ductile and copious" as Greek, the greatest literary language of antiquity, Jefferson sees Burns not in terms of a Scottish ending but as indicative of an American beginning. The distinctive grain of Burns's language was important for writers seeking to develop an American grain, and Burns's fidelity to community voice as well as his play with registers can be seen as prefacing, directly or indirectly, the poetics of Walt Whitman, then later William Carlos Williams, Robert Frost, and even the Robert Creeley for whom Burns's poems were "first delights in hearing and reading poetry as a boy" and "never forgotten."[12]

If we think of Burns's language not simply in terms of dialect but of fidelity to—and modification of—the vernacular, we can see how and why this poet continued to matter to many American readers, not least politicians and poets across the nineteenth-century United States. Sometimes the enthusiasts are surprising. One was Edgar Allan Poe, whose guardian was Scottish, who went to school for a short time in 1815 in Burns's Irvine, and who in the 1830s, his sweetheart Mary

---

[11]   *Thomas Jefferson: Writings*, Merrill D. Peterson (ed.) (New York, 1984), pp. 1295–6.
[12]   Robert Creeley, editorial introduction to *The Essential Burns* (New York, 1989), p. 15.

Devereaux recalled, "used often to quote from Burns, for whom he had a great admiration."[13] Poe is not remotely a "ploughman-poet," but he is a poet of lost loves and of haunted darknesses: these things too are part of Burns's work with its sentimental tears and depressive plunges. Poe's Mary and Burns's Mary may be closer than we think, and Poe's admiration is a reminder that Burns in the States did not simply become a bard of Yankee patriotic poetic optimism.

Burns was, though, a poet who appealed to those who were seen to epitomize nineteenth-century American ideals in public life. Growing up in 1820s Indiana among folksongs and farm-rhymes, Abraham Lincoln absorbed the Scottish poet's work: "After Abe read poetry," wrote Carl Sandburg in his 1926 *Abraham Lincoln: The Prairie Years*, "especially Bobby Burns's poems, Abe began writing rhymes himself."[14] Whether that "Bobby" is what Lincoln would have called Burns, or simply what Sandburg and other Americans in the 1920s called him, it shows how Burns was assimilated into American vernacular culture. Burns's Scots vernacular impulse had him termed "Rab," "Rob," and "Robie," rather than "Bob" or "Bobby." The American, *Greyfriars Bobby*-like familiarity of "Bobby Burns" signals a distancing from the particular grain of Scots vernacular, but also the way that Burns had become part of that American vernacular impulse strong in popular, though now sometimes scorned poets such as the Sandburg who collected the folksongs of *The American Songbag* in 1927 and whose poetry in *Good Morning, America* (1928) and elsewhere sought to continue to be in touch with vernacular life. This, surely, is the Burns whose "Auld Lang Syne" became so important to Hollywood cinema.[15]

Lincoln's admiration for Burns was not Sandburg's creation, though. Another biography has Lincoln reading Burns "assiduously" in 1830s Illinois.

> Next to Shakespeare ... Lincoln was fondest of Burns. He constantly recited Burns's immortal satire on unction and hypocrisy, "Holy Willie's Prayer." That attack of the Scottish poet on religious conceit, together with his "Address to the Unco Guid, or Rigidly Righteous," may almost be said to have stated Lincoln's views on the religion of the times ...[16]

---

[13] Mary Devereaux, qtd. in Hervey Allan, *Israfel: The Life and Times of Edgar Allan Poe* (2 vols, London, 1927), vol. 1, p. 333.

[14] Carl Sandburg, *Abraham Lincoln, The Prairie Years* (2 vols, New York, 1926), vol. 1, p. 72.

[15] Professor James Chandler of the University of Chicago is completing a study of Adam Smith and Hollywood cinema, which includes striking material on Burns; some of this was presented in a lecture by Professor Chandler at the Royal Society of Edinburgh's conference on "Robert Burns in Global Culture" on 23 January 2009.

[16] Albert J. Beveridge, *Abraham Lincoln* (2 vols, Boston, 1928), vol. 1, p. 300.

Lincoln quotes from "Address to the Deil" in a letter and elsewhere recorded his admiration for Burns.[17] Fred Kaplan, in his 2008 *Lincoln: The Biography of a Writer*, and Ferenc Morton Szasz, in his *Abraham Lincoln and Robert Burns* (2008), make the fullest, most persuasive cases for Burns's inspirational and intimate importance to the Lincoln who knew the Scottish poet's work thoroughly. The intensity of that importance is most clearly signaled not in Lincoln's public oratory but in the names given to his sons: Robert Lincoln and William Wallace Lincoln. The Robert Burns who had hymned "Scots, wha hae wi' WALLACE bled" and inveighed against "Chains and slaverie!" was one of Lincoln's greatest literary inspirations; Burns's mind-set, argue Kaplan and Szasz, shaped Lincoln's own.[18] Though it is not quoted by Kaplan or Szasz, the newspaper account of the "Burns' Festival" [*sic*] at which a toast was given by "the Hon. Abraham Lincoln" in Springfield, Illinois, on 25 January 1859 ended with another toast characteristic in its linking of "the Plowman Bard ... Bob Burns" to an icon of "American ... liberty": "I give you on this centennial anniversary of the birth of Burns—the name of GEORGE WASHINGTON—may his memory be ever as green in all our hearts as the fern and the laurel on the brow of Ben Vorlich."[19] As a poet who had grown up in but who also critiqued a centrally Presbyterian society, Burns might attract Lincoln and many other nineteenth-century Americans who were holding Burns suppers from at least the 1820s onwards. It is easier still to see how Burns's ideas of brotherhood might appeal to Lincoln and others (males in particular) if we accept that the poet's readiness to be a "Negro-driver" in Jamaica tended to be glossed over.

While Burns's high standing among nineteenth-century American cultural elites has yet to be fully researched, there is even more work to be done on his appeal to other sectors of American society. How far was his work known among African Americans, for instance? The first book Frederick Douglass bought after his release from slavery was a copy of Burns, which he passed on to his own son, and in 1846 Douglass visited both Ayr and Alloway, meeting Burns's youngest sister and writing to a friend about being "an enthusiastic admirer of Robt. Burns ... Scotland's noble bard"; one of Burns's nieces told Douglass that "her uncle was more highly esteemed in America than in Scotland," while Douglass himself, still described as a "Runaway Slave," saw Burns as someone who "broke loose

---

[17]   See Abraham Lincoln, "Memoranda on Robert Burns, [January 25 1865]," in *The Collected Works of Abraham Lincoln*, Roy P. Basler (ed.) (8 vols, New Brunswick, 1953–1955), vol. 8, p. 237; see also vol. 1, p. 106.

[18]   Fred Kaplan, *Lincoln: The Biography of a Writer* (New York, 2008), pp. 62–71; Szasz, *Abraham Lincoln and Robert Burns*, pp. 49–86.

[19]   [Anon.,] "The Burns' Festival," *Daily Illinois State Journal* (27 January 1859): 3; the speaker is "Mr. Blaisdell"; the words of Lincoln's toast are not recorded. I am grateful to Dr David A. Taylor, Head of Research and Programs at the American Folklife Center, Library of Congress, for a transcript from this newspaper, published in Springfield, Illinois.

from the moorings which society had thrown around him."[20] Clearly, Douglass could identify with Burns. Yet Virginian Booker T. Washington nowhere mentions Burns in *Up from Slavery*, and it was Christian hymns rather than the poetry of the Scottish bard that swayed the crowd of Bostonians when Booker T. Washington celebrated "the Brotherhood of Man" in the Boston Music Hall in 1879.[21] Maya Angelou in our own time has spoken of her lifelong love of Burns's work, and not least of her admiration for his song "The Slave's Lament," in which a Virginian plantation slave sings of exile and exhaustion; the Ghanaian Kofi Annan, delivering the inaugural Robert Burns Memorial Lecture at the United Nations headquarters in New York in 2004, celebrated Burns's assertion that "Man to Man the world o'er / Shall brothers be for a' that"; but we need to know more about Burns and earlier generations of African Americans.[22]

For Douglass, as for many white Americans, Burns could be an example of revolutionary energy. He also exemplified hard work. Emerson spoke of Burns at a Boston centenary dinner in 1859, arguing that

> [h]is organic sentiment was absolute independence, and resting as it should on a life of labour ... Not Latimer, not Luther struck more telling blows against false theology than did this brave singer. The Confession of Augsburg, the Declaration of Independence, the French Rights of Man, and the "Marsellaise," are not more weighty documents in the history of freedom than the songs of Burns.[23]

So Burns is mapped on to an American Protestant work-ethic, enlivened with a trill of French music. Emerson sees Burns's poetry as more rebelliously political than did Jefferson, but, while registering that it is far from his own, he also perceives that Burns's vernacularity is crucial:

> He grew up in a rural district, speaking a *patois* unintelligible to all but natives, and he has made the Lowland Scotch a Doric dialect of fame. It is the only example in history of a language made classic by the genius of a single man. But more than this. He had that secret to draw from the bottom of society the strength of its speech, and to astonish the ears of the polite with these artless words, better than art, and filtered of all offence through his beauty. It seemed odious to Luther that the devil should have all the best tunes; he would bring them into

---

[20]   Frederick Douglass, letter to "a friend, dated April 23, 1846" in "A Fugitive Slave Visiting the Birth-place of Robert Burns," *New York Weekly Tribune*, 18 July 1846; this piece is available at http://library.sc.edu/spcoll/ douglass/fugitive.pdf.

[21]   Booker T. Washington, *Up from Slavery* (Oxford, 1965), p. 186.

[22]   Maya Angelou, "Angelou on Burns," 1996 BBC TV documentary directed by Elly M. Taylor; Kofi Annan's Inaugural Robert Burns Memorial Lecture of 13 January 2004 can be found on the United Nations website at http://www.unis.unvienna.org/unis/pressrels/2004/sgsm9112.html, accessed 15 June 2009.

[23]   Ralph Waldo Emerson, "Speech at Burns Centenary Dinner in Boston, January 1859," in *Robert Burns: The Critical Heritage*, Donald A. Low (ed.) (London and Boston, 1974), pp. 434–6 (pp. 434–5).

the churches; and Burns knew how to take from friars and gypsies, blacksmiths and drovers, the speech of the market and street, and clothe it with melody ...[24]

This Martin Luther Burns is in some ways a misreading and an enervated purification of Burns—"filtered of all offence through his beauty"—yet it does relate to what Walt Whitman heard in the Burns whom he regarded as "to-day, in some respects the most interesting personality among singers." For Whitman

> there are many things in Burns's poems and character that specially endear him to America. He was essentially a Republican—would have been at home in the Western United States, and probably become eminent there ... Without the race of which he is a distinct specimen, (and perhaps his poems) America and her powerful Democracy could not exist today ...[25]

Whitman misreads Burns, but, as I have argued in *Devolving English Literature*, his misreading is an act of translation: when he calls Burns "an average sample of the good-natured, warm-blooded, proud-spirited, amative, alimentive, convivial, young and early middle-aged man of the decent-born middle classes everywhere and any how," the term "middle-class" grates on a British ear, but Whitman intends, surely, only to suggest that Burns is a regular guy.[26] Such people Whitman sees as fundamental to his own country, so that while he does call Burns a "Scottish bard," he wants to translate him: "I take my observation of the Scottish bard by considering him as an individual amid the crowded clusters, galaxies, of the old world—and fairly inquiring and suggesting what out of these myriads he too may be to the Western Republic."[27] For Whitman, who had read Burns's letters as well as his poetry, what is most immediately striking about Burns is that "no poet on record so fully bequeaths his own personal magnetism." Addressing Burns as "Dear Rob!" and stating that "Probably no man that ever lived—a friend has made the statement—was so fondly loved, both by men and women, as Robert Burns," Whitman implies perhaps a homoerotic attraction. Excited by Burns's "I, Rob, am here," and pronouncing the Scottish poet an "'odd-kind chiel'" who "remains to my heart and brain as almost the tenderest, manliest, and (even if contradictory) dearest flesh-and-blood figure in all the streams and clusters of by-gone poets," Whitman likes to present not just Burns but also himself as "Poet and Person":[28]

---

[24] Ibid., pp. 435–6.

[25] Walt Whitman, "Robert Burns as Poet and Person" from *November Boughs*, in *Walt Whitman: Complete Poetry and Collected Prose*, Justin Kaplan (ed.) (New York, 1982), pp. 1152–61 (pp. 1152–3).

[26] See Robert Crawford, *Devolving English Literature*, 2nd edn (Edinburgh, 2000), pp. 208–14.

[27] Whitman, *Complete Poetry and Collected Prose*, Kaplan (ed.), p. 1154 (*November Boughs*).

[28] Ibid., pp. 1154, 1155, 1154, 1161, 1152.

"Walt Whitman, an American, one of the roughs."[29] Whitman's perception that "one best part of Burns is the unquestionable proof he presents of the perennial existence among the laboring classes, especially farmers, of the finest latent poetic elements in their blood" is what makes it essential for this American poet to translate and re-embody Burns in a North American environment. If Whitman is naive or self-serving in his discerning of "unfinish, careless nudity, slovenly hiatus" in Burns's work, he appreciates Burns's crucial love of vernacular language—"His brightest hit is the use of the Scotch patois"—and he relishes "the home-brew'd flavor of the Scotch vernacular" so that in Burns, surely, he detects his own lineaments: aspects of Scotland's bard which can be translated, re-formed, re-sounded by America's bard. Whitman sings Burns's praises in order to boost his own vernacular bardship.[30] Whitman's repeated revisions of his published comments on Burns, each time moderating his criticisms, signal attempts to come to terms with a persistent anxiety of influence.[31]

Whitman's Burns, a potential citizen of the Western United States and "loved, both by men and women," suggests a poet whose appeal might range beyond that of male heterosexual Anglo-Saxon Protestant New England Americans. It may be among these, though, that Burns's late nineteenth-century admirers were concentrated. Longfellow's poem "Robert Burns" uses the Standard Habbie or "Burns stanza" and locates a political strain in Burns's work:

> But still the music of his song
> Rises o'er all, elate and strong;
>   Its master chords
> Are Manhood, Freedom, Brotherhood;
> Its discords but an interlude
>   Between the words.[32]

But where for Whitman Burns is a strong, charismatic physical human presence, for Longfellow he has lost his own male body and come to merge with the Scottish natural environment where "His voice is in each rushing brook, / Each rustling bough," while in America he is welcomed as a "Dear guest and ghost," revered as insubstantial, only transcendentally bardic: "A form of mingled mist and light / From that far coast."[33] This is a Burns who appeals strongly to the New England poet, but whose apparently misty ephemerality could potentially fade and be replaced by assertions of more familiar, less "far" and remote, voices of America itself. Longfellow, even as he pays tribute to Burns, surely hopes to be one of those voices.

---

[29] Ibid., p. 50 (*Leaves of Grass*).

[30] Ibid., pp. 1155, 1159 (*November Boughs*).

[31] See Gary Scharnhorst, "Whitman on Robert Burns: An Early Essay Recovered," *Walt Whitman Quarterly Review*, 13 (Spring 1996): 217–20.

[32] Henry Wadsworth Longfellow, "Robert Burns," *The Poetical Works of Henry Wadsworth Longfellow*, Walter Jerrold (ed.) (London, n.d.), p. 526.

[33] Ibid., pp. 526–7.

Burns may appeal both because he speaks of Presbyterian democratic virtues and because he unleashes the Presbyterian unconscious. Emily Dickinson makes references to Burns songs in her letters, but her liking for Burns remained private and it is generally easier to trace the more public enthusiasm of male poets. A note of New England purification is present in Longfellow's version of Burns, and in John Greenleaf Whittier's. Part of Whittier's poetic apprenticeship involved trying on Standard Habbie for size, not just the stanza form but also the Scots dialect so associated with it:

> Ye thievin', cheatin' auld Cheap Jack,
> Peddlin' your poison brose, I crack
> Your banes against my ingle-back
>   Wi' meikle pleasure.
> Deil mend ye i' his workshop black
>   E'en at his leisure![34]

The Scots is not bad, but it is hard for Whittier to translate Burns into an advocate of total abstinence, even if it is a testament to Burns's American importance that Whittier feels the need to recruit him. Thirty years after this early poem was written, as well as delivering his own oration at the Boston Burns centenary dinner of 1859, Emerson read to the assembled company Whittier's later poem "The Memory of Burns," which, like Emerson's own speech, invokes Martin Luther alongside the Scots bard, stressing Burns's assimilable Protestantism.

The autodidact Whittier, son of a poor Massachusetts farmer, loved Burns's verse from boyhood. Whittier's poem "Burns" recalls his childhood reading of the Scottish bard out in the meadow under a maple's shadow and sees Burns's work as attuned to the setting and creatures of farm life. This Burns is very much a poet of "Nature" with a capital "N":

> New light on home-seen Nature beamed,
>   New glory over Woman;
> And daily life and duty seemed
>   No longer poor and common.[35]

Whittier's Burns sounds terribly virtuous, but his perceived ability to connect with a world of American "daily life and duty"—and not least New England farm life— is what matters. For all his sophistication, Whittier was an instinctive small-town person or villager, settling near his own birthplace in Massachusetts and, in books such as his 1831 *Legends of New England*, identifying with that local territory as Burns had done with his.

In their different ways, then, the four men who were the four most celebrated poets of later nineteenth-century America—Poe, Longfellow, Whittier, and Whitman—all drew strength from Burns's work. If Poe's "great admiration" for

---

[34]   John Greenleaf Whittier, "The Drunkard to his Bottle," *The Poetical Works of John Greenleaf Whittier* (London, 1904), p. 530.

[35]   Whittier, *Poetical Works*, p. 215.

Burns did not find its way into his published writings, Longfellow's public verse tribute to Burns is an imaginative pilgrimage. In writing about Burns, Whitman devoted more attention to the Scottish bard than to any other poet (except himself). Whittier wrote more verse tributes to Burns than to any other poet. In nineteenth-century America, poet after ambitious poet sought to pay tribute to Burns and so situate him as a potential poetic ancestor. In political life, giants such as Jefferson and Lincoln grew up with Burns's work and can be seen to have shared some of his ideals. Burns was vital to the dominant culture of nineteenth-century America, and further work is likely to establish his presence in American subcultures too. This American sympathy with Burns was also recognized in nineteenth-century Scotland. On the same night in 1859 that Emerson's and Whitman's praises of the bard were applauded in Boston, at the Burns Birthday Centenary celebrations in Paisley in the West of Scotland a toast was proposed to "American Poetry and Longfellow" by a speaker who, while praising Longfellow and others, maintained that "America has yet to produce *her* national poet, *par excellence*"—there was no mention of Walt Whitman.[36]

In the Romantic period and after, Americans certainly visited Alloway and other Burns sites, liking or disliking the monuments. William Cullen Bryant knew Burns's work well, though when visiting Ayr and Alloway in 1845, he thought "[t]he wild rose and the woodbine ... in full bloom in the hedges ... were a better memorial of Burns than any thing which the chisel could execute."[37] Burns in nineteenth- and early twentieth-century America, as in Scotland, was literally a chiselled, monumental presence. Whitman had paid considerable attention to the erection of what he describes as the "Sicilian marble" Dumfries Burns statue ("unveiled in April 1881 by Lord Roseberry" [*sic*]), as if to imply that monuments to the poet in America might be no bad thing.[38] New York had already got its Burns statue in Central Park in 1880. Albany got one in 1888, Chicago in 1906, while Atlanta came to boast a full-scale replica of Burns Cottage at Alloway. There are more public monuments to Robert Burns in America than there are monuments to any American poet, and Burns mattered to both North and South, to the down-at-heel but also to the well-heeled.

In 1869, to celebrate "Robert Burns's Natal Day" 150 men and 100 women dined in New York's Metropolitan Hotel on "Buffalo Tongue" and "Calf's Head" with "tomato sauce." "Poor Burns!" read a note on the menu, "how he would have enjoyed *such* a dinner."[39] That last phrase picks up on Burns's own praise of "sic a dinner" as haggis (p. 113). In replacing Burnsian haggis with "Buffalo tongue," the New York diners were again confidently translating their bard into an American idiom. After the ladies had left the room, the gentlemen started drinking their many toasts. When William Cullen Bryant, introduced as "the greatest of American poets," toasted "Minstrelsy," "The audience then rose to their feet" with

---

[36]   Robert Brown, *Paisley Burns Clubs, 1805–1893* (Paisley, 1893), pp. 192, 210.

[37]   William Cullen Bryant, *Letters of a Traveller* (London, 1850), p. 197.

[38]   Whitman, *Complete Poetry and Collected Prose*, Kaplan (ed.), p. 1159.

[39]   [Anon.,] *A History of the Celebration of Robert Burns's 110th Natal Day, at the Metropolitan Hotel, New York* (Jersey City, 1869), n.p. Hereafter referred to as *A History*.

"loud cheers, clapping of hands and waving of handkerchiefs, and the wildest demonstrations of love and joy." Yet these increasingly excited drinkers knew their bard. Bryant presented Burns as one who "in an age of formalism in poetry, of cold and feeble imitation and parrot-cry repetition, first led the way back to truth and nature ... to clothe strong emotions in unborrowed words, which carried them directly to the heart." In effect, Bryant presents Burns as one of the great initiators of the Romantic movement, a rightful position from which Burns would be dethroned by such influential twentieth-century critics as M.H. Abrams. Such critics replaced Burns's primacy with that of Burns's admirer, Wordsworth. This is an odd view, very different from that of Keats, Byron, or Jane Austen. It represents a tunnel vision developed by modern academics and is tellingly out of step with Burns's international popularity.

It might seem that the advent of modernism also swept Burns aside. Yet the T.S. Eliot who wrote an unpublished Scots parody of Burns and the Ezra Pound who, as a provincial outsider in London, presented himself as a young "birkie ca'ed a lord" had clearly absorbed a good knowledge of one of America's favorite poets.[40] If Pound and Eliot knew Burns, he seems to have been of far less imaginative use to them than he had been to their nineteenth-century American predecessors, but Burns's stance and example continued to matter in other areas of American poetry that modernism overshadowed. These included not only the village verse of the *Spoon River Anthology* and the sub-Whitmanian folksy verse and song-collecting of poets like Sandburg, but also the much more substantial and culturally central achievement of America's greatest twentieth-century vernacular poet, Robert Frost.

The point is not that Frost in any sense directly imitates Burns's style, but he does very much adopt Burns's stance and, like so many of his ambitious American poetic predecessors, wishes to situate himself as a successor to Burns. Burns was probably the first major poet Frost's Scottish mother read to him in his Californian childhood, and long before Frost came to be accepted by a wide international public as New England's, or even America's, bard, he was writing in 1894 to a New York magazine editor, making the most of his Burnsian position as a rural farmer-poet. "A daimen icker in a thrave's a sma' request," quotes Frost in one of these letters, drawing on the most thornily Scots line of Burns's "To a Mouse," that poem of a young ploughman-poet anxious about future prospects.[41] This is just the position the young Frost was in, and he maps himself on to Burns. Frost's deliberate positioning of himself as rural villager and poet-farmer while negotiating with the cultural center (in this case New York, and, later, the English Literature world of universities) followed to an extent the example of Whittier, whose name and place of residence are mentioned in passing in Frost's poetry. Not for nothing had Whittier been termed "the American Burns." When Frost visited Britain in 1913 to 1914, he formed his most important, if short, connection with a living poet—Edward Thomas. But Frost's attitudes were also shaped by poets

---

[40] *Collected Early Poems of Ezra Pound*, Michael L. King (ed.) (London, 1977), pp. 214–5.

[41] *Selected Letters of Robert Frost*, Lawrence Thompson (ed.) (London, 1965), p. 39.

with whose work he had long been familiar. As I have argued in *Identifying Poets*, critics have paid insufficient attention to the 1913 letter to Sidney Cox in which Frost writes,

> The common people in the south of England I don't like to have around me. They don't know how to meet you man to man. The people in the north are more like Americans. I wonder whether they made Burns' poems or Burns' poems made them.[42]

Here Frost uses the common, idiomatic phrase "man to man," but it is as if that phrase—familiar from one of Burns's most famous poems in which "Man to Man the warld o'er, / Shall brothers be for a' that"—leads him naturally to the thought of Burns as he speculates on how British northerners have a more American attitude than have British southerners. When Frost goes on immediately to "wonder whether they made Burns's poems or Burns's poems made them," what he displays is a strong interest in the way poetry and a distinctive local identity might nurture and even create one another. Given Frost's upbringing, it is not surprising that Burns should be in his mind in this context. This 1913 letter suggests very much the trajectory Frost's own poetry will take. Its next sentences—"And there are stone walls (dry stone dykes) in the north: I liked those. My mother was from Edinburgh ..."—point strikingly toward the future direction of Frost's work, for "Mending Wall" would be the opening poem of *North of Boston*, published the following year. A strong yet ironically "man to man" poem, it is also Burnsian in that it is vernacular verse by a would-be farmer-poet drawing on the actual business of farm-work. Wordsworth was never a farmer-poet; Burns very much was. It was as self-styled farmer-poet that Frost became a staunchly regional voice and then, most obviously in his reading at John F. Kennedy's presidential inauguration, very much a national bard.

Frost's sentence-sounds do not echo Burns's. Yet, like Whitman and Burns, Frost champions vernacular language: no "Shantih shantih shantih" for him. Burns's stance and his love of the language of working people, as well as the language of English poetry, were continuing sources of nourishment. Oliver Wendell Holmes had written in the nineteenth century that

> Burns ought to have passed ten years of his life in America, for those words of his:
>   'A man's a man for a' that'
> show that true American feeling belonged to him as much as if he had been born in sight of the hill before me as I write—Bunker Hill.[43]

---

[42]   William R. Evans (ed.), *Robert Frost and Sidney Cox, Forty Years of Friendship* (Hanover, NH, 1981), p. 31; see Robert Crawford, "Robert Frosts," in *Identifying Poets: Self and Territory in Twentieth-Century Poetry* (Edinburgh, 1993), pp. 17–41.

[43]   Oliver Wendell Holmes, qtd. in Low's introduction to *Robert Burns: The Critical Heritage*, pp. 1–57 (p. 45).

For the Burns who had once joked that "I'd better gaen an' sair't the king, / At Bunker's hill," this is both ironic and just.[44] Frost's perception of the Scots as somehow both more like Americans and as bound up with Burns's poetry is a later version of Holmes's thought, as is Whitman's conviction that Burns would have thrived in the Western United States. In 1897 in Wisconsin, an American Scot could even argue that "Burns is more in sympathy with American than with Scottish life."[45] No one would argue that today; it was misguided then. Yet it shows how markedly Burns could be read as America's bard.

If Burns has something to say to twenty-first century America, this is also related to his stance as farmer-poet. For all that as the poet of "Auld Lang Syne" he remains a staple of American popular culture from *It's a Wonderful Life* to *Sex and the City*, Burns projects also a voice of caution and warning. One of the most vital things he has to say to present-day America is something not all Americans want to hear. It is bound up with that almost Hesiodic facet of Burns which has always attracted readers and which inflects some of his greatest poetry. John Muir in the late nineteenth century and John Steinbeck writing of the Depression alike responded to one of Burns's best-known poems in their American writings. One of Burns's favorite poems was Alexander Pope's "Essay on Man," which he quotes frequently in his letters. Pope, with all his urbanity, writes, as he puts it, of "The whole Universe [as] one system of Society" and of how man came "from Nature rising slow to Art!" with Nature instructing,

> Go, from the Creatures thy instructions take:
> Learn from the birds what food the thickets yield;
> Learn from the beasts the physic of the field;
> Thy arts of building from the bee receive;
> Learn of the mole to plow, the worm to weave;
> Learn of the little Nautilus to sail,
> Spread the thin oar, and catch the driving gale.
> Here too all forms of social union find,
> And hence let Reason, late, instruct Mankind.[46]

In "To a Mouse," Burns takes what sounds like the confident Enlightenment Progressivism of these poised couplets and gravitates to the less stable verse movement of the Standard Habbie stanza. He makes his poem not a lecture but a prayerful work poem, situated in a time, season, and farming activity. Its full title is "To a Mouse, On turning her up in her Nest, with the Plough, November, 1785." This is a poem whose famous first line sounds in its human language the

---

[44]   *The Poems and Songs of Robert Burns*, James Kinsley (ed.) (3 vols, Oxford, 1968), vol. 1, p. 62.

[45]   John G. Dow, "Burns in America," in vol. 6 of J.D. Ross (comp.), *Burnsiana* (1897), in Low (ed.), *Robert Burns: The Critical Heritage*, pp. 439–40 (p. 440).

[46]   Alexander Pope, "Essay on Man," in *The Poems of Alexander Pope*, John Butt (ed.) (London, 1965), pp. 525, 531 (Third Epistle, lines 172–80).

"ee" "ee" "ee" sounds of the startled creature it addresses and so subliminally establishes a bond between man and nature from the start: "Wee, sleeket, cowran, tim'rous *beastie*." "To a Mouse" can be read as one of Burns's cuddliest poems, but it is not. Like "Tam o' Shanter," it is humorous, while drawing on that darker, even Poe-ishly depressive side of Burns's temperament. Composed not long after Burns was complaining how since the American War his country was "decaying very fast," written while his family was facing ruin connected with a banking crash, and just after the death of one of the poet's teenage brothers, it is a poem of fear and uncertainty.[47] Its second stanza, especially in the first two lines, probably resonates with us to produce a greater anxiety than at any time since it was written. Here Burns becomes the first major poet to sound a note of ecological anxiety with which we identify all too readily. Reading his lines today, not least in America, we commune with the earlier generations who have enjoyed them; yet the same lines of necessity mean something disturbingly urgent to us here and now:

> I'm truly sorry Man's dominion
> Has broken Nature's social union,
> An' justifies that ill opinion,
>   Which makes thee startle,
> At me, thy poor, earth-born companion,
>   An' *fellow-mortal*! (p. 47)

If Burns in any sense today might be America's bard, I wish it were as one of the world's great love poets; as a poet of community; as a poet of radically democratic politics; but most of all I wish it were specifically in this stanza and this poem where, in common with poets in America and in Scotland the eighteenth-century farmer-poet tells us in Scots and in vernacular English not about our national glories or even about our political ideals, but about something we want to hear less, yet which, with all his poetic skill as well as with conviction, he articulates unforgettably and still resoundingly:

> I'm truly sorry Man's dominion
> Has broken Nature's social union ...

In a Scots-English, fellow critturly, democratic accent, as elsewhere in his work, Burns for his day and for ours also is articulating, as bards must sometimes do, a vital, inconvenient truth.

---

[47]   *The Letters of Robert Burns*, J. De Lancey Ferguson (ed.), 2nd edn, G. Ross Roy (ed.) (2 vols, Oxford, 1985), vol. 1, p. 19.

Chapter 7
The Presence of Robert Burns in Victorian and Edwardian Canada

Carole Gerson and Susan Wilson

> I brought four books wi' me;
> I read them by turns:
> The Bible, Scott's Worthies,
> John Bunyan, and Burns.[1]

In *Rapt in Plaid: Canadian Literature and the Scottish Tradition*, Elizabeth Waterston claims that "[i]n Canada, in the early nineteenth century, there was hardly a household that did not treasure a copy of Burns's poems."[2] W.M. MacKeracher's "To a Copy of Burns' Poems (Found in the house of an Ontario farmer)" (1900), speaks to the esteem in which many held the Scottish poet's works:

> …
> Large book, with heavy covers worn and old
>   Bearing clear proof of usage and of years,
> Thine edges yellow with their faded gold,
>   Thy leaves with fingers stained—perchance with tears!
> ….
> With reverent hands I lay aside the tome,
>   And to my longing heart content returns,
> And in the stranger's house I am at home,
>   For thou dost make us brothers, Robert Burns.[3]

Burns's staying power proved consistent through the nineteenth century and well into the twentieth, as signaled by the ongoing popularity of Burns-related social events and celebrations and long-standing affection for his poems. Noting that statues of Burns are to be found in Halifax, Fredericton, Montreal, Toronto,

---

[1]   Alexander McLachlan, "The Old Settler, or, The Trials and Troubles of Paisley John," *Poems* (Toronto, 1856), p. 88.

[2]   Elizabeth Waterston, *Rapt in Plaid: Canadian Literature and the Scottish Tradition* (Toronto, 2001), p. 19.

[3]   W.M. MacKeracher, "To a Copy of Burns' Poems," in *Selections from Scottish-Canadian Poets, Being a Collection of the Best Poetry Written by Scotsmen and their Descendants in the Dominion of Canada*, Daniel Clark, Rev. William Clark, and George Kennedy (eds) (Toronto, 1900), pp. 242, 245.

Winnipeg, Vancouver, and Victoria, literary historian John Robert Colombo surmises that "There are more statues of Robert Burns in Canada than of any other literary figure" and "probably more Burns memorials in Canada than in Scotland."[4] Characteristic is the view of Lucy Maud Montgomery, author of the best-selling novel *Anne of Green Gables* (1908), that Burns transcended national boundaries and "gave voice to the song that sings itself in *all* human hearts, whether in Scottish braes or Canadian prairies."[5] Alongside this notion of the universal Burns, Montgomery believed she had inherited her own literary ability from her father's distant cousin, poet Hector Macneill, reputedly an acquaintance of Burns. As a child, she had memorized "The Cottar's Saturday Night" for recitation, and her 1911 honeymoon journey to Scotland included visits to a number of Burns sites.[6] It is therefore not surprising that Burns figures among the many quotations and literary allusions that pepper Montgomery's fiction, from "Auld Lang Syne," to "Highland Mary," "To a Louse," and "A Man's a Man for a' That."[7]

Evidence that Montgomery's taste was shared by many Canadians of her era appears in a write-in literary poll conducted by one of Toronto's major newspapers in 1908. Here, Burns held the middle rank among readers' favorite poets—behind Tennyson, Shakespeare, Browning, and Longfellow, but ahead of Scott, Wordsworth, Byron, Shelley, and Milton. A question about favorite poems garnered similar results: "The title oftenest given was Gray's 'Elegy,' and next to it came 'In Memoriam.' Scott's 'Lady of the Lake' followed in order of preference, then 'Crossing the Bar' and Burns's hymn to humble domestic piety, 'The Cottar's Saturday Night'."[8] However, Burns pulled ahead in response to "The book I most often turn to"; in this category, his poems tied with Browning's, behind Shakespeare and Tennyson. Additional references to "The Cottar's Saturday Night" abound in Canadian documents, from an 1885 Burns anniversary sermon[9] to the autobiography of Charles W. Gordon, better known as "Ralph Connor," the spectacularly popular novelist of the first decades of the twentieth century. Gordon was a Presbyterian minister who idealized the Highland immigrant community

---

[4]   John Robert Colombo, *Canadian Literary Landmarks* (Willowdale, ON, 1984), p. 281.

[5]   L.M. Montgomery to G.B. MacMillan, 23 Aug. 1905, in Francis W. Bolger and Elizabeth R. Epperly (eds), *My Dear Mr. M: Letters to G.B. MacMillan from L.M. Montgomery* (Toronto, 1992), p. 12.

[6]   Mary Henley Rubio, *Lucy Maud Montgomery: The Gift of Wings* (Toronto, 2008), pp. 22, 37, 154.

[7]   Rea Wilmshurst, "L.M. Montgomery's Use of Quotations and Allusions in the 'Anne' Books," *Canadian Childrens' Literature*, 56 (1989): 15–45; Rea Wilmshurst, "Quotations and Allusions in L.M. Montgomery's Other Novels," ts. Toronto, November 1990.

[8]   "Canadian Standards of Literary Tastes," *Globe* (Toronto), 5 Sept. 1908, Saturday Magazine section, p. 8.

[9]   D.D. (Duncan Darroch) McLeod, "Sermon Preached on the Occasion of Burns's Anniversary, January 23, 1885" (Barrie, ON: 1885?) (Canadian Institute for Historical Microreproductions [hereafter CIHM] 24578).

of Glengarry County, in eastern Ontario, through what John Richthammer has described as "[i]mperial adventure fiction,"[10] in order to promulgate the values of muscular Christianity.[11] Such examples illustrate Canadians' prevailing construction of Burns as a recorder of patriotic inspiration, egalitarian sentiment, and emotional universals.

The preferences of Montgomery and Gordon, Canada's most internationally successful authors at the beginning of the twentieth century, demonstrate the Scottish influence on mainstream English-Canadian culture and suggest that much of Burns's popularity may be attributed to nostalgia among the large proportion of Canadians from families that had immigrated from Scotland.[12] In the Canadian imaginary, Scottishness was often aligned with Canadianness due to the upward mobility of many Scots in the emerging Canadian power structure over the course of the nineteenth century. In the words of literary critic Daniel Coleman, "the Scots were the primary inventors of English Canada through their leading roles in business ... in politics ... in religion ... and in [higher] education."[13] In less than humble moments, some advocates claim that the Scots created Canada, beginning with the Orcadians and Lewismen[14] whose stoic skills underpinned the success of the fur trade.[15] It is therefore not surprising that there is little evidence of interest in Burns on the part of French-speaking Canadians.[16]

Canadians of Scottish descent fostered links through Caledonian Societies, St Andrews Societies, North British Societies, Highland Societies, Saltire Societies, and Burns Clubs.[17] These groups sponsored lectures, the installation of statues,

---

[10]   John Richthammer, "Ralph Connor/The Rev. Dr Charles W. Gordon: The Role of Archives in the Memorialization of a Canadian Literary and Theological Giant," *Miscellanea Manitobiana*, No. 4 (Winnipeg, 2004), online edn, 1 Jan. 2005, http://cybrary. uwinnipeg.ca/people/dobson/manitobiana/issues/004.cfm, accessed 29 April 2009.

[11]   Charles W. Gordon, *Postscript to Adventure: The Autobiography of Ralph Connor* (Toronto, 1975), p. 177.

[12]   "In 1961, the last census year in which the category was recorded, over 1,800,000 Canadians declared themselves of Scottish origin, thus constituting the Scots as the third largest ethnic group in Canada, exceeded in number only by the English and French" (J.M. Bumstead, *The Scots in Canada* [Ottawa, 1982], p. 3).

[13]   Daniel Coleman, *White Civility: The Literary Project of English Canada* (Toronto, 2006), pp. 5–6.

[14]   *Leodhasaich* in Gàidhlig.

[15]   Matthew Shaw, *Great Scots! How the Scots Created Canada* (Winnipeg, 2003), p. 9; also see Ken McGoogan, *How the Scots Invented Canada* (Toronto, 2010).

[16]   Very few translations of Burns into French are to be found in Canadian libraries.

[17]   There is no complete inventory. The microfiche collection created by the Canadian Institute for Historical Microreproduction includes printed constitutions and/or by-laws for the Burns Club of Hamilton (1858), the Burns Club of Montreal (1959), the Halifax Caledonian Club (1861), and the Burns Literary Society of Toronto (1901). *The Burns Chronicle and Club Directory* for 1935 (2nd series, vol. 10) lists seven Canadian Burns clubs whose membership ranges from 40 (Brantford, ON) to 489 (Victoria, BC).

and convivial evenings in celebration of Scotland's national poet that constituted focal points of social cohesion, providing both a sense of communal identity and a means of social networking. Such organizations also played "a vital role in promoting knowledge of Scottish history and literature ... [as evident] in the stated aims of the majority of the Scottish organizations in [nineteenth-century] Canada."[18] Historian Michael Vance points out that "[a]spects of Scottishness were employed to empower immigrant communities, to reinforce class power, or to exert cultural influence ..."[19] However, in the aftermath of the Confederation of 1867, as a sense of Canadian identity emerged, such cultural dominance was also occasionally challenged. Vance cites Alexander Fraser's address to the Caledonian Society of Montreal in 1903 as evidence that Scottish-Canadians' "exercise of power and influence" was perceived as threatened.[20] Under the title of *The Mission of the Scot in Canada*, Fraser stated, "We are assailed because we have organized Scottish societies in Canada ... The position which has been taken is that our societies tend to keep alive racial divisions, that they hark back to the Old Land, and consequently are obstacles in the way of and a menace to Canadian national sentiment and national unity."[21] Fraser's response to this critique was to argue that Canadian nationality was as yet unformed, and that "the mission of the Scot in Canada" was to "infuse his character into the life of the people of Canada."[22] To this end, Fraser advocated "a federation of Canada's Scottish societies to promote Scottish history, literature, and music, Scottish games and customs, and Scottish fraternal and benevolent organizations; and to preserve the records of Scottish pioneer settlers."[23]

Typically, in the early days of their inception, these Scottish societies were

> essentially ... elite all-male drinking club[s] that met ... on St Andrew's Day [or on Robbie Burns's birthday] for a bacchanalian dinner. ... These occasions were ... marked by heavy drinking and speeches from invited and local worthies, but by the end of the [nineteenth] century the events had evolved into society balls ... used to raise funds for benevolent purposes.[24]

Such events drew large crowds. In Halifax, Nova Scotia, some 1600 participants joined the celebration of Burns's centenary on 25 January 1859, organized by the North British and Highland Societies. They assembled in the Temperance Hall for a procession and speeches, followed by a banquet for some 300 at the Mason

---

[18]   Michael Vance, "A Brief History of Organized Scottishness in Canada," in Celeste Ray (ed.), *Transatlantic Scots* (Tuscaloosa, 2005), pp. 96–119 (p. 103).

[19]   Ibid., p. 97.

[20]   Ibid.

[21]   Alexander Fraser, *The Mission of the Scot in Canada* (Toronto, 1903), p. 6.

[22]   Ibid., p. 11.

[23]   Ibid., pp. 16–17.

[24]   Vance, "A Brief History," pp. 100–101.

Hall with wine and many toasts.[25] While Burns birthday celebrations regularly occurred throughout the English-speaking world, their timing in late January was particularly welcome to snow-bound Canadians. In the understated words of a resident of Winnipeg (the prairie city sometimes dubbed "Winterpeg" because of its extreme climate), "It is found very convenient in most communities, as winter is getting through, to have a national festival."[26]

Before turning to Burns's literary influence on the young Dominion of Canada, it is worth noting certain characteristics of the "renegotiation[,] ... transmission and performance"[27] of the transnational tradition of Burns clubs and suppers. While Burns festivities clearly forged a connection between Scotland and Canada, the old world and the new, they also reflected, in the words of Michael Vance, "the patriarchal nature of Scottishness itself, as seen in the all-male character of the early drinking clubs and in the celebrations of male figures like Robert Burns."[28] Along with the politics of gender, the politics of location are also in evidence, in terms of both geography and social class, as most of the men who enjoyed full membership in these societies "were from the Lowlands rather than the Highlands of Scotland."[29] This is significant in terms of the construction of a Scottish-Canadian identity, for the Burns clubs provided a sense of community and cultural ties largely for members of the middle class,[30] while poorer immigrants of Highland origin bonded through their shared Gaelic cultural and linguistic traditions. A special locus for Gaelic culture in Canada, as Jonathan Dembling observes, was "Cape Breton Island, at the eastern end of Nova Scotia ... [which] occupies a unique place in the Scottish diaspora."[31] He notes that "[w]hen Canadian Confederation was completed in 1867, Gaelic was the third most widely spoken [European] language in the new country,"[32] and in post-Confederation Canada, Cape Breton has served as the largest *Gàidhealtachd*, or Gaelic-speaking area, outside of Scotland. In her thesis on "Scots in Groups: the Origin and History of Scottish Societies With Particular Reference to Those Established in Nova Scotia," Patricia Lotz suggests that "[t]he absence of Burns Societies [in Nova Scotia] is accounted for by the dominance of Highland rather than Lowland immigration

---

[25]   *Celebration of Burns' Centenary* (Halifax, 1859) (CIHM 14108).

[26]   George Bryce, *The Scotsman in Canada* (2 vols, Toronto, 1911), vol. 2, p. 416.

[27]   Celeste Ray, editorial introduction to *Transatlantic Scots*, pp. 1–20 (p. 12).

[28]   Vance, "A Brief History," p. 107.

[29]   Ibid., p. 100.

[30]   In private conversation during the Transatlantic Burns Conference (8 April 2009), Vance suggested that social class was more influential than language in determining the appeal of Burns clubs to Scottish immigrants.

[31]   Jonathan Dembling, "You Play It as You Would Sing It: Cape Breton, Scottishness, and the Means of Cultural Production," in Ray (ed.), *Transatlantic Scots*, pp. 180–197 (p. 180).

[32]   Ibid., p. 181.

to the province."[33] Thus, whereas Gaelic provided the cultural ties which bound Scots together in the "Highland enclave communities that were established in Nova Scotia, Cape Breton, Prince Edward Island, the Eastern Townships of Quebec, and in Ontario,"[34] the familiar vernacular of Burns's writing created a cultural link for middle-class Scots in larger urban communities. Dembling further suggests that "Lowlanders may actually serve as a buffer between Gaelicness and Englishness, a safe zone where linguistic and cultural assimilation can take place without sacrificing a Scottish identity."[35]

Several examples demonstrate how Burns clubs could provide a sense of home and community for Gaelic-speaking immigrants who found themselves bereft of their linguistic communities when they joined Canada's middle class. The same Alexander Fraser who advocated a federation of Scottish societies in the early twentieth century founded the Gaelic Society of Canada in 1897, served as president of the Toronto Burns Society, was a life member of the Toronto Caledonian Society, and edited the *Scottish Canadian* for some twenty years.[36] Evan MacColl, a native Gaelic-speaker from Lochfyne-side who settled in Kingston and later moved to Toronto, contributed the only Gaelic poem to be published in the Toronto Caledonian Society's anthology, *Selections from Scottish-Canadian Poets* (1900).[37] Patrick Sinnott, another native Gaelic-speaker who immigrated from Inverness to Montreal in 1912, worked his way across the country to Victoria, British Columbia, where he eventually co-founded the Saltire Society which held an annual Burns supper.[38] The society still meets on a monthly basis, and the longevity of Burns's cultural influence remained evident in January 2009, when it paid tribute to Burns's 250th birthday with a celebratory laying of heather at the Burns statue in Beacon Hill Park, Victoria.

While commemorations of Scotland's national bard tended to avoid controversy, some Canadians debated his reputation. One surviving condemnation appeared in a lecture delivered by Rev. W. McKenzie in 1859 at the Mechanics' Institute in the town of Ramsay, Quebec. "Great genius has great responsibilities," he intoned, and Burns suffered the consequences of his transgressions: "what a sight of pity and of fear we have in that fitful life, and darksome death of his."[39] Whether or not such direct attacks were common, the defensive position assumed by many

---

[33] Patricia A. Lotz, "Scots in Groups: The Origin and History of Scottish Societies with Particular Reference to Those Established in Nova Scotia" (unpublished MA thesis, St Francis Xavier University, 1975), p. 178.

[34] Vance, "A Brief History," pp. 97–8.

[35] Dembling, "You Play It as You Would Sing It," p. 194.

[36] Vance, "A Brief History," p. 113n1.

[37] Evan MacColl, "*Beannachd Dheireannach An Eilthirich Ghaelich/The Last Farewell of a Gaelic Emmigrant*," in *Selections from Scottish-Canadian Poets*, pp. 36–9.

[38] Patrick John Paterson Sinnott (1888–1977), a native Gaelic-speaker and member of the Fraser clan, was the maternal grandfather of Susan Wilson, co-author of this article.

[39] Rev. W. McKenzie, *Centenary of Robert Burns: A Lecture* (Montreal, 1859), pp. 13, 24.

lectures and publications in Canada's printed record from the second half of the nineteenth century suggests a climate of uneasiness about Burns's biography and suspicion regarding his potential to inspire subversion. This is significant if one bears in mind the country's political environment at the time of Confederation in 1867. The Fenian Raids and the North-West Rebellion which marked the decades of the 1860s through the 1880s resulted in the creation of the North-West Mounted Police. Political expedience also caused the mustering of a volunteer militia which ultimately evolved into the Canadian Expeditionary Force that would win the country international recognition through its role in the First World War. In the latter half of the nineteenth century, when the Dominion's oldest military regiment, the Queen's Own Rifles of Canada, was deployed to quash attempts at Irish, First Nations and Métis political insurgency, Scottish-Canadians sought to enhance their reputation as nation-builders rather than as rebels by serving in their country's armed forces.[40]

Despite Burns's radicalism, there were also those ready to champion the Scottish poet, and support for him countered the opinions of his detractors. In the eyes of Rev. Robert Grant of Great Village, Nova Scotia, Burns could do no wrong. His 1883 pamphlet, *Robert Burns: Vindicated*, proved so popular that he issued an expanded and retitled version the following year.[41] In his effusive comparisons of Burns to Moses and of Burns's writing to the Bible, Grant celebrated the poet's exertions "in the sacred cause of freedom" and asserted that his "excesses were the *exception*."[42] Particularly striking is a pamphlet titled *Robert Burns As Thinker, Seer, Poet*, which was issued in Winnipeg in 1913 by an author identified only as "C., Fort Rouge," who was more interested in Burns's ideas than his poetry. Claiming that "The great lesson that his life and writing ought to have for us is to teach us that in order to live happily we have to get into closer touch with nature," C. identified Burns as a predecessor of "the Socialist or Labor movement" and argued that he was "a philosopher and thinker in the first place, and chose a metrical form of expression because it suited his temperament best."[43]

This defensive spirit also penetrated Canadian travel literature.[44] Letters written to friends at home in Seaforth, Ontario, by J. Campbell, a medical doctor who toured Scotland, were printed in a local newspaper before appearing as a book in 1884. Campbell explained that the volume was prepared at the request of the newspaper editor, who "urged us to write a defense of the life and character of the

---

[40] See "The Queen's Own Rifles of Canada: A Brief History," *The Rifleman Online—The QOR of C*, http://qor.com/history/history.html, accessed 1 May 2009.

[41] Rev. Robert Grant, *Robert Burns, Scotia's Immortal Bard: His Life and Labours* (Halifax, 1884); some libraries cite a "fourth edition" from 1886.

[42] Ibid., pp. 12, 15.

[43] C., Fort Rouge, *Robert Burns as Thinker, Seer, Poet* (Winnipeg, 1913), pp. 25, 15, 2.

[44] According to Cecilia Morgan in *"A Happy Holiday": English-Canadians and Transatlantic Tourism, 1870–1930* (Toronto, 2008), sites related to Sir Walter Scott attracted more Canadian tourists than those related to Burns (pp. 71–5).

poet, which would make the subject complete and very acceptable to the readers of the [Stratford] *Beacon*."[45] Campbell added, "[W]e never thought that the life and works of Robert Burns needed a defence, if properly understood" and attributed Burns's personal difficulties to a broken heart: "Had [Highland Mary] lived to become his wife ... her influence would have been exerted for good and ... many of those indiscretions which clouded his after-days would have been prevented."[46] Like Campbell, many Canadians who admired Burns as a poet saw his human failings as symptomatic of what would later be termed the Romantic agony. In the words of Agnes Maule Machar,

> 'Twas his to feel the anguish keen
> Of noblest powers to mortals given,
> While tyrant passions chained to earth
> The soul that might have soared to heaven.[47]

Or, in the more folksy style of Alexander McLachlan,

> Burns wasna perfect to a dot
> An' wha among us a'
> But has some hole in his ain coat
> An' maybe some hae twa?[48]

In addition to inspiring celebration and commentary, Burns offered models for many nineteenth-century Canadian writers, particularly those of Scottish descent. Elizabeth Waterston's list of Scottish-Canadian poets influenced by Burns[49] is amplified by copious additional references to Burns in the online Chadwyck-Healey database of Canadian Poetry. This dialogical transnational literary relationship, the cultural influence of the old world writer upon that of the new and the latter's adaptation and redirection of traditional elements, is one of the characteristics of the "Double Voicing" which Stephen Scobie identifies as a distinctive feature of Canadian poetry[50] and which presumably characterizes the literature of most settler cultures. For example, in his collection of poems issued in Montreal in 1857, Andrew Learmont Spedon demonstrated his skill with the Standard Habbie stanza

---

[45]   J. Campbell, *The Land of Robt. Burns, and Other Pen and Ink Portraits* (Seaforth, ON, 1884), pp. 4–5, 10.

[46]   Campbell defended Burns again in "The Nature of Robert Burns," *Canadian Magazine*, 6 (March 1896): 395–402.

[47]   Agnes Maule Machar, "An Evening With Burns," *Century Illustrated Magazine*, 27/3 (January 1884): 479.

[48]   Alexander McLachlan, "Burns," *The Poetical Works of Alexander McLachlan* (Toronto, 1900), p. 401.

[49]   Waterston, *Rapt in Plaid*, pp. 24–8.

[50]   Stephen Scobie, "Double Voicing—a View of Canadian Poetry," in Jorn Carlson (ed.), *O Canada: Essays on Canadian Literature and Culture* (Arhus, Denmark, 1995), pp. 38–49.

popularized by Burns,[51] and emulated Burns's addresses to humble creatures in his own verses, "To a Fire-Fly" and "To a Mosquito." Spedon also composed a poem titled "Auld Lang Syne," noting that he "has attempted to imitate Burns, but not with the slightest pretensions to compete with him."[52] With other poets, the connection may be more subtle; for example, Burns seems to be reflected in poems titled "The Ploughman" and "Stanzas to a Scottish Thistle in Nova-Scotia" by an earlier Scottish immigrant poet, Andrew Shiels.[53] In the analysis of Waterston, "In general, early Scottish poets in Canada wrote more patriotic songs but fewer love songs than Burns, more egalitarian songs but fewer drinking songs, more on nature's details (flowers, animals, waterways), but fewer satires on people; more songs of sentiment, fewer of passions."[54] As well as sponsoring festive events like Burns suppers, Scottish social organizations promoted Burns through poetry prizes and publications; not surprisingly, Burns figures significantly in *Selections from Scottish-Canadian Poets*, issued by the Caledonian Society of Toronto in 1900. One poet who regularly celebrated Burns was William Beattie, a man otherwise unknown for his writing, who composed an annual Burns birthday ode each year from 1909 to 1916.[55] More familiar is the name of Robert Service, whose eight years (1904–1912) in the Canadian North qualify him as a Canadian writer, and whose indebtedness to Burns has been demonstrated in a critical assessment of his war poetry.[56]

While Canadian references to Burns abound, the "Burns of Canada" was indisputably Alexander McLachlan, who was born in Johnstone (now a suburb of Strathclyde) in 1817 and immigrated to Upper Canada in 1840, where he variously worked as a farmer, tailor, and emigration agent. Critic D.M.R. Bentley notes that "[b]etween McLachlan and Burns there were doubtless affinities born of nationality, political orientation, and similar experiences, but hardly of temperament. McLachlan was a provincial Victorian with a strong Presbyterian

---

[51]   Burns was not the first Scottish poet to adopt this metrical pattern. Although used by several of Burns's literary predecessors such as Sir Robert Sempill of Beltrees (1590?–1660?), Allan Ramsay (1684–1758), and Robert Fergusson (1750–1774), the "Standard Habbie" or the "Habbie Simson stanza" later became known as the "Burns stanza" due to Burns's technical mastery of the form.

[52]   Andrew Learmont Spedon, *The Woodland Warbler; A Volume of English and Scottish Poems and Songs* (Montreal, 1857), p. 113.

[53]   Andrew Shiels, *The Witch of Westcot; A Tale of Nova Scotia, in Three Cantos* (Halifax, 1831), pp. 159, 189. For additional examples, see Fred Cogswell, "The Maritime Provinces 1815–1880," in Carl F. Klinck (ed.), *Literary History of Canada* (Toronto,1965), pp. 102–24 (p. 117).

[54]   Elizabeth Waterston, "The Lowland Tradition in Canadian Literature," in W. Stanford Reid (ed.), *The Scottish Tradition in Canada* (Toronto, 1976), p. 208.

[55]   William Beattie, *Odes of Appreciation of Robert Burns* (Toronto, n.d.) (CIHM 66549).

[56]   Edwina Burness, "The Influence of Burns and Fergusson on the War Poetry of Robert Service," *Studies in Scottish Literature*, 21 (1986): 135–46.

background" who drew "abundantly" on "Burns's descriptions of Scottish plants and landscapes" but left "untouched his ribald celebrations of sensual life."[57] Indeed, McLachlan's refraction of Burns outlines the construction of Burns that Canadians chose to celebrate. In his poem entitled "Robert Burns," McLachlan writes,

> Hail to thee, King of Scottish song,
>   With all thy faults we love thee;
> Nor would we set up modern saints,
>   With all their cant, above thee.
> There hangs a grandeur and a gloom
>   Around thy wondrous story,
> As of the sun eclipsed at noon,
>   'Mid all his beams of glory.[58]

At the banquet of the Burns Centennial Festival organized by the Toronto Burns Club in 1859, McLachlan's reputation as a Burnsian poet brought him to a podium otherwise dominated by illustrious political and professional figures, including members of parliament George Brown and Thomas D'Arcy McGee, and future prime minister John A. Macdonald.[59] In 1885, McLachlan won the gold medal offered by the Toronto Caledonian Society with his poetical tribute which opens by praising Burns's advocacy of "the Britherhood o' Man." Lauding by turns Burns's wise, romantic, comic, and patriotic verse, the poem's touchstone remains Burns's "universal Heart."[60] In addition to the mastery of vernacular Scots evident in his six published volumes, McLachlan himself shared Burns's interest in social reform, proclaimed in poems whose titles speak for themselves. These include "Old England is Eaten by Knaves," "The Man Who Rose From Nothing," and "Young Canada; or, Jack's as Good as His Master." And, like Burns, McLachlan presents contradictions to the modern critic. On the one hand, in line with his advocacy for the underdog, McLachlan wrote sympathetically of the destruction of the Indigenous peoples of North America: in "To an Indian Skull," he praises his "uneducated" "red brother" as one who may be "the least contaminated, / From civ'lization's trammels free."[61] On the other, he sounds like a white supremacist in his poem "The Anglo-Saxon," which opens, "The Anglo-Saxon leads the van, / And never lags behind, / For was he not ordain'd to be / The leader of mankind?"[62] Such racism remained evident as many as three decades after McLachlan's death

---

[57]   D.M.R. Bentley, introduction to *The Emigrant* by Alexander McLachlan (London, ON, 1991), p. xvi.

[58]   Alexander McLachlan, "Robert Burns," *Poetical Works*, p. 94; also in *Selections from Scottish-Canadian Poets*, p. 72.

[59]   Program, *Burns Centennial Festival* (CIHM 43354).

[60]   McLachlan, "Burns," *Poetical Works*, pp. 397, 401.

[61]   McLachlan, "To an Indian Skull," *Poetical Works*, p. 71.

[62]   McLachlan, "The Anglo-Saxon," *Poetical Works*, p. 33.

in 1896. Citing the militant response to the 1924 murder of Scottish nursemaid Janet Smith in Vancouver, a still unsolved crime that was initially blamed on a Chinese servant who was abused in efforts to obtain a confession, Vance observes that at times "organized Scottishness could be mobilized to reinforce racism and white supremacy."[63] However, such reactions were the exception rather than the rule.

Alongside McLachlan's invocation of Burns, whose "noble work" was "to lift the poor and lowly,"[64] the democratic Burns was a common reference point among Canada's social reformers from various classes. Working-class poet and labor organizer Marie Joussaye adulated Burns in "Two Poets" (1895), which contrasts the obscurity of Browning with the accessibility of Burns. In her view, the "hardy, humble ploughman of the soil" whose "name was known in palace and in cot" because his poems represented "The grandest thoughts couched in the simplest words" will "live on Fame's immortal scroll" because his "lyrics touched the heart of all mankind."[65] Burns similarly appears as a touchstone of class unity in Agnes Maule Machar's Knights of Labor novel, *Roland Graeme: Knight* (1892). Advocating peaceful reconciliation between factory workers and factory owners, the book twice cites his stanza that concludes "man to man, the warld o'er, / Shall brothers be, for a' that."[66] In the modernist era, Scottish-born Jessie Sime took the title of her book of stories, *Sister Woman* (1918), from Burns's poem, "Address to the Unco Guid."

Despite the apparent ubiquity of Burns in Canadian life and print, his presence in Canadian schoolbooks from the 1880s through the 1920s seems to have been surprisingly sparse.[67] His representation was greatest in the fourth *Ontario Reader* of 1885, which exemplified the patriotic, democratic and lyrical Burns with "Bruce to his Troops Before the Battle of Bannockburn" (i.e., "Scots Wha Hae"), "For a' That and a' That," "To Mary in Heaven," and "Flow Gently Sweet Afton." Among a sampling of school readers approved by various jurisdictions from 1881 to 1929, this was the only text in which Burns was not vastly outnumbered by selections from Scott, Wordsworth, Longfellow, and Tennyson. Later readers reduced their offerings; the fifth *Victorian Reader* (1898), authorized for use in Manitoba's schools, included both "A Man's a Man" and "The Cottar's Saturday

---

  63   Vance, "A Brief History," p. 106.

  64   McLachlan, "Robert Burns," *Poetical Works,* p. 95.

  65   Marie Joussaye, "Two Poets," in Carole Gerson and Gwendolyn Davies (eds), *Canadian Poetry: From the Beginnings through the First World War* (Toronto, 1994), p. 321. The comparison between Browning and Burns seems to have been common. See Bliss Carman's facetious "The Two Bobbies," in Bliss Carman and Richard Hovey, *Songs from Vagabondia* (Boston, 1894).

  66   Agnes Maule Machar, *Roland Graeme: Knight: A Novel of our Time* (1892) (Ottawa, 1996), pp. 15, 120.

  67   Many thanks to Dr Penney Clark (University of British Columbia) and Dr Nancy Vogan (Mount Allison University) for their assistance in researching the presence of Burns in Canadian schoolbooks and songbooks.

Night," with a lesson plan for the latter appearing in the *Educational Journal of Western Canada.*[68] Most others offered just one Burns poem—sometimes "The Cottar's Saturday Night," but more often a shorter selection such as "Scots Wha Hae," "A Man's a Man," or "Flow Gently Sweet Afton." One Catholic reader that seems to have remained in print from 1865 until 1891 chose "Lament of Mary Queen of Scots."[69] The Burns poem selected for *The Canadian Elocutionist* (1885) was "Highland Mary." Equally sporadic was Burns's appearance in school songbooks, where he was most frequently represented by "Auld Lang Syne."[70] This disjunction between the widespread popularity of Burns and his apparent lack of official sanction in the classroom during the late nineteenth century and into the twentieth offers grounds for speculation. Was this gap due to Burns's controversial personal life or to his democratic radicalism? Did his use of vernacular Scots fail to fulfill the standard usage that the public education system wished to promote to an increasingly diverse student body? Might this disparity represent a class division between the elitist appeal of Sir Walter Scott, who at one time was offered the poet laureateship of England, and the populist appeal of Burns? Perhaps Burns's reputation as a distinctly Scottish poet meant his work could not be subsumed into the dominant English canon which served as the literary benchmark for the young Dominion of Canada, and this, in turn, resulted in his marginalization in formal literary studies in Canadian schools.

Another absence concerns the lack of concrete evidence to support the desire of some critics to attribute virtually all Canadian instances of oral and/or "dialect" poetry to the influence of Burns.[71] Dialect verse was generally popular among the many amateur and professional recitalists who entertained Canadians before the days of radio and film, and the notion that Burns directly inspired later poets who specialized in the vernacular of other ethnic groups would seem to be largely wishful thinking. For example, early in her writing career Sara Jeannette Duncan chose a North American working-class idiom for her dialect poem "My Washerwoman's Story."[72] Despite her own Scottish descent, which she warmly depicted in her Canadian novel, *The Imperialist* (1904), Duncan does not seem to mention Burns in her copious output of sophisticated realistic fiction. Another example which challenges this assumed Burnsian influence involves the oral

---

[68]   E. McFarlane, "A Suggestive Lesson Plan. The Cotter's Saturday Night," *Educational Journal of Western Canada*, 4/4 (June/July 1902): 114–6.

[69]   *The Metropolitan Fifth Reader ... Arranged Expressly for the Catholic Schools in Canada* (Montreal, 1891).

[70]   This song was not always attributed to him: the fifth reader of Charles E. Whiting's *New Public School Music Course* (Toronto, 1912) identifies the song titled "Should Auld Acquaintance" as "Scotch Folk Song" (p. 66).

[71]   As Scots is now recognized as a language in its own right, "dialect" is a contentious term no longer used to describe vernacular Scots.

[72]   Sara Jeannette Duncan, "My Washerwoman's Story," *The Week* (Toronto), 5/13 (23 Feb 1888): 203.

tradition underlying William Henry Drummond's once popular verses in French-accented English (the Canadian equivalent of "blackface," now vanished for similar reasons). Drummond's adaptation of the oral tradition more likely derives from his early childhood in Ireland than from the model of Burns[73] and was later manifested in such poems as "We're Irish Yet," which he read to the annual dinner of the St Patrick's Society of Montreal in 1907.[74] In a similar fashion, a prominent Canadian historian overstates the connection between the charismatic Mohawk poet, E. Pauline Johnson, and Burns by describing Johnson as "a Canadian reader of Burns,"[75] when in fact Burns does not figure in the list of canonical British poets that Johnson devoured as a child.[76] Despite their common inheritance of oral culture, Burns did not particularly appeal to Aboriginal Canadians, as indicated by the lack of comment by Ojibwa George Henry when he was taken to Burns's cottage during his 1844 visit to Britain.[77] Where Burns does factor into the practice of popular Canadian poets such as Drummond and Johnson is less as a direct influence on their writing, and more as a creator of the receptive climate for oral verse that contributes to a popular national literary identity. Like their Scottish cousins, Canadians wanted national bards, and the example of Burns may well have enabled Pauline Johnson and William Henry Drummond to partially fulfill that role.

How, then, to summarize the legacy of "Transatlantic Burns" in Canada? In Daniel Clark's introduction to the Toronto Caledonian Society's *Selections from Scottish-Canadian Poets* (1900), he observes, "Of all the forms of poetry, the songs of a country wield the greatest influence on the mind-life of a people."[78] Clark continues, "The Scots who have made Canada their home ... were and are so permeated with the literature of Scotland, especially the poetry of Burns and Scott, that they are almost intuitively led to adopt to some extent the form and prominent constructive features of these song writers."[79] However, Burns's influence in Victorian and Edwardian Canada extended beyond the literary; his humanitarian ideals served as the impetus for benevolent work and social justice,

---

[73]   As suggested by Waterston, *Rapt in Plaid*, pp. 29, 33.

[74]   Mary Jane Edwards, "Drummond, William Henry," in the *Dictionary of Canadian Biography Online*, http://www.biographi.ca/, accessed 1 May 2009. For the Irish tradition in Canada, see Carl F. Klinck, "Literary Activity in Canada East and West 1841–1880," in Klinck (ed.), *Literary History of Canada*, pp. 145–62 (p. 156).

[75]   Veronica Strong-Boag, "'A People Akin to Mine': Indians and Highlanders within the British Empire," *Native Studies Review*, 14/1 (2001): 27–53 (27).

[76]   Veronica Strong-Boag and Carole Gerson, *Paddling Her Own Canoe: the Times and Texts of E. Pauline Johnson (Tekahionwake)* (Toronto, 2000), p. 149. The actual statement in Strong-Boag and Gerson's book on Johnson is that Johnson's medium of oral performance meant that her verses, like the poems of Burns, "would engrave themselves in public memory."

[77]   Penny Petrone (ed.), *First People, First Voices* (Toronto, 1985), p. 91.

[78]   Daniel Clark, introduction to *Selections from Scottish-Canadian Poets*, p. 6.

[79]   Ibid., p. 14.

while festivities in his honor reinforced a sense of communal identity for middle-class Scottish immigrants and provided occasion for celebration of their ethnic origins. Perhaps the Scottish-Canadian poet John Mortimer best describes this legacy in his tribute to Burns, "After a Hundred Years" (1900):

> For many a soul-ennobling thought,
>   And many a maxim deep and sage,
> Thou in the furnace of thy grief
>   Has coined to bless each future age.
>
> And they shall bless thee in return,
>   And hold thy honored mem'ry dear,
> For thy great human heart, and all
>   That claims the tribute and the tear![80]

---

[80]   John Mortimer, "After a Hundred Years," in *Selections from Scottish-Canadian Poets,* p. 197.

Chapter 8
Robert Burns and Latin America

Nigel Leask

Any study of "transatlantic Burns" that lacked a perspective on Latin America would be geographically and culturally partial; accordingly, my task in this chapter is to complement other work published in this volume that address Robert Burns's reception and influence in the United States and Canada. Yet I have to confess at the outset that Burns's poetry is not deeply rooted in the soil of Latin America. Given the dominance of Spanish and Portuguese languages and literatures in these national cultures, access to Burns, as to other Scottish and British writers of the romantic period, was contingent upon translations; and these, it turns out, were few and of recent date. The poetry of Robert Burns was translated into Hungarian, Norwegian, Finnish, Esperanto, and even Japanese before Spanish and Portuguese. I will therefore start by commenting on the question of translation before moving on to consider some of the broader issues concerning Burns's Latin American connections.

Given the challenge raised by "Poems, chiefly in the Scottish Dialect" to Standard English, it is appropriate that Burns's poetry appears to have been translated into Catalan before Castilian. Andrew Monnickendam has located a Catalan translation of "Ae Fond Kiss" published in the journal *L'Avens*, dating to 1890.[1] A scan of the *Bibliography of Scottish Literature in Translation* (BOSLIT) suggests that no poem by Burns was translated into Castilian until 1919, when "A un ratón del campo" (a translation of "To a Mouse") appeared in a collection entitled *Manojo de Poesías Inglesas* (but published in Cardiff).[2] Notably, this volume of translations by Salvador de Madariaga (Spanish professor at Oxford, liberal statesman and writer) was introduced by the writer and Scottish nationalist "Don Roberto" Cunningham Graham, who had strong personal links with Argentina. A second collection entitled *Poetas Líricos Ingleses*, also including a translation of "To a Mouse," was published in 1949 in Buenos Aires; amongst the translators was Jorge Luis Borges, although the blind librarian of Babel does not seem to have been responsible for "A un ratón del campo."[3]

---

[1]   Andrew Monnickendam, "Burns in Spain," paper presented at the Robert Burns in European Culture Conference, Charles University, Prague, 6–8 March 2009.

[2]   *Manojo de Poesías Inglesas*, puestos en verso castellano por Salvador de Madariaga, proluguillo de R.B. Cunningham Graham (Cardiff, 1919), pp. 21–3.

[3]   *Poetas Líricos Ingleses*, selección de Ricardo Baeza; estudio preliminar por Silvina Ocampo; traducciones de Ricardo Baeza, Silvina Ocampo, J.R.Wilcock, R.B. Hopenhaym, Jorge Borges, Alcala Galiano, Diez-Canedo y Salvador de Madariaga; noticias biobibliográficas de Ricardo Baeza y José Manuel Conde (Buenos Aires, 1949), p. 161.

According to Monnickendam, five publications entirely dedicated to selections of Burns's poetry translated into Spanish were published in 1940, 1954, 1990, 1998, and 2008 respectively, but all from Spanish, rather than Latin American, publishing houses.[4] I have been unable to find evidence of a single Latin American imprint solely dedicated to the poetry of Burns, although clearly the above-mentioned Spanish editions had some Latin American circulation. When I taught a course in British romanticism at the National Autonomous University of Mexico (UNAM) in Mexico City in the late 1990s (UNAM is the biggest university in Latin America), Burns was not widely studied, and when he was, usually at the behest of a Scottish lecturer, students worked from original language texts, and accompanying language glosses, rather than from translations. On a recent visit to "Gandhi" (the main bookstore in Mexico City) in 2008, I found not a single text of a single poem by Burns, either in the original or in translation, on the shelves, although Byron and Keats were available, and contemporary Scottish writing was well represented by large runs of the novels of James Kelman, Ian Rankin, and Alexander McCall Smith.

By comparison with Scott and Byron, Burns comes off very badly in the Iberophone translation stakes: BOSLIT shows that Scott's poem "Don Roderick" was translated into Portuguese as early as 1811, and his novels *Ivanhoe* and the *Talisman* translated into Spanish in 1825 and 1826 respectively by José de Mora, and distributed in Latin America by the London-based publishing and trade network of Rudolph Ackermann. John Ford speculates that both novels "perhaps struck a chord in the martial crusading zeal of the [Latin American] Liberators and their supporters."[5] Byron's *Siege of Corinth* was translated into Spanish in 1818, and the other "Turkish Tales" followed over the next decade: even *Childe Harold* and *Don Juan* were available in Spanish before 1830. More unexpectedly, William Blake's plates illustrative of Blair's *The Grave*, commissioned by Robert Cromek in 1808, were widely distributed in Latin America by Ackermann, accompanied by Mora's poetical interpretations, in the latter's *Meditaciones Poéticas* (1826).[6] Although the absence of translations of Burns's poetry into Spanish during this period is striking, it is largely explained by the fact that his poems were written "chiefly in the Scottish Dialect," raising problems for any translator seeking a Spanish equivalent of the demotic "feel" of the original. A more rigorous scrutiny of the archive than I have been able to conduct might reveal new data, but it is probably not too rash to conclude that Burns's poetry (unlike his fellow Scottish writers Byron and Scott) had zero, or at least minimal, influence on nineteenth-century Latin American poetry and literary criticism. This is all the more marked

---

[4]   Monnickendam, "Burns in Spain": the places of publication are Barcelona, Zaragoza, and Madrid.

[5]   John Ford, "Rudolph Ackermann: Culture and Commerce in Latin America, 1822–1828," in John Lynch (ed.), *Andrés Bello: The London Years* (Richmond, Surrey, 1982), pp. 137–52 (p. 149).

[6]   Ibid., p. 144.

when we consider Burns's profound influence on Anglophone North American writing of the same period.

In a recent paper entitled "Burns in Brazil," John Corbett notes that all four translations of Burns into Portuguese listed on BOSLIT date from the twentieth century, when "English succeeded French as the second language of cultured Brazilians."[7] Contemporary Brazilian readers are however fortunate in having a good 1994 bilingual translation of a selection of fifty Burns poems by Luiza Lobo, a former student of G. Ross Roy at the University of South Carolina, one of the leading Burns scholars in the world.[8] Lobo translates the Scots language poems into standard Portuguese, "with a few slight touches to indicate archaism"; but as Corbett points out, her translations are rather in the nature of glosses which allow the reader some sense of the original poems published on the facing page. Lobo admitted that "the challenges posed by Burns's Scots were often too great."[9]

Corbett speculates that the delay in translating Burns in Latin America was largely due to the fact that prior translation into French was a precondition for nineteenth-century translation into both Spanish and Portuguese.[10] But given that a reasonable selection of Burns's poetry was in fact available in French by the mid-nineteenth century (from as early as 1826, according to BOSLIT), this hardly explains the long delay until the appearance of the first Spanish translation of Burns in 1919, or Portuguese, as late as 1952. A more likely reason for the delay might be what Brazilian critic António Cândido calls the "cultural weakness" of [nineteenth-century] Latin America, the "non–existence, dispersion, and weakness of publics disposed to literature, due to the small number of real readers"; but also "the lack of the means of communicating and diffusion (publishers, libraries, magazines, newspapers)."[11] In the language of Pascale Casanova's *World Republic of Letters*, nineteenth-century Latin America was a long way from the "Greenwich Meridian of Literature" (in her view Paris), the "relative aesthetic distance from the centre of the world of letters of all those who belong to it": or, translating a geographical into a temporal metaphor, "*it is necessary to be old in order to have any chance of being modern or of decreeing what is modern.*"[12]

---

[7] John Corbett, "Burns in Brazil," p. 3 (unpublished paper). Thanks to Professor John Corbett for a copy of this paper, and for discussions of the subject.

[8] *50 Poemas de Robert Burns*, seleccionados e traduzidos por Luiza Lobo, edição bilingüe, Seleção e Colaboração de G. Ross Roy (Rio de Janeiro, 1994). See also Lobo's essay "The Reception in Brazil of the First Portuguese Translation of Robert Burns," *Studies in Scottish Literature*, 30 (1998): 249–60.

[9] Corbett, "Burns in Brazil," p. 3.

[10] Ibid.

[11] Qtd. in Pascale Casanova, *The World Republic of Letters*, trans. M.B. DeBevoise (Cambridge, MA, 2004), p. 16.

[12] Casanova, *The World Republic of Letters*, pp. 88, 89. Nonetheless, as I have argued above, the currency of both Byron and Scott in Spanish translation reveals that there was some absorption of British romantic poetry, usually via prior French translations, so the Casanova's "distance" effect is intermittent.

Thwarted by the translation records, and on the point of admitting defeat, I resorted to the more nebulous realm of Burnslore. I recalled an enterprising tourist guide in Burns's Mauchline who in 2002 showed my wife (from Mexico) and our daughters round the Ayrshire kirkyard where four of the poet's children, and many of his friends and acquaintances, lie buried. Having ascertained my wife's nationality, he pointed out the grave of a Mauchline family whose sons, he claimed, had died in the siege of the Alamo in 1836, at the hands of the Mexican army led by General Santa Anna. (Like all good tourist guides, he had a story up his sleeve for every nationality.) He then repeated the anecdote—I had heard a version of it before—about the origin of the word "gringo," which turns up a Burns connection, albeit of a rather apocryphal nature. During the U.S. invasion of Mexico from 1846 to 1848 (itself prompted by the U.S. annexation of the newly independent republic of Texas in 1845) a favorite marching song for the U.S. troops was Robert Burns's "Green Grow the Rashes O"—hostile Mexicans quickly dubbed the invaders "Gringos," parroting the opening words of their marching song.[13] There may be some truth in this—the *OED* records its first usage in 1849, on the U.S./Mexican border—and the Mexicans certainly had good reason to be bitter, given that fifty-five percent of their sovereign territory was ceded to the U.S. government at the Treaty of Guadalupe Hidalgo in 1848. But if the story is true, it is ironic that Burns's tender love lyric in praise of the female sex should have been converted into a marching song, and then provided ammunition for Mexican resentment of their northern neighbours.

Unwilling to give up on the trail of Burns in Latin America, I recalled ritual singing of "Auld Lang Syne" at Mexican "año viejo" parties. We had always sung the Scots words, but I decided to check on what the Mexicans were singing—was this (at last) a case of a widely disseminated, albeit subliminal, Burns translation into Spanish? To my disappointment, not at all. The words commonly sung across both Spain and Latin America are entitled "Despedida" ("Farewell") and bear little relation to Burns's original lyric. Their author is unknown, but probably wrote in the twentieth century and was a native of Spain. The words are strongly Roman Catholic in sentiment, and derive from the Boy Scout movement, where they are sung around the campfire on the eve of striking canvas. Here are some stanzas from "Despedida," sung to the common melody of "Auld Lang Syne":

> ¿Por qué perder las esperanzas
> de volverse a ver?
> ¿Por qué perder las esperanzas
> si hay tanto querer?
> (Chorus) No es más que un hasta luego,
> no es más que un breve adiós,

---

13   The *Wikipedia* entry on "Gringo" classifies this as one of many "unsupported etymologies" popular in Mexico and Latin America, but gives its official derivation (supported by the *Diccionaria de la lengua española de la Real Academia Española*) from "griego," or Greek, denoting any foreign person (http://en.wikipedia.org/ wiki/Gringo).

muy pronto junto al fuego
nos reunirá el Señor.
Con nuestras manos enlazadas
en torno al calor,
formemos esta noche
un círculo de amor. (Chorus)

Pues el Señor que nos protege
y nos va a bendecir,
seguro que otra noche
nos habrá a reunir. (Chorus)[14]

This does not look very promising. One big exception to the Latin American "Burns black-out," however, is the Bard's importance as a focus of cultural identity among Scottish expatriates and diaspora descendents. Like other parts of the New World, Latin America experienced significant Scottish immigration from the time of the liberation wars, although of course nothing on the scale of the U.S. or Canada. One of the best-documented cases of an organized Scots colony is that of Topo, in Venezuela. In 1825, 200 Scots emigrants were recruited in Aberdeen and the Inverness area and set sail to settle a designated plot of land at Topo, near Caracas. But it turned out that the land allocated by the Columbian government (as it was then) was barren hilly scrub, and the sponsor body, the Columbian Agricultural Society, suffered badly in the economic crash of 1826. After a major political scandal, the British government financed the colonists' resettlement in Guelph, Ontario, where the "La Guayra Settlers" formed the nucleus of the new community founded by the novelist John Galt.[15] Marginally more successful was the Scottish colony founded near Buenos Aires by the Robertson brothers in 1825; although the investors received no return for their money, most of the emigrants did settle in Argentina after the colony broke up.[16] In the century that followed, thousands of Scottish miners, railway engineers, soldiers, planters, and merchants made their lives in Latin America; successfully assimilated into their host countries, many retained (and retain) a strong sense of their Scottish roots.

One manifestation of this presence in modern cultural memory is the existence of "St Andrews Societies" (and cognate organizations) across the length and breadth of Latin America; in Mexico City (founded 1893), in Argentina (also the "Buenos Aires Tartan Army"—piping and Highland dancing—and the "Scotland in Argentina" Society), in Uruguay (the Montevideo St Andrews Society), and Chile (Santiago St Andrews Society, founded 1924). All of these societies, and their smaller sister organizations in other Latin American capitals, hold annual

---

[14]   www.siemprescout.org/pdf/cancionero.pdf, accessed 25 March 2009.

[15]   Hans P. Rheinhamer, *Topo: The Story of a Scottish Colony near Caracas, 1825–27* (Edinburgh, 1988).

[16]   Joseph Dodds, *Records of the Scottish Settlers in the River Plate and their Churches* (Buenos Aires, 1897).

Burns suppers, St Andrews Dinners, and ceilidhs. The Mexican society, about which I am best informed, has this year struck a commemorative coin for Burns's 250th anniversary, bearing a handsome portrait of the Bard with the slogan "A Man's a Man for a' That"; it can be yours for 500 pesos (bronze) or 1000 pesos (silver).[17] Mexico City "St Andrews" is also linked to the "St Patrick's Battalion Pipe Band" who sport the Mackenzie of Seaforth tartan, combining the green, white, and red of the Mexican tricolor with the blue and white of the saltire, "symbolizing the unity and fraternity of these two nations." The St Patrick's Pipe Band performed well at the Glengarry Highland Games in 2007 and 2008, held in Maxville, Ontario. According to its website, the Band's mission statement is "to promote Highland Bagpipe Music in Mexico and to honour the members of the St Patrick's Battalion that died far away from their land of birth defending their newly adopted country."[18]

This represents an interesting act of cultural syncretism, because the St Patrick's battalion was composed of Irish American solders, recent immigrants to the U.S. from famine-gripped Ireland, drafted into the U.S. army and dispatched to invade Mexico in 1846 (some of them may have sung "Green Grow the Rashes" as they marched along). Principally Catholics, they were denied the right to hold Mass and were poorly treated by their Presbyterian officers (doubtless many of whom were of Scottish descent). It did not take them long to realize that the Mexican enemy were Catholics like themselves, and fought under a rather familiar green, white, and red republican tricolor; unsurprisingly, nearly 800 Irish soldiers defected to the Mexican side, led by Captain John Riley. But although they were fierce fighters and caused heavy U.S. casualties, they had unfortunately backed the wrong horse, and when General Santa Anna (victor of "Los Alamos" in the previous decade) was defeated at the battle of Churubusco, fifty were lynched by the U.S. army, while others were branded on the face with the letter "D" for "deserter." There is still a moving memorial to the soldiers of the St Patricio brigade in San Angel, Mexico City, although many of the Irish names are misspelled: the episode is the basis for the 1999 film *One Man Hero* starring Tom Berenger.[19]

Interesting as this is as an example of the fusion of Scots and Irish cultural identities in Mexico, it has a tangential bearing on the main subject of my chapter. In what remains, I will explore some significant (albeit indirect) contemporary links between the Ayrshire Bard and the cause of Latin American independence that got under way the decade after his death, as well as briefly considering some parallels between the agrarian poetry of Burns and two Latin American near-contemporaries, the Guatamaltec Jesuit Rafael Landivar and the Venezuelan exile and patriot Andrés Bello. During Burns's lifetime, the Iberian colonies in the New

---

17   www.standrewsmexico.synathsite.com, accessed 25 March 25 2009.

18   www.bandadegaitas.com.mx/historicalEng.html, accessed 27 March 2009.

19   www.proudtoliveinamerica.com, accessed 27 March, 2009; for a fuller historical treatment, see Karl Bauer and Robert W. Johannsen, *The Mexican War: 1846–1848* (Lincoln, 1992).

World were jealously guarded by their Spanish and Portuguese masters: few travel books were available until the magisterial works of Alexander von Humboldt, and a spate of publications in the independence decades of the 1810s and 20s associated with what Mary Louise Pratt calls the invasion of the Anglo-Saxon "capitalist vanguard."[20] There are only two references to Spanish America in Burns's poetic corpus: the first is Coila's address to the poet in lines 261 to 264 of "The Vision":

> "And trust me, not *Potosi's mine*,
>   Nor *King's regard*,
> Can give a bliss o'ermatching thine,
>   A *rustic Bard*."[21]

This allusion to Potosi, the world-famous silver mines in Peru (now Bolivia) from which 45,000 tons of pure silver were extracted in three centuries, is a conventional trope for fabulous wealth in eighteenth-century poetry, so perhaps hardly counts. But Burns's second allusion is more interesting, and occurs in "Address of Beelzebub" (probably written in 1786). The eponymous Beelzebub, after offering MacDonald of Glengarry advice in how to brutalize his recalcitrant "Highlan hounds" who had sought to emigrate to North America "in search of that fantastic thing—LIBERTY," promises Glengarry and John Campbell, 4th Earl of Breadalbane, seats in "the benmost neuk" of hell:

> At my right hand, assign'd your seat
> 'Tween HEROD's hip, an' POLYCRATE;
> Or, if ye on your station tarrow,
> Between ALMAGRO and PIZARRO;
> A seat, I'm sure ye're weel deservin't; (vol. 1, p. 255)

Here Breadalbane[22] keeps company with Pizarro and Almagro, notorious conquistadores of Peru, alongside King Herod and the Sicilian tyrant Polycrates. Pizarro and Almagro were of course central villains in the so-called "Black Legend" of Spanish colonial cruelty in the New World, with which Burns was probably familiar from William Robertson's *History of America* (1777) (his friend Alexander Cunningham was Robertson's nephew) as well as other sources; for

---

[20] See Mary Louise Pratt, *Imperial Eyes: Travel Writing and Transculturation* (London and New York, 1992) pp. 144–71; and Nigel Leask, *Curiosity and the Aesthetics of Travel Writing, 1770–1840: "From an Antique Land"* (Oxford, 2002), pp. 243–314.

[21] *The Poems and Songs of Robert Burns*, James Kinsley (ed.) (3 vols, Oxford, 1968), vol. 1, p. 113; subsequent quotations from Burns's poetry, and Kinsley's commentary, are from this edition and will be cited in the text by volume and page number.

[22] Only the following year Burns visited Taymouth Castle, seat of Baron Breadalbane, and penned his poem "Admiring Nature in her wildest grace" in pencil over the chimney of the inn at Kenmore, Loch Tay. See Raymond Lamont Brown (ed.), *Robert Burns's Tours of the Highlands and Stirlingshire, 1787* (Ipswich, 1973), pp. 35–6. No mention is made here of Breadalbane's political crimes.

instance, James Kinsley notes that Marmontel's "*Histoire des Incas de Peru* was among the books owned by Burns at his death" (vol. 3, p. 1186).

Tracing the Latin American connection through Burns's intellectual and epistolary networks yields richer fruit however than the sparse allusions in his verse, associating him at only one remove from some of the major actors on the historical stage. I will mention two of the more substantial connections here, his correspondent the poet Helen Maria Williams (they never actually met), and his personal acquaintance Dr John Allen, stepson of Robert Cleghorn, Burns's friend, Midlothian farmer, and fellow "Crochallan fencible." Burns began corresponding with Helen Williams at the behest of his patrons Frances Dunlop and Dr John Moore, the Glaswegian-born novelist and travel writer who employed Helen Williams as his amanuensis in London, where he had settled. Helen Williams's mother hailed from Kilmeny in Fife, and after her Welsh husband's early death in 1762, she had moved with her children to Berwick-upon-Tweed, where Helen grew up within the Presbyterian community. Returning to London with her family in 1781, she quickly made her name as a poet with *Edwin and Eltruda: A Legendary Tale* (1782), *An Ode on the Peace* (1783), and the anti-colonial epyllion *Peru* (1784), largely inspired by Marmontel's sentimentalized defense of the Incas against Spanish conquest, as we have seen another possible source for Burns's knowledge of Peruvian history.

In a letter of 15 February 1787 to Moore, Burns expressed his admiration of Williams's writing, which he felt was characterized by "the wild, unfetter'd flight of native Poesy, and the querulous, sombre tenderness of 'time-settled sorrow'."[23] His admiration was fully reciprocated; in June, Williams wrote to Burns exclaiming that she had felt "the power of your genius":

> I believe no one has yet read oftener than myself your Vision, your Cotter's Evening, the Address to the Mouse, and many of your other poems. My mother's family is Scotch, and the dialect has been familiar to me from my infancy: I was, therefore, qualified to taste the charm of your native poetry, and, as I feel the strongest attachment for Scotland, I share the triumph of your country in producing your laurels.[24]

Deborah Kennedy has shown how each poet lavished compliments on the other's "native genius," a category embracing poetry written by "women of feeling" like Williams as well as (supposedly) unlettered ploughmen.[25] Certainly by 1788 Williams was steeped in Burns's poetry, and after that date Burns was well acquainted with hers. In 1788, Williams sent him a copy of her 364-line *Poem on the Bill Lately Passed for Regulating the Slave Trade* in tetrameter couplets. Burns, unusually, responded with a lengthy and appreciative critique in a letter

---

[23]   *Letters of Robert Burns*, J. De Lancey Ferguson (ed.), 2nd edn by G. Ross Roy (ed.) (2 vols, Oxford, 1985), vol. 1, p. 96.

[24]   Deborah Kennedy, *Helen Maria Williams and the Age of Revolution* (Lewisburg, 2002), p. 39.

[25]   Ibid., p. 38.

dated July or early August 1789; "I know very little of scientific criticism," he pleaded, "so all I can pretend to in that intricate art is merely to note as I read along, what passages strike me as being uncommonly beautiful, & where the expression seems to me perplexed or faulty."[26] This letter, which I have discussed elsewhere, is almost unique in offering insight into Burns's real thoughts on the slave trade.[27]

Like Burns an enthusiast for the French Revolution, Williams moved to France in 1791 and adopted French citizenship, making her name in the following decade with her popular and partisan chronicle *Letters from France*, her 1797 *Travels in Switzerland*, and translations of Bernardin St Pierre's *Paul et Virginie*, and, in the 1810s, the South American travel writings of her close friend Alexander von Humboldt, entitled *Personal Narrative of Travels to the Equinoctial Regions of the New Continent, During the years 1799–1804* (1814–1829). (Williams's translation of Humboldt accompanied Charles Darwin on his famous *Beagle* voyage in the following decade.) In Paris, Williams was celebrated for her Sunday night *salons* in the Rue Helvetius, which ran from 1792 until as late as 1819, surviving all the storms of revolution, war, and state surveillance (she had quickly fallen foul of Napoleon), frequented by many of the cosmopolitan luminaries of romantic period Europe and America.[28]

One consistent theme was Williams's involvement with Latin American exiles, and especially the Venezuelan revolutionary General Francisco de Miranda, "El Precursor" (1750–1816). (Miranda was also a friend of Tom Paine, and also Burns's connections Dr John Moore, Col William Fullarton and Dr William Maxwell.) Born into a wealthy Caracas family, Miranda had served in the Spanish army on the side of the American colonists during the Revolutionary War, whose example inspired similar aspirations for his oppressed homeland. In the 1780s he travelled in Europe, schemed with Pitt and other European leaders to send an expeditionary force to liberate Spain's American colonies, and served as a general in the section of the French Revolutionary army commanded by General Charles Dumouriez, fighting in the 1792 campaign in the Netherlands. The story of Dumouriez's defection to the Royalist forces will be familiar to many Burnsians, and clearly disgusted the poet:

> You're welcome to Despots, Dumourier;
> You're welcome to Depots, Dumourier.—
>
> …
>
> Then let us fight about,
> 'Till freedom's spark is out,
> Then we'll all be damned no doubt—Dumourier. (vol. 2, p. 680)

---

[26]   *Letters*, Ross Roy (ed.), vol. 1, p. 428.

[27]   Nigel Leask, "Burns and the Poetics of Abolition," in Gerry Carruthers (ed.), *The Edinburgh Companion to Robert Burns* (Edinburgh, 2009).

[28]   Nigel Leask, "Salons, Alps and Cordilleras: Helen Maria Williams, Alexander von Humboldt, and the Discourse of Romantic Travel," in E. Eger, C. Grant, C. O'Gallchoir, and P. Warburton (eds), *Women, Writing and the Public Sphere 1700–1830* (Cambridge, 2001), pp. 217–38.

Although Miranda remained loyal to the Republican side, he was arrested in 1793 and publicly denounced by Marat. Sporadically imprisoned and persecuted, he fled to London in 1798, where over the next fourteen years he continued tirelessly to lobby for the formation of an independent Latin American empire (which he termed "Colombia") ruled by a hereditary emperor to be designated "the Inca." In the early 1790s Miranda had frequented Helen Williams's salon in Paris, and in the 1793 volume of her *Letters from France* she published translations of his letters back from the front, representing him as a republican hero and fully exonerating him from any involvement in Dumouriez's defection.

In London, Miranda's home at 27 Grafton St (famous for its extensive library) became the nerve center of a group of exiled Latin American revolutionaries, most notably his fellow Caraqueño Simón Bolivar and Andrés Bello—much to the embarrassment of the British Tory government, it should be said, who after 1809 pursued an official policy of support for its new Spanish ally against Napoleon. After an abortive attempt to liberate Venezuela in 1806, Miranda eventually returned to lead the first republic of Columbia, which declared itself independent in 1810, but he died in prison in Caracas in 1816 after defeat by Spanish counter-revolutionary forces. During his absence and after his death, 27 Grafton St (now home to Andres Bello and his English family) became a center for the recruitment of English, Irish, Scots, and Welsh mercenaries and liberal sympathizers; under the banner of the "British Legion," led by Simon Bolivar, they played a crucial role in defeating the Spanish armies at the battles of Boyaca and Carbobo in 1821, in what is now Columbia, although they took heavy casualties.[29]

Miranda also provides a link to Robert Burns's other significant Latin American connection, John Allen (1771–1843). After the death of her husband, Allen's mother had married Burns's friend and correspondent Robert Cleghorn, who farmed at Saughton Mills near Edinburgh. Cleghorn, a keen member of the Crochallan Fencibles, is mainly remembered as recipient of Burns's bawdry and "old Cloaciniad song[s],"[30] but the poet also consulted him on agricultural matters and introduced him to his friend the farming expert Tennant of Glenconner. In August 1795, Cleghorn and his stepson John Allen (who, after qualifying as a medical doctor at Edinburgh University in 1791, was lecturing on medical topics and translating Cuvier's *Study of the Animal Economy*) visited Burns in Dumfries, where they made up a party with John Syme and Dr Maxwell.[31] In 1801, Allen was employed as physician to accompany Lord Holland (C.J. Fox's nephew and

---

[29]   See José Luis Salcedo-Bastardo, "Bello and The 'Symposium' of Grafton Street," in Lynch (ed.), *Andres Bello: The London Years*, pp. 57–65; and Joseph F. Thorning, *Miranda: World Citizen* (Gainesville, 1952).

[30]   *Letters*, Ross Roy (ed.), vol. 2, p. 126.

[31]   The visit is described in *Letters of Robert Burns*, vol. 2, pp. 365–6, 373–4 ("To Robert Cleghorn," 21 August 1795 [Letter 680] and January 1796 [Letter 687] respectively). To my knowledge the "Mr Allan" mentioned by Burns here has never before been identified as being Dr John Allen.

intellectual focus of the Whig opposition) on his tour of Spain and Portugal: they visited Helen Williams's Paris salon *en passant*. The trip, repeated in 1809 on the eve of the Peninsular campaign, laid the foundation for Allen's expertise in Hispanic language, history, and politics. The relationship prospered to the extent that Dr "Jack" Allen was permanently employed as Holland's secretary and librarian at Holland House, playing an active part in forging the influential links between the *Edinburgh Reviewers* and Holland's London circle. It was here that in 1813 Allen befriended Lord Byron and showed him some of Burns's letters to his stepfather, including the scatological song "There was twa wives," eliciting Byron's famous comment, "What an antithetical mind!—tenderness, roughness—delicacy, coarseness—sentiment, sensuality—soaring and grovelling, dirt and deity—all mixed up in that one compound of inspired clay!"[32]

Allen published five seminal articles on Latin American affairs in the *Edinburgh Review* between 1806 and 1810, making him perhaps Britain's leading expert in the field and giving him an important role in forming British public opinion regarding Latin American independence. Perhaps the most famous of the *Edinburgh*'s essays was the 1809 "Emancipation of Spanish America" by another Scot, James Mill, and co-authored by Miranda himself: it appears immediately after Jeffrey's notorious review of Cromek's *Reliques of Robert Burns*, but its republican animus set off alarm bells in the minds of Francis Jeffrey, Holland, and other prominent Whigs.[33] Allen's own earlier pro-emancipationist views underwent a change after his second tour of Spain with Lord Holland in 1809, when he encountered many of the Spanish Liberals who sought to convene (in Cadiz) the first modern Spanish Cortes, including representation for the American colonies. This converted Allen from the cause of independence to that of reconciling the rebellious colonies with the mother country, partly in the fear that Napoleon had his eyes on Spanish America. Allen's change of heart explains why his later *Edinburgh Review* essays repudiated the policies of revolutionaries such as Miranda, denouncing his political intrigues after his return to Caracas in 1810; they also proposed a confederation of American states ruled by the Spanish crown (but not from the European metropolis), complemented by complete freedom of commerce.[34] (This was a view surprisingly close to that aired in the *Edinburgh*'s rival *Quarterly Review*, written by Coleridge's friend Joseph Blanco White, recommending constitutional monarchy and reconciliation with Spain.)

The case of John Allen leads me to my final Latin American Burns connection, the Venezuelan intellectual and poet Andrés Bello; despite the fact that Bello was

---

[32] George Gordon, Lord Byron, "Extracts from Byron's journal" (1813), in *Robert Burns: The Critical Heritage*, Donald A. Low (ed.) (London and Boston, 1974), pp. 257–8 (pp. 257–8).

[33] *Edinburgh Review*, 13 (January 1809): 333–53.

[34] José Alberich, "English Attitudes Towards the Hispanic World in the Time of Bello as Reflected by the *Edinburgh Review* and *Quarterly Review*," in Lynch (ed.), *Andrés Bello: The London Years*, pp. 67–81 (p. 72).

twenty-two years Burns's junior, and there was no direct contact between the two men, his career and writing suggest some interesting analogies with the Ayrshire poet. Andrés Bello arrived in London in July 1810 in company with Bolivar and Luis Lopez Mendez as part of a diplomatic mission to the British Foreign Secretary, the Marquis Wellesley. He stayed rather longer than he had planned, until February 1829, when he returned to Latin America to assume a senior political post for the Chilean government, accompanied by his English second wife and their children. Bello is perhaps the archetypal romantic exile: Rafael Caldera writes that during his nineteen years in London, Andrés Bello "became fully aware of a sense of American identity, of what his America was, of what it could and could not achieve."[35] His friendship with the other Spanish American exiles in London reinforced his notion of the *patria*, and the need to give it form and features; his vehicle for this ambitious task was the launch of two journals, the *Biblioteca Americano* (1823) and the *Repertorio Americana* (1826). Amongst their miscellaneous and patriotic articles,[36] the journals featured two fragments of Bello's unfinished epic poem *America*, entitled *Alocución a la Poesía* and *Silva a la agricultura de la zona tórrida*. The latter, deeply inspired by the example of Francisco Miranda, is the most interesting for my present purposes, as it reveals the agrarian and georgic foundations upon which Bello's ideology of *americanismo* was constructed. Beyond the all-pervasive influence of Virgil's *Georgics* lay the model of Rafael Landivar's wonderful *Rusticatio Mexicano* (1772), a patriotic celebration of Mexican and Guatamalan nature and agriculture composed in 5,000 Latin hexameters. *Rusticatio* was written in Bologna after the author, a Jesuit priest, had been expelled from Mexico at the suppression of the order by Carlos III in 1765.[37] While Landivar's poem seems oblivious of the political storm ahead, Bello's openly saluted the triumph of Spanish American independence as an era of georgic prosperity: "Salve, fecunda zona";

> Tú tejes al verano su guirnalda
> De granadas espigas; tú la uva
> Das a la hirviente cuba;

[35]   Rafael Caldera, "Bello in London: the Incomprehensible Sojourn," in Lynch (ed.), *Andrés Bello: The London Years*, pp. 1–6 (p. 4).

[36]   The *Reportorio* was divided into sections dealing with "Humanities," "Sciences," and "Moral Sciences." Articles in the former section include "Use of the Barometer," "Description of the Orinoco between the Falls of Guaharivos and the Straits of Guaviare," "Instructions for improving the production of Cotton," "Description of Mixtec Cochineal, its husbandry and uses," "Census of the population of the Republic of Colombia." Literary material includes, in addition to Bello's poem, Olmedo's "Canto a Bolivar," J.V. Garcia's "Canto a la independencia de Guatamala," "Las poesías de Horacio" traducido por D. Javier de Burgos, "Bibliografia Espanola, Antigua y moderna" etc. (Aristobulo Pardo, review of *El Repertorio Americano, Thesaurus, BICC*, 30 [1975]: 176–9).

[37]   For a modern edition with parallel Latin and Spanish texts, see Rafael Landivar, *Rusticatio Mexicana: Por los Campos de México*, Prólogo, Versión y Notas de Octaviano Valdés (Mexico, 1965).

No de purpúrea fruta, o roja o gualda,
A tus florestas bellas
Falta matiz alguno; y bebe en ellas
Aromas mil el viento y greyes van sin cuento
Paciendo tu verdura desde el llano
Que tiene por lindero el horizonte, hasta el erguido monte,
De inaccessible nieve siempre cano.

(You weave for the summer its garland
of heavy grain; you give the grape
to the bubbling cask;
not a single shade of fruit, purple, red or white
lacks in your beautiful forests, where the wind
drinks in a thousand fragrances,
where herds without number
graze your pastures, from the plains
whose boundary is the horizon
to the uplifted mountains,
eternally white with inaccessible snows.)[38]

Although Bello's female personification of the "fecunda zona" here resembles Burns's tutelary local muse Coila in "The Vision," his poetic form and syntax is a far cry from Burns's more characteristic verse. Mary Louise Pratt, in her fine discussion of Bello's *Silva* in *Imperial Eyes*, notes the irony that the poem's

> claims for rusticity are made in the least rustic, most learned poetic rhetoric Spanish afforded at the time; [although] this cultivated Spanish is peppered with Americanist historical and material referents—*Aztec, yarravi, Caupolican, yucca*—that Bello rightly felt obliged to explain in footnotes.[39]

(She forebears from mentioning that in 1847 Bello published a *Gramática de la lengua castellana, destinada al uso de los americanos* [*Grammar of the Spanish Language for the use of Americans*] equivalent to the work of Noah Webster in North America, in an attempt to "americanise" the Spanish language of his native continent).

Pratt also writes perceptively about the manner in which Bello's poem transculturates Humboldt's romantic representation of American nature as part of a "creole process of self-invention."[40] In stark contrast to the historical reality of the Anglo-American "capitalist vanguard" inaugurating the boom and bust economy of mining, sisal, and rubber in the newly independent Latin

---

[38] This passage and the poem in general are discussed by Mary Louise Pratt in *Imperial Eyes*, pp. 172–82. I use Pratt's translation here. Her text is based on the 1952 edition of Bello's *Obras Completas*, vol. 1 (Caracas, 1952), pp. 65–74.

[39] Pratt, *Imperial Eyes,* p. 174.

[40] Ibid., p. 175.

American republics, Bello's America was agrarian and non-capitalist. (In contrast to *Rusticatio Mexicano*, there is no reference to mineral wealth.)[41] Although this suggests a "dialogic response to the commodifying, greed-glazed gaze of the English engineers,"[42] the poem exemplifies the common tendency of the syntax of georgic poetry to leave the agency of labor unspecified. As Pratt indicates, Creole civic consciousness found it difficult to represent those Americans (indigenous, mestizo, afro-American) "in whose names, and by whose bodies, the wars with Spain were fought, whose labours would build the new republics, and whose continued subjugation formed the basis for EuroAmerican privilege. In the esthetic as in the political realm, the unquiet American multitudes could not be dealt with."[43]

Both Bello and Burns would have endorsed Arthur Young's remark in his essay "On the Pleasures of Agriculture": "We may talk what we please of lilies and lions rampant, and spread eagles in the fields d'or or d'argent; but if heraldry were guided by reason, a plough in a field of arable would be the most noble and antient arms."[44] Bello sought to create a new poetic voice and agrarian identity for post-colonial, creole Latin America, whereas Burns's poetry engaged the Scots language and cultural tradition with the forces of capitalist modernity, especially as represented by the revolutionary social changes wrought by agricultural "improvement." Although no direct influence can be proven, there are other affinities between Bellos's *Agricultura de la zona tórrida* and Burns's most georgic poem "The Vision" beyond the presence of a female tutelary muse, especially in the passage where Coila's sisters inspire Scotland's patriotic statesmen, improvers and poets:

> "They Scotia's Race among them share;
> Some fire the *Sodger* on to dare;
> Some rouse the *Patriot* up to bare
>   Corruption's heart:
> Some teach the *Bard*, a darling care,
>   The tuneful Art." (vol. 1, p. 110)

The agricultural theme is also strongly marked here:

> "When yellow waves the heavy grain,
> The threat'ning *Storm*, some, strongly, rein;
> Some teach to meliorate the plain,

---

[41] The durability of the agrarian ideal in the discourse of Latin American patriotism is still evident in Mexican critic Alfonso Reyes's essay "Virgil in Mexico" (1930) when he asks, in a discussion of Father Miguel Hidalgo, the great Mexican *insurgente*: "the Virgilian union of agriculture and poetry—was that not perhaps the dream of Hidalgo, the dream of the father of his country?" (Alfonso Reyes, *The Position of America, and Other Essays*, trans. Harriet de Onis [New York, 1950], pp. 154–5).

[42] Pratt, *Imperial Eyes*, p. 178.

[43] Ibid., p. 180.

[44] Qtd. in Kenneth MacLean, *Agrarian Age: A Background for Wordsworth* (New Haven, 1950), p. 11.

With *tillage-skill*;
And some instruct the Shepherd-train,
  Blythe o'er the hill." (vol. 1, p. 111)

Yet there is a difference: Burns was able to give the discourse of nation a distinctively democratic and modern inflection through the use of Scots vernacular, and by reinventing the generic possibilities of both pastoral and georgic.[45] As Coila expresses it, Burns can offer a poetic voice that cannot simply be overshadowed by English Augustan convention as represented by Thomson, Shenstone or Gray;

"Yet, all beneath th' unrivall'd Rose,
The lowly Daisy sweetly blows;
Tho' large the forest's Monarch throws
  His army shade,
Yet green the juicy Hawthorn grows
  Adown the glade." (vol. 1, p. 113)

One can imagine that this would have resonated with Andrés Bello in his attempt to inaugurate the georgic muse of "Gran Columbia," a voice newly emancipated from the shadow of the imperial Spanish poetic canon, and the dominance of *peninsular* culture. Yet, we might ask in conclusion, what would Bello the creole poet have made of Burns's syntax of labor, and his critical questioning of social hierarchy, so signally absent from his own patriotic georgic vision, as in these lines from "Man was Made to Mourn":

The Sun that overhangs yon moors,
Out-spreading far and wide,
Where hundreds labour to support
A haughty lordling's pride;
...
If I'm design'd yon lordling's slave,
By Nature's law design'd,
Why was an independent wish
E'er planted in my mind? (vol. 1, pp. 117, 118)

Burns here interrogates the meaning of the word "independence" with more rigor than could Bello in presaging a democratic future based on emancipated labor as well as national self-determination. Perhaps in this light it is easier to understand why Latin America had to wait until that century of social revolutions, the twentieth, before Burns was translated into its own native idiom.

---

[45] See Nigel Leask, *Robert Burns and Pastoral: Poetry and Improvement in Late Eighteenth-Century Scotland* (Oxford, 2010).

PART 4
Robert Burns and
Transatlantic Cultural Memory

Chapter 9
Robert Burns's
Transatlantic Afterlives

Susan Manning

I see amid the fields of Ayr
A ploughman, who, in foul and fair,
  Sings at his task
So clear, we know not if it is
The laverock's song we hear, or his,
  Nor care to ask.
…
For now he haunts his native land
As an immortal youth; his hand
  Guides every plough;
He sits beside each ingle-nook,
His voice is in each rushing brook,
  Each rustling bough.
His presence haunts this room to-night,
A form of mingled mist and light
  From that far coast,
Welcome beneath this roof of mine!
Welcome! This vacant chair is thine,
  Dear guest and ghost![1]

I was talking about time. It's so hard for me to believe in it. Some things go. Pass
on. Some things just stay. I used to think it was my rememory. You know. Some
things you forget. Other things you never do. But it's not. Places, places are still
there. If a house burns down, it's gone, but the place—the picture of it—stays,
and not just in my rememory, but out there, in the world. What I remember is a
picture floating around out there outside my head. I mean, even if I don't think it,
even if I die, the picture of what I did, or knew, or saw, is still out there.[2]

Henry Wadsworth Longfellow and Toni Morrison write about the inseparability of
memory from imagination, the shaping process that the past exerts on the present,
and the present on the past. Longfellow's "Robert Burns," first published in
Harper's New Monthly Magazine in August 1880, is a vision of an event somewhere

[1] "Robert Burns," *The Complete Poetical Works of Henry Wadsworth Longfellow*
(Boston and New York, 1894), p. 397.
[2] Toni Morrison, *Beloved* (London, 1987), pp. 35– 6.

between memory and projection; the poet never visited Scotland, although the opportunity might have presented itself on one of several trips to England. His immortal ploughman, laverock, and ingle-nook are literary tokens that would have been immediately familiar to his American readers, for they were the currency of hundreds of tributes to Burns. Longfellow's poem contributes to a larger phenomenon identified by cultural critics. "[T]he same restricted range of images, tones, rhetorical tropes, and ideological tendencies," writes Colin McArthur, has tended to define discourse about Scotland and Scots. This he calls the Scottish "discursive unconscious ... that may be tapped consciously or unconsciously by those seeking to assert or describe their relation to 'Scottishness'."[3] Although it does not feature amongst McArthur's instances, the transatlantic afterlife of "Robert Burns"—man and poet—looks like a perfect example of the workings of the "Scottish Discursive Unconscious," promulgated through poetic imitations, Burns Club suppers, biographies, and political citation. As we know, the Burns cult gained momentum through the nineteenth century, associating itself with (and contributing to) the celebratory Kailyardism and Highlandism derided by Scottish Modernists and more recently deconstructed by cultural studies.

Exposing the discursive markers of international Scottishness through Burns's transatlantic afterlives as at best expressions of unthinking conventionality and at worst a kind of bad faith is, sadly, easily done. But if we want to understand *why* tropes and images of plowman laddies, laverocks wild, and sprigs of heather proved so powerful and so adaptable to new conditions, we need to unbind the taxonomies and consider individual instances. What does it mean to map a poetic afterlife, and more particularly, a transposed or dislocated afterlife? We have sound methods for mapping demographic and bibliographic migration: when people and books travel, we can enumerate, situate, and evaluate their movements. Tracing the transatlantic editions and biographies of Burns suggests some measure of the popularity of the poet; it is a significant fact that people, often not wealthy, thought it worth their while to fork out sometimes substantial sums from meager resources to acquire a relic of the national bard of a faraway land.[4] These records enable us to infer quite a lot about migration patterns, the reading habits of emigrants, the material forms of tradition and transmission, and many other things. They do not, however, tell us about *affect*, except in a quantitative sense—and this was clearly considerable around "Robert Burns" in nineteenth-century North America. Who was "Robert Burns" to his transatlantic readers, and what did his poems mean to them?

---

[3]   Colin McArthur, "Transatlantic Scots and the Scottish Discursive Unconscious," in Celeste Ray (ed.), *Transatlantic Scots* (Tuscaloosa, 2005), pp. 339–56 (p. 340).

[4]   See, for example, James Grant Wilson, *American Editions of Robert Burns's Poems* (New York, 1900), and Anna M. Painter, "American Editions of the *Poems* of Burns before 1800," *The Library*, 4th series, 12 (1932): 434–56. See also Fiona Black's chapter in this volume.

If these are not questions that can be addressed through bibliographic records, neither are they necessarily best approached through the testimonies of the nineteenth-century public figures whose voices have become canonical. In his centenary Burns Night address of 1859, Ralph Waldo Emerson praised Burns's poetry for "giving voice to ... middle-class Nature."[5] Carol McGuirk has noted astutely that the reality of Burns's near-hopeless poverty, his social status, and his rage against these was unavailable to middle-class inheritors of upwardly mobile American ideology.[6] The image of Burns received by Emerson, Longfellow, Whitman, and Margaret Fuller may be readily traced to James Currie's biography and collection of 1800, whose parameters were set by a Scottish Enlightenment debate on the character of genius and its relation to morality. The full title of Henry Mackenzie's review, after all, was *"Surprising effects of Original Genius, exemplified in the Poetical Productions of* Robert Burns, *an Ayrshire Ploughman."*[7] This was the image of Burns which fitted the conceptual framework of the Scottish literati; it was scarcely surprising that it should also appeal to a generation of American writers brought up on the *Lectures* of Hugh Blair and the criticism of *The Mirror* and *The Lounger*.[8]

Poetic ideas travel in rather different ways from intellectual ideas, however: rhythms, echoes, voices, and images disperse "influence" beyond the reach of documentary trace but are still available to that combination of memory and imagination which constitutes emotional familiarity. Some images and some lives seem to carry huge resonance for large numbers of people in a way that others do not. Samuel Taylor Coleridge, for example, was an immensely important figure for American nineteenth-century Romanticism, and a would-be emigrant who, enamored of American freedoms, planned at one stage to settle in the Susquehanna valley. Thus far, quite similar to Burns. But he did not become the subject of poems by emigrants, nor did his poems pervade popular verse. Burns's "life," in contrast, was integral to the broadly based reception of his poetry, on both sides of the Atlantic. "Life" has to be in inverted commas here, and should probably be in the plural, because there were many versions of the biographical story, answering in each case as much to the needs of the construer as to the actual life

---

5   Ralph Waldo Emerson, "Speech at Burns Centenary Dinner in Boston, January 1859," in Donald A. Low (ed.), *Robert Burns: The Critical Heritage* (London and Boston, 1974), pp. 434–6 (p. 435).

6   Carol McGuirk, "Haunted by Authority: Nineteenth-Century American Constructions of Robert Burns and Scotland," in Robert Crawford (ed.), *Robert Burns and Cultural Authority* (Iowa City, 1997), pp. 136–58 (p. 145).

7   Henry Mackenzie, *"Surprising effects of Original Genius, exemplified in the Poetical Productions of* Robert Burns, *an Ayrshire Ploughman,"* in the *Lounger*, 97 (9 December 1786), qtd. in Low (ed.), *Robert Burns: The Critical Heritage*, pp. 67–71.

8   Blair's *Lectures on Rhetoric and Belles Lettres* (1783) was part of the Harvard curriculum and a popular college text in Britain and America throughout the nineteenth century. His Lecture 38 "On the Origin and Progress of Poetry" gives an account of poetry as the passionate utterance of natural man.

of the subject. Burns himself was the most significant of these fabricators. In this essay I shall argue that two of his self-images in particular color his transatlantic poetic "afterlives": two versions chronologically separated by the publication and Edinburgh success of his poetry.

Emerson declared in his address to the Burns Club of Boston that "The people who care nothing for literature and poetry care for Burns"; an obvious statement, perhaps, but a significant one. A compound resonance of biography and memory structures the transatlantic afterlives of the "figure of Burns" which simultaneously instantiated and diverted the political implications of the class and economic pressures driving nineteenth-century emigration. Burns's transatlantic afterlives emerge in the writing of emigrants who may have carried copies of the poet amongst their precious and scant possessions, who may have bought copies of the early American reprints of his works—or who may simply have heard stories of the poet, or recited or sung his work. Emigrant admirers whose experience of hardship in Scotland reflected (or came, in retrospect, to reflect) Burns's own, created a distinctive version of their Bard from an image initially shaped by the poet himself.

The National Library of Scotland holds an extensive archive of emigrants' correspondence and personal narratives. A collection of thirty-two letters related to the family connections of the Kerrs of Dalry in Ayrshire between 1820 and 1883 includes an interesting example from 1822. The writer, emigrant James Boyle, has no literary or stylistic pretension; his main concern is to convey information about agriculture and the market, but—or and—the documentary account concludes with a poem that, looking backwards towards Scotland, adds an emotional dimension apparently inconsistent with the enterprise and aspiration of the prose description:

> ... specie or barter is the basis of commerce but the withdrawing of so much of the circulation Medium has reduced the p[ric]e of property one halph[.] A fine time to purtches property hear and also a good time to draw mony from Scotland as ther is 13 per cent of premium abuve par but we can get littel mony hear but our litle [w]ants is suplied by Barter[,] but our wants is few the woods supl[y] ing us with fuel shugar tea soap from our ashes and the Offal of Hogs milk beef lether of skins of our cattle f'lax hemp corn wheat rye Oats tobaco Potatoes buce wheat cotton onyone by field [?]cuttor with a variety of Mellons coucombers […] pumkings pomreganets goavas castor oyle Beans besides culinary herbs and Medical plants besides fruits piches Aples grapes cherrys Plumes Pears Squinches &c Ther is a spirit of Emulation in our country for trading to New Orle[ans] with our produce[.] I woud go myself if I could live long and I think mony will soon get more plentiful[.] Ther is a great many steam boats trading on the Ohio which makes [?] easy and expeditious. I can add no more but ever remain your sincer Brother[.] My compliments to all freands and inquirers a[cq] uaintances[.] May god prosper you and all my welwishers
>
>   James Boyle

There is no break—graphic or textual—between this and the verse squeezed into the bottom of the page:

O Scotia dear though far awa
Some times a silent tear will fa
Whin eer we fondly think on a
We left in Caledonia
Our father's home we cant forget
Thy sun though clouded is not set
Bright may it shine in glory yet
Like lang syne Calledonia.
Ever happy may thow be
Caledonia, Caledonia
Ever virtuous ever free.[9]

A scribbled note up the side of the page indicates "Tune Dainty Davie." The best known words to this jaunty tune are Burns's, published in the *Merry Muses of Caledonia*. It is also known as an alternative tune for Burns's signature song "Rantin Rovin Robin." Although expurgated editions of *The Merry Muses* began to be published around 1800, it is more likely that the tune was known to James Boyle from other sources; "Dainty Davie" was familiar to fiddlers, and is also found in William Vickers's collection of fiddle music.[10] It is amongst the tunes Harry R. Stevens identified as being commonly known in Cincinnati by 1824.[11] Its tone is resolutely upbeat: despite the nostalgic lyric set to it here, the implication (endorsed by the prospects for prosperity expressed in the body of the letter) must be that emigration has not been a mistake. Old "Scotia dear" is a fond and familiar memory but not an unhappy one. Words of apparent lamentation are belied by the manner of performance: what Boyle's fellow-Ayrshireman, fellow-emigrant and poet Hew Ainslie would call "the land far awa'" is the location of sorrow, viewed from a perspective of betterment.

As verse, "O Scotia dear" seems strikingly adept in relation to the workaday prose that precedes it; the marking of "Chorus" on the right-hand side of the transcription suggests that the song may not have been original to the letter writer. It was not uncommon for poems to be shared and circulated freely amongst emigrants; whoever the original author, the echoes of "The Cotter's Saturday Night" are surely meant to be heard:

---

[9]   Kerr Family Correspondence, Manuscripts Division, National Library of Scotland, Acc. 11416. I am grateful to Kevin Halliwell of the National Library of Scotland for drawing my attention to this letter and to Maria Castrillo (also of the National Library) for help with the Kerr Family Correspondence.

[10]   William Vickers's original manuscript is now held in the collection of the Newcastle-upon-Tyne Society of Antiquaries.

[11]   Harry R. Stevens, "Folk Music on the Midwestern Frontier, 1788–1825," *Ohio Archaeological and Historical Quarterly*, 57 (1948): 126–46.

O Scotia! my dear, my native soil!
　　For whom my warmest wish to Heaven is sent!
Long may thy hardy sons of *rustic toil*
　　Be blest with health and peace and sweet content![12]

Or, even more clearly, Burns's "Farewell to the Brethren of St James's Lodge, Tarbolton," of 1786, an intensely empathetic, if proleptic, evocation of the feelings of the emigrant, from the moment when Burns viewed his own future as lying across the Atlantic:

Adieu! a heart-warm, fond adieu!
　　Dear brothers of the *mystic tye*!
Ye favour'd, ye enlighten'd Few,
　　Companions of my social joy!
Tho' I to foreign lands must hie,
　　Pursuing Fortune's slidd'ry ba',
With melting heart, and brimful eye,
　　I'll mind you still, tho' far awa'.

Oft have I met your social Band,
　　And spent the chearful, festive night;
Oft, honor'd with supreme command,
　　Presided o'er the *Sons of light*:
And by that *Hieroglyphic* bright,
　　Which none but *Craftsmen* ever saw!
Strong Mem'ry on my heart shall write
　　Those happy scenes when far awa'
...
And *You*, farewell! whose merits claim,
　　Justly that *highest badge* to wear!
Heav'n bless your honor'd, noble Name,
　　To Masonry and Scotia dear!
A last request, permit me here,
　　When yearly ye assemble a',
One *round*, I ask it with a *tear*,
　　To him, *the Bard, that's far awa'*. (vol. 1, p. 271)

The imaginative intensity contained within the perfect rhyme pattern is compelling, inevitable; it might readily become an emotional vehicle for less articulate, but actual, emigrants.

　　Here is an example of how Burns's poetry was internalized and carried into new worlds in ways more intimate than bibliographic evidence can suggest. It involves more than the idea of conscious memorizing; the echoes of Burns a reader will

---

[12]　*The Poems and Songs of Robert Burns*, James Kinsley (ed.) (3 vols, Oxford, 1968), vol. 1, p. 151; subsequent quotations from Burns's poetry are from this edition and will be cited in the text by volume and page number.

hear in "O Scotia dear though far awa" are embedded more like the layered "re-memorying" that Toni Morrison writes about in *Beloved*, which for her character Sethe is a matter of survival through unremittingly hostile circumstances. It entails an imaginative level of engagement with the past that goes beyond mere memory, keeping places and people alive in the mind, sometimes by reinventing them or oneself. It acts as both a form of resistance to and a form of acknowledgement of new circumstances. When Scots emigrants engaged in this kind of re-memorying they simultaneously projected their own experience onto Burns and his poetry, and used these to give meaning and shape to that experience. In the case of this letter, it might in principle be possible to establish a documentary connection between the poet and the correspondent: was the James Boyle who wrote to his "brother" a fellow Ayrshire mason as well as a family member?[13] Did he possess or purchase or hear these poems either prior to emigration, or subsequently in America? Whether or not he had firsthand experience of Ayrshire masonry, what is significant in the present context is that the emigrant correspondent is living Burns's own might-have-been: James Boyle's is the kind of letter Burns himself might have written back to *his* kin in Ayrshire, had his plans to emigrate not been turned aside by the success of the Kilmarnock edition. And without the poems echoed in the letter, Boyle's understanding and evocation of his own experience would have been differently shaped.

The poignancy of the emigrant experience was a popular theme on both sides of the Atlantic throughout the nineteenth century. Michael Vance has noted that a prize was offered at the first Caledonian Games in Toronto in 1859 for the best poem in "broad Scots" on the theme of "The Emigrant," for example.[14] The *soi-disant* "Burns of Canada," Alexander McLachlan, was a Chartist sympathizer who emigrated in 1840, later sublimating his radicalism in collections of poetry including *The Emigrant and Other Poems* (1861). In Britain, a broadside ballad from around 1880 called "The Song of the Emigrant" printed by the "Poet's Box" of the Overgate, Dundee and sold for a penny, offers a reprise of both vocabulary and mood. The ballad embeds extensive references to Burns's songs as markers of Scotland and Scottishness held in the childhood memories of a now-distant homeland:

> I'm lying on a foreign shore,
> An' hear the birdies sing,
> They speak tae me o' Auld Langsyne,
> And sunny memories bring.
> Oh, but to see a weel-kent face,
> Or hear a Scottish lay,
> As sang in years lang, lang bye-gane,

---

13 Hugh and John Kerr are recorded as founder members of the Dalry Burns Club in 1826. See http://www.dalryburnsclub.org.uk/founders/founders.html.

14 Michael Vance, "Organized Scottishness in Canada," in Celeste Ray (ed.), *Transatlantic Scots* (Tuscaloosa, 2005), pp. 96–119 (p. 104).

They haunt me nicht and day.
My hair ance like the raven's wing,
Noo mixed wi' siller threeds,
Mind me o' ane wha used to sing
O' Scotia's valiant deeds;
She sang, while I stood at her knee,
The dear sangs o' langsyne,
  "Auld Robin Gray," an' "Scots Wae Hae,"
Or "Myrtle Groves," sae fine.

She sang to me "The White Cockade,"
She sang "The Rowan Tree,"
"There was a lad was born in Kyle,"
An' "Bonnie Bessie Lee."
Whaur is the sang can melt the heart,
Or gaur the saut tear fa',
Like auld Scotch sangs sae dear to me,
Noo that I'm far awa'.
I've watched the sun at morning tide
Strike o'er the lofty Ben,
I watch him yet wi' greedy e'e,
To where he sets again.
I ken he shines on Scotia's shore,
Though far across the sea,
While I being have I'll sing—
My native land of thee.[15]

Like others of its type, the ballad would have circulated locally at market days and feeing days; sung in the street by hawkers and sold for a penny, it would have resonated particularly with relatives of emigrants, recipients of letters like James Boyle's to his Kerr relatives. As Morrison's Sethe puts it, "Places, places are still there. If a house burns down, it's gone—but the place—the picture of it stays." Ballads like this acted as a kind of collective re-memory, articulating a "picture" of the past and keeping the places left behind differently alive in the memories of individual readers and hearers. General tropes allow a particular image of a "lofty Ben" or a stretch of "Scotia's shore" to form in the mind. The songs, rather than the person, of Scotland's bard "haunt" this ballad, as they are assumed already to permeate the imaginations of its performer and audience. "'Auld Robin Gray' an' 'Scots Wae Hae'" [*sic*] are mnemonics of affect rather than precise memories, the shared baggage of those bound together by the momentous emotional upheaval of the transatlantic crossing. Again, the empathetic texture is complex: reminiscences of loss and past time blend with familiarity, community, and belonging. The

---

[15]   Information about the ballad and its circulation is drawn from the following website: "The Word on the Street," National Library of Scotland, http://www.nls.uk/broadsides/broadside.cfm/id/14940, accessed 8 May 2009.

hardship of the life remembered is occluded in nostalgia, but tacitly acknowledged in the refusal to wish oneself back in it.

This and other relatively late examples (broadsides had begun to decline as a popular medium of information following the lifting of tax on newspapers in 1855) suggest that the transferable power of Burns's verse remained strong in the transatlantic imaginary towards the end of the nineteenth century. Tags such as "Scotia dear," "auld langsyne," and "far awa'" gained in intensity through repetition; they speak less of the kind of semantically lazy sentimentalism disparaged by McArthur than of a shared lexicon for an experience that had little precedent for ordinary people before the late eighteenth century. Near the beginning of this Scottish exodus, Burns's capacity to intuit and to inflect so precisely the emotional freight of a journey he was never in the event to make established the terms in which it would be articulated by generations who did cross the Atlantic in the following century. Trying to account for the popularity of Burns in America near the end of the nineteenth century, John G. Dow, a Scottish immigrant to Madison, Wisconsin, wrote of the intensifying power of memory amidst "strange scenes, strange faces, and alien tongues": "Then it is that Burns's poetry, and more especially his songs, offer a rallying ground for troops of affectionate reminiscences and vague emotions that arise from instincts of the blood."[16] Dow insists that Burns's poetry does not simply "reflect" the country life of Scotland, but "gathers up" and "interprets" it, intensifying and clarifying its effects in the memories of emigrant readers and audiences, and validating their hardships.[17] J.G. Whittier's testimony in 1840 was echoed by others throughout the century:

> With clearer eyes I saw the worth
>   Of life among the lowly;
> The Bible at his Cotter's hearth
>   Had made my own more holy.[18]

Why did people believe this to be so? Both Burns's farewell to his fellow freemasons published in 1786 and the anonymous ballad circulated in Scotland a century later are verbally and emotionally contiguous at many points to Boyle's unpublished letter of 1822: the memory of Burns's poetry was reconfigured formally and generically and given new significance in a transatlantic context of circulation. It hardly seems appropriate to talk about influence here; neither would it make sense to trace a genealogy when direct connections are unlikely and so many different examples might have been adduced. Gilles Deleuze and Felix Guattari's

---

[16]   John G. Dow, "Burns in America," in vol. 6 of J.D. Ross (comp.), *Burnsiana* (1897), in Low (ed.), *Robert Burns: The Critical Heritage*, pp. 439–40 (p. 439).

[17]   Ibid.

[18]   J.G. Whittier, "Burns. On receiving a sprig of heather in blossom," in *The Complete Poetical Works of Whittier*, H.E. Scudder (ed.) (Boston, 1894), pp. 196–7, qtd. in Low (ed.), *Robert Burns: The Critical Heritage*, pp. 432–3 (p. 433).

metaphor of the rhizome, an underground root network that may bud or shoot far from its visible source, offers a better model for kinds of connection that are difficult to document and require an imaginative act of engagement. It also allows us to consider the interwoven nature of biographical and poetic responses to "the figure of Burns."[19] The rhizomatic image captures the permeation of an idiom, a medium of evocation, with Burns's poetry at the generative center of an emotional matrix, and Burns's life (actual, imagined, and might-have-been) rewritten in the experience of settlers. What might-have-been in Burns's life conferred legitimacy on the experience of aspirant bards; the poet's evocation of his life as an emigrant itself appears as a pervasive model and repeated trope in their verse. There would be many to assent to Oliver Wendell Holmes's assertion that "Burns ought to have passed ten years of his life in America."[20]

The nineteenth-century group gathered in 1889 by the Scottish-American writer John D. Ross as *Scottish Poets in America* were self-modeled in the image of a Burns who might have been, settled in the land of promise but always with a tear for the memory of "far awa'." In this way, "Burns" became a posthumous model and advocate for settlers who needed both to establish a relationship to their chosen or imposed new environment and to articulate continuing ties to the life they left behind. The Ayrshire poet Hew Ainslie was a paradigmatic case. Unable to provide for his family in Scotland, Ainslie emigrated to America, where, living out the might-have-been, he wrote the exemplary emigrant song "The Lads an' the Land Far Awa'," which integrates the spirit of "Auld Lang Syne" with the remembered "social joy" of the "Address to the Masons":

> When I think on the lads an' the land I ha'e left
> An' how love has been lifted an' friendship been reft;
> How the hinnie o' hope has been jumbled wi' ga',
> Then I sigh for the lads an' the land far awa'.
>
> When I think on the days o' delight we ha'e seen,
> When the flame o' the spirit would spark in the een;
> Then I say, as in sorrow I think o' ye a',
> Where will I find hearts like the hearts far awa?
>
> When I think on the nights we ha'e spent hand in hand,
> Wi' mirth for our sowther, and friendship our band,
> This world gets dark, but ilk night has a daw'!
> And yet I may rejoice in the land far awa'![21]

---

19   Deleuze and Guattari make several key points about the rhizome: "The rhizome is an antigenealogy"; it "deterritorializes" and "reterritorrializes"; "it always has multiple entryways"; "the map has to do with performance" (Gilles Deleuze and Félix Guattari, *A Thousand Plateaus: Capitalism and Schizophrenia*, trans. Brian Massumi [1987; London, 2004], pp. 12, 14).

20   Oliver Wendell Holmes, "Some Aspects of Robert Burns," *Cornhill Magazine* (October 1879): 408–9.

21   Qtd. in John D. Ross, *Scottish Poets in America* (New York, 1889), p. 56.

One of Ainslie's claims to fame (as indicated in his *Pilgrimage to the Land of Burns* [1820], repeated at a meeting of the Burns Club of Brooklyn and reiterated in Ross's account of the poet), was that "before he left Scotland for the first time, [he] had had the honor of kissing Burns' 'bonny Jean' by the banks of the Nith, on the spot where he had composed one of his deathless lyrics."[22] The confusion of pronouns accomplishes the elision—recurrent in Ross's book as in that of his subjects—between Burns and his transatlantic Scottish followers. Where they cannot (as here) in effect *become* Burns, they study his work and ventriloquize his voice: the "fire of Burns" is in the brain of William Cant Sturoc, who "though [in his own words] 'owre the seas an' far awa'… take[s] a hearty interest in all that concerns Scotland"; "Burns became [the] earliest model" for Daniel McIntyre Henderson; Dr John M. Harper writes "after the manner of Burns's 'Twa Dogs'"; Malcolm Taylor's return to Scotland and excursion through Ayrshire in 1874 inspires "a very fine poem on Robert Burns"; Duncan MacGregor Crerar is "Secretary of the Burns Society of [New York]" and "[p]robably the finest of his productions is his poem on Robert Burns"; "'Burns' Poems' was one of the first books placed in [James D. Crichton's] hands as soon as he had learned to read"; and Donald Ramsay is a collector of fine Burns editions, and amuses himself in writing poems on "incident[s] in the life of the Ayrshire Bard."[23] *Scottish Poets in America* reveals the transferable power of this trope: the mind of Andrew Wanless finds "'room only for contemplation of the songs of the old Scotch Bards'"—indeed, "[i]n many points he resembles Burns"; James Kennedy "devoted whatever time he could spare in carefully reading the works of Ramsay, Fergusson, Burns, Scott … and as a result his mind gradually conformed to their style of composition."[24]

This composite figure of the Scottish bard, and its magnetic charm for emigrant poets and readers, is a very particular image, conditioned by Burns's own attempt—after the Edinburgh *éclat* of the Kilmarnock edition of his poems altered his decision to leave Scotland—to formulate a biographical "story" for himself in the aversive re-memory of the life of another Scottish poet.[25] Again, we may approach it through the re-memorying of Ross's American Scots. The first of these is the emigrant Scot Thomas C. Latto, whose three sonnets celebrating Ramsay, Fergusson, and Burns are quoted by Ross in sequence. Common tropes of excess, neglect, abuse, and the triumph of merit connect the latter two:

> Poor, ill-starr'd Robert! I have grieved for thee,
>   Kind, joyous, fired with genius' generous glow,
>   And, save the pendulum too fast would go—

---

[22] Ibid., p. 59.

[23] Ibid., pp. 61, 63, 90, 99, 148, 29, 35, 198, 206.

[24] Ibid., pp. 127, 39.

[25] On Emerson's idea of the aversive stance to authority, see Stanley Cavell, *Emerson's Transcendental Etudes*, David Justin Hodge (ed.) (Stanford, 2003); see also my conference paper "'Ae spark o' Nature's Fire': Was Robert Burns a Transcendental Philosopher?" delivered at Robert Burns 1759–2009 Conference, University of Glasgow, 15–17 January 2009.

Embodiment of mirth's wild witchery;
From Ramsay's lays oft snatching inspiration,
   Indeed, improving upon honest Allan,
     He kythed into the daintiest "rhyming callan',"
Helping e'en Burns to his immortal station.
The "Daft Days" will receive the meed of praise,
   Until "The Holy Fair" with age grows dim;
The "Farmer's Ingle" shed its cheery blaze,
   While Robin's "Cottars" chant their evening hymn;
High Priest of Nature! nobler was the tone
Caught up by thee from lowly Fergusson.[26]

The first line leaves ambiguous the identity of "ill-starr'd Robert" (which one?), and the poet's own first person presence immediately following associates Latto with Burns grieving for Fergusson, his and their posthumous poetic forebear. "Mirth's wild witchery" immediately recalls *Tam O'Shanter*, rather than anything in Fergusson's verse; even the reference to "honest Allan" comes from Burns's poem on pastoral poetry: "Yes! there is ane; a Scottish callan! / There's ane: come forrit, honest Allan!" (vol. 1, p. 192). The sonnet is a poetic palimpsest in which Ramsay, Fergusson, Burns, and Latto echo and impersonate each other until authorship is compounded and confounded in the pairing of their poems with Burns's. In this transatlantic refraction, each poet partakes of and takes further his immediate forebear; the biographical afterlife generates the poetic effect. Afterlife is also pre-life (through another): Ramsay, Fergusson, and Burns all merge in the transatlantic cultural imaginary into an "ideal" Scots poet, what I have been calling the "figure of Burns":

Dying at thirty-eight, two feverish years,
   He snatched, in which to pour those deathless lays
     That 'tis in vain to emulate or praise,
So surely have they distanced all compeers;
It is a marvel, did we but reflect
   How many cultured failures struck the lyre,
Till at one swoop his mountain-muse of fire
Hailed him as God's anointed—sole elect.
And now where is the man, save he alone,
   With immortality's bright singing robe;
Whose songs are sung to earth's remotest zone—
   Whose birthday is a joy throughout the globe?
A simple ploughman from the braes of Ayr
Enjoys a triumph that no king can share.[27]

A single chronological trajectory cannot do justice to this complex weave of associations.

---

[26]   Qtd. in Ross, *Scottish Poets in America*, p. 17.
[27]   Ibid.

We should be aware that the biographical image is carefully crafted and multi-layered. Thomas Latto, like Fergusson, was educated at St Andrews; in 1894, six years after Ross's account, Latto's obituarist in the *New York Times* structured the poet's life around the conflict between his chosen profession of Scotch Law and his poetic proclivities: "literature had more attraction for him than law, and, as several of his poems in local publications attracted wide attention, his future prospects as a lawyer were thereby impaired."[28] This incompatibility of law and poetry may have been a fact of life in early nineteenth-century Scotland; it is certainly a story that the aspiring poet told himself and then to others when he emigrated to America in 1851. There is an oblique and teasing relationship between this account and that of Hew Ainslie, whose *Pilgrimage to the Land of Burns* Latto edited with a biographical memoir, and who Ross described as "enter[ing] upon the study of the law [in Glasgow], but this proving too uncongenial an occupation for one of his temperament, he soon resigned his position."[29] Latto's case proves paradigmatic: the "Scottish Poets" typically make the crossing to America either because they are unable to scratch a living—or a good-enough living—in Scotland, or because their money-getting occupations there are incompatible with the poetic vocation to which they feel called. The association of poetry with hardship in the Old World ("Is there for honest poverty?") ties their experience as emigrants back into Burns's verse with specific intensity unavailable to genteel admirers such as Longfellow and Emerson, with their educational roots in the meliorist traditions of the Scottish Enlightenment. It is impossible at this distance to distinguish between biographical fact and the bio-critical trope of the Romantic poet blasted in his worldly prospects by the uncomprehending hostility of prosaic minds. The categorical difference between the events of a life and the shaping constructions of biography make this not simply an imponderable but a meaningless question. The tale of impoverished merit and ineptitude for worldly gain was certainly true in that this was the life-story believed by and of these transatlantic poets.

Further connections emerge when we align Ross's and the anonymous obituarist's account of Latto's story with Burns's reading of Fergusson's life:

> (O *Ferguson*! thy glorious *parts*,
> Ill-suited *law*'s dry, musty arts!
> My curse upon your whunstane hearts,
>   Ye Enbrugh Gentry!
> The tythe o' what ye waste at *cartes*
>   Wad stow'd his pantry!)
> ("To William Simson, Ochiltree," vol. 1, p. 94)

---

[28] "The Obituary Record," in *The New York Times*, 14 May 1894, *New York Times* Article Archive: 1851–1980, http://query. nytimes.com/mem/archive-free/pdf?_r=1&res= 9D03E7DA1630E033A25757C1A9639C94659ED7CF, accessed 8 May 2009.

[29] Ross, *Scottish Poets in America*, p. 55.

It is this powerful invocation, I suggest, that would later shape the early biographies of Fergusson reprinted on both sides of the Atlantic as prefaces to his poems, and which determined his poetic reputation as unhappy precursor to the equally unfortunate Burns. Burns probably imbibed this view from Thomas Ruddiman's Preface to *Poems on Various Subjects by Robert Fergusson, Part II*, published in Edinburgh in 1779, seven years before his own arrival in the city. Ruddiman declared Law "a study the most improper for him, and in which he made little or no progress; for a genius so lively could not submit to the drudgery of that dry and sedentary profession."[30] Again, it appears, Burns's biographers respond to and reproduce a poetic genealogy established by the poet himself. His negative association of poets and lawyers (late eighteenth-century Edinburgh was pre-eminently a city of lawyers) also stuck: Fergusson's first biographer David Irving dismissed the story that the poet had studied Law with the view that "Poetry and Law, are things too heterogeneous in their nature, ever to unite in the same individual."[31] When Alexander Grosart published his "Life of Fergusson" in 1851 (the year Latto emigrated to America), he emphasized the theme of uncomprehending worth neglected by those bound to worldly status.[32]

In early 1787 Burns was in Edinburgh following the unexpected success of his *Poems, Chiefly in the Scottish Dialect* (1786), and preparing for a second edition. His poetic biography was already being crafted by the literati who brought him to notice as a "Heaven-taught ploughman."[33] The Ayrshire poet quickly stepped in to change the course of the "genius" debate. Transferring the epithet conferred on him by Henry Mackenzie, Burns invoked "ILL-FATED GENIUS! Heaven-taught *Fergusson*" (vol. 1, p. 323; italics mine). His poems on Fergusson, all directly or indirectly invoking the poet's own vocation, were composed within two years of this time—at the point when "Robert Burns" might first be said to have a biography: that is, a life of interest to those who did not know him personally, a life whose contours could be shaped and told for the edification of others. Writing the poems to Fergusson, Burns dispelled the myth of natural genius and established for himself a poetic genealogy of an entirely earthbound kind. He kicked out, indirectly, at the literary caste of the Establishment and its power to kill with kindness or indifference, and he voiced a figure of the Bard as neglected genius, devoted to celebration of Scotland's beauties:

---

[30] Thomas Ruddiman, Preface to *Poems on Various Subjects by Robert Fergusson, Part II* (Edinburgh, 1779).

[31] David Irving, ed. *The Poetical Works of Robert Fergusson, with the Life of the Author* (Glasgow, 1800), p. 8.

[32] Grosart later revised and expanded his account for a volume in the "Famous Scots" series (1898).

[33] Mackenzie, "*Surprising effects of Original Genius*," qtd. in Low (ed.), *Robert Burns: The Critical Heritage*, pp. 67–71 (p. 70); see also Robert Crawford, "Robert Fergusson's Robert Burns," in Robert Crawford (ed.), *Robert Burns and Cultural Authority* (Iowa City, 1997), pp. 1–22 (p. 2).

My senses wad be in a creel,
Should I but dare a *hope* to speel,
Wi' *Allan*, or wi' *Gilbertfield*,
    The braes o' fame;
Or *Ferguson*, the writer-chiel,
    A deathless name.
…
Ramsay an' famous *Ferguson*
Gied *Forth* an' *Tay* a lift aboon;
Yarrow an' *Tweed*, to monie a tune,
    Owre Scotland rings,
While *Irwin*, *Lugar*, *Aire* an' *Doon*,
    Naebody sings.
…
The warly race may drudge an' drive,
Hog-shouther, jundie, stretch an' strive,
Let me fair Nature's face descrive,
    And I, wi' pleasure,
Shall let the busy, grumbling hive
    Bum owre their treasure.
("To William Simson, Ochiltree," vol. 1, pp. 93, 94, 96)

Against the Mandevillian image of self-interested activity, Burns sets the figure of poetic vocation. Similarly, the second stanza of "Heaven-taught Fergusson!" associates ill-fated genius directly with poetic worth:

O why should truest Worth and Genius pine
    Beneath the iron grasp of Want and Woe,
While titled knaves and idiot-greatness shine
In all the splendour Fortune can bestow? (vol. 1, p. 323)

What seems to be happening here is not a negation but a radical reorientation of the Scottish Enlightenment debate on genius. Intertwining his experience of poverty with Fergusson's, Burns shifts the emphasis from the untutored, perhaps divine, nature of genius to its plight in a world devoted to gathering gear. The "ill fate" of genius is to be expected to subsist on poetry alone. This projection of the unhappy life of his namesake Robert Fergusson was the product of Burns's own suspicion and distrust of the real comprehensiveness of the "Enbrugh Gentry['s]" benevolence, as their figure of the mad, dissipated Fergusson was a manifest of anxiety about the negative shadow-side of Moderatism and Enlightenment. Burns's diatribe against the neglect of poetic worth, "Apostrophe to Fergusson, Inscribed Above and Below his Portrait"—"O thou, my elder brother in Misfortune, / By far my elder Brother in the muse!" (vol. 1, p. 323)—ensured that their names would be inseparable in nineteenth-century reputation both in Britain and America. The bio-poetical conflation would also authorize a shape and meaning for the lives of the emigrant poets who left Scotland to escape hardship and practice their vocation in America.

Burns's alignment of himself and Fergusson took effect immediately in Scotland: that same spring the twice-weekly *Edinburgh Advertiser* for 13–17 April 1787 carried an advertisement for Burns's "Poems, Chiefly in the Scottish Dialect" (the "Edinburgh Edition"). The front page of the following number held two extracts from the poems of "this Heaven-taught Bard": "Man was made to Mourn," and "When Guilford Good," and referred readers "who wish to be better acquainted with this original genius, to the new edition of his Poems, just published."[34] An inner page of the same number of the Advertiser announced *"Poems, Chiefly in the Scottish Dialect*, by the late Robert Ferguson [*sic*], of facetious memory." The bookseller, Charles Elliot, may simply have been riding on the current vogue for Burns; there was no work by Fergusson with this title.[35] But the association—or confusion—carried over into American publications: the Edinburgh Edition of Burns's *Poems, Chiefly in the Scottish Dialect* of 1787 was reprinted twice in America in 1788; in Philadelphia by Stewart & Hyde (July), and in New York, in December an edition printed by J & A. McLean, *"To which Are Added, Scots Poems, Selected from the Works of Robert Fergusson."*[36] The advertisement for this edition in the publishers' *Independent Journal* announced:

> This American Edition of Burns' Poems will be ornamented with a HEAD of the Author, neatly engraved by Mr. Scott, of Philadelphia, and, to render the work more worthy of public patronage, will be added, without any additional Expence [*sic*] a number of POEMS selected from the works of the celebrated R. FERGUSON.[37]

The addition of a "HEAD of the Author," and the poems by Fergusson distinguish this edition. "More worthy of public patronage" means, certainly, "more saleable," but associating Burns with the "celebrated" but unfortunate Fergusson may also imply a social duty to support neglected worth. A later advertisement for the same volume in the *Norfolk and Portsmouth Journal* of 26 November transferred the epithet "celebrated" from Fergusson to Burns, denominating the earlier poet instead as "of noted memory."[38] The Contents page of this volume made no

---

[34]   *Edinburgh Advertiser*, 17–20 April 1787; see also Rhona Brown's chapter in this volume.

[35]   The 1785 (Edinburgh) edition of Fergusson's works was entitled *Poems on Various Subjects, by Robert Fergusson. In two parts.* In small print at the bottom of the same advertisement appears "Allan Ramsay's GENTLE SHEPHERD, with the Original Music."

[36]   See Richard B. Sher, *The Enlightenment and the Book: Scottish Authors and Their Publishers in Eighteenth-Century Britain, Ireland and America* (Chicago and London, 2006), p. 669. A copy of the volume is held in the National Library of Scotland, shelfmark RB.s.419.

[37]   Painter, "American Editions," p. 447.

[38]   Ibid., p. 448. According to Painter, John and Archibald McLean had emigrated from Glasgow in 1783. In July 1787 the *Independent Journal* had carried an advertisement from John Reid, a new Scottish bookseller in New York, whose wares included "Burn's [*sic*] *Poems, Chiefly in the Scottish Dialect*." This must have been an imported copy of the Edinburgh Edition. Painter shows that McLean's text for Fergusson's poems was the third edition of 1785 (Painter, "American Editions," pp. 435–6). See Rhona Brown's chapter in

separation, and indicated no change of authorship, between the final Burns poem ("A Bard's Epitaph") and the first poem by Fergusson ("An Eclogue"); a single Glossary covered the work of both poets. Not all of the Fergusson poems included in the volume were in fact—in a linguistic sense—"Scots poems"; there is no indication of the source or the principles of choice, and the reader is left to infer the nature of the poetic connection between the two poets. George Washington owned and probably subscribed to this edition.

The compounded expression of Burns's poetry and figure of neglected worth wrested from the control of the E'nbrugh gentry was unique, and uniquely empowering for emigrants to North America throughout the nineteenth century. My final example corroborates the compound afterlives. William Wye Smith, born in Jedburgh in 1827, was the son of Scottish immigrants who became a popular Canadian poet. When he revisited Scotland as an adult in 1862, he re-traced the route of Robert Burns's tour of the Borders;[39] both before and after this visit Wye Smith wrote poems in Scots with the poet in mind, songs like "The Highland Laddie,"

> O the bonnie Highland laddie!
>   On his hills beside the sea; —
> Wi' his cheek sae fair and ruddy,
>   And the love-light in his ee: —[40] (p. 132)

and competent experiments in Habbie Simson; his poems frequently gesture towards the failings so inseparable from the poetic myth of Burns, only to dispel them in a vision of Burnsian independence and equality realized on transatlantic shores, as in "Burns. For a Scottish Gathering":

> Aih, Sirs! could Robin been advised
>   To life's amended issue!
> A *new edition*, read, revised,
>   Correct in every tissue!
> But they who might his mentors been,
>   Were tempters all beside him;
> They tippled wi' him morn and e'en,
>   But never sought to guide him!
>
> I tell you, friends! we'll look nae mair
>   At ilk lamented failing—

---

this volume for details of the advertisement for this volume in the *Freeman's Journal or, The North American Intelligencer*.

[39]   Scott A. McLean and Michael Vance (eds), *William Wye Smith: Recollections of a Nineteenth-Century Scottish Canadian* (Toronto, 2008), p. 18.

[40]   *The Poems of William Wye Smith* (Toronto, 1888), http://www.archive.org/details/poems williamwye00smitgoog, accessed 8 May 2009; all quotations from Wye Smith are taken from the version on this site. I am grateful to Michael Vance for alerting me to this archive.

But like the laverock high in air
  Beside some cloudlet sailing,
We hae his thoughts, his words, his sang,
  Like some sweet story olden,
To fire us as we plod alang
  Toward our sunset golden!

If Independence in the heart
  Has ever won its measure—
If loves and lives of manly men
  Have given the world a treasure—
If on the brow of honest Worth
  A halo e'er has lighted,
Thank Burns! who taught that nevermore
  Should man by man be slighted! (pp. 119–20)

The sources of the poem's rhetorical authority are lateral and indirect, deriving—paradoxically—from pastiche; its displaced allusions catch slightly at the edges of poetic memory: "the brow of honest Worth" ... "[s]hould man by man be slighted." Wye Smith's Burns is a politically quiescent figure in this translated context: no longer the angry embodiment of neglected Worth, he takes on the mantle of triumphant prophet of New World equality, his afterlife if not his actual life lived out in transatlantic sociability:

To us, in cabins of the West,
  Or some young city viewing,
With Scottish lore Burns gives a zest
  To all that's worth pursuing!
We stand, with him, for God-given right
  Of life, and love, and labor!
And every man's a Scot to-night,
  And every Scot "Our Neighbor!" (p. 120)

Burns's compound afterlife receives a final twist in an intriguing invocation to Robert Fergusson, based on:

An incident strikingly illustrative of the unhappy destiny of the young poet, and at the same time of the honorable esteem in which he was held by those who knew him, [and which] must not remain untold. Shortly after his death a letter came from India directed to him, enclosing a draft for £100, and inviting him thither, where a lucrative situation was promised him. The letter and draft were from an old and attached school-fellow, a Mr. Burnet, whose name deserves to be forever linked with Fergusson's for this act of munificent, though fruitless, generosity. *Whitelaws Book of Scottish Song: Introduction.*[41] (p. 90)

---

[41] This anecdote had been recounted in Fergusson biographies since that of David Irving in 1800; it was further elaborated by Alexander Grosart's expanded version of his 1851 biography of Fergusson in the "Famous Scots" series in 1898.

The poem imagines a saving emigration that would—had it occurred—have re-written Fergusson's story as one of merit rewarded in the new world of Empire:

> "O come to the Indies, Rab!
>   For the skies of the East are aglow;
> There's hope for thy bosom, and light for thine eyes,
>   There's wealth at thy bidding to flow!"
> 'Twas thus to the Minstrel he sent,
>   With a pledge from his brotherly hand;
> As he lay at noon in his sultry tent,
>   And dreamed of his native land!
>
> Swift sails the message bore
>   Through spicy isles of the sea;
> But the bard, or ever it reached the shore,
>   Had laid down his head to dee!
> They could kindle and glow at his strains,
>   Or weep 'neath his minstrel wand,—
> But they left him to die amid clanking chains,
>   In the heart of his native land!
>
> Alas, for a friend at hand,
>   Wi' a bosom as tender and true—
> And a cheering word for the hopeless bard,
>   Like the lad ower the ocean blue!
> Soon, soon was thy harp untuned
>   That might lang hae been strung wi' glee—
> And mony wakened to find thee fled,
>   They wad hae gien gowd to see!
>
> O sweetest and kindliest Rab!
>   Heart-broken, yet brither to a';
> How young and how fair thy brow to bear
>   The sorrows that were thy fa'!
> Like the Minstrel wha set thee a stave,
>   The Plowman Laddie o' Ayr,
> We'll drap a saut tear ower thy lowly bier,
>   And a' that lies buried there!* ("Robert Fergusson," pp. 90–91)

The address in the first and last stanzas is direct, and familiar; Wye Smith must have been aware that "Rab" would immediately evoke another Robert in his readers' minds: indeed, the association with "the PLOWMAN LADDIE o' Ayr" leaps out at the close. The note at the end of the verse explains:

> The late true-hearted Scottish Poet, James Ballantine, took Fergusson's grave under his special care, and had a margin of shells round it brought from Ayr. After reading the above, he wrote to the author, "Should we have met when you were here, I should have joined you in your pilgrimage to Fergusson's grave, and shed tears together over the poor dear fellow and true Scotsman." (p. 91)

The posthumous decoration of Fergusson's tomb is re-located and re-memorialized through the figure of the ploughman from Ayr. Burns's transatlantic afterlives reach forward and back to create a might-have-been as an emigrant poet for his elder brother in the muse.

Chapter 10
Burns and Aphorism; or, Poetry into Proverb: His Persistence in Cultural Memory Beyond Scotland

Carol McGuirk

Jacques Derrida's deconstruction of Juliet's "What's in a name?" speech in *Romeo and Juliet* considers aphorism and the immortality of names in terms of the tragic "contretemps" that they introduce in Shakespeare's play:

> [A]phorism separates, and in the first place separates me from my name. I am not my name ... Non-coincidence and contretemps between my name and me, between the experience according to which I am named or hear myself named and my "living present" ... The absolute aphorism: a proper name.[1]

Aphorism is for Derrida a "discourse of dissociation": "One aphorism ... can come before or after the other, before *and* after the other ... Its encounter and its contact with the other are always given over to chance."[2]

I consider here the lucky chance by which later authors outside Scotland have drawn on aphorisms from Burns as touchstones for their own work. These are Burns's posthumous *linguistic* adventures, and many of them transpired in North America. First, however, I will discuss Burns's own adaptations of Scots adages and his "aphorization"—sententious isolation and condensing—of memorable moments from canonical English poets and scripture. As is well known, Burns's career is marked by a self-conscious separation of his signed poems from his anonymous, informally circulated songs. To consider aphorisms, by which Burns's wordings live on in contexts not necessarily linked to his name, is one way of exploring a disjunction ("I am not my name") that the poet himself evidently recognized: "Word and deed are *overtaken*. Aphorism outstrips."[3]

The Scots are drawn to aphorism. During the 1730s, the vernacular poet Allan Ramsay compiled an alphabetically organized, forty-four chapter assortment of

---

[1]   Jacques Derrida, "Aphorism Countertime," in Derek Attridge (ed.), *Acts of Literature*, trans. Nicholas Royle (London, 1992), pp. 414–34 (pp. 432–3); see *Romeo and Juliet* (II, ii).

[2]   Ibid., p. 417.

[3]   Ibid., p. 416.

Scots Proverbs. Although published twenty-three years before Burns was born, some express sentiments that will sound familiar to Burns's readers:

> "He has mickle Prayer but little devotion."
> "If we hae little Gear we hae less Care."
> "Love's as warm among Cotters as Courtiers."
> 'The simple Man's the Beggars [*sic*] Brother."
> "We are bound to be honest but no to be rich."[4]

Burns uses such folk sayings to illustrate a speaker's passing mood; a measure of character for him is the type of aphorism—whether kindly or caustic, literary/ biblical or folk/proverbial—on which a speaker relies. In Burns's adaptation, then, truisms are offered to readers not as "truths" but as representative utterances. Moreover, no matter how homely their speech, his proverb-users are engaging in a proto-literary activity, for aphorisms, although they come to hand readymade, nonetheless must first be selected and approved, as a poet chooses words and rhymes, from a near infinite menu of potentially conflicting possibilities. One of the proverbs from Ramsay quoted above, "The simple Man's the Beggars Brother," is preceded by the very different proposition that "The lazy Man's the Beggar's Brother."[5]

In a Burns song published in 1792, the betrayed speaker consoles himself with stereotypes and proverbs:

> Whae'er ye be that woman love,
>   To this be never blind;
> Nae ferlie 'tis tho' fickle she prove,
>   A woman has't by kind:[6]

That last line, though the gender is changed, recalls a proverb in Ramsay: "He has't of kind, he coft [purchased] it not."[7] The sententious narrator of "Tam o' Shanter" (1790), too, aside from lifting phrases from the English poets, adapts one of Ramsay's proverbs ("Time and Tide will tarry for nae Man"),[8] which resurfaces in Burns's "Nae man can tether time or tide" (vol. 2, p. 559). The adage in Ramsay

---

    [4]   Allan Ramsay (comp.), *A Collection of Scots Proverbs* (1737), in *The Works of Allan Ramsay*, Alexander M. Kinghorn and Alexander Law (eds) (6 vols, Edinburgh, 1944–1974), vol. 5, pp. 59–133 (pp. 81, 90, 98, 112, 118); subsequent quotations from *Scots Proverbs* are from volume 5 of this edition.

    [5]   Ibid., p. 111.

    [6]   "She's fair and fause &c.," *The Poems and Songs of Robert Burns*, James Kinsley (ed.) (3 vols, Oxford, 1968), vol. 2, p. 655; subsequent quotations from Burns's poetry are from this edition and are cited in the text by volume and page number.

    [7]   Ramsay, *Scots Proverbs*, p. 81.

    [8]   Ibid., p. 116.

itself can be traced to "the tide tarieth no man,"[9] first collected and printed by John Heywood in 1546.

Aphorism and poetic speaking are not as antithetical as might be assumed. An aphorism user *remembers* a saying and passes it along; a poet *devises* a saying striking enough to descend to posterity as memorable. Heywood, the first to print old English adages, was a notable playwright; incidentally he also was the maternal grandfather of John Donne.[10] Samuel Taylor Coleridge, even as he distinguishes prose from poetry (prose = words in their best order; —poetry = the *best* words in the best order[11]) marks their strong affinities and perhaps recalls a dictum of Swift's: "Proper Words in proper Places, makes the true Definition of a Stile."[12] Swift and Coleridge are agreed in seeing prosaic and poetic diction as points along a continuum of pithy word choices. In *Table Talk*, Coleridge muses on "good sense" versus a poet's less practical but, if successful, more powerful imaginings: "Poetry is certainly something more than good sense, but it must be good sense, at all events; just as a palace is more than a house, but it must be a house, at least."[13]

Burns's writings sometimes conjoin but sometimes separate poetic speech from common-sense expression. In "Epistle to Hugh Parker," he imagines riding off into the night sky on his mare Jenny Geddes, his "Pegasean pride":

> ... when auld Phebus bids good-morrow,
> Down the zodiac urge the race,

---

[9]   John Heywood, *The Proverbs of John Heywood*, Julian Sharman (ed.) (London, 1874), p. 11.

[10]   Julian Sharman describes Heywood's collection as "the most popular of all popular books ... [P]oets, play-writers, and statesmen made capital of its mine of proverbs. The Elizabethan dramatists are brimming with them" (*The Proverbs of John Heywood*, p. xv). Among the adages already old in 1564 when Heywood printed them (given here in modern form) are: "the more the merrier"; "better late than never"; "the fat's in the fire"; "one good turn deserves another"; "beggars can't be choosers"; "a penny for your thoughts"; "haste makes waste"; "out of sight, out of mind"; "make hay when the sun shines"; "strike while the iron is hot"; "look before you leap"; "can't see the forest for the trees"; "two heads are better than one"; "love me, love my dog"; "many hands make light work"; and (Shakespeare remembered this one) "all's well that ends well."

[11]   Samuel Taylor Coleridge, *Specimens of the Table Talk of the Late Samuel Taylor Coleridge*, H[enry] N[elson] Coleridge (ed.), 2nd edn (London, 1836), p. 45.

[12]   Jonathan Swift, *A Letter to a Young Gentleman*, in *The Prose Works of Jonathan Swift*, Herbert Davis et al. (eds) (14 vols, Oxford, 1939–1968), vol. 9, p. 65. Jonathan Swift adds a disclaimer: exploring the elements of style in any deep way "would require too ample a Disquisition to be now dwelt on" (p. 45). Like Coleridge, Swift is interested in both colloquial and formal literary expression; unlike Coleridge, his interest in daily speech is largely satiric, as in *A Complete Collection of Genteel and Ingenious Conversation, According to the Most Polite Mode and Method now used at Court, and in the Best Companies of England. In Three Dialogues. By Simon Wagstaff, Esq.* (London, 1738).

[13]   Coleridge, Specimens of the Table Talk, p. 78.

And cast dirt on his godship's face;
For I could lay my bread and kail
He'd ne'er cast saut upo' thy tail.— (vol. 1, p. 413)

Burns's last line echoes a proverb in Ramsay's collection: "Ye'll never cast Saut on his Tail";[14] in an English rhyme that may be even older, "Simple Simon," the hero plans to catch a small bird by this means.[15] Burns's and Ramsay's Scottish version again appears in Sir Walter Scott's *Redgauntlet* (1824).[16]

For Burns's speakers, to talk in proverbs is to establish credentials as a rustic. For the poet himself, however, Scots aphorisms often serve as a counterpoint to high-flown poetic language. "My Farm gives me a good many uncouth Cares and Anxieties," he wrote to Robert Ainslie during the same month (June 1788) that his epistle to Parker dreams of escaping the earth altogether, racing past Phoebus Apollo, god of poetry, and kicking dirt in his face.[17] A Scots adage that echoes an older rhyme about how not to catch a bird ends this fantasy of flight; the aphorism brings him back. And there he sits, marooned in reality, a vale of proverbs rather than the Pegasean empyrean of poetry—a train of thought, at any rate, suggested by the lines in "Epistle to Hugh Parker" that follow those just quoted:

Wi' a' this care and a' this grief,
And sma', sma' prospect of relief,
And nought but peat reek in my head,
How can I write what ye can read?— (vol. 1, p. 413)

---

[14]   Ramsay, *Scots Proverbs*, p. 125.

[15]   Here is the stanza about Simple Simon and the bird: "He went to catch / A dickey bird, / And thought he could not fail, / Because he had got / A little salt / To put upon his tail" (*History of Simple Simon* [York, c. 1820], p. 6). "Simple Simon" was printed first as a chapbook in 1764; it is one of the rhymes in *Mother Goose* (1780; U.S. rpt. 1786), which postdates Ramsay's collection. Cotton Mather used the proverb about salting a bird's tail in New England in 1744, a reference still postdating Ramsay's Scottish variation, in which no bird is mentioned. *The Imperial Dictionary of the English Language*, John Ogilvie and Charles Annandale (eds), new edn (4 vols, London, 1883), assigns "Simple Simon" and the bird's tail to "hoary antiquity," while in the more scholarly *Oxford Dictionary of Nursery Rhymes*, Iona and Peter Opie (eds) (1951; Oxford, 1997), the editors, printing a short version of the rhyme, speculate that "Simon might have been a name for a simpleton for several centuries ... Boyd Smith (*Mother Goose*, 1919) repeats the statement that a tale of Simple Simon formed one of the chapbooks of the Elizabethan era; ... and a tune, 'Simple Simon,' is included in the third edition of Playford's *The Dancing Master* (1665)" (p. 459).

[16]   Scott's re-use of the Scottish version occurs in Ch. 11 of *Redgauntlet* (Edinburgh, 1824), in which Fairford is warned that Redgauntlet's network of spies is "so good, that were you coming near him with soldiers, or constables, or the like, I shall answer for it, you will never lay salt on his tail." See Walter Scott, *Redgauntlet*, G.A.M. Wood and David Hewitt (eds) (Penguin, 2000), p. 227.

[17]   *The Letters of Robert Burns*, J. De Lancey Ferguson (ed.), 2nd edn, G. Ross Roy (ed.) (2 vols, Oxford, 1985), vol. 1, p. 287.

Defined here is a dissonance not only between poetic inspiration and practical necessity but also between spoken, social speech (the realm of proverbs) versus writing and reading.

More happily enmeshed in the realm of the proverbial is the pert country girl who speaks in broad Scots in Burns's late song "Scottish Ballad." She rapidly narrates the tale of her courtship, darkly revisiting her indignation, several weeks after spurning his first marriage proposal, when she learned that her "braw wooer" had been seen with her cousin:

> But what wad ye think? in a fortnight or less,
>   The deil tak his taste to gae near her!
> He up the lang loan to my black cousin, Bess,
>   Guess he how, the jad! I could bear her, could bear her,
>   Guess ye how the jad! I could bear her.
> ...
> I spier'd for my cousin fu' couthy and sweet,
>   Gin she had recover'd her hearin,
> And how her new shoon fit her auld shachl't feet;
>   But, heavens! how he fell a swearin, a swearin,
>   But, heavens! how he fell a swearin. (vol. 2, p. 796)

This unnamed speaker energetically applies to Bess an insulting adage in Ramsay—"Ye shape shoon by your ain shachled feet"—unconsciously revealing her possessive love for the wooer with whom she has been toying.[18]

Burns uses homely Scots proverbs just as he uses echoes from prior poets or Scripture: to bring his characters to life. When portraying exalted speakers, he is likely to turn instead to the English poets, as a stanza in "Scots Wha Hae" suggests:

> Wha will be a traitor-knave?
> Wha can fill a coward's grave?
> Wha sae base as be a Slave? —
>   — Let him turn and flie:— (vol. 2, p. 708)

The song, especially when performed to its old Scottish air, sounds unequivocally "Scots," but Burns is drawing on a famous scene in Shakespeare. In Act 3 of *Julius Caesar*, Brutus, Caesar's adopted son and his assassin (he kills Caesar to stop him from being acclaimed emperor), poses a parallel series of rhetorical questions: "Who is here so base that would be a bondman? If any, speak, for him have I offended. Who is here so rude that would not be a Roman? ... Who is here so vile that will not love his country?"[19] In Burns's song, a Roman forum becomes the field at Bannockburn, republican Brutus becomes Robert Bruce, a Roman mob becomes a fiercely loyal army, and the diction shifts from formal

---

[18]   Ramsay, *Scots Proverbs*, p. 128.
[19]   William Shakespeare, *Julius Caesar*, in G. Blakemore Evans et al. (eds), *The Riverside Shakespeare*, 2nd edn (Boston, 1997), III, ii, 29–33 (p. 1166).

English to idiomatic Scots. Shakespeare's revolutionary context is retained, but Burns moves the point of national crisis from the last days of the Roman republic to June 1314, eve of the Battle of Bannockburn, the military victory that restored Scottish independence. A large part of Burns's art or craft lies in such submerged but seismic shifts in the register and context in which he re-purposes both received wisdom and literary language.[20]

Sometimes he introduces contradictory aphorisms, as in a coat of arms he designed in 1794 to replace a lost seal. He wanted the design inscribed on a "Highland pebble":

> On a field, azure, a holly bush, seeded, proper, in base; a Shepherd's pipe & crook, Saltier-wise, also proper, in chief.—On a wreath of the colors, a woodlark perching on a sprig of bay-tree, proper, for Crest.—Two Mottoes: Round the top of the Crest—"Wood-notes wild"—At the bottom of the Shield, in the usual place—"Better a wee bush than nae bield"—[21]

"Wood-notes wild" echoes line 134 of Milton's "L'Allegro"; Milton is praising Shakespeare. In the upper image, a native wood-lark alights on a sprig of bay, but "in base" stands a tree of northern growth. The species of holly native to Scotland is deciduous, not an evergreen like the Mediterranean bay; it is nonetheless apt for Burns in flourishing despite harsh weather and (like two other of Burns's favorites, the hazel and hawthorn) growing best on higher ground. Any coat of arms brings together the disparate history of male and female ancestors: Burns selects a visual image well designed to represent his own poetic project as a crisscrossing (a display "Saltier-wise") of divergent elements. This is especially true of the mottos: Burns's quotation of Milton is countered by a proverb collected in Ramsay as "A wee Bush is better than nae Bield."[22] If aphorism "separates," as Derrida argues—"it marks dissociation (*apo*), it terminates, delimits, arrests (*horizō*)"[23]—Burns, in reusing familiar phrases (whether from literary classics or anonymous folk sources), often brings them back in this way as elements in a pair or series. Rather than settling

---

[20]   Another revision of Shakespeare by Burns is discussed in *Allusion to the Poets* (New York, 2002) by Christopher Ricks, who considers echoes of *King Lear* in "A Poet's Welcome to His Love-Begotten Daughter," an early Burns poem whose "allusions range wildly ... Burns embraces *King Lear*. His pair of lines, "tho' ye come here a wee unsought for" and "Tho' ye come to the world asklent," is itself paired with the opening scene of *King Lear*: "though this Knave came somthing [*sic*] sawcily to the world before he was sent for…" (p. 64). Gloucester also reminisces in this scene that "there was good sport at his making" (ibid., p. 65), a matter Burns's lines may reflect when he addresses newborn Elizabeth as the "sweet fruit of monie a merry dint." Ricks observes the shift in genre and emotional register between tragedy in *Lear* and celebration in Burns: "the world of tragedy is there in Burns but as reminder and contrast" (ibid.).

[21]   Burns, *Letters*, Ross Roy (ed.), vol. 2, p. 285.

[22]   Ramsay, *Scots Proverbs*, p. 70.

[23]   Derrida, "Aphorism Countertime," p. 416.

things as aphorisms do, such serial quotations raise questions. Do these "mottos" compete, or is Burns promoting the cozy cohabitation of contraries? Milton's phrase is, perhaps significantly, placed higher than the proverb—as high as can be on the top. Yet the literal grounding of the folk-saying at the base of the image could be read as marking the phrase not as lesser but as foundational.

The aphorisms extracted from Burns's own poems that still circulate today, separated from their original and often equivocal matrix of counter-statement, therefore preserve only a partial view even of Burns's characters, let alone of the poet himself. Burns is often widely removed from his speakers, whether historically (King Robert Bruce), in gender and age (the adolescent country girl in "Scottish Ballad"), or in temper, as in "Holy Willie's Prayer," the dramatic monologue whose speaker, almost in the same breath, confesses to habitual drunken adultery and boasts of his affinities with the apostle Paul:

> Maybe thou lets this fleshly thorn
> Buffet thy servant e'en and morn,
> Let he o'er proud and high should turn,
>   That he's sae gifted;
> If sae, thy hand maun e'en be borne
>   Untill thou lift it.— (vol. 1, p. 76)

William Fisher deftly perverts the spirit of Paul's second letter to the Corinthians: "of myself I will not glory, but in mine infirmities ... And lest I should be exalted above measure ... there was given to me a thorn in the flesh, the messenger of Satan to buffet me, lest I should be exalted above measure" (2 Cor. 12:5, 7 AV). Such prehensile shifts in meaning and adapted micro-allusions are precisely what are lost in posterity's aphoristic reductions of Poet Burns to a handful of memorable phrases.

Nonetheless, the stripped-of-context or proverbial Burns soon became— especially in North America—an important element in posterity's memory of him. Wise sayings drawn from Burns were, like his songs, conveniently portable links to the home-culture for the uncounted Scots emigrants of the nineteenth century. The naturalist and emigrant Scotsman John Muir had memorized Burns, reciting whole poems to himself as he strode alone through the North American wilderness.[24] But many nineteenth-century emigrant Scots remembered Burns mainly as a coiner of phrases, some of which they may have encountered in secondary sources. The original edition of Bartlett's *Familiar Quotations*, self-published in 1855 by Cambridge, Massachusetts, bookseller John Bartlett, included a section on Burns. The ninth edition (1891), the last edited by Bartlett before his death in 1905,

---

[24] In a diary entry for 25 January 1906 (Burns's birthday) Muir wrote that "On my lonely walks ... [Burns] was always with me, for I had him by heart" (*John of the Mountains: The Unpublished Journals of John Muir*, Linnie Marsh Wolfe [ed.] [Boston, 1938], pp. 434–5).

incorporates seventy Burns passages and cites forty poems and songs.[25] Bartlett's selection is made across a broader range than one might expect, broader than the selections of most anthologists today. Burns's aphoristic *tour de force* "Tam o' Shanter" generates eleven entries, while the sententious "The Cotter's Saturday Night" is cited five times; yet less famous works are included, too—"A Winter Night," "The Twa Dogs," "Ode, Sacred to the Memory of Mrs Oswald," "Epistle from Esopus to Maria"—along with songs that are today all but forgotten.

The epigraph of Bartlett's ninth edition records a shy demurral: "I have gathered a posie of other men's flowers, and nothing but the thread that binds them is mine own."[26] A certain modesty is probably called for in introducing a project in which literary language is trimmed down so neatly: posies, like greeting cards but unlike poems, are tidy, pretty things. Yet though Bartlett's window into literary language was narrow, still it was a window, shedding some light for busy, upwardly mobile nineteenth-century Americans. *Familiar Quotations* is set up chronologically by author rather than alphabetically or thematically by topic, and early editions were focused on literary and biblical sayings (the subtitle is *A Collection of Passages, Phrases, and Proverbs. Traced to their Sources in Ancient and Modern Literature*). By offering samples of the style of each successive school of writers, the work offered among other things a concise outline of the literary history of the British Isles as well as more recent examples of American eloquence. Bartlett was himself a diligent if self-taught student; too poor to attend Harvard, he began his working life at age sixteen as a clerk in the Harvard bookstore and by age 30 had purchased the business. He retailed years of private study into a reference work that sketched a shortcut to literary discrimination, a stock of peak moments from classic texts far more wide-ranging than any that his equally self-made readers could have hoped to acquire on their own.

If phrases from Burns were still current only by means of such genteel compendia as *Familiar Quotations*—still the hunting ground of anxious amateur orators—we would have to think of Burns's words as surviving today, at least outside Scotland, on artificial life-support. But aphorisms drawn from Burns were also culled by writers. Just as Burns re-shaped Brutus's speech from Shakespeare to bring Robert the Bruce to life, the twentieth-century writers to whom I now turn adapted "familiar quotations" from Burns to delineate their own characters and settings. None of their works is set in Scotland; it is not local color but Burns's memorable wording that attracts these writers.

Some sense of how Burns's poems and songs lived on in the pioneer imagination may be seen in the "Little House" stories of Laura Ingalls Wilder (1867–1957), written beginning in the 1930s but based on Wilder's childhood experiences during the 1870s and 1880s on a series of struggling farms in Wisconsin, Kansas, Minnesota, and South Dakota. Burns's name is never mentioned in these

---

[25]   Bartlett, John (comp.), *Familiar Quotations: A Collection of Passages, Phrases, and Proverbs. Traced to their Sources in Ancient and Modern Literature*, 9th edn (Boston, 1891).

[26]   Ibid., p. i.

children's novels—Tennyson is the only poet named[27]—and the Scottish roots of the family are only implied. Yet the father regularly performs Burns's songs on his fiddle, while the mother, intent on maintaining an orderly life despite the family's isolation, until the final books, on precarious and lonely steadings, is a habitual speaker of proverbs. In *Little Town on the Prairie* (1941), when a vast flock of blackbirds devours the corn crop, the family gather the birds they have managed to shoot before running out of bullets. While preparing to cook them for supper, Ma quietly observes that "There is no great loss without some small gain," a Scottish adage given in Ramsay as "Nae great loss but there's some sma' Advantage."[28] Another proverb of Ma's is quoted by Laura in a later volume: "as Ma would say, 'Least said, soonest mended'"; this is likewise an adage in Ramsay: "Little said is soon mended."[29] The repertory in Wilder's stories extends to English proverbs collected by Heywood, from "all's well that ends well" to "as Ma would say, enough is as good as a feast,"[30] although that last probably originated in Scotland; it occurs in Barbour's *Bruce* (c. 1375).

Folkish proverbs, as in Burns, coexist with out-of-context literary phrases—

"Modulate your voice, Laura," Ma said gently.

"Remember, 'Her voice was ever gentle, soft, and low, an excellent thing in woman'"[31]

—an aphorism drawn from *King Lear* (V, iii) that is among the quotations from Shakespeare included in *Bartlett's*. Proverbial sayings from scripture are also introduced, on one occasion by Pa to tease his serious-minded wife:

"That's right, Laura, listen to your Ma," said Pa. "'Wise as a serpent and gentle as a dove'."

"Charles!" said Ma.[32]

---

[27] Laura discovers a volume of Tennyson hidden in a drawer; opening it, she is entranced by the first lines of "The Lotos Eaters" before she realizes that she may be spoiling a Christmas surprise and hastily replaces the book. When finally able to finish the poem on Christmas day, she strongly disapproves of it: "in the land that seemed always afternoon the sailors turned out to be no good. They seemed to think that they were entitled to live in that magic land and lie around complaining. When they thought about bestirring themselves, they only whined, 'Why should we ever labor up the laboring wave?' Why indeed! Laura thought indignantly. Wasn't that a sailor's job, to ever labor up the laboring wave? But no, they wanted dreamful ease. Laura slammed the book shut" (Laura Ingalls Wilder, *Little Town on the Prairie* [New York, 1971], p. 235).

[28] Wilder, *Little Town*, p. 102; Ramsay, *Scots Proverbs*, p. 101.

[29] Laura Ingalls Wilder, *These Happy Golden Years* (New York, 1971), p. 53; Ramsay, *Scots Proverbs*, p. 98.

[30] Wilder, *Happy Golden*, pp. 76, 118.

[31] Wilder, *Little Town*, p. 97.

[32] Wilder, *Happy Golden* p. 54; Wilder slightly rewords Matthew 10:16 (AV).

Wilder, like Burns, sometimes introduces dueling proverbs, as in an exchange between Laura's parents as they admire her new home-made dress.

> [Pa] said, "They say that fine feathers make fine birds, but I say it took a fine bird to grow such feathers …"

> "You look very nice," praised Ma, "but remember that pretty is as pretty does."[33]

A buffer-zone of time-honored sayings envelops the family, connecting them to more settled ways of life and mitigating their solitary struggle by supplying reminders of broader social experience. Burns is just one among this host of unnamed yet instrumental voices, but his role is central in delineating the contrasting personalities and fates of the elder Ingalls girls. Mary Ingalls is associated with Burns's "Highland Mary" (1792), a tender elegy written for Margaret Campbell, who died at age twenty of typhus.[34] While it is unlikely that Wilder invented the detail of her sister's preference for this song—the stories are based on the lives of her family—in repeatedly introducing Burns's tribute to his lost love she strongly conveys the family's otherwise unspoken grief over their own Mary's early misfortune. Although she does not die when, like most of the

---

[33]   Ibid., p. 163; Pa's saying reverses the moral of Aesop's "Fable of the Peacock and the Crane": "fine feathers do not make fine birds." Ma's rejoinder, a common saying at that time and place, can be traced back to medieval times, for it was already old when dramatized by Chaucer in "The Wife of Bath's Tale."

[34]   According to James Mackay, "Highland Mary" was born Margaret Campbell in Dunoon and baptized in March 1766 (*RB: A Biography of Robert Burns* [Edinburgh, 1992], p. 213): if so, she was twenty when she died in 1786 (she had contracted typhus while nursing her brother Robert through it). Her death was unknown to the poet until some weeks after it had occurred. Robert Crawford quotes from Burns's narrative in the *Glenriddell Manuscript*, which affirms their "most ardent reciprocal attachment ... We met by appointment, on the second Sunday of May [1786], in a sequestered spot by the banks of Ayr, where we spent a day in taking a farewel [*sic*], before she should embark to the West Highlands, to arrange matters among her friends for our projected change of life" (*The Bard: Robert Burns, A Biography* [Princeton, 2009], p. 215). Crawford accepts the account offered by Margaret Campbell's mother in 1823: "Burns wrote repeatedly to the Highlands, but could obtain no information ... At length he addressed a letter of inquiry to her uncle at Greenock, and by him the striking and melancholy truth was unfolded" (qtd. in Crawford, *The Bard*, p. 230). Snyder and Carswell introduced into the Highland Mary legend the possibility that an infant's coffin unearthed when the Campbell family grave was opened at Greenock (when the cemetery was moved during the 1920s) might have been that of Mary's infant child by Burns. This was a large family plot, however, and quantities of remains were uncovered; moreover, the infant was buried in a separate coffin. See Hilton Brown (*There Was a Lad: An Essay on Robert Burns* [London, 1949], p. 251) and Mackay (*RB*, pp. 222–7) for fuller details. There is no way to determine whether Margaret Campbell bore Burns's child. The only evidence is contextual—the agonized guilt that imbues all of Burns's elegies for her. That the immediate cause of her death was typhus fever is not in question.

family, she is severely stricken by scarlet fever, the fever causes her to go blind at around age 14. In a scene set a few months after this catastrophe, Pa takes out his fiddle:

> He looked at Mary sitting quietly with beautiful empty eyes and folded hands in her rocking chair by the oven. "What shall I play for you, Mary?"
>
> "I would like to hear 'Highland Mary,' Pa."
>
> Softly Pa played a verse. "Now, Mary! Help sing!" he said, and they sang together:
>
> > ... "The golden hours on angel wings
> > Flew o'er me and my dearie
> > For dear to me as light and life
> > Was my sweet Highland Mary!"
>
> "It's sweet," Mary said when the last note died away.
>
> "It's sweet, but it's sad," said Laura. "I like 'Coming Through the Rye'."[35]

Because the later books tell of Laura's courtship and eventual marriage, the younger sister's choice of a light-hearted love song foreshadows her future, just as "Highland Mary" addresses Mary's blindness, though indirectly. Wilder never quotes the Burns lines that most plainly parallel: "clos'd for ay, the sparkling glance, / That dwalt on me sae kindly!" (vol. 2, p. 660).

During her years of absence attending a college for the blind, the oldest daughter is remembered by performances of "Highland Mary." By contrast, Laura's maturing and changing character is conveyed by a shifting group of Burns songs:

> Laura had never been so happy, and for some reason she was happiest of all when they were singing,
>
> > "Ye banks and braes of Bonny Doon,
> > How can ye bloom sae fresh and fair?
> > How can ye chaunt ye little birds,
> > And I sae weary, full of care?"[36]

Burns, as always, remains unidentified in this scene, but this preference for "Bonie Doon" suggests that Laura is developing the tender sensibilities of adolescence. In the later novels, song-lyrics by Burns assist the readers' recognition that she has fallen in love. She unconsciously reveals her emotions, for instance, in a scene in

---

[35] Laura Ingalls Wilder, *By the Shores of Silver Lake* (New York, 1971), pp. 154–5.

[36] Ibid., p. 213.

which she is conversing with Almanzo Wilder, who has been courting her, and her best friend, Ida Brown:

> [Laura] "I think it's a pity we don't all go in a crowd any more ... What fun the sleighing parties were, but now we're all paired off."
>
> "Oh, well," Ida said, "In the springtime a young man's fancy lightly turns to thoughts of love."
>
> "Yes, or it's this," and Laura sang,
>
> > "Oh whistle and I'll come to you, my lad,
> > Oh whistle and I'll come to you, my lad,
> > Though father and mither and a' should gae mad,
> > Oh whistle and I'll come to you, my lad."
>
> "Would you?" Almanzo asked.
>
> "Of course not!" Laura answered. "That's only a song."[37]

Wilder, in her own voice rather a terse narrator, introduces stanzas from Burns to enlighten readers as to the true feelings of silently watchful Laura. During a long separation occurring just after her engagement, Laura's worries about Almanzo are underscored in this displaced way when Pa plays "For the sake o' Somebody," a late Burns song, at the Ingalls's Christmas Eve gathering:

> "Let's have a little music ... What shall I play?"
>
> "Play Mary's song first," Laura answered. "Perhaps she is thinking of us."
>
> Pa drew the bow across the strings and he and the fiddle sang:
>
> > "Ye banks and braes and streams around
> > The castle of Montgomery,
> > Green be your woods and fair your flowers,
> > Your waters never drumlie;
> > There summer first unfolds her robes
> > And there the langest tarry,
> > For there I took my last fareweel
> > Of my sweet Highland Mary."

---

[37]   Wilder, *Happy Golden*, pp. 183–4. Ida Brown is quoting line 20 of Tennyson's "Locksley Hall." "The whole poem," said Tennyson, "represents young life, its good side, its deficiencies, and its yearnings" (Hallam Tennyson, *Alfred Lord Tennyson: A Memoir by His Son* [2 vols, London, 1897], vol. 1, p. 195). Wilder, as in other scenes, introduces an apt literary reference to suggest Ida's own deepening attachment to the young man who is courting her.

One Scots song reminded Pa of another, and with the fiddle he sang:

> "My heart is sair, I dare na tell,
> My heart is sair for somebody.
> Oh! I could make a winter night,
> A' for the sake o' somebody."[38]

First the father first plays Mary's unchanging melody, but his next Burns song is chosen for his second daughter, forlorn because she has received no letter from Almanzo Wilder for several weeks.

In Wilder's stories, phrases from Burns retain the anonymity of aphorism but are often quoted at length. Most later writers employ Burns in more fleeting ways, in moments brief as a phrase. Still, they reanimate Burns's images and expressions by finding them useful in their own projects. A comic example can be seen in *How Right You Are, Jeeves* (1960) by P.G. Wodehouse. Born a British subject, son of a judge in Hong Kong, Wodehouse was naturalized as a U.S. citizen in 1955. In the scene below, his most famous character, Jeeves, a super-intelligent valet, quotes the wisdom of Poet Burns to his employer Bertie Wooster, who has hatched a typically harebrained plot to scare off an unwanted fiancée. Jeeves has been away on his annual holiday, shrimping at Herne Bay, but has been fetched back to assist Wooster in this emergency. He does not approve of his employer's master-plan:

> "I distrust these elaborate schemes. One cannot depend on them. As the poet Burns says, 'the best laid plans of mice and men gang aft agley'."
>
> [Wooster] "Scotch, isn't it, that word?"
>
> "Yes, sir."
>
> "I thought as much. The 'gang' told the story. Why do Scotsmen say 'gang'"?'
>
> "I have no information, sir. They have not confided in me."
>
> "... So you think the poet Burns would look askance at this enterprise, do you? Well, you can tell him from me he's an ass."[39]

Bertie Wooster is a perfect example of the idle rich; his London club is aptly named The Drones. Burns's aphorism—"the best laid plans of mice and men gang aft agley"—makes good sense to working-class Jeeves.[40] Yet different classes

---

[38]   Wilder, *Happy Golden*, p. 226.

[39]   P[elham] G[renville] Wodehouse, *How Right You Are, Jeeves* (New York, 2000), pp. 148–9.

[40]   Richard Usborne writes that "Jeeves's origins were 'of the people' ... [He] has a cousin who is a constable ... and another cousin who is a jeweler ... He had an understanding with the present Lady Bittlesham, the then Jane Watson who was Bingo Little's uncle's cook" (*Plum Sauce: A P.G. Wodehouse Companion* [London, 2002], p. 91). Wooster's club, The Drones, is contrasted with Jeeves's London sanctuary, a club for butlers and valets called (after Zeus's beloved cup-bearer) the Junior Ganymede Club. Members of

have different conceptions of wise behavior, and Bertie Wooster, with his inherited wealth, his social connections, and above all his certainty that Jeeves will always save the day, is the last man in the world to appreciate this adage from Burns, who witless Bertie assumes is still alive in 1960. Wooster will hardly recognize these as wise words addressed to a newly homeless mouse who, like the plowman speaker in "To a Mouse," has no safety net at all. The phrase from Burns (incidentally, a poet frequently quoted by Jeeves) cannily sketches the gulf between a masterful servant and a comically clueless Drone.

"The best laid schemes o *Mice* an' *Men* / Gang aft agley": a tragic adaptation of the same phrase occurs in John Steinbeck's *Of Mice and Men* (1937), in which allusions to Burns's "To a Mouse" go well beyond the title. In this spare, symbolic novel, George Milton and gigantic but feeble-minded Lennie Small, day-laborers, dream of owning a ranch together. Lennie fantasizes about the kind care he will lavish on the rabbits that he plans to breed. The novel, like the second stanza of Burns's poem, considers "Man's dominion" as a disruptive force that shatters "Nature's social union" (vol. 1, p. 127). Yet in Steinbeck, "Nature" is represented by, among other things, childlike Lennie, who kills without realizing what he does. George discovers that he, too, is a killer: he shoots Lennie even though he sees their bond as his remaining link to humanity itself: "I seen the guys that go around on the ranches alone," George says in his American vernacular. "That ain't no good. They don't have no fun. After a long time they get mean. They get wantin' to fight all the time."[41] George protects but constantly scolds Lennie, who is gentle yet does not know his own strength. Lennie likes to keep a dead mouse in his pocket to stroke while he works. He much prefers them alive, but when they struggle to escape, he breaks their necks to quiet them.

Steinbeck's intention was "to see how like a play he could write a short novel."[42] What he dramatizes is, as in Burns's "To a Mouse," the perils faced by those with no margin for error, no hedge against sudden disaster. Steinbeck's ranch hands, like Burns's ploughman speaker, inhabit a semi-domesticated borderland. In Burns the mouse is threatened by the ploughman's cultivation of her space: the destruction of her nest by the coulter of the plough decreases her chances of surviving the coming winter. Burns's ploughman-speaker allows the mouse

---

the club can consult a book about the idiosyncrasies of prospective upper-crust employers. Finally, Usborne traces Jeeves's numerous literary allusions: "I ... can establish Lucretius, Pliny the Younger, Whittier, Fitzgerald, Pater, Shelley, Kipling, Keats, Scott, Wordsworth, Emerson, Marcus Aurelius, Shakespeare, Browning, Rosie M. Banks, Moore, Virgil, Horace, Dickens, Tennyson, Milton, Henley, the Bible, Stevenson, Gray, Burns, Byron, and whoever it was who wrote 'The Wreck of the Hesperus'" (ibid., p. 92). (He is playfully suppressing Longfellow, author of the last-named poem.) "Rosie M. Banks" is a recurring Wodehouse character, a novelist whose successful if cloying titles include *Only a Factory Girl* and *Mervyn Keene, Clubman*, along with the Dryden-inflected *All for Love* and the Burns-infused *A Red, Red Summer Rose*.

41   John Steinbeck, *Of Mice and Men*, Joseph Henry Jackson (intro.) (New York, 1937), pp. 73–4.

42   Joseph Henry Jackson, introduction to *Of Mice and Men*, pp. v–xix (p. xviii).

to escape unhindered; by contrast, at the end of Steinbeck's novel, George kills Lenny for reasons that remain ambiguous. There is a lynch mob bearing down on them intent on hanging Lenny, who has inadvertently broken the neck of a young woman who has invited him to stroke her hair; but George may also be expressing his refusal to continue shielding his friend.

Steinbeck's characters try to live up to Burns's imperative of human kindness; this is evident in George's years of tending to Lennie and in Lennie's dim appreciation of soft and helpless creatures like mice, rabbits, and puppies. But scanty resources doom their efforts—and not only a shortage of money to buy a ranch and settle in a home. Lenny lacks the judgment and forethought to avoid recurrent episodes of violence, and George runs out of patience. As if putting an animal out of its misery, he shoots Lenny, who trusts him entirely, in the back. Burns's analogy between mice and men as equally helpless against unforeseen disaster is the ironic fulcrum of Steinbeck's Depression-era tragedy.

A lyric recollection of Burns occurs in a song of 1994 by singer/songwriter Sting (Gordon Sumner), whose "Fields of Gold" evidently remembers Burns's "Corn Rigs." Here are stanzas from Burns's early song:

> I lock'd her in my fond embrace;
>   Her heart was beating rarely:
> My blessings on that happy place,
>   Amang the rigs o' barley!
> But by the moon and stars so bright,
>   That shone that hour so clearly!
> She ay shall bless that happy night,
>   Amang the rigs o' barley.
>
> I hae been blythe wi' Comrades dear;
>   I hae been merry drinking;
> I hae been joyfu' gath'rin gear;
>   I hae been happy thinking:
> But a' the pleasures e'er I saw,
>   Tho' three times doubl'd fairly,
> That happy night was worth them a',
>   Amang the rigs o' barley.
>   CHORUS
> Corn rigs, an' barley rigs,
>   An' corn rigs are bonie:
> I'll ne'er forget that happy night,
>   Amang the rigs wi' Annie. (vol. 1, p. 14)

Burns's chorus can be traced to earlier sources whose phrasing is, however, less striking.[43] Burns, many of whose earliest poems were verse renditions of the

---

[43] Ramsay's last song in *The Gentle Shepherd*—it is printed also in *Tea Table Miscellany*—includes Burns's phrase "corn rigs are bonie"; another pre-Burns version of the song celebrates "corn rigs and rye rigs." Kinsley traces several seventeenth-century English songs that use "corn rigs," but because their hero is invariably named "Sawney," he

Psalms, here writes a hymn to the body, remembered in a moment of perfect harmony with nature. Indeed, his speaker swears a vow not to God but by natural entities, the moon and stars that "shone" "that happy night." The vow itself is not a lover's pledge to remain faithful but a poet's promise *never to forget*. In Scotland in Burns's day, barley was called "corn," so his phrase "corn rigs and barley rigs" is tautological, emphatic. The couple make love on a rig or ridge, explained in the *OED*'s fifth, agricultural, definition as "a raised or rounded strip of arable land": on a high ground, the young lovers reap a harvest of mutual pleasure. A more ancient sense of "ridge" is implied as well: in the *OED*, the word's first listed meaning is "the back or spine in man or animals." The lovers' bodies are at one with the landscape; they are "among" the rigs, embedded in fertile ground. The speaker lists many things that have made him happy since that night, but still it stands as his peak moment, at least six times—"three times doubl'd"—more joyous than any other joy.

Sting's lyrics for "Fields of Gold" remember the chorus of Burns's song:

> You'll remember me when the west wind moves
> Upon the fields of barley
> You'll forget the sun in his jealous sky
> As we walk in fields of gold
> …
> Will you stay with me, will you be my love
> Among the fields of barley
> We'll forget the sun in his jealous sky
> As we lie in the fields of gold
>
> See the west wind move like a lover so
> Upon the fields of barley
> Feel her body rise when you kiss her mouth
> Among the fields of gold[44]

The repeated "fields of barley"—especially the odd, almost awkward phrasing of "among the fields"—echoes Burns, and Sting's melody retains the Scottish tune's upward lilt: "fields of bar-ley" ends on a rising note in both. Sting's setting is summer, not harvest, and the sun, not the moon, governs his landscape. The union is consensual and alfresco in both, but the encounter is blessed by nature in Burns's song, while in Sting's the lovers steal their pleasure under a jealous sky. Burns's repetition of "I have been" in his final stanza shows that his song looks back, but Sting's song specifies that "many years have passed." Sting's lyrics, evidently addressed to a long-time partner, suggest that summer joys will return in "the days still left," yet with its admission of broken promises, the song is elegiac where Burns's is celebratory. "Fields of Gold" is addressed directly to a lover:

---

concludes that the song's origins are Scottish. See *The Poems and Songs of Robert Burns*, Kinsley (ed.), vol. 3, pp. 1009–10.

[44]   Sting, "Fields of Gold," http://www.elyrics.net/read/s/sting-lyrics/fields-of-gold-lyrics.html, accessed 8 June 2009.

"You'll remember me."[45] Burns, though he fondly remembers, does not address Annie, who is part of a moment now passed. Burns was at most twenty-three when he wrote his song;[46] Sting's is more of a mid-life song.[47]

"By a name
I know not how to tell thee who I am."[48]

In "Ulysses Gramophone," Derrida considers the *yes* and the signature in Joyce's *Ulysses*, but in tracing the patterns of that hyper-allusive novel, he alights on the affirmative process of aphoristic re-inscription:

> A signature is always a *yes*, *yes*, the *synthetic* performative of a promise ... [A]ny writing in the widest sense of the word, involves a *yes* ...Only another event can ... countersign ... This event, that we naively call the first event, can only affirm itself in the confirmation of the other: a completely other event.[49]

Those authors considered here who have brought back the sayings of Burns—identified specifically or not—in Derrida's terms affirm his poet's task *as it was*, precisely if paradoxically by introducing his words in "completely other" contexts. Wilder and Wodehouse, Steinbeck and Sting: all write from different outlooks yet all resort to Burns, affirming his currency even as they change his contexts.

The poems that Burns signed were addressed to the literati at large; his autobiographical letter remembers his awe in adolescence at the thought of making "verses like printed ones, composed by men who had Latin and Greek."[50] His unsigned and informally circulated songs were, however, turned toward a broader public who, as the nineteenth- and twentieth-century reception shows, heard in his words a decisive expression of their own tentative thoughts—not about Scotland

---

[45] Sting's phrase "You'll remember me" itself inspired Eva Cassidy, whose 1996 cover of "Fields of Gold" was recorded shortly before she died: "Eva first heard the song on a cassette tape of the Sting solo album 'Ten Summoner's Tales' ... [S]he went through a ... phase where she listened to that every time we were in the car ... Eva developed her own guitar arrangement ... and played it for Keith Grimes ... Grimes recalls ... I had heard Sting's recording, but the way she put it across ... overwhelmed me" (*Eva Cassidy: "Fields of Gold,"* http://www. evacassidy.org/eva/fog.htm, accessed 8 June 2009).

[46] See Burns, *Letters*, Ross Roy (ed.), vol. 1, p. 142.

[47] Other popular singer-songwriters have drawn on Burns. Christopher Ricks discusses Bob Dylan's echoes of Burns: "[He ...] begins his songs 'Highlands' with the words of Burns ('My heart's in the Highlands'); in 'Lay, Lady, Lay' he shows himself the heir of Burns in the loving comedy of a third person/first person turn: 'Stay, lady, stay with your man awhile / Until the break of day / let me see you make him smile'." Robert Burns puts in an appearance in *Tarantula* (Ricks, *Allusion to the Poets*, 43–4 n3).

[48] *Romeo and Juliet*, II, ii, 55–6, as quoted by Derrida in "Aphorism Countertime," p. 424.

[49] Jacques Derrida, "Ulysses Gramophone: Hear Say Yes in Joyce," in Attridge (ed.), *Acts of Literature*, pp. 253–309 (pp. 279, 298, 309).

[50] Burns, *Letters*, Ross Roy (ed.), vol. 1, p. 137.

itself so much as about love, work, and life. For that broader public outside Scotland, Burns's words long outlived his name by descending as wise adages. To be sure, Burns's name is still annually spoken each late January around the world. Frederick Douglass, said to have made Burns's *Complete Works* his first book purchase after escaping from slavery in Maryland, gave the toast to Burns's "Immortal Memory" on 25 January 1849 in a speech that began with a description of Douglass's recent pilgrimage to Ayrshire but that concluded with one of Burns's most often quoted phrases, selected by Douglass as especially pertinent: "if any think me out of my place on this occasion (pointing at the picture of Burns), I beg that the blame may be laid at the door of him who taught me that 'a man's a man for a' that'."[51] More than a century later, the *Autobiography* of Martin Luther King, Jr., cites Burns's phrase "Man's inhumanity to Man" ("Man was Made to Mourn," vol. 1, p. 118) no fewer than six times, including as part of the epigraph of Ch. 21: "Man's inhumanity to man," writes Dr King, speaking of the murder of four children in a Birmingham, Alabama church-bombing, "is not only perpetrated by the vitriolic actions of those who are bad. It is also perpetrated by the vitiating inaction of those who are good."[52]

Whether the "yes" of aphoristic echo—in Derrida's terms, the countersigning that affirms the anterior "event," Burns's poetic career itself—is linked, as in Douglass, to Burns's name or remains, as in King, unspoken, is not as important today as it must have been for Burns himself during his lifetime. For like the lovers he depicts in "Corn Rigs," his words are at this point fully embedded in the general landscape of literary and colloquial speech. This was already the case when Emerson spoke at a centennial celebration of Burns's birth in January 1859:

> [E]very boy's and girl's head carries snatches of his songs, and they say them by heart, and, what is strangest of all, never learned them from a book, but from mouth to mouth. The wind whispers them, the birds whistle them, the corn, barley, and bulrushes hoarsely rustle them, nay, the music-boxes at Geneva are framed and toothed to play them; the hand-organs of the Savoyard in all cities repeat them, and the chimes of bells ring them in the spires. They are the property and the solace of mankind.[53]

"The Immortal Memory," the invariable toast of Burns suppers, is repeated in annual celebrations that honor a particular person, Robbie Burns, and a particular nation, Scotland. Yet Emerson may have been nearer the mark in locating the essence of Burns's "immortal memory" not in his life or works per se but rather in the *memory of mortals*, the interactive matrix of living cultural exchange.

---

[51]   Frederick Douglass, "Speech at a Burns Supper, January 1849," http://www. bulldozia.com/ projects/ index.php?id= 256, accessed 12 June 2009.

[52]   Martin Luther King, *The Autobiography of Martin Luther King, Jr.*, Clayborne Carson (ed.) (New York, 1998), p. 220.

[53]   Ralph Waldo Emerson, "Speech at Burns Centenary Dinner in Boston, January 1859," in Donald A. Low (ed.), *Robert Burns: The Critical Heritage* (London and Boston, 1974), pp. 434–6 (p. 436).

Chapter 11
The Robert Burns 1859 Centenary: Mapping Transatlantic (Dis)location

Leith Davis

The year 2009, the "Year of Homecoming" in Scotland, was designed to highlight "Scotland's great contributions to the world": whisky, golf, ancestry, innovators, and, of course, its national poet, who was marking his 250th anniversary.[1] As part of its global campaign, Homecoming Scotland, the organization responsible for encouraging Scots and Scotophiles to visit Scotland during the year, sponsored a virtual "World Famous Burns Supper" in partnership with the Famous Grouse Whisky Company with a website that tracked Burns Night celebrations around the globe. Anyone holding a Burns celebration on 25 January 2009 was encouraged to "complete our simple two-step registration to ... become part of the World's largest ever Burns Night celebration!"[2] The website featured an interactive "Global Hosts Map" with 3,673 pinpointed sites, mostly clustered in Great Britain and North America, but with examples from as far away as Azerbaijan and Zimbabwe. The technology used to represent this "World Famous Burns Supper"—Google Maps—was new. But the sentiment behind it—creating a sense of connectedness between Burns enthusiasts from different locations around the world—actually dates back 150 years earlier to the first centenary celebration of Burns's birth.[3] While Burns served as symbol of Scottish identity for Scots at home and abroad before 1859, the centenary served to globalize Burns, drawing on the new technologies of the time in order to represent him as a modern phenomenon linking individuals around the world.[4] At the same time as it promised to unite different groups in an international celebration, however, the centenary also made it apparent that "Burns" could look very different depending on which side of the Atlantic he was being toasted. In *Virtual Americas*, Paul Giles examines "the ways specific local

---

[1]   http://www.homecomingscotland2009.com/default.html.

[2]   http://www.burnssupper2009.com/this-year/default.aspx.

[3]   Carol McGuirk suggests that the centenary was "the point at which the transformation of Burns from controversial literary celebrity into 'immortal memory' seems to have been completed" ("Burns and Nostalgia," in Kenneth Simpson (ed.), *Burns Now* [Edinburgh, 1994], pp. 31–69 [p. 32]).

[4]   See Ann Rigney, "Embodied Communities: Commemorating Robert Burns, 1859," *Representations*, 115/1 (2011): 71–101, for a fascinating account of this globalization in terms of the work of literature in cultural memory. I am grateful to her for sharing this work with me while it was in process.

conditions and cultural landscapes reconstitute transnational networks in different ways."[5] The Burns Centenary offers a unique opportunity to consider how the "local conditions" influencing the representation of one particular literary figure at one particular time "reconstitute" transatlantic networks. Building on the work of Giles, this chapter examines the discourse surrounding the centenary events, suggesting the way in which Burns served in 1859, not only as a "mediator between memory communities" on either side of the Atlantic, to invoke Ann Rigney's theories regarding cultural memory,[6] but also as a marker of local, national and transatlantic differences.

During the first half of the nineteenth century, Burns became, as Alex Tyrrell suggests, "what Pierre Nora has called a 'lieu de mémoire,' the focus of a form of public memory that appropriates not only places, but historical figures, literary works, and artistic objects to consecrate them as the quintessence of a nation."[7] The process through which this was achieved was complex and multi-faceted. The circulation of books such as James Currie's *The Works of Robert Burns* and Allan Cunningham's *The Life and Land of Burns* in international print networks helped make Burns and Scotland synonymous.[8] The evolution of Burns clubs from local gatherings of friends of the poet to national and international sites where ex-patriot Scots joined together with non-Scots served to encourage worldwide familiarity with Burns.[9] In addition, the construction of memorials and statues to Burns made locations such as Dumfries and Ayr focal points "for continuing worldwide interest in Burns."[10] Despite the fact that Burns's reputation steadily expanded both in Scotland and abroad, however, celebrations of the Scottish poet and songwriter, although clearly demarcating a worldwide influence, were confined to discrete locations.

---

[5]   Paul Giles, *Virtual Americas: Transnational Fictions and the Transatlantic Imaginary* (Durham, NC, 2002), p. 11. Specifically, he suggests that "conceptions of national identity on both sides of the Atlantic emerged through engagement with—and, often, deliberate exclusion of—a transatlantic imaginary, by which I mean the interiorization of a literal or metaphorical Atlantic world in all of its expansive dimensions" (p. 11).

[6]   Ann Rigney, "Plenitude, Scarcity and the Circulation of Cultural Memory," *Journal of European Studies*, 35/1 (2005): 11–28 (26).

[7]   Alex Tyrrell, "Paternalism, Public Memory and National Identity in Early Victorian Scotland: The Robert Burns Festival at Ayr in 1844," *Historical Association*, 90/297 (2005): 42–61 (43).

[8]   See James Currie, *The Works of Robert Burns; with an Account of his Life and Criticism on his Writings* (4 vols, London, 1800); and Allan Cunningham, *Life and Land of Burns* (New York, 1841). For further discussion of Currie's contribution to the reception of Burns, see my "Negotiating Cultural Memory: James Currie's *Works of Robert Burns*," *International Journal of Scottish Literature*, 6 (2010), http://www.ijsl.stir.ac.uk/issue6/davis.htm.

[9]   See James Mackay, *The Burns Federation, 1885–1985* (Kilmarnock, 1985), p. 37.

[10]   Ibid., p. 25.

Apart from two dinners in Edinburgh and London in 1816 that James Mackay suggests hinted at a "Burns celebration on a national scale," it was not until 6 August 1844 that there was a wider celebration of Burns.[11] The Ayr Burns Festival was prompted by the return of Burns's three remaining sons to Scotland. James Glencairn Burns and William Burns had been serving in India for the previous twenty years, while Robert Burns, Jr., had held a position at the Stamp office at Somerset House in London. Organized by Christopher North and Lord Eglinton, with committees formed in Edinburgh, Glasgow, and Ayr, the Ayr Burns Festival was modeled, according to one participant, on the Shakespeare Festival held at Avon.[12] It featured a huge procession, public speeches, and a banquet for approximately 2,000 guests in a pavilion specially erected for the occasion in a field next to the Burns Monument (see Figure 11.1). The September 1844 edition of *Blackwood's Edinburgh Magazine* covered the event, marveling at its popularity and likening the spectacle to that produced on the occasion of a royal visit: "The streets of Ayr were swarming with people, and sounding with the crash of music. There were arches on the bridge, flags streaming from windows, and bells tolling from the steeples—symptoms of a jubilee as great as if Royalty had descended unawares, and the whole district had arisen to pay honour to its Queen."[13]

"Stanzas for the Burns' Festival" by "Delta," published in the same issue of *Blackwood's*, suggests that audience members came from England and Ireland for the occasion:

> Sons of England!— Sons of Erin!
> Ye who, journeying from afar,
> Throng with us the shire of Coila,
> Led by Burns's guiding star—[14]

The celebration did attract at least one visitor from outside Britain: the American poet and journalist, Bayard Taylor, who was traveling around Europe in the employ of the *New York Tribune*.[15] But the Festival was primarily a national event, as Lord Eglinton's speech on the occasion suggested: "every *town* and every *district*; every class, and every sex, and every age, has come forward to pay homage to their poet."[16]

In fact, in the pages of *Blackwood's*, the Burns Festival is presented as a national recovery program for Scotland, an antidote to the "perilous influences" of

---

[11]   Ibid., p. 37.

[12]   Ibid., p. 39.

[13]   "The Burns' Festival," *Blackwood's Edinburgh Magazine*, 56 (September 1844): 371.

[14]   Ibid., p. 399.

[15]   Taylor writes about his experiences of the Ayr Festival in *Views A-Foot or Europe Seen with Knapsack and Staff* (New York, 1847).

[16]   Qtd. in *The Knickerbocker, or New York Monthly Magazine*, 24 (October, 1844): 386; italics mine.

Fig. 11.1   "View of the Grand Procession," *Illustrated London News*, 10
            August 1844 (Issue 119, p. 93).

the Chartist movement that Scotland had been "exposed to" in recent years: "Thus
agitated and disturbed, the Scottish people, once jealously national, and so proud
of that nationality that it had passed into a byword throughout Europe, might have
lost their cohesive power, loosened the cord which bound the social rods together,
and formed themselves into separate sections with apparently hostile interests."[17]
Luckily, just in time, *Blackwood's* suggests, the Burns Festival was able to provide
"a strong counteracting influence" by concentrating the Scottish people's attention
on "stirring memories of the past." The Burns Festival, *Blackwood's* asserts, serves
as a reminder that "the interests of Scotland" are alike in all classes: "It was a
stirring and exciting spectacle, such as no other country could have exhibited—to
behold peer and senator, poet and historian, and peasant—the great and the small,
the lettered and the simple of the land—unite ... in deep and sincere homage to
the genius of once humble man."[18] The *Blackwood's* author further emphasizes the
"commonality among the participants" by describing their spontaneously joining

---

[17]   "The Burns' Festival," p. 370. Arguing that "public memory is pluralist and
'conflictural', not monolithic," Tyrrell suggests that the 1844 festival "was moulded to
reinforce an important political development in Scotland and England—an attempt by
conservatives to construct a version of aristocratic paternalism during the late 1830s and
the early 1840s" ("Paternalism," p. 44).

[18]   "The Burns' Festival," pp. 370, 371.

in song following the speeches: "One of the bands struck up the beautiful air—"Ye Banks and braes o' bonny Doon"; and immediately the People, as if actuated by one common impulse, took up the strain, and a loftier swell of music never rose beneath the cope of heaven."[19]

The national agenda of the Burns Festival can be contrasted with the global perspective that characterized the Centenary celebration of the poet fifteen years later. Instead of being focused in one geographic location, the Centenary was celebrated in a network of connected locations. Circulars were distributed between locations urging participants to co-ordinate efforts. As Ralph Waldo Emerson suggested from his transatlantic vantage point at the celebration in Boston: "At the first announcement, from I know not whence, that the 25th of January was the hundredth anniversary of the birth of Robert Burns, a sudden consent warmed the great English race, in all its kingdoms, colonies, and states, all over the world, to keep the festival."[20] The *Illustrated London News* for 29 January 1859 indicated its sense of the global quality of the celebration as well, noting that "all who speak the English language, whether scattered over the United States and Canada, or cherishing in the Southern Hemisphere the name and the traditions of the Old Country—united on this remarkable occasion to recognise and to glorify a Poet."[21]

The Burns Centenary, as Rigney points out, must be seen in the context of other nineteenth-century public festivals of commemoration that provided "occasions ... for bringing people together in civic spaces in order to act out their loyalties in a pleasurable way."[22] According to Rigney, these public festivals represented a temporal mixture, as "they allowed people to actually share lived experiences (song, dance, spectacle, exhibitions, drinks) in the here and now of civic space while also celebrating a particular imagined tradition and performing their affiliation to it."[23] The extent of the "co-memoration," in the case of Burns, was truly staggering.[24] James Ballantine, a stained-glass artist and writer from Edinburgh who served as the Secretary of the Burns Centenary celebration at Edinburgh's Music Hall, collected descriptions from 872 celebrations in his immense *Chronicle of the Hundredth Birthday of Robert Burns*. Ballantine logged 676 events from Scotland, 76 from England, 10 from Ireland, 48 from the Colonies, 61 from the United States, and

---

[19]   Ibid., p. 375. Tyrrell suggests, in the context of the Ayr Festival, that "[i]n life Robert Burns had been a radical; in death he would be the potent symbol of a Scotland that was resistant to the values of Whiggism, Chartism and the Anti-Corn League" ("Paternalism," p. 50).

[20]   James Ballantine (ed.), *Chronicle of the Hundredth Birthday of Robert Burns* (Edinburgh and London, 1859), p. 551.

[21]   *Illustrated London News* (29 January 1859): 97.

[22]   Rigney, "Embodied Communities," p. 78.

[23]   Ibid.

[24]   See Peter Burke, "Co-Memorations: Performing the Past," in Karin Tilmans, Frank Van Vree, and Jay M. Winter (eds) *Performing the Past: Memory, History, and Identity in Modern Europe* (Amsterdam, 2010), pp. 105–18.

l from Copenhagen. As Ballantine observes, however, his work represents only a "condensation" of the actual number of festivities that took place.[25]

The *Chronicle* itself constitutes an extremely self-conscious process of "co-memoration" of the Burns centenary. Using an impressive network of sources who sent information and newspaper clippings from local papers, Ballantine published his work—in Edinburgh and London—a mere four months after the January celebration. In his Preface, Ballantine remarks on the "unanimity of sentiment" that runs through the numerous celebrations, and indeed, the celebrations do seem unanimous in their focus on Burns's humble origins, the hardships he bore, and his indomitable spirit. Following a convention that had begun with Currie's inclusion of the biography of Burns and his poetry, virtually all speeches emphasize Burns's hard life and perseverance as a Scottish "peasant poet." He is seen as a model rural laborer who arose from his "unlettered peasantry" and "opened up a new and inexhaustible realm of fancy and sentiment—a new and bright creation which the sons of toil have since enjoyed." There are occasional allusions to his "errors" or "jovial habits," but the overwhelming sense is that these weaknesses were either a necessary accompaniment to his "genius and strength" or an opportunity for the current audiences to learn a "lesson of charity" to forgive rather than to "pass too severe a sentence" on "Rantin', Rovin' Robin."[26]

In addition to indicating the "unanimity of sentiment" that connected events at the many diverse geographical locations, the *Chronicle* also reveals other kinds of connections that were built, connections forged through bodies, material goods, and information. These connections take two forms. On the one hand, a radial pattern joins places associated with Burns to outlying areas. Most obviously, Burns's relatives and friends offered such a link. William Nichol Burns attended the celebration at Dumfries, while James Glencairn Burns attended the Glasgow City Hall celebration, and the daughter and grand-daughter of Robert Burns, Jr. honored the Belfast Music-Hall celebration with their presence. Meanwhile, as far away as New York, people who knew Burns or people who knew people who knew Burns gained currency for the celebration they were attending by touting their connections, however tenuous. Burns's belongings also helped form radial connections. The New York celebration, for example, included "[a] piece of bark, elegantly framed, cut from a tree on Burns's farm ... [a] lock of Burns's hair, and an impression of his seal,"[27] while the Boston celebration featured "a haggis, which had been made for the occasion in the cottage in which Burns was born."[28]

Ballantine's *Chronicle* also indicates a less centralized network, however, as peripheral groups form connections together. Joseph Howe of Nova Scotia attended the celebration in Boston, A. M'Alpin of Cincinnati found his way to

---

[25]   Ballantine (ed.), *Chronicle*, p. v.

[26]   Ibid., pp. v, 527, 261, 61, 282.

[27]   J. Cunningham (ed.), *The Centennial Birth-day of Robert Burns as Celebrated by the Burns Club of City of New York* (New York, 1860), p. 43.

[28]   Ballantine (ed.), *Chronicle*, pp. 550–551.

New Orleans for the occasion, and Mr. H. Fuller, editor of the *New York Mirror*, crossed the Atlantic to join the celebration in Dumfries. If connections could not be conveyed in person, they were conveyed by letter or by the new technology of the time: the telegraph. The description of the Burns celebration in Hamilton, Canada West, notes that the event featured its own "telegraph apparatus, fitted up on purpose, for carrying on correspondence with the various admirers of Burns throughout the continent." James Ballantine's collection includes numerous accounts of how messages of universal brotherhood were delivered by telegraph. The Burns Club of Montreal seems to have been particularly active in utilizing this new medium. It sent a "telegraphic dispatch" to the Burns Club of New Orleans, asking to be "remembered in your festivities to-night: though distance divides us, we are animated by the same spirit, reverence and pride for and in the name of Burns, and love to bonnie Scotland! Please reply" (see Figure 11.2). The celebration in Montreal also included the reading of a question received from Hamilton, "We are getting on finely. How's a' wi' ye," while "the answer of the meeting"—"Gaylies brawlies. Thanks to ye for speerin"—was "ordered to be sent by telegraph." "Telegraphic greetings" were also read out from Brockville, Kingston, Quebec, Ottawa, and Prescott while, appropriately, the band played the "Telegraph Gallop."[29] Given this interest in the technology of modernity, it is fitting that the Montreal event was the only transatlantic locale visually recreated for readers of the *Illustrated London News*.

Ballantine's *Chronicle* was designed to bring both official and unofficial sites to the eye of the general public. As the "Preface" announces, "The utmost enthusiasm [for the centenary] pervaded all ranks and classes. Villages and hamlets, unnoticed in statistical reports, unrecorded in Gazetteers, had their dinners, suppers and balls. City vied with clachan, peer with peasant, philanthropist with patriot, philosopher with statesman, orator with poet, in honouring the memory of the Ploughman Bard."[30] The narrative of the *Chronicle* weaves the celebrations together into one vast experience. The occasional slippage of accounts of the speeches from third person to first person and back again gives readers the sense of an omniscient perspective that zooms occasionally to the ground, a Victorian "Google Earth."

While Ballantine's *Chronicle* was the most compendious publication to result from the Burns Centenary, there were many other publications in British and transatlantic venues that outlined the details of individual celebrations. Rigney posits that the celebration of the figure of Burns in 1859 offered "not just an exercise in conviviality, but also a way of performing affiliations within the framework both of local, embodied communities and large-scale imagined ones, formed variously along national, diasporic, imperial, linguistic, and ideological lines."[31] The rest of this essay takes up Rigney's challenge to analyze the "different geopolitical framings of Burns in 1859," concentrating in particular on the connections and

---

29 Ibid., pp. 522, 573 and 532.
30 Ibid., p. v.
31 Rigney, "Embodied Communities," p. 93.

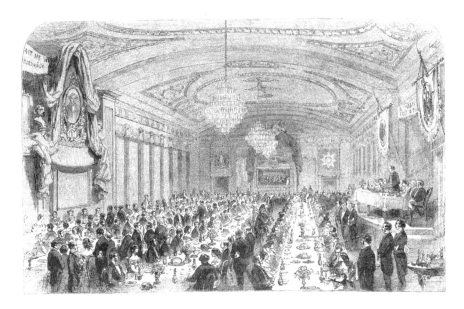

Fig. 11.2   "The Burns Banquet at Montreal," *Illustrated London News*, 26 February 1859 (Issue 961, p. 205).

disjunctions involved in the transatlantic circulation of the poet's memory. As I shall argue, Burns's transatlantic appeal was in part a reflection of the unstable role he came to play in the imagining of Britain itself.

The Centenary was celebrated, if one were to judge by the sheer number of celebrations, most enthusiastically in Scotland. The *Illustrated London News* notes, "few were the towns [in Scotland] that did not make centenary demonstrations to their national poet."[32] Numerous Scottish cities and villages declared 25 January 1859 a holiday as they prepared to honor the man who, more than any other, had been "instrumental in nurturing the love of country and maintaining the national spirit and honour."[33] However, celebrations of Burns as "the glorious representative of the genius of his people" and the "personification of the genius and glory of his country" happened as much outside of Scotland as inside.[34] The audience at the Belfast Music-Hall hailed him as "the most thoroughly and intensely Scotch" of all famous Scotsmen.[35] Such identifications suggest what Susan Manning has referred to as a "model of complicity, where literary texts"—and in this case, a literary figure—"are deployed to shore up and enforce a national image."[36]

---

[32]   *Illustrated London News* (29 January 1859): 106.

[33]   Ballantine (ed.), *Chronicle*, p. 77.

[34]   Ibid., p. 246; *Illustrated London News* (29 January 1859): 115.

[35]   Ballantine (ed.), *Chronicle*, p. 497.

[36]   Susan Manning and Andrew Taylor, "What Is Transatlantic Literary Studies?" in Manning and Taylor (eds), *Transatlantic Literary Studies: A Reader* (Edinburgh and Baltimore, 2007), pp. 1–16 (p. 1).

But the Centenary celebrations also suggest the way that Burns proved useful in the articulation of a British imperial identity. The *Illustrated London News*, for example, indicated that "[t]hough Scotland, as was to be expected, was more fervent in the expression of her loyalty and affection to the name of her illustrious son, the English people were not wanting in due appreciation of his genius or in sympathy for the national feeling which prompted the celebration."[37] Many speeches presented at the Centenary elide Burns's Scottishness into a celebration of Britishness. In Glasgow's City Hall event, Burns's works are praised as forming "an unseen bond which will for ever unite Britons and their children in every part of the world," while "Auld Langsyne" is tasked with "hold[ing] together the widespread descendants of the British empire." At the Belfast Music-Hall celebration, Hugh M'Call effused that "[t]here is not a spot of earth trod by Saxon or Celt—not a country or clime inhabited by men with British hearts and sympathies—that will not enjoy its own peculiar burst of enthusiasm" on this occasion. In M'Call's speech, Burns is the national poet not of Scotland, but of the "United Kingdom," which, he suggests, "[i]n the wise dispensation of Providence" has "been set apart as the great coloniser of the world, sending forth its industry and energy, its language and its literature from one end of the universe to the other, and carrying its national habits to the remotest regions of the earth." Burns is described as a "public benefactor, and public property"; he is "not only a man of Scotland—not only a native of Great Britain, but a cosmopolitan—a man of the world—the poet of all countries and of all times."[38] Burns here is not the kind of "cosmopolitan patriot" celebrated by Kwame Anthony Appiah as engaged in a positive linking of the local and global.[39] Rather, Burns's cosmopolitanism serves as a metaphor for the dissemination of British values abroad in the British colonial project—a project in which the Scots were particularly prominent.[40]

The biggest celebration of Burns outside of Scotland took place in the metropolitan center of empire, London, with roughly 15,000 people in attendance at the Crystal Palace. A contest for the best poem about Burns had been organized for the event, and the winning entry, by one Miss Isa Craigs, was announced and read aloud. Relics of Burns were also placed on display for participants to view: the Naysmith portrait, the Taylor portrait, locks of Burns's and Jean Armour's hair, Burns's writing table, a rough draft of one of his ballads, and "pages from his account book, in which the gains of his earlier works were carefully summed up."[41] The crowning glory of the day, however, was the revelation of a Burns bust "of heroic proportions ... having a column and a pedestal to itself" which

---

[37] *Illustrated London News* (29 January 1859): 106.

[38] Ballantine (ed.), *Chronicle*, pp. 43, 498, 499, 526, 538.

[39] Kwame Anthony Appiah, "Cosmopolitan Patriots," in Bruce Robbins and Pheng Cheah (eds), *Cosmopolitics: Thinking and Feeling Beyond the Nation* (Minneapolis, 1998), pp. 91–114.

[40] See, for example, Douglas S. Mack, "Introduction: Can the Subaltern Speak?" in *Scottish Fiction and the British Empire* (Edinburgh, 2006), 1–13.

[41] *Illustrated London News* (5 February 1859): 137.

"occupied a distinguished central position in front of the court" (see Figure 11.3).[42] I would like to consider this monument to Burns a little more carefully, taking into account the particular way in which it performs Burns in the nation's capitol. For one thing, this display of Burns accrues additional meaning when we recall that the Crystal Palace, a vast glass structure encompassing 70,000 square meters of land, had actually been built to house that first of all Victorian "spectacles" of colonial power, the Great Exhibition of the Works of Industry of All Nations held in 1851. If the Great Exhibition had the effect of reducing national cultures "to the products and materials they exhibited," as Kylie Message argues,[43] the exhibition of Burns eight years later fulfilled a somewhat similar function, reducing Scotland and Scottish identity to a recognizable object that could be consumed in the imperial metropolis. Appropriately, the *Illustrated London News* indicated that the Burns celebration at the Crystal Palace had "all the crowd and bustle of a fair, the illusion being further strengthened by the stall with which the nave was lined, and all of which offered for sale appropriate little souvenirs of the poet. On one, of a literary nature, might be had a complete edition of his works; and on another neat little busts, in parian, of Burns."[44] The celebration at the Crystal Palace had the effect of rendering both "literary" and the less "literary" items into "souvenirs" which could be taken home for private consumption.

But the Crystal Palace display also suggests a more complicated rendering of Burns and Scotland than just simple incorporation. The festival featured a "Court of the Poets," with the bust of Burns in the center of "well-executed busts of the poets from whom Burns might have been supposed to have received some of his early inspiration, or who were contemporary with him."[45] Burns towers over his predecessors and contemporaries, who are indistinguishable in the illustration, and the arrangement suggests both the way in which he is circumscribed and defined in relation to them *and* the way in which he stands out from them. In *Tropicopolitans*, Srinivas Aravamuden examines the creation of Britishness through the construction of a literary canon: "Predicated on the triple scheme of nation, language and culture," he suggests, English Literature "invents a 'Britain' as a collective subject who authors *a* literature, proceeding diachronically with authorial highlights, from Spenser to Shakespeare to Milton" and beyond.[46] In the Crystal Palace celebration, Burns is built visually into the "collective subject"

---

[42] Ibid.

[43] Kylie Message, *New Museums and the Making of Culture* (Oxford, 2006), p. 86; see also Jeffrey Auerbach, *The Great Exhibition of 1851: A Nation on Display* (New Haven, 1999).

[44] *Illustrated London News* (5 February 1859): 137.

[45] Ibid.

[46] Srinivas Aravamudan, *Tropicopolitans: Colonialism and Agency, 1688–1804* (Durham, 1999), p. 234. Aravamudan suggests that "[t]exts circulated within a system that reified nation, language, and culture, conferring the sphere of print with the representative powers of the 'daily plebiscites' that, according to Ernest Renan, perpetuate nationalism" (p. 233).

Fig. 11.3   "Festival at the Crystal Palace, Sydenham," *Illustrated London News*, 5 February 1859 (Issue 958, p. 137).

of Britain, but not as a "highlight" of the chronological development of a British canon. Rather, he is constituted as a remarkable exception.

Speeches delivered at the centenary celebrations also encouraged this view, emphasizing Burns's exceptional relationship to canonical English writers. Speaking at the Belfast Music-Hall celebration, for example, Professor Craik tells the tale of a "mendicant poetess" who accosts his literary friend in London and asserts the importance of Burns: "there's plenty o' your book poets—Pope, and Milton, and Cammell, and sic like; but Burns and me, ye see, we're pure nature."[47] In mid-nineteenth-century Britain, Burns stands out as a poet of "pure nature," of vernacular speakers, of cultural mendicants in a circle of "book poets." For many of his nineteenth-century promoters, he represents the persistence of the local within a rapidly expanding colonial imperium.[48] Burns occupies an ambivalent place,

---

[47]   Ballantine (ed.), *Chronicle*, p. 496.

[48]   For a concise overview of the changes in British overseas activity and the ideology of empire during the nineteenth century, see Douglas Peers, "Britain and Empire," in Chris Williams (ed.), *A Companion to Nineteenth-Century Britain* (Malden, MA, 2004), pp. 53–78.

then, as a figure who represents both "a heightened articulation of geopolitical location" and the loss of that location in the wider process of globalization.[49]

It is precisely this unstable position that Burns occupied as symbol of both local insistence and global incorporation that made him most valuable in the Centenary celebrations across the Atlantic. The 1859 Burns celebrations provided a perfect opportunity for the display of the concentric identities that were in the process of being formed and reformed in the British North American provinces and in the United States in the mid-nineteenth century. In the British North American territories (Nova Scotia, New Brunswick, and the recently united Canadas), Burns served as a figure who helped to connect the inhabitants to the larger British project of empire at the same time as suggesting the primacy of the local. The celebration in Halifax, Nova Scotia, for example, began with a toast to "The QUEEN—reigning in the affections of a free and loyal people, and ruling over the most extensive and powerful empire the world has ever seen."[50] In particular, the speaker congratulated the Queen on her recent colonial acquisition, India: "The calm and almost severe simplicity with which our Queen has assumed the empire of India, and of more than a hundred millions of human beings, has something in it approaching to the sublime."[51] In the Haligonian context, Burns becomes an example of how someone from a geographically marginal location can have a wider influence, with the Lieutenant Governor suggesting that, "Such was the case with Burns, and such I hope may be the case with many of the inhabitants of this Province."[52] In fact, he goes on to argue, perhaps Burns has already had an influence on the men "whose names will be illustrious in History" whom Nova Scotia has already given "to the world": "Who can tell the effect, who can judge the influence which the history of a man like Burns has exerted upon these men? Who can say what a contemplation of his untiring assiduity may lead the sons of Nova Scotia to achieve in the future? (Cheers)."[53] The celebration also included a rendition of "The Garb of Old Gaul," a song, which, in Nova Scotian context, appears quite ambiguous. The lyrics, which originally celebrated the feats of the Scottish regiments in North America during the Seven Years War, suggest on the one hand the similarities between Scotia and Nova Scotia as northern nations with a "love of liberty" who live a rough and hardy life:

> No effeminate customs our sinews unbrace,
> No luxurious tables enervate our race;

---

[49] Editorial introduction to *Global/Local: Cultural Production and the Transnational Imaginary*, Rob Wilson and Wimal Dissanayake (eds) (Durham, 1996), pp. 1–18 (p. 3). In their introduction, Wilson and Dissanayake suggest the way in which the local in our contemporary era has become co-opted, micromanaged, and manipulated by global capital.

[50] *Celebration of Burns' Centenary, Halifax, Nova Scotia* (Halifax, 1859), p. 9 (CIHM 14108).

[51] Ibid., p. 8.

[52] Ibid., p. 13.

[53] Ibid.

Our loud-sounding pipe breathes the true martial strain
And our hearts still the old Scottish valour retain.[54]

The song thus suggests the loyalty of Nova Scotians to the British imperial cause, as the chorus proclaims:

Such is our love of liberty, our country and our laws,
And teach our late posterity to fight in Freedom's cause,
That, like our ancestors of old, we'll stand in freedom's cause:
We'll bravely fight, like heroes bold, for honour and applause
And defy the French, with all their force, to alter our laws.[55]

However, the assertion of martial power must also be considered in the context of the contemporary political situation in the British provinces in North America. Nova Scotia had just become the first of the provinces to obtain self-government in 1848, following a decade of legal struggles against an entrenched colonial system by reformists like Joseph Howe. "Our country" and its "laws" thus read ambiguously, as do the "arts" which might alter those laws.

At the celebrations in Toronto in Canada West, too, Burns did double duty as a marker of imperial loyalty and of local assertion. At the Rossin House Hotel celebration, the speaker commented that "[t]he songs of Burns are already a part of the living language of our common race" and noted the connection between the gathering "on a spot hewn in our own day out of the old savage-haunted pines of Ontario's wooded shores" and gatherings held "wherever the free banner of England floats on the breeze." But this celebration in this "distant nook of Britain's world-wide empire" also served the purpose of promoting Canadian culture and institutions. Toasts were made to "The Bench and Bar of Canada," the "Universities and Schools" of Canada, and the "The Canadian Institutions and the Scientific Associations of Canada." The toast to "The Mother Country" began with the hope that "her Canadian sons" may "prove worthy of their sires," but shifted to protest, "But why should they prove unworthy of their sires" and to indicate the benefits of living in Canada.[56] A toast to "The City of Toronto" became an opportunity to write back to the empire's notion of it outlying areas, as the speaker humorously quoted *Bell's Gazeteer*'s entry for Toronto: "Toronto, a town in Upper Canada, with one hundred wooden houses, and eight thousand inhabitants." The response by the audience in their elegant surroundings in the Rossin House Hotel, was, not surprisingly: "Laughter."[57] A more pointed demonstration of local interests occurred

---

[54] "The Garb of Old Gaul," in *The Songs of Scotland, Ancient and Modern*, Allan Cunningham (ed.) (4 vols, London, 1825), pp. 263–4 (p. 263). Cunningham notes that the words are by Henry Erskine with music added by General Reid. Erskine was grandson of the Charles Erskine of Alva who was created a baronet of Nova Scotia in 1666.

[55] Ibid., p. 264.

[56] Ballantine (ed.), *Chronicle*, pp. 542, 543, 544.

[57] Ibid., pp. 544, 555.

at the St Lawrence Hall down the road, where one of the keynote speakers invited by Burns Club President Donald Ross was the radical reformer William Lyon Mackenzie King, a Scottish emigrant who had founded the reformist newspaper *The Colonial Advocate* in 1824 and then spearheaded the Upper Canada Rebellion in 1837. Also in attendance on the platform was Thomas D'Arcy McGee, who had been outlawed by the British government for his part in the Young Ireland Rebellion of 1848 before becoming a Member of the Legislative Assembly in the newly formed Parliament of Canada. In the British provinces in North America then, Burns celebrations, while acknowledging a connection to the "Mother Nation," also provided opportunities to promote local political interests and culture.

While the Canadian celebrations drew on a Burns who represented the importance of the local within a larger imperium, celebrations in the United States reformulated him as a spokesperson for the republican ideals on which the American constitution was formed. In his oration in Boston, Massachusetts, Emerson lauded Burns as a "the poet of the middle class" who

> represents in the mind of men to-day that great uprising of the middle class against the armed and privileged minorities—that uprising which worked politically in the American and French Revolutions, and which, not in governments, so much as in education and in social order, has changed the face of the world. [58]

In addition, he asserted that "The 'Confession of Augsburg,' the 'Declaration of Independence,' the French 'Rights of Man,' and the 'Marseillaise,' are not more weighty documents in the history of freedom than the songs of Burns."[59] Emerson's employment of the term "middle-class" here to extend Burns's appeal can be explained by the fact that he is addressing an audience which is made up of comfortably middle-class if not upper-class citizens. But Emerson was by no means the first or the only American commentator to emphasize Burns's democratic side. The Boston Burns Club, which sponsored the Parker House celebration, had enshrined in its constitution—written nine years earlier—the fact that Burns represented "Liberty—American liberty!" and averred,

> Enjoying as we do the full advantages of that liberty of speech and action he was fated to see but partly established, our admiration of their benefits will always be enhanced by associating ourselves with the name of one of their boldest and ablest promoters.[60]

A speaker at the New York Centenary celebration at the Astor House expressed almost identical sentiments to Emerson's in declaiming that "[h]is famous song, "A Man's a Man for a' that," is the Declaration of Independence set to music."[61]

---

[58] Ibid., p. 551.

[59] Ibid.

[60] *Celebration of the Hundredth Anniversary of the Birth of Robert Burns, by the Boston Burns Club* (Boston, 1859), p. 6.

[61] Cunningham (ed.), *Centennial Birth-day*, p. 74.

Burns celebrations in the United States were used as an excuse to showcase national cultural and literary efforts too. Anyone who was anyone in literary circles appeared at the celebrations. William Cullen Bryant and Fitz-Greene Halleck gave orations at the New York Celebration. A speaker at the Boston celebration noted, "As the home and head-quarters of so many American poets, the voice of poetry was not wanting on this occasion to do honour to the memory of the Scottish Bard, and no fewer than four original poems were composed for the occasion, one by Oliver Wendell Holmes, two by Professor James Russell Lowell, and one by Mr. John G. Whittier."[62] If writers could not appear in person, then they sent their regrets that were then read out at the event, as was the case for Washington Irving, Henry W. Longfellow, Dion Boucicault, and Bayard Taylor (the same Bayard Taylor who had participated in the earlier Ayr Festival). In addition to the requisite toasts made to Burns and to Scottish Literature, there were also toasts to American Literature, American Poets, and the American Press. Thomas Fraser's poem on Burns, which won the Burns Club of Baltimore's contest for the centenary, suggests the literal translation of Burns to North American soil:

Dear bonny Doon, clear gurglin' Ayr,
Pure Afton an' the Lugar fair,
Can claim his sangs their ain nae mair,
      Sin' lang years syne,
Braw Hudson an' thrang Delaware
      Kenn'd every line![63]

America here is styled as the New World recipient not only of Burns's republican values, but also of his poetic muse, since the very rivers have memorized his songs.

This use of Burns to promote American values and culture is, of course, complicated. Although Burns is used to gesture toward a fundamental political difference between the United States and Britain, that difference is expressed in terms which suggest the close relationship between the two. Burns may have been the originator of "American Liberty," but he was, after all, technically British. By marking him as a representative of "the great uprising of the middle class against the armed and privileged minorities," American commentators thus also suggested their reliance on their colonial parent. At the same time, however, Burns's unusual position within the British canon (as we saw embodied in the Crystal Palace display) made him an appropriate model for a nation whose identity was based on a myth of exceptionalism. By identifying with Burns, Americans were able to further stake out their singular position in relation to their British predecessors. In 1859, celebrations in America, as in Canada, capitalized on the fluidity of Burns's identity in order to stake out their own national positions.

---

[62] Ballantine (ed.), *Chronicle*, pp. 552–3.
[63] Thomas Fraser, *Prize Poem, Written for the Baltimore Burns Club Centennial Celebration of the Birthday of Burns* (Baltimore, 1859), p. 4.

As well as gesturing toward a wider national consolidation, however, the Burns celebrations in America also suggested the different regional interests beneath the surface of the supposedly United States, interests that would erupt in a bloody civil war two years later. In New York, a speaker used Burns for an abolitionist message, denouncing the idea that he would have actually gone "to Jamaica as an overseer of a plantation": "I think I see Robert Burns following a gang of slaves, and chanting 'A man's a man for a' that.' Poor Burns was in a very bad way, but he was not as bad as that." Similarly, at the meeting in the Revere House in Boston, a Mr. John Wilson asserted, "His was not the maxim, 'My country, right or wrong!'—his, not the feeling which would laud a declaration of independence, without applying its ground-truths to all, irrespective of their condition, their colour, or their clime."[64] Meanwhile, in Milwaukee, Wisconsin, the occasion of Burns's centenary was useful in promoting the expansion of the Western frontier, as Judge Hubbell, in responding to the toast to America, proclaimed,

> Heaven, in mercy, gave to man this Western Continent ... that he might try to lift up the whole human family; and he has lifted up this portion of the family, high on the hills of science, of art, of practical freedom, of unrivalled prosperity, and resistless progress, until we hear the distant voices of the nations, far down in the vallies below, calling to us for a helping hand, to lift them up to our American level.[65]

As I have suggested, Burns's unstable position—suggesting both the incorporation of the local in the promotion of imperial interests and the resistance to the imperium—proved useful in constructing the varied kinds of identities being negotiated in the British North American provinces and in the United States in the mid-nineteenth century. Given the impulse to reinvent Burns on the other side of the Atlantic, it is not surprising, perhaps, to find out that the idea for the international Burns celebration apparently originated in North America—in New York. Although this fact is not mentioned in Ballantine's *Chronicle*, and even Emerson seems to have been vague about the origin of the connected celebrations, the *Illustrated London News* for 29 January 1859 asserts that it is in America that "the idea of the Centenary seems to have originated, and afterwards in the British Isles, where it was taken up as soon as suggested."[66] *The Centennial Birth-Day of Robert Burns as Celebrated by the Burns Club of New York* confirms this, stating that the notion of a global celebration originated with the New York Burns Club "several months previous to the close of the year 1858" when the club was seeking to honor the birthday of Robert Burns "in a manner worthy the occasion

---

64   Ballantine (ed.), *Chronicle*, pp. 580, 556.

65   G.W. Featherstonehaugh, *The Centennial Anniversary of the Birthday of Robert Burns, As Commemorated by his Countrymen in the City of Milwaukee, Wisconsin, January 25th, 1859* (Milwaukee, 1859), p. 21.

66   *Illustrated London News* (29 January 1859): 98.

and creditable to the chief city of the Western Hemisphere."[67] In October, 1858, the New York Club sent a circular out to "kindred associations in the cities of Great Britain, the United States and the British Provinces" requesting recipients to

> make arrangements ... for such co-operation as may be practicable for the purpose of giving united expression to those sentiments of reverence for the memory and admiration for the genius of the Poet of Humanity, which, while especially natural and becoming to his countrymen, find an echo and a sympathy in the hearts of the people of America, and of every civilized nation.[68]

The circular, which was also published in "the leading newspapers of London, Edinburgh, Glasgow, and other places in Great Britain," reads like a nineteenth-century equivalent of the instructions for "Global Burns Hosts" as it indicates what interested parties could do to join in: "Communications with reference to the proposed arrangements may be addressed to Vair Clirehugh, Corresponding Secretary of the Burns Club of the city of New York, at the Astor House."[69] If Scotland had produced the original Burns, then it was the Americans who set out to create global Burns.

In *Virtual Americas*, Giles offers the notion of an "ideology of exchange" from which "estranged perspectives on particular cultures can appear at their most rewarding."[70] America, he suggests, "introduces an element of strangeness into British culture, just as British traditions, often in weirdly hollowed out or parodic forms, shadow the democratic designs of the American republic."[71] In the case of the Burns Centenary, this "element of strangeness" is rendered even stranger by the fact that it also involves not just Britain and America, but also Scotland and Canada. Examining the Centenary suggests how the identity of transatlantic locations—both in Canada and the United States—is established not just through the process of selectively incorporating and rejecting elements of Britishness, but also using representations of Britishness that are themselves highly ambivalent.

The Centenary celebrations both in Britain and across the ocean in North America also effected a fundamental change in the nature of how Burns was understood and consumed after 1859. For what is striking in all the events is the degree of simulation involved, simulation which draws on both old and new technologies. We have already considered the display of Burns in London and the dispersal of Burnsian relics. But equally important are the representations of Burns at those locations which lacked actual objects connected with the poet and so resorted to simulation. At Belleville, Canada West, for example, a replica of Burns's cottage made of Canadian fir boughs was "mounted on runners" for the "special feature of the day": "a sleigh ride" with "over sixty sleighs." In Ottawa,

---

[67]   Cunningham (ed.), *Centennial Birth-day*, p. 9.
[68]   Ibid., p. 9–10.
[69]   Ibid., p. 10.
[70]   Giles, *Virtual Americas*, p. 5.
[71]   Ibid.

Burns was made to loom large over the whole city: "The entire range of windows fronting on Sussex and George Streets were brilliantly illuminated, and on the front of the building were placed three transparencies, one being a well-executed full-length portrait of the immortal bard."[72] The Mechanics' Hall celebration in Hamilton, Canada West, also included "a transparency" of a stanza of Burns's famous poem, "A Man's a Man":

> "It's coming yet, for a' that,
> That man to man, the world o'er,
> Shall brothers be, for a' that."

Both the man and his words, then, were metonymically relocated to new venues in 1859. Such relocations and recontextualizations suggest a process of virtualization, a process that Pierre Levy identifies as producing a fundamental "change in identity, a displacement of the center of ontological gravity of the object being considered."[73] Although it would be erroneous to speak of the pre-1859 Burns as constituting a clear "center of ontological gravity," an original from which subsequent simulacra were produced, the first Burns Centenary resulted in a proliferation of representations of Burns. Burns became useful not only as an object but also as a technology of communication. Significantly, many of the speeches held on 25 January 1859 liken Burns to the "electric fluid" running along the telegraph cable.[74] At Glasgow's City Hall celebration, for example, one speaker suggested that the "songs of Burns are the electric sparks which flash along" the telegraph cable, while, similarly, the Chairman of the New Orleans celebration effused, "The electric flash blends our feelings in one current, as the magic songs of Burns unite the hearts of his countrymen throughout the world."[75] The 1859 Centenary was a celebration of global connection with Burns reconceived as the message and the medium of that connection.

It was a global vision of technological unification that was, however, constrained by physical limits. The telegraphic connection of which Burns was both symbol and conductor was in fact limited to operating between the eastern cities of North America and between British and European cities. There had been a transatlantic telegraph cable operative in 1857, but it had faltered, only to be followed by several more disastrous attempts.[76] For George Hally, Chairman of the gathering at the Masonic Hall in Auchterarder, however, Burns's poetry both anticipated the transatlantic cable and in some ways compensated for its failure:

---

[72]   Ballantine (ed.), *Chronicle*, pp. 512, 532.

[73]   Pierre Levy, *Becoming Virtual: Reality in the Digital Age*, trans. Robert Bononno (New York and London, 1998), p. 26.

[74]   Ballantine (ed.), *Chronicle*, p. 536.

[75]   Ibid., p. 573.

[76]   See Henry Martyn Field, *History of the Atlantic Telegraph* (New York, 1869).

although the Atlantic telegraph cable lately laid by the energy, capital, and skill of two great nations, is now silent and dumb, there is a cable of poetry and song, laid nearly a hundred years ago by a simple ploughman, which neither the length, the depths, nor the storms of the Atlantic can ever sever, and through which this day the electric sparks flow, making hearts in America beat warmly and in unison with those in Scotland.[77]

In 1859, the "electric flash [that] blends our feelings in one current" stopped short at the Atlantic even as it gestured symbolically, albeit ambiguously, toward the "energy, capital, and skill" on the opposite shore.[78]

---

[77] Ballantine (ed.), *Chronicle*, p. 170.
[78] Ibid., pp. 573, 170.

PART 5
Remediating Burns in Transatlantic Culture

Chapter 12
Burns in the Park:
A Tale of Three Monuments[1]

Michael E. Vance

James Inglis Reid's butcher shop on Granville Street in the heart of downtown Vancouver, British Columbia, had a version of the "Selkirk Grace" lit up in neon over the entry way until the business was closed and the building torn down to make way for the expansion of a downtown shopping mall in 1986. The illuminated marquee, with the line "We Hae Meat That Ye Can Eat" on each side, was a well-known local landmark. The allusion proved to be a powerful marketing tool with Burns Night being the biggest sales day of the year for the firm.[2] Reid, a native of Kirkintilloch, very likely provided the haggis for the Immortal Memory that followed the unveiling of the Burns statue in Stanley Park in 1928. As one of the founding members of the Vancouver Scottish Society, Reid offered the response to one of the toasts made that evening, and he would certainly have been in the crowd that witnessed the unveiling. Reid's butcher shop is gone, but photographs of the Vancouver unveiling survive as they do for other Burns monuments in North America. As Chris Whatley has recently demonstrated with photographs of unveilings in nineteenth-century Scotland, such images can provide an indication of the intentions of those who erected the monuments as well as the response of contemporaries to their creation.[3]

In this light, David J. Martin's photograph of the Vancouver proceedings in Stanley Park, taken on 25 August 1928, can be compared with H.D. McClellan's

[1]   I wish to thank the staff of the Vancouver City Archives, the Toronto City Archives, the Archives of Ontario and the Public Archives of Nova Scotia for the assistance they provided while I was researching this chapter. I also wish to thank Douglas Gibson, Geoff Hudson and Renée Hulan for their advice and suggestions. This chapter has also benefited from Sharon Alker's careful editing, for which I am grateful. All errors and omissions, however, are mine alone.

[2]   Reid opened his landmark shop in 1925 with the help of another immigrant Scot and experienced butcher, Horatio Nelson Menzies (Christoph Voss, "James Inglis Reid, Ltd. Fonds," *City of Vancouver Archives Newsletter*, 3 [October 2006]: 1–2, http://vancouver.ca/ctyclerk/archives/about/NewsNo3.pdf, accessed 25 October 2009).

[3]   Christopher A. Whatley, "Robert Burns, Memorialization, and the 'Heart-beatings' of Victorian Scotland," in Murray Pittock (ed.), *Robert Burns in Global Culture* (Lewisburg, 2011). I am grateful to Professor Whatley for allowing me to read an earlier version of his essay.

Fig. 12.1   David J. Martin's photograph of the crowd at the Vancouver unveiling ceremony in 1928. City of Vancouver Archives, CVA 518–13.

photograph of the Toronto unveiling ceremonies in Allan Gardens on 21 July 1902. Both photographers direct the viewer's attention to the statute and the speaker standing at the base of the monument in the act of giving a formal address (see Figures 12.1 and 12.2). The two statues portray Burns in a standing position and are elevated on pedestals, but the two crowds are very different. McClellan's Toronto photograph shows a stiff formal event with the participants in their finest Edwardian dress, while Martin's photograph records a large informal crowd in relaxed 1920s fashions stretching out over the lawn and the roadway in front of the monument.[4] In contrast to the Vancouver and Toronto images, the only photograph

---

    [4]   H.D. McClellan appears to have worked only briefly in Canada since he is recorded in neither the 1901 nor the 1911 census, but the Toronto City Directory for 1903 lists him as the proprietor of View Photo Company in a building on Yonge Street that also served as a boarding house for single working men. David J. Martin apprenticed to a professional photographer in Calgary after his family had immigrated to Canada in 1905 following the failure of their Glasgow hardware business. His collection of more than 12,000 photographs is housed in the National Archives in Ottawa, but copies of some images are also held by the City of Vancouver Archives (CVA). See "David Martin Fonds" R7612–0–8–E, National Archives of Canada, and CVA 518.

Fig. 12.2   H.D. McClellan's photograph of the Toronto unveiling in 1902. City of Vancouver Archives, Mon P62.

of the Halifax Burns statue that appears to have survived from 1919, the year of that monument's erection, was taken by a Notman Studio photographer sometime after the unveiling and has no people in it. Like the statue itself, the image is essentially a portrait of Burns in the empty Victoria Park setting (see Figure 12.3).[5]

These contemporary photographic images of the Toronto, Halifax and Vancouver statues, erected in each of the first three decades of the twentieth century respectively, provide the starting point for this chapter, which places these particular Burns monuments in their historical context.[6] The discussion begins with the unveiling ceremonies and the iconography of the monuments themselves—both of which reveal transatlantic and local aspects of the statues' design and reception. The committees responsible for the erection of each city's statue are then examined in order to illustrate the local and international influences reflected in their monument selections and fundraising efforts. Finally, the impact of the three monuments is assessed with a discussion of their siting and subsequent history, revealing how the Burns statues are situated within the broader legacy of colonization in Canada.

The transatlantic character of all three unveiling ceremonies was reflected in the invitations extended to Scottish speakers to provide the main address on each occasion, but the speeches, the crowd arrangements, and event programs all reveal a tension between the organizers' desire to celebrate Burns as an outstanding Scot and the poet's universal relevance. The two objectives are readily apparent in Ramsay MacDonald's address given at the Vancouver unveiling. MacDonald's status as leader of the opposition and recent Prime Minister of Britain made him a particularly welcome speaker, and given his Labour party affiliation and humble Lossiemouth origins, it is not surprising that he chose to emphasize Burns's democratic spirit in his address (see Figure 12.4).[7] According to MacDonald,

---

5   The Halifax Notman Studio was established by the Scottish immigrant William Notman as a branch of his highly successful Montreal business, which specialized in providing portraits of the elite. Oliver Hill, the owner of the Halifax branch in 1919, started as an apprentice with Notman before finally purchasing the business in 1891, which he ran until his death in 1923.

6   Much of the following account is based on the records of the Toronto Burns Monument Committee held by the Archives of Ontario (F1150–MU449 and 450); *The Annals of the North British Society of Halifax,* 1904–1923 (Halifax, 1943); and *Vancouver's Tribute to Burns, published to commemorate the unveiling of a statue to Scotland's immortal bard in Stanley Park* (Vancouver, 1928). Subsequent footnotes indicate when additional sources have been consulted.

7   The invitation to provide an address at the Vancouver unveiling coincided with a Canadian holiday that MacDonald was undertaking with his daughters Ishbel and Sheila at a time when he was attempting, as Leader of the Opposition, to rebuild the Labour Party's political fortunes after the defeat of their first government in 1924. See David Marquand, "MacDonald, (James) Ramsay (1866–1937)," *Oxford Dictionary of National Biography* (Oxford University Press, September 2004, online edn, http://www.oxforddnb.com, accessed 25 October, 2009.

Fig. 12.3   Notman Studio's 1919 photograph of the Halifax Burns in Victoria Park, Nova Scotia. Archives and Records Management, Notman Studio Collection, 1983–310/A-129.

Fig. 12.4   David J. Martin's photograph of Ramsay MacDonald addressing the crowd in Stanley Park. City of Vancouver Archives, CVA 518–14.

"Burns ... told the world that in Scotland there is a sturdiness of heart that belongs to the man of independent mind, the man who can lift up his head in the eyes of the world, poor and down-trodden, but still remaining, 'A Man for a' that'." But MacDonald also emphasized the role of Burns in maintaining Scottish identity overseas by invoking the Canadian Boat Song, "still seeing in your dreams the Hebrides," and the image of the emigrant's well-thumbed copy of Burns, consulted "long after they had committed it almost completely to memory."

Another Scot, the Edinburgh-born historian Prof. James Eddie Todd, was asked to provide an address for the Halifax unveiling, but his speech was read by another speaker when he chose not to return to his Dalhousie University post after wartime service in India. Todd's address for the Halifax unveiling does not appear to have survived, but in a previous speech given to the North British Society on St Andrews day in 1913 he had, like MacDonald, emphasized Burns's influence on Scottish identity, claiming that no individual had done as much as Burns to "serve Scottish nationality" and that, as a result, "the language in which he wrote his poetry would never die."[8] However, George H. Murray, the Premier of Nova Scotia and the only speaker to address the Halifax crowd in person, stressed the universal appeal of Burns's sentiment:

> He lives in our hearts because with all his genius he was entirely human. And by reason of his wealth of human understanding he was enabled in his poetry to tap the universal well-springs of love and sympathy ... [the] unfailing affection for the poetry of Burns proves that the world craves the sympathy that the heart of Burns yielded without measure. Nevertheless we are all too apt to leave out the human element in our dealings with one another, in our business, in our politics, in our national relationships.[9]

Such an appeal to universality had earlier been voiced by the Rev. Prof. William Clarke, the Aberdeenshire-born Professor of Mental and Moral Philosophy at Toronto's Trinity College. In his 1902 address before that city's monument, Clarke quoted "A Man's a Man for a' that" but reduced the poem to a broad statement about shared humanity and ignored the explicit demand for social equality contained within its lines. Like the other addresses, Clarke's speech also highlighted Burns's poetic genius and humble Scottish origins, though for the clergyman scholar it was

---

[8]   Viscount Robert Bannatyne Finlay, another native of Edinburgh and the former Vice Chancellor of Britain, was also invited to give an address, but his speech was read by another speaker when illness prevented his attendance at the Halifax ceremony. Prof. Todd, who had joined Dalhousie in 1913, remained in Britain after the war and became head of the History Department at Queen's University in Belfast (J.E. Todd, "The Apprenticeship of a Professor of History, 1903–1919," *History*, 44/151[June 1959]: 115–98).

[9]   The author of the article in which Murray's comments were reported went further, stating that Burns, "the poet of freedom," should be studied by "all of us in this community, for the development of a broader vision, and deeper sense of brotherhood" while at the same time suggesting that the recent Great War had been fought for the sentiment contained in Burns's "A Man's a Man for a' that" (*Morning Chronicle*, 15 September 1919).

the poet's sense of morality that had particular appeal. According to Clarke, "It had been claimed that Burns was a singer and nothing more, but he maintained that [Burns] was a great teacher" and that "it would help every clergyman if he would meditate upon the presentation of hell in 'The Epistle to a Young Friend' before going to the pulpit."[10] That poem's evocation of one's conscience, rather than fear of damnation, as a guide to personal conduct resonated with Clarke's theology and social conservatism. Edwin Muir claimed that in Scotland, conservative commemorations like Clarke's had transformed Burns from the "poor man's poet" into a figure that resembled "Holy Willie."[11]

Certainly, there is little evidence in the Canadian ceremonies, as Chris Whatley has found with the nineteenth-century Scottish unveilings, for alternative readings of Burns from labor organizations or even their participation in the events. Indeed, a proposal to move the day of the Toronto unveiling from Monday to Saturday so that "working men" could attend was, in the words recorded in the monument committee minute book, "not entertained." The organizers of all three Canadian unveilings sought to ensure that their events were "respectable" occasions, but the Toronto committee went further by seeking to make their ceremony exclusive. A roped enclosure was created around the Toronto monument, and only individuals who had been given tickets printed especially for the unveiling were admitted. Among those issued invitations were the committee members and their wives, the heads of the city's various Scottish Societies, as well as leading clergyman, political figures, and military leaders from both Toronto and Montreal. The self-conscious respectability of the crowd is readily discernable in H.D. McClellan's photograph (see Figure 12.2), but the guest list was not without controversy. Various Ontario branches of the Sons of Scotland, an insurance and social society open to Scots and their descendants that survives to this day, contributed to the statue fund but only their "chief," Col Alexander Fraser, was admitted to the reserved area, provoking a sharp exchange of letters between the parties. A compromise was worked out, and on the day of the unveiling, 220 members of the Sons of Scotland led by the 48th Highland Regiment Pipe Band marched to Allan Gardens and assembled as a body outside the enclosure. At the Vancouver unveiling a reserved area for invited guests was also created, and leading military and political figures, such as Vice Admiral Sir Cyril T.M. Fuller and Dr Simon Fraser Tolmie, the Premier of British Columbia, were seated there, but the group also included Miss Mary Isdale's class of young Highland dancers. Indeed, David Martin's photograph (see Figure 12.1) shows no obvious demarcation between the reserved area and the crowd. The use

---

[10] *The Mail and Empire*, 22 July 1902. Born in Inverurie, Clarke had studied at Aberdeen and Oxford universities, holding a series of church appointments, including deacon of Wells Cathedral, before emigrating to Canada. Several well-known orators were considered for the Toronto unveiling including the Scottish-Canadians George William Ross and Duncan C. Fraser, Liberal Members of Parliament for Middlesex West, Ontario, and Guysborough, Nova Scotia, respectively. Fraser was initially the favored choice.

[11] Muir was responding to another speech by Ramsay Macdonald given at a Dumfries unveiling in 1936. See "Burns and Holy Willie," in Andrew Noble (ed.), *Edwin Muir: Uncollected Scottish Criticism* (London, 1982), pp. 189–92.

of loudspeakers ensured that all those assembled in Stanley Park would have been able to hear the speeches, perhaps requiring less formal seating arrangements, but the decision to pass out event programs and commemorative badges to the crowd as souvenirs reflected a more inclusive approach by the organizers at the outset.[12] The Toronto committee also had badges made but these were reserved for the exclusive use of the Executive Committee, and event programs were only distributed to invited guests. Programs for the Halifax unveiling were also printed, but these were only circulated to members of the North British Society, which had raised the money for the statue. A platform was constructed in Halifax for the speakers and invited guests, but the inclusion of the Belgian, French, and American consuls in addition to the usual political, clerical, and military leaders among the guests was as much a reflection of the immediate post-war circumstances of the event as the desire to give it a respectable appearance.

While crowd arrangements differed, the programs for all three ceremonies had many similarities. "A Man's a Man for a' that" was performed at both the Toronto and Vancouver unveilings, but all three ceremonies commenced with "There was a lad was born in Kyle" and ended with "Auld Lang Syne" and "God Save the King." A shift toward a more Scottish focus, however, can be seen by the selection of "Ye banks and braes o' bonie Doon" for the Halifax event and more particularly with the choice of "Scots Wha Hae" for the Vancouver program. The latter song had been sung at the North British Society's St Andrews Festivals and by members of the Toronto monument committee at the end of their meetings, but, perhaps because of the song's overt Scottish patriotism, it was excluded in favor of Burns's more autobiographical and universal songs—echoing the theme of the addresses given by both Clarke and Murray. The shift in emphasis from the universal to the clearly Scottish can also be detected in the draping of the monuments themselves. The Toronto Burns had been merely covered with plain linen cloth while the Halifax statue was draped in the Union Jack. In Vancouver, however, the Saltire hid the monument until the moment of unveiling, reflecting the claims made in MacDonald's address about the link between Burns and Scottish identity overseas. The association of Highlandism and Scottish identity forged in Victorian Scotland was also evident in all three programs, despite Burns's own identification with his native Ayrshire. Two militia unit bands, the 48th Highlanders in Toronto and the Seaforth Highlanders in Vancouver, provided both kilts and bagpipes at their city's ceremonies, while the North British Society's own pipers provided both at the Halifax event.[13]

---

[12] A newsreel was also made and shown later in Vancouver's Capitol, Pantages, Orpheum and Dominion theatres "as well as throughout the province and Dominion" (*Vancouver's Tribute to Burns*).

[13] Despite their prominent place in the program, pipers are not in view in McClellan's photograph, perhaps reflecting the fact that the Toronto Committee at first planned to use the brass and choral sections of the 48th band and only changed its plans after objections were raised by the Sons of Scotland. In contrast, kilted pipers can clearly be seen in Martin's photograph beside the Vancouver monument and a piper, James Alexander, was featured at the Burns Supper held in the Hotel Georgia after the unveiling.

Newspaper reports of the unveiling ceremonies also reflect a shift in emphasis from Burns as a universal poet to Burns as representative of Scottish identity. In 1902, the *Daily Star* announced the unveiling of the Toronto monument with the headline "Burns The Poet Of Humanity," while two and half decades later the *Sunday Province* headline for the article on the Vancouver ceremonies read "Scotsmen Pay Tribute to Burns." The quantity and focus of the coverage also changed over time. In Toronto, the *Mail and Empire*, *Daily Star*, and *The Globe* all provided extensive reports on the unveiling, giving verbatim accounts of the speeches and detailing the features of the statue as well as providing numerous Burns quotations.[14] The Halifax press devoted less space to the story, but the *Morning Chronicle* gave an account comparable to the earlier Toronto coverage including the publication of a poem written by the Rev. Alexander Louis Fraser commemorating the event, "To Robert Burns":

> Death does not Freedom's force demobilize,
> > So thou art linked with these great times of ours,
> And here today our hearty plaudits rise
> > In recognition of thy deathless powers.

In the nineteenth century, Canadian newspapers had regularly published local poets such as Fraser, including Alexander McLachlan, the "Burns of Canada," and John Imrie, the Glasgow-born printer and Burns Monument Committee member, who tried to raise funds for the Toronto Statue with "A Monument to Burns we will Raise" published in several local Ontario papers:

> Toronto Scots have said,—
> Young Canada's first Cairn of praise,
> > To Scotland's honor'd dead!
> Let grateful hearts, and willing hands,
> > Pay tribute to his name,
> Till soon within Toronto stands
> > His Monument of fame!

Several poems were also composed for the Vancouver Burns in Scots dialect, including W.S. Mitchell's tribute:

> O Robin, could ye see the day
> When buirdly Scots in great array,
> On Britain's shores that face Cathay
> > Your Memory mark
> Wi' nine fit bronze, on granite base,
> Such as the toon o' Ayr doth grace;
> Wi' Presidents you've got your place
> > In Stanley Park.

---

[14]   *Sunday Province*, 26 August 1928; *Toronto Daily Star*, *The Mail and Empire*, and *The Globe*, 22 July 1902.

Unlike Scottish immigrant poet James Anderson, whose songs had been published by newspapers in British Columbia's gold fields, Mitchell's tribute only found publication in the event's commemorative book published by the Vancouver Burns Fellowship. The Vancouver press was much more interested in Ramsay MacDonald's politics—reminding readers of his previous 1906 visit to the province when he met with socialist miners' organizers in Nanaimo, reprinting his comments regarding British Liberal leader Lloyd George, and analyzing his address to the Canada Club on empire and immigration given the day before the Burns ceremony. Even Noel Robinson's lengthy and appreciative editorial on the unveiling in the *Morning Star* emphasized MacDonald's political career, drawing parallels with Burns's life story in order to illustrate his points, while the *Vancouver Sun* merely provided photos and captions of the Stanley Park proceedings.[15] In marked contrast to the Toronto reports at the start of the century, it appears that by 1928 the press agreed with the *Province*, which only devoted four short paragraphs to the unveiling, that it was essentially a "Scottish" event.

The iconography of the statues themselves, however, was the product of a series of remarkable transatlantic exchanges. The first Burns statue commissioned early in the nineteenth century for Calton Hill in Edinburgh was designed in marble by the London sculptor John Flaxman, but as early as the 1840s the Tarbolton mason-turned-sculptor, James Crawford Thom, had erected an "imposing statue of Robert Burns" in Newark, New Jersey, where he had settled. Thom's statue is apparently now lost, but the Flaxman Burns remains in the National Portrait Gallery in Edinburgh. Like the statues in Vancouver, Halifax, and Toronto, the Flaxman Burns is in a standing position as is the first bronze of Burns executed by George Ewing for Glasgow's George Square in 1877. Both the Flaxman and Ewing statues have Burns holding daisies in one hand—a clear allusion to "To a Mountain Daisy" and an obviously romantic interpretation of the poet that was developed further in transatlantic statuary most notably by Sir John Robert Steell's monumental statue in New York's Central Park. Unveiled in 1880, with versions appearing shortly after in Dundee, London, and Dunedin, New Zealand, Steell's Burns shows the poet in a seated position, pen rather than daisy in hand, with his gaze fixed to the sky. Andrew Carnegie thought that the sculptor had shown "Burns as a humpback simpleton" but what Steell was trying to recreate was the moment when Burns composed "To Mary in Heaven" as recounted by Jean Armour via James Lockhart and John MacDiarmid.[16] The reimagining of Mary Campbell as Burns's muse reached its apogee in the late nineteenth century, particularly in North America, but clearly influenced the Aberdeen-born and Edinburgh-based

---

[15] *Vancouver Daily Province*, 25 August 1928; *Morning Star*, 26 August 1928; *Vancouver Sun*, 27 August 1928.

[16] See Mark Stocker, "'The head o' the Bard sweeps the Southern Sky!' Sir John Steell's Statues of Robert Burns: From Dundee to Dunedin," *Journal of the Scottish Society for Art History*, 11 (2006): 18–25 (p. 19); James A. Mackay, *Burnsiana* (Alloway, 1988); and Edward Goodwillie, *The World's Memorials of Robert Burns* (Detroit, 1911).

Steell. The pedestal for his Dundee Burns, also unveiled in 1880, was inscribed with the lines "Thou lingering star—My Mary from my soul was torn" and, along with the statue itself, can be seen as a forerunner to the Highland Mary statues later erected at Dunoon and Liverpool in 1896. The most transparent sculptural representation of the cult of Highland Mary, however, is the Burns Monument unveiled in 1900 in Beacon Hill Park, Victoria, British Columbia. The bronze sculpture, designed by the London-born Royal Canadian Academy sculptor Hamilton MacCarthy, extended Steele's design by creating a pair of figures with a seated Burns staring up at Mary standing beside him (see Figure 12.5).[17] As a consequence, the Victoria Burns monument, the first erected in Canada, reflected both the romantic interpretation of Mary and the seated convention for Burns figures established by Steele.

Mark Stocker has suggested that Steell seated Burns simply in order to match the position of Central Park's Walter Scott statue, which stands directly opposite; nevertheless, for a time it became the standard pose on both sides of the Atlantic.[18] The Dumfries monument, the only one executed by a female artist, Amelia Hill (née Paton) and unveiled two years after Steele's New York monument, has a marble Burns in a seated position, as does the bronze statue in Albany, New York, unveiled in 1888. But by the 1890s the standing position was once again favored, commencing with George A. Lawson's bronze Burns erected in Ayr in 1891 which would prove to be the most popular representation of the poet. The Halifax and Vancouver statues were molded in Lawson's original casts, and replicas were also made for Melbourne in 1904, Detroit in 1921, Montreal in 1930, Winnipeg in 1936, and the Sorbonne in Paris in 1938.[19] Unlike Steell's seated Burns or the earlier standing figures of Flaxman and Ewing, the Edinburgh-born Lawson depicted Burns in a strikingly masculine pose with crossed arms, clenched fists, and fixed gaze. Fellow Edinburgh sculptor David W. Stevenson depicted Burns in a similar manly pose for the Leith monument, unveiled in 1898 and reproduced for Newcastle-upon-Tyne in 1901 and Toronto in 1902. While Lawson crossed the poet's arms, Stevenson has one arm crossing Burns's chest grasping his coat and the other by his side gripping his bonnet as he takes a forward stride. Both Lawson and Stevenson modeled their sculptures on James Nasmyth's 1786 portrait, and Stevenson published his reasoning for preferring that representation in 1892, stating that "[t]he manly forehead; the stamp of individual character in every

---

[17]   *The Colonist* (Victoria, British Columbia), 11 November 1900.

[18]   Stocker, "Sir John Steell's Statues of Robert Burns," p. 19.

[19]   The Sorbonne monument was hidden during the war and thus escaped the fate of many other bronzes that were melted down during the occupation (Mackay, *Burnsiana*, pp. 40–41); see also Kirrily Freeman, *Bronzes to Bullets: Vichy and the Destruction of French Public Statuary, 1941–1944* (Stanford, 2009).

Fig. 12.5   Hamilton MacCarthy's statue of Burns and Highland Mary erected
              in 1900 in Beacon Hill Park. Photographer: M. Vance.

feature, the mobile mouth, the eloquent eye, and the general look of engaging frankness are all here."[20]

While the Canadian-designed Victoria monument had taken the earlier transatlantic romantic fascination with Mary to the extreme, the Toronto, Halifax, and Vancouver copies of the Stevenson and Lawson statues were clearly connected to the shift toward more masculine representation that had first occurred in Scotland. Nevertheless, local characteristics were given to each statue by both the design and construction of the pedestals and by the attached bronze plaques depicting scenes from Burns's poems. All three monuments used local stone carved by local craftsmen with designs chosen by the statue committees. The Vancouver committee selected a Columbia grey granite pedestal, "in keeping with the trend of modern thought," modeled on Whitney Warren's base for the Dante statue in New York, while the local firm McIntosh Granite & Marble Company designed and carved Toronto's monumental granite pedestal that features decorative thistles surrounded by laurels in bas relief. Johnson P. Porter, a mason from Pictou, Nova Scotia, was responsible for carving the Halifax pedestal of Nova Scotia granite that bears the inscription "A man's a man for a' that" on the front face. The panels attached to these monuments have some common themes. All three statues have scenes depicting "The Cotter's Saturday Night," "Tam O' Shanter," and "To a Mountain Daisy." While the Halifax and Vancouver panels arrived with the statues from their London foundry, the Toronto plaques were designed by Emanuel Otto Hahn, a German immigrant who had studied at the Ontario College of Art and Industrial Design. At one point, the Toronto statue committee asked that the panel designs be redrawn because the figures were too German looking and required "Scotch faces," but the selection of images, which also included a scene representing "John Anderson, My Jo," was undoubtedly in the hands of the committee rather than the artist. The fact that the Halifax monument also has an additional scene depicting the "Jolly Beggars" suggests that even when the images were supplied, rather than commissioned, local committees were involved in their selection.

Attaching panels to the statues was also a transatlantic development. While the first pedestal scene, showing Burns being crowned by his Muse, appeared on the Flaxman monument, only inscriptions of Burns's poetry appeared on Scottish monuments until the 1890s. The bronze plaques on the Glasgow Burns were added by James Ewing at the turn of the century, and those that adorn the Leith and Ayr monuments were also added at a later date. Given the scenes depicted on the monuments, however, it appears likely the panels were added to the Ayr monument before 1896 when the Irvine and Paisley monuments were erected, the only Scottish statues with contemporaneous panels. Two of the Ayr panels designed by Lawson himself, of "The Cotter's Saturday Night" and "Tam O' Shanter," are those which also appear on the Halifax and Vancouver monuments.

---

[20] "The Portraits of Burns," *Burns Chronicle and Club Directory*, 1 (25 January 1892): 79–95.

A third panel of the "Jolly Beggars," a gift of the Freemasons of Scotland, was executed by the Ayr artist D. McGill, but the fourth panel, the gift of "twenty–five Americans" illustrating the parting of Burns and Highland Mary flanked by the muses Fate and Fame, was designed by the New York sculptor George Bissell.[21] Ayr's "American panel" not only reflected the ongoing fascination with Mary, but also the fact that the idea of attaching bronze scenes appears to have originated in the United States. The panels attached to Charles Calverley's Burns, unveiled in Albany, New York, in 1888, illustrate both "The Cotter's Saturday Night" and "Tam O' Shanter," ubiquitous scenes in all subsequent monuments, as well as "To a Mountain Daisy" found on the Vancouver, Halifax, and Toronto monuments (see Figure 12.6).[22]

The influence of Calverley's Burns on Toronto planners was evident as early as May 1891 when Peter Kinnear, a prominent Albany resident who had persuaded the local heiress Mary McPherson to fund the statue, provided Col Alexander Fraser with information about the monument and an introduction to the artist. At the time, Fraser, the editor of the *Mail and Empire* as well as Grand Chief of the Sons of Scotland, was serving as the secretary of the city's first Burns Statue Committee formed in March of that year. He would later become a member of the statue design subcommittee of the subsequent Burns Monument Committee which actually commissioned the Toronto Burns.[23] As the nearest statue at the time, it was natural that Toronto organizers would study Calverley's design, but Peter Kinnear also ensured that this would be the case by writing once again to the new committee when it formed in 1897.

Kinnear's correspondence with the Toronto Monument committee reflects the fact that there was a lively transatlantic network of lobbying at the turn of the twentieth century, with sculptors based in both North America and Britain seeking commissions. The committees included a large proportion of members with transatlantic connections who made use of their commercial and professional contacts to raise funds for the statues in the United States and Britain as well as in their own cities. The sculptors were aware of these connections and incorporated this knowledge into their lobbying efforts, which often began after reading about a plan to raise a monument in a newspaper announcement. For example, early in 1898, William Grant Stevenson, the younger brother of David Stevenson, wrote from Edinburgh to the committee after seeing "a cutting from a Toronto paper."[24] As evidence of his suitability for the commission, Stevenson included photographs

---

[21] Mackay, *Burnsiana*, pp. 33–42 and Goodwillie, *The World's Memorials of Robert Burns*, pp. 33–86.

[22] A fourth panel on the Albany monument illustrates lines from "Auld Lang Syne" ("The Burns Statue Number," *The New Albany*, 1/2 [July 1891]: 40).

[23] "Burns Statue Correspondence, 1891–92," *Fraser Papers*, Archives of Ontario, F1015 Mu1063.

[24] "Toronto Burns Monument Committee Fonds," Archives of Ontario, F1150–MU449 and 450.

Fig. 12.6   Photograph of the Albany Burns with Charles Caverley's annotations
               supplied to Col Alexander Fraser by the sculptor. Burns Monument,
               Washington Park (*c.* 1888). Archives of Ontario, F 1015–1.

of his monumental sculpture of William Wallace erected at Aberdeen as well as his Burns in marble for Kilmarnock and in bronze for Chicago. While unsuccessful in getting the Toronto commission, which went to his elder brother, a replica of Stevenson's Chicago Burns, erected in 1906, was unveiled in Fredericton, New Brunswick, in the same year. In his letter to the Toronto committee, Stevenson indicated that he was in communication with Burns Statue committees in San Francisco, where an American sculptor was eventually chosen, and Denver, where his Burns was selected and unveiled in 1904.

The Toronto and Vancouver committees also considered submissions from local sculptors, but all three cities ultimately chose Scottish models for their monuments.[25] The Toronto committee appears to have been influenced by the activities of Robert Barron, a local Scottish-born grocer, who collected photographs and models of Burns monuments during a 1901 tour of Scotland that included a visit to David Stevenson's Edinburgh studio. The committees, however, may have been predisposed to favor Scottish models given the fact that they were mainly comprised of Scottish immigrants, especially in Toronto and Vancouver, or individuals with particularly strong personal connections to Scotland, as was the case with the North British Society. The Toronto Burns Monument committee was led by the hotelier David Walker, who had emigrated from Scotland in 1850, while Mr. P. McAuslin Carrick, the President of the Vancouver Burns Fellowship, was a member of Glasgow's Clarinda Burns Club before arriving in British Columbia. Eben MacKay, a Chemistry Professor at Dalhousie University and the Vice-President of the North British Society who chaired the Halifax unveiling, was typical of the membership, being a Nova Scotian of Scottish descent born in Pictou County, while the society's ongoing links to Scotland were exemplified by Dugald Macgillivray, who headed the Burns Memorial Committee and also employed two Scottish domestics, Katie Fraser and Georgina Ross, in his household.[26]

Generally, the membership of all three committees was comprised of local professionals, businessmen, and civil servants who had professional dealings across North America and overseas and an interest in all things Scottish. Indeed, while individuals such as Alexander Fraser and John Imrie were members of both Toronto's Burns Literary Society and the Burns Monument Committee, only in Vancouver did an organization devoted to celebrating the works of the poet, the

---

[25] Before opting for the Lawson design, the North British Society considered a model for a Burns statue from the Edinburgh sculptor William Birnie Rhind whose younger brother John Massey Rhind had also lobbied for the Toronto commission. The younger Rhind had pursued a very successful career in the United States and, as with Stevenson, included in his letter photographs of his work and a printed prospectus illustrating his winning design for a monument in Pittsburgh that was finally completed in 1914. The Toronto committee considered a submission from the local sculptor, Mr. Dunbar, as well as the designs of the Ayr and Paisley statues and a Burns monument proposed for Boston.

[26] For David Walker, see the 1901 Census of Canada, Toronto City Centre, Ward No. 3 A–24 p. 1, line 38; for Dugald Macgillivray see the 1911 Census of Canada, 45 Halifax, p. 15, line 20.

Vancouver Burns Fellowship, spearhead the movement to erect a statue, but the Fellowship also appealed to groups such as St Andrews and Caledonia Society for assistance. Similarly, the first Toronto committee drew members from a broad range of organizations including the St Andrews, Caledonian, Orkney and Shetland, and Gaelic societies, various "camps" of the Sons of Scotland, and the Toronto Shinty-club. Its successor organization self–consciously recruited from the city's elite, printing up a circular letter inviting targeted individuals to participate, but the North British Society made no such effort since their membership already contained a high proportion of leading Halifax citizens.

While the committee memberships were clearly drawn from the local community, their fundraising efforts took them much further afield and even across the Atlantic.[27] The Toronto committee wrote to Andrew Carnegie while he was residing at Skibo Castle, Ardgay, and received a $100 contribution for their effort. They were also able to obtain transatlantic corporate donations from Ward, Lock & Company in London, as well as the distillers, John Walker & Sons in Kilmarnock and Whyte & McKay in Glasgow. Toronto businesses such as the O'Keefe Brewing Company, the Crystal Ice Company, and the Toronto Foundry Company also contributed to the fund, while some local individuals such as S.F. Mckinnon, A.E. Ames, and David Walker himself contributed sums equivalent to Andrew Carnegie's and that of Lord Strathcona, the Montreal railway magnate who contributed $150. After his death, the North British Society received $1000 from Strathcona's estate for their statue, but most of the funds were raised from the society's own membership. Two individuals, the Scottish-born British Columbia MLA William Dick and the Province's Lt Gov. Walter C. Nichol, subscribed more than $500 each for the Vancouver Burns, and the Fellowship also reported receiving contributions from Scotland, the United States, and elsewhere in the Dominion. This reflected the committee's own local fundraising efforts that, in addition to teas, whist drives, dances, and a music festival in Stanley Park, included the publication of a pamphlet by James Taylor, the statue fund secretary, entitled *Robert Burns, Patriot and Internationalist* that claimed Burns was an "inspired Seer" who "looked forward to the time when sanity and concord would prevail, when warfare would cease, and the nations would live together in bonds of international amity."[28]

Although all three committees claimed international or universal relevance for Burns, there are relatively few examples of engagement with the poet's legacy in the subsequent history of the Canadian monuments, despite the fact that all three were erected in prominent locations. The placing of the Burns statue in Stanley Park, however, had created some minor controversy when the Parks Board proposed a site near the inconspicuous duck ponds rather than the prominent position it now

---

[27] Subscription or membership lists are available in printed and manuscript form for all three groups, but space does not permit a full analysis of them here.

[28] James Taylor, *Robert Burns: Patriot and Internationalist* (Vancouver, 1926), pp. 6–7.

occupies near the entrance to the park on high ground overlooking Coal Harbour and downtown Vancouver. The current site was chosen by members of the Burns Fellowship who ensured that they would get their desired location by accompanying the Parks Board engineer as he assessed proposed sites for their suitability. One contemporary editorial used the dispute as an opportunity to question the entire idea of placing public statues in a park that was meant to preserve the forest in pristine condition as a natural retreat from the baneful influence of urban life.[29] But in the end, the Parks Board readily approved the Fellowship's site, perhaps because the precedent had already been made with the monument that commemorates President Warren Harding's visit to the city in nearby Malcolm Bowl and, on the road side immediately adjacent the Burns statue, the memorial to Queen Victoria. The Imperial monarch was also commemorated in Halifax by Victoria Park, a portion of the original Commons where the Burns monument is located. The siting of the statue there was uncontroversial and received unanimous approval from the city council. Indeed, the city engineer stated that the location, at the north end of the park near the corner of Spring Garden and South Park Streets facing the Public Gardens, "was ideal."[30] The Public Gardens, originally known as the Horticultural Gardens, which had also been carved out of the Halifax Commons, emulated London's Kew Gardens not only in collecting exotic plant species but also in displaying them in public space suited to Victorian ideas of rational and respectable recreation. As with the Halifax Burns, the Toronto monument was also linked to these *bourgeois* notions by virtue of its location. Allan Gardens, which was also imitative of Kew, emerged early as the location favored by the Toronto committee, and their choice also won easy approval from city council.[31] The statue was located facing outward in the northeastern corner of the park, ensuring that Burns would be the first sight visitors saw as they entered from the busy tramcar intersection at the corner of Carlton and Sherbourne streets.

The Toronto committee had selected Allan Gardens because of its location near the downtown core, but, because of its centrality, the park was also frequented by those on the margins of Toronto society. As early as 1909, the Parks Commissioner recommended that a special constable be assigned to Allan Gardens in order to prevent vandalism, and by the 1940s the *Globe* was reporting that the area surrounding the park had become the haunt of "bootleggers, prostitutes and dope

---

[29]   A. Fraser Reid, "Scots Won Site For Burns' Statue," *Vancouver Sun*, 24 January 1948. "A City of Memories," *Vancouver Sun*, 13 March 1928. Despite the "natural state" claims, there had been considerable manipulation of Stanley Park's ecology. See Sean Kheraj, "Improving Nature: Remaking Stanley Park's Forest, 1888–1931," *BC Studies*, 158 (Summer 2008): 63–90.

[30]   Halifax City Council Minutes, 18 July 1915, pp. 113–4.

[31]   Other locations considered by the Toronto committee included Queen's Park behind the Provincial legislature and a site in front of the Toronto Normal School. Allan Gardens was also known as the Horticultural Gardens until it was renamed in 1901 upon the death of George William Allan, a former President of the Horticultural Society and Mayor of Toronto, who had donated the land in 1857.

peddlers" who resided in the district's rooming houses.[32] Such problems persist to this day in the park, where the presence of members of Toronto's homeless community is obvious to any visitor. Indigenous people are disproportionately represented among Toronto's impoverished, and the Anishawbe Health Centre is located right beside Allan Gardens. In August 1999, members of the Allan Gardens Project organized an occupation in order to highlight the condition of the city's homeless population, but were forcibly removed by police. This was not, however, the first violent confrontation in the park. In the summer of 1933, police dispersed a demonstration numbering over two thousand organized Canadian Communists protesting the outlawing of their party, and in the spring of 1965, police arrested a number of rioters among a crowd of several thousand who had come to protest a planned Neo-Nazi rally in the park.[33] The right to publicly exercise free speech was at issue in both cases, but the only occasion in which the Burns Monument was specifically incorporated into Allan Gardens' demonstrations was in the summer of 1962 when Interpoet staged a series of readings in front of the statue.[34]

Milton Acorn, Gwendolyn MacEwen, Luella Booth, and several other poets, who were also regulars at the Bohemian Embassy on Yonge Street, chose the Burns Monument as the ideal site to protest a city by-law that allowed the preaching of sermons in Allan Gardens but required all other speakers to obtain a permit. The group, led by Acorn, challenged the regulation by reading their poetry in front of the Burns statue, and the police responded with tickets and court summonses—provoking a poetic response from Luella Booth:

> A dead poet stands in the
>   park
> And underneath his feet
> Living poets aren't allowed
>   to speak.

For a brief time, the controversy generated a series of front-page articles, editorials, cartoons, and letters to the editor. One correspondent with the *Toronto Star*, M.V. Drummond, who thought that the poets were part of a left-wing Communist conspiracy, suggested that the Burns monument was having a disturbing influence on young people and that "City Council should have it demolished and replaced with one of Kipling." The charges against Acorn and the other poets were eventually dropped, and the city modified the by-law—first by issuing free permits

---

[32]   Toronto City Council Minutes, 1909, Appendix A, 1507; *Globe and Mail*, 21 December 1946.

[33]   See the *Globe and Mail*, Tuesday, 10 August 1999; John Manley, "'Starve, Be Damned!' Communists and Canada's Urban Unemployed, 1929–39," *Canadian Historical Review*, 79/3 (1998): 466–91 (477); and Franklin Bialystok, "Neo–Nazis in Toronto: The Allan Gardens Riot," *Canadian Jewish Studies*, 4–5 (1996–1997): 1–38.

[34]   For Interpoet and the Bohemian Embassy, see Rosemary Sullivan, *Shadowmaker: The Life of Gwendolyn MacEwen* (Toronto, 1995), pp. 125–6.

to anyone requesting one and then by designating the area adjacent to the Burns statue, identified as "poets' corner" as a result of the dispute, as a free speech area where no permits were required. Poetry had attracted Interpoet to the monument, but others ranging from evangelical preachers to "ban-the-bomb" advocates used the base of the statue merely as a convenient platform.[35] As a consequence of more recent park redevelopment efforts, however, the statue is no longer sited at the prominent corner that had attracted speakers in the early 1960s, and it now sits, facing into the park, in a relatively isolated location halfway down Sherbourne Street across from the Palm House.

In contrast to the Toronto monument, the Burns statue in Halifax's Victoria Park was not the focus of public gatherings until 2002 when the monument was moved back thirty feet in order to create a public square.[36] The new space in front of the statue has since been a stage for a number of protests, including the Halifax Peace Coalition's mock trial of President George W. Bush in 2004, but is more frequently used as a gathering spot for pipers during the tourist season. Since the 2002 relocation, individuals who donate to the local food bank, Feed Nova Scotia, can have an inscription placed on one of the square's bricks, but the opportunity to link Burns to the food bank project was missed. Although a stone inscribed with the "Selkirk Grace" was placed in the brickwork at the foot of the monument, neither the press reports about the fund raising scheme nor the Feed Nova Scotia website, which still offers the "Victoria Park Legacy Bricks" to the public, mentions Burns's poetry. The interpretive sign, placed beside the monument as part of the redevelopment, while indicating that Burns was "a champion of the common man," merely gives a brief biographical sketch of "Scotland's National Bard," identifies each of the monument's panel scenes, and provides background information on the North British Society. Although interpretation was apparently not required when the monuments were erected, such an explanation was also believed to be necessary in Vancouver in 1996 when the statue received new plaques identifying the panel scenes and the poet himself as part of a rededication organized by the Vancouver Burns Club.[37]

---

[35] For M.V. Drummond's letters, see the *Toronto Star*, 29 August and 7 September 1962. Further reports and commentary can be found in the *Toronto Star*, 9, 16, 17, 21, 23, 28, 30 July, 31 August, and 14 September 1962; the *Globe & Mail*, 23, 27, 30 July, 3 August, 1962, 12, 14 January, and 1, 29 June 1963; and the *Evening Telegram*, 20 July 1962 and 31 May 1963.

[36] The statue was first cleaned by volunteer members of the North British Society, in full Highland regalia.

[37] Echoing MacDonald's speech at the unveiling, the new plaque on the front of the Vancouver monument, that quotes "A Man's a Man for a' that," declares to the passersby that "Robert Burns's sincere desire for friendship and brotherhood among all peoples is clearly shown in his many poems and songs. His poetry and letters, both serious and humorous, are worthy of study by those who value liberty and freedom." The Toronto Burns was rededicated in 1985, but the monument has not had any interpretative plaques or signs added to it ("Burns Statue Rededication," City of Toronto Archives, Series 1327, File 67).

Of the three monuments considered here, the Vancouver Burns is the only statue that is in its precise original location, but it was not the first monument to a poet in Stanley Park—that honor went to Pauline Johnson, whose memorial cairn was erected near Ferguson Point in 1922. After the unveiling of the Burns statue, Ramsay MacDonald was presented with a copy of Johnson's retelling of local indigenous knowledge, *Legends of Vancouver*, that had associated her so closely with the park. As Victoria Strong-Boag and Carole Gerson have shown, Johnson's work was extremely popular in large part due to the manner in which she naturalized the relationship between white settlers and the First Nations.[38] The irony of both her monument, which celebrates her indigenous origins, and the Burns monument, ostensibly a testament to the poet's universal humanity, is that they were both erected at the time when the Parks Board was forcing the original inhabitants out of Stanley Park. The fishing boat beached on the shore of the park in the background of David Martin's photograph of the unveiling ceremony (see Figure 12.7) ably illustrates the fact, as Jean Barman has shown, that Squamish and Musqueam people, along with others of mixed European, Hawaiian and indigenous origin, were still residing in the park when the Burns statue was erected.[39] In Halifax and Toronto, it was the monument that later shifted position, but in Vancouver it was the people who were relocated.

The Burns statues considered in this chapter continue to receive annual visits on January 25th from, among others, the St Andrews Society in Toronto, the North British Society in Halifax, and, most recently, in Vancouver by Todd Wong's "Gung Haggis Fat Choy" celebrants, as part as their Burns Night-Chinese New Year fusion event, but this represents only a small minority of those who pass by the monuments. As early as 1898, Dr Daniel Clark, member of the St Andrews Society and the superintendent of the Asylum for the Insane, in refusing a request to join the Burns Statue Committee, had argued that any memorial would merely "decorate a city park" and predicted that such statues, despite the intention of their sponsors, would not serve to promote Burns's memory.[40] Clarke's assessment appeared to be corroborated by Brian Fleming, a Halifax columnist, who wrote at the time of the monument's relocation in 2002 that few who passed by on the "Atlantic region's busiest thoroughfare know either who Burns was or why he rates one of the largest statues in town." Fleming, who would have preferred a statue to food bank director Dianne Swinemar, attributed the presence of Burns to the lingering influence of the British Empire, whose heroes are commemorated in numerous street names and monuments in the city at the expense of Nova Scotian

---

[38]   Victoria Strong-Boag and Carole Gerson, *Paddling Her Own Canoe: The Times and Texts of E. Pauline Johnson (Tekahionwake)* (Toronto, 2000), 178–217.

[39]   Jean Barman, *Stanley Park's Secret: The Forgotten Families of Whoi Whoi, Kanaka Ranch and Brockton Point* (Vancouver, 2005), and "Erasing Indigenous Indigeneity in Vancouver," *BC Studies*, 155 (Autumn 2007): 3–30.

[40]   For Clark's career, see Barbara L. Craig, "Clark, Daniel," *Dictionary of Canadian Biography Online*, http://www.biographi.ca, accessed 25 October 2009.

Fig. 12.7   Beached boats in the background of David J. Martin's photograph of the crowd at the Stanley Park unveiling. City of Vancouver Archives, CVA 518–13.

figures.[41] While this is undoubtedly the case, the present discussion has shown that the erection of the Halifax Burns was part of a transatlantic movement in public statuary that not only included Scottish, English, and Canadian contributions, but was also deeply influenced by developments in the United States. The committees who sponsored the erection of monuments were largely comprised of the upper middle class, often with wider connections in both the British and North American business communities, but also with particularly strong attachments to Scotland, if not to Burns himself. It is also clear, however, that it was a movement that drew support from the elite of each city and, unlike in Scotland itself, appears to have had little appeal among the general laboring population—which in part may account for the lack of interest in the monuments once they were erected. Brian

---

[41] "Monumental Mistakes," *Halifax Daily News*, 31 July 2002. A more recent Mi'kmaq protest, staged in front of the Edward Cornwallis statue during the 2008 First Nation's "Day of Action," commented further by making the link between Halifax's public statuary and the colonization of the region's indigenous people ("Cornwallis Statue Hurtful," *Metro Halifax*, 30 May–1 June 2008).

Fleming's commentary, however, highlights an aspect of the Burns statues that is only apparent in an overseas context and one that has little or nothing to do with the poet himself. In Canada, the Burns monuments are part of a collective colonial legacy that not only speaks to the influence of British imperialism, but more specifically to the dispossession of indigenous peoples. The connection between the erection of monuments and colonial dispossession is, however, most obvious in Stanley Park where, like the other monuments in the park, the Burns statue presides over the erasure of the memory of the land's first inhabitants.

Chapter 13
"Magnetic Attraction":
The Transatlantic Songs of Robert Burns and Serge Hovey

Kirsteen McCue

Burns's songs became my hobby: I spent every spare minute arranging the songs. This was the magnetic attraction and still is: what could be done harmonically with these challenging, entrancing melodies?[1]

Serge Hovey's "The Robert Burns Song Book" is without doubt one of the most interesting and important of transatlantic projects concerning Robert Burns. This is a major musical work spanning the years from around 1952 until 1973, and even longer if one considers the recordings which were made between 1976 and 1989.[2] It is the story of an artistic collaboration between two men of different cultures both fascinated by folk song yet living some 200 years apart—a project which, in the words of Timothy Neat, "links people, places, nations, things and ideas across many centuries."[3] But fundamentally, it is a story about the power of a "magnetic attraction," as American composer Serge Hovey (1920–1989) himself described it, to the old tunes associated with more than 300 of the songs we have come to connect with the Scottish poet Robert Burns (1759–1796). How and why Hovey became so interested in Burns's songs and song-writing methods is the focus of this chapter, but an exploration of his "hobby" has even further-reaching effects on the understanding and appreciation of Burns's songs as we celebrate the 250th

---

[1]   See Serge Hovey's letter to Hamish Henderson of 14 September 1972 in "A Robert Burns Rhapsody," *Edinburgh Review*, 96 (Autumn 1996): 121–31 (123). This is part of a major feature on Hovey with a number of articles by friends and colleagues.

[2]   The recording project produced seven albums comprising some eighty-seven songs, recorded by the Scottish singer Jean Redpath and a variety of both Scottish and American musicians. While these recordings were initially made by Philo and Rounder Records in the USA, they were re-released on CD by the Scottish company Greentrax in the bicentenary year of Burns's death in 1996. My thanks to Jo Miller for her discussions about Redpath during and after her paper on Redpath and Burns at the International conference, Robert Burns 1759 to 2009, held by the Centre for Robert Burns Studies at the University of Glasgow, 15–17 January 2009 (http://www.gla.ac.uk/departments/ robertburnsstudies/ conference/).

[3]   Timothy Neat, "Serge Hovey Remembrances January 1996," *Edinburgh Review*, 96 (Autumn 1996): 141–5 (144).

anniversary of the poet's birth and begin the project of editing anew all of Burns's songs.[4] Notably absent in any major critical work on Burns during the final decades of the twentieth century,[5] Hovey's project has yet to receive the critical attention it deserves, as do the personal connections he forged with artists and academics living and working in Scotland. During the creation of his project Hovey inspired traditional Scottish singers and ethnomusicologists to think again about the place of Burns's songs in their wider cultural context. Hovey's "Robert Burns Song Book" opened up the debate, drawing attention not just to the quality of Burns's songs, and to the intricate processes of collecting, amending, and arranging or setting songs but, most of all, to the role Burns played as protector of a tradition of songwriting and performing in Scotland. For Hovey, as a composer, this project allowed him to establish a musical hybrid—combining old Scottish tunes with his own contemporary American musical language. And the recordings of the songs, with Scottish traditional singer Jean Redpath, who was herself resident in the United States by this time, further illustrates the transatlantic nature of this project.

While Burns's biography is all too well-known, Hovey's is less so. But like Burns, Hovey has an "autobiographical letter" (directed to Mr Joseph A. Diana of 11 August 1982) and an inspiring life story. Born in New York in 1920, Hovey talks of his early childhood being a time of great energy and enquiry, with his parents having taken up "interesting positions in the new movie industry" in Los Angeles.[6] In fact his mother, Sonia Levien (1888–1961), was one of the first American women to graduate with a law degree and was an active participant in the suffragist movement, yet she became a major screenwriter, most prominently for MGM. His father, Carl Hovey (1875–1956), had been the editor of the liberal magazine *The Metropolitan* and was a writer of some note, having penned *The*

---

⁴   A team from the University of Glasgow, headed by Gerard Carruthers, has just begun work on *The Collected Works of Robert Burns* to be published by Oxford University Press. The songs for Johnson's *Scots Musical Museum* will be edited by Murray G.H. Pittock and the songs for George Thomson's *Select Collection of Original Scottish Airs* by Kirsteen McCue. There will be a further volume of miscellaneous songs.

⁵   There are several published articles about Hovey's project in the 1980s and 1990s, but all written by friends or family. Hovey's songs are not discussed in any major work on Burns or in any of the major collections of critical essays on the poet produced in the last three decades.

⁶   Hovey wrote his letter to Joseph A. Diana on 11 August 1982, p. 2. This is a long letter describing Hovey's life and his artistic development and discussing all the major events which shaped his work as an artist. I would like to express my thanks to his widow Esther Hovey and son Daniel Hovey for giving me permission to quote from this letter from their personal archive, and also for providing so much help in answering queries and sharing information with me. Grateful thanks also to Thomas Keith in New York for furnishing me with some critically important archival materials relating to Hovey's "Robert Burns Song Book" and its possible publication in the early 1980s. Sections of this letter are republished in the special edition of the *Edinburgh Review* referenced above, in a section entitled "Serge Hovey: The Strongest Possible Roots," pp. 134–9.

Life Story of J. Pierpont Morgan in 1911.[7] The house, says Hovey, "became an intellectual oasis in the Hollywood desert. My sister and I grew up in a home where people such as Aldous Huxley, Thomas Mann, Bertrand Russell, Mabel Dodge Luhan and Leopold Stokowski dropped by for Sunday teas and lively discussions."[8]

Stokowski was not the only visiting musician, and Hovey tells the story of his mother asking her friend George Gershwin for advice about a piano for the young Serge. Hovey's musical education was then conducted by a group of Jewish immigrant musicians. Most important were the composition lessons Hovey received from both Arnold Schoenberg[9] (who was to write a letter of introduction for him to Harvard) and Hanns Eisler. Eisler's influence was far-reaching, and his personal friendship with Bertolt Brecht secured Hovey the job of providing the score for the Hollywood production of *Galileo* in 1947. Hovey notes that working with Schoenberg, who had left war-torn Europe so recently, "gave me an understanding of the connection between the terrible events of World War II and the way one composer created new musical means to express his personal turmoil."[10] And Hovey strove to develop musical language himself throughout his life, always maintaining, even through acute physical disability in his later years, a deep interest in new developments which expanded musical linguistics in the new computer age. His plan, he tells Diana in 1982, is to develop his own brand of electro-acoustic music while retaining "the strongest possible roots in nature, folk music and the great classical traditions."[11]

Having spent the first years of his career as a composer mostly writing for theatre—notably for the Jewish musical *Sholem Aleichem* in 1953—Hovey's first foray into American Roots music seems connected to his work in the 1940s as the Secretary of the Executive Board of "The Musician's Congress," whose aim was "to further the ideals of democracy through music."[12] It is notable that amongst musicians and composers involved in the Congress, such as Ira Gershwin, Benny

---

[7]   Louis Filler's book *The Muckrakers* (Stanford, 1994) mentions Hovey's role as editor of *The Metropolitan* which he describes as "a quasi-Socialist periodical" which was "radical" and which strove to give space to more "advanced" material (p. 370). For information about Hovey's family, see Esther Hovey, "The Genesis of Serge Hovey's *The Robert Burns Song Book*," *Studies in Scottish Literature*, 30 (1994): 287–9. See also Esther Hovey, "Burns's Songs: An American Connection," written for an exhibition by G. Ross Roy for the 2001 Robert Burns World Federation Annual conference in Atlanta, Georgia, and available online at http://www.worldburnsclub.com/expert/ burns_songs_an_american_connection.htm, accessed 15 June 2009.

[8]   Hovey, letter to Joseph A. Diana, p. 2.

[9]   Serge Hovey's home movie of Schoenberg taken in Malibu and Brentwood c. 1938 can be viewed on YouTube at http://www.youtube.com/watch?v=v7QbWP1rpIg, accessed 15 June 2009.

[10]   Ibid.

[11]   Hovey, letter to Joseph A. Diana, p. 6.

[12]   Ibid., p. 2.

Goodman, Charles Ives, Aaron Copland, Otto Klemperer, and Darius Milhaud, there is also one Alan Lomax, who in 1937 had begun working with his father at the Archive of American Folksong at the Library of Congress. Lomax's activities were to take him across America and also to Britain, Italy, Spain, and beyond. Suffice it to say Hovey believed that his involvement with this group had "an overwhelming impact on my life and its direction."[13] He began writing scores for documentary films which focused on democratic or humanitarian themes, but other scores expanded Hovey's fascination with national musics—focusing initially on Jewish music and song, and then expanding to the music of West Africa and Afro-American themes as well as including Scottish melodies.

With a developing interest in things humanitarian, it should be unremarkable that Hovey would identify his own ideas with those of Robert Burns, often referred to as the greatest of humanitarian poets and the author of anthems such as "A Man's a man for a' that." But in fact Hovey's introduction to Burns was altogether different, coming through a friend who was confused by James Barke's 1955 tartan-clad edition of *The Poems and Songs of Robert Burns*. Hovey explained this in his letter to Hamish Henderson of 14 September 1972:

> My interest in Burns's songs, from the musical angle, started about twenty years ago. At the time I was living in New York, very much involved with Jewish music and off-Broadway theatre. I knew next to nothing about Scots songs. Then a friend, a Burns enthusiast, kept after me on a point of curiosity, i.e., what in the world were all these little tune indications under the titles of Burns's songs? He showed me, opening up the Barke edition to p. 584: THE TAILOR and asked, what did that mean: "Tune: *The Drummer?*" Or page 600: O, THAT I HAD NE'ER BEEN MARRIED, "Tune: *Crowdie?*": Did these notations refer to tunes that still existed? Or tunes that had disappeared? Were they folk tunes? Or what? It's hard to recapture the state of total innocence and naiveté with regard to the music for Burns's songs that I had then, or for that matter, most people in the United States (I won't speak for Scotland!) still possess. Most people? Most U.S. scholars as well, even in "English" departments of great universities! Sheer curiosity led me to *The Scots Musical Museum* and Thomson's *Scotish* [sic] *Airs* but once I realized that the tunes were still extant, that they were mostly Scots folks songs, and, above all, that they sounded marvelous in conjunction with Burns's lyrics, then I was hooked.[14]

His creative obsession with Burns began with his "Robert Burns Rhapsody," subtitled "A Scottish-American Fantasy," written to celebrate the bicentenary of Burns's birth in 1959 and premièred that year, through the auspices of Eisler, by the Berlin Radio Orchestra. By the time of the letter to Henderson, Hovey had completed his "Robert Burns Song Book"—which he referred to as "a 'definitive' collection of the songs of Burns, from the musical point of view."[15] It initially

---

[13]   Ibid., p. 3.
[14]   "A Robert Burns Rhapsody," pp. 122–3.
[15]   Ibid., p. 123.

comprised some 324 settings of songs for piano and voice, but by the time of the recording project in the late 1970s, many of these settings were arranged for a variety of instrumental forces, and sometimes a small chorus too. Hovey's recordings give a much more impressive idea of his compositional scope than do the simpler arrangements for voice and piano. These fuller settings span the simplest, most unobtrusive arrangements such as one finds for "The Lea Rig" or "Red, red rose" to the more sophisticated choral settings he wrote for "A Man's a man for a' that" or "Up wi' the carls o' Dysart." They expand to incorporate wonderfully American-Scottish settings such as that for "My love she's but a lassie yet," with its Coplandesque square-dance interlude, and touches popular music, as is the case of "Where angry winter's braving storms" with its statuesque tune by Niel Gow, which is reminiscent of the work of The Carpenters. Some settings employ a repeat and fade ending, also much more akin to pop songs than art songs. Others allow Hovey to experiment and improvise and are sometimes more avant-garde in nature, yet always nodding respectfully to Burns's initial choices of tunes.

The "Song Book" runs to 1200 pages of manuscript and is still in family hands in Los Angeles, but Hovey did create a single-volume work on the project entitled "The Retrieval and Performance of the Songs of Robert Burns"[16] which explained his aims. This volume provides a fascinating account of how he developed his knowledge of Burns's songs and how he created his new settings. As his wife Esther has written elsewhere, "when Serge Hovey became interested in ethnic music, that meant total immersion."[17] It seems that Hovey's initial discovery led him first to extant literature on Burns, for his opening chapter is impressive in its breadth and depth of knowledge of secondary sources. Moreover, his appreciation of what he refers to as "the Burns myth," which struggles to "separate fact from fiction"[18] both in Britain and the United States, is notable. Hovey is able to give a fluent and detailed account of the plight of Burns's songs in the twentieth century, when music and lyrics became separated and Burns's original song publications by James Johnson and George Thomson were forgotten. Hovey even provides tables of selected songs to show which of Burns's tunes were replaced, which became popular, and which songs gained prominence in the "saccharine cult" of

---

[16]   Serge Hovey, "The Retrieval and Performance of the Songs of Robert Burns." This is an undated typewritten document, clearly created to entice a publisher on board. It includes four major sections: I: Background of the Songs; II: Contribution of the Present Author; III: Projected Publications; IV: Projected Recordings; and a supplementary section containing musical excerpts from the larger "Robert Burns song Book" and recommendations for its publication. There is a separate archive of personal correspondence with supporting letters for the publication project, but these span the period 1971 until the early 1990s, just after Hovey's death. I was able to cite only a copy at the University of Mississippi.

[17]   Esther Hovey, "The Genesis of Serge Hovey's *The Robert Burns Song Book*," p. 288.

[18]   See Hovey, "The Retrieval and Performance of The Songs of Robert Burns," p. 14.

Victorian sentimentality.[19] Hailing the appearance of James Chalmers Dick's 1903 study *The Songs of Robert Burns* as, quite rightly, a "stunning breakthrough," Hovey understands that most scholars, not to mention the wider public, have no real knowledge of what Burns's songs are and that this must be rectified.[20] With the republication of Dick's study by the American Folklore Associates in 1962, and James Kinsley's new Oxford edition of the poems and songs just a few years later (which, like Dick's, included musical notation), Hovey notes a new dawn for Burns's songs. But he is also quick to point out that much more careful work needs to be done in musical terms with these songs, and that both Dick and Kinsley, who remove the melodies from their respective musical publications and rarely think of performance, often fail to notice when a lyric does not quite scan with its melody, or where all-important repetition marks are missed out. Hovey argues that his work as a composer makes it possible for him to spot such things more easily and thus to correct them where necessary. And it is this contribution to which Robert D. Thornton draws attention.[21] Thornton believed that Hovey moved the whole project on, because although Dick's study contributed greatly to scholarship, it was Hovey's practical settings for performance which finally did justice to Burns's songs. Ever forceful in his opinions, Thornton rather complicates things with his suggestion. Hovey, above all else, is a creative artist, a composer who is giving his own very personal interpretation of these songs. Dick and Kinsley are editors, presenting facts and evidence and avoiding interpretation—they never intended to produce a text for performance purposes. But Hovey does occasionally spot things which the editors have missed, such as the lack of repetition marks in the *Scots Musical Museum* for "O my love's like a red, red rose" (no. 402), which have accounted for singers misreading this melody for decades. In this case, Hovey correctly notes that his new setting is the first to rectify this.[22]

Hovey is also keen to emphasize the truly transatlantic nature of his project, for he wished to throw "new light on the vital relationship that has existed between Scottish folksongs and the roots of our American musical heritage."[23] These Scottish tunes of Burns's time were not wholly new to his ears, for,

---

[19]   See Ibid., p. 11. The tables are found on pp. 10–11. A further table of mismatched tunes in George Thomson's *A Select Collection of Original Scotish [sic] Airs* in 1799 is given on pp. 63–5.

[20]   Hovey contributes to wider public awareness himself in general articles on Burns's songs; see Serge Hovey, "Bobby Burns Songs," *Music Journal*, 33/10 (December 1975): 14–15 (cont. 25 and 39); Serge Hovey, "The Songs of Robert Burns," *Burns Chronicle and Club Directory*, 4/4 (1979): 19–23.

[21]   See Robert D. Thornton, "Serge Hovey and the Others," *Studies in Scottish Literature*, 30 (1994): 277–85.

[22]   See Hovey's notes on this song in *The Robert Burns Song Book* (2 vols, Pacific MO, 2001), vol. 2, p. 174.

[23]   See Hovey, "The Retrieval and Performance of The Songs of Robert Burns," p. 15. This section is entitled "Contribution of the Present Author."

The Burns and Scottish tunes worked their way into the bloodstream of American music. Scottish tunes came over to North America with the European settlers. In the late 18th century there appeared in a Philadelphia newspaper an advertisement of <u>The Scots Musical Museum</u> to be printed in the United States. Names of typical Burns tunes appeared regularly on the programs of concerts in Early Boston, New York, Philadelphia and Richmond. Traditional Scottish ballads settled and evolved new variants in the Appalachians. The hopes and dreams of early America found many forms of cultural expression and, together with the writings of Paine and the spirit of the Enlightenment, we also find the songs of Burns.[24]

His description of what he wishes to do with his own musical realization of the songs also highlights this transatlantic thoroughfare. Hovey acknowledges the importance of an unaccompanied singing tradition in Scotland, but comments that even in Burns's day his songs were heard in a variety of places from the field to the drawing room. Consequently there is, in Hovey's opinion, "ample room for a multiplicity of interpretations of the songs," providing "Burns's intentions are well understood."[25] Hovey is happy to work with a Scots tune, from "a modern American point of view."[26] He explains that after much experimentation he thinks that it is acceptable to use, in the accompaniment, "harmonies and rhythms that are characteristically 'American,' though always for the purpose of bringing out the beauty of the air" which is "the carrier of tradition." And herein lies the core of Hovey's success. His respect for the notion of a living tradition, both during Burns's lifetime and in his own, is unwavering. And his detailed research allows him to tackle these songs with a depth of understanding and respect for both their oral roots and their early printed variants which he blends smoothly with his own contemporary musical language. While most Scottish ethnomusicologists and traditional singers with whom he worked far preferred unaccompanied singing of their songs, all of them were clearly impressed by Hovey's project and its ethos. All acknowledged that what Hovey achieved was something quite special, "an out-of-the-ordinary artistic phenomenon" which was "an amalgam of creative flair and scholarly exactitude," making these new settings "a formidable achievement."[27]

While Hovey's discussion and "Background of the Songs" is fascinating, the main component of the "Song Book" is the new settings of the songs themselves arranged into six "thematic" song chapters:

1. "Country Life"—"Songs portraying farmers, millers, shepherds, weavers, flax-dressers, tinkers, colliers, coopers, shoemakers, tailors and even excisemen"

---

[24] Hovey, "The Retrieval and Performance of The Songs of Robert Burns," p. 15.

[25] Ibid., p. 19.

[26] Ibid., p. 20.

[27] "A Robert Burns Rhapsody," p. 131.

2. "The Lasses"—"Songs associated with Nelly, Tibbie, Peggy, Alison, Mary, Annie, Betty, Phemie, Nancy, Lesley, Maria, Jessie, Jean (Armour), &c, &c"

3. "High Society"—"Songs of garden fetes, Pomp and Circumstance, Boswell and Johnson...of Scottish lairds for whom Burns had genuine affection, such as the Duke of Gordon"

4. "Friends"—"bacchanalia"

5. "The Banks of Nith"—"Songs that build magic visions of Nature sometimes—though not invariably—introducing the female figure into the landscape"

6. "Scotland's Freedom"—"divided into 5 sections"
    a) Old Scotland and its Ballads
    b) The Jacobite Risings
    c) Love and Liberty—A Cantata
    d) The Election Ballads
    e) More Freedom Songs[28]

Hovey presents a detailed "commentary" alongside each of his new musical settings, as exemplified by "Blythe hae I been on yon hill." Here Hovey provides his new setting for voice and piano alongside the original tune from Robert Bremner's *Reels* of 1759. He gives a lengthy quotation from Burns's letter to George Thomson of 30 June 1793, which talks about the tune Burns encloses and about the fact that it is played by the hautboy (or oboe) player Mr Fraser in Edinburgh. Alongside the full set of lyrics is another quotation from Burns to Thomson of September 1793 which discusses the creation of his new song. Hovey then gives his own little pictorial sketch of Lesley Baillie (for whom Burns wrote the song) and comments that the tune he has used for his setting is "the variant by Thomas Fraser (Edinburgh oboe player) that Burns mailed to publisher George Thomson." Finally, he includes, below his setting, Thomson's comment on the Fraser variant of this well-known tune, in which Thomson states that the second half of the tune is altogether different from that commonly known.[29] So, although Hovey is projecting his own new setting, the reader is thus very aware of how the song came into being, for whom it was written, and how Burns chose and adapted the melody for his lyric. Hovey deals with every song in this way, often adding his own explanations of how he has tackled his setting in musical terms. He explains, for example, that the melody he uses for "Corn Riggs" is an

---

[28] See Hovey, "The Retrieval and Performance of The Songs of Robert Burns." This information is taken from the introductions to the individual chapters of this text. These listings are then interspersed with examples of the song settings themselves. The first two "chapters"—"Country Life" and "The Lasses"—were published in 1997 and 2001 respectively by Mel Bay Publishing in the U.S.

[29] See Hovey, "The Retrieval and Performance of The Songs of Robert Burns," pp. 48–9.

amalgam of several eighteenth-century variants of the tune which he has found during his research. Sometimes more factual notes about the history of a melody are given, as is the case with "Behold my love," where the melodic connections with American popular music are also noted (as they frequently are elsewhere) and incipits of manuscripts of Burns's lyric and related correspondence appear. Often his own sketches (rather like doodles) are presented as his visual response to the song—a fine example being his setting of "The Fête Champêtre" beginning "O wha will to St Stephen's house / To do our errands there man" (to the tune "Killiecrankie") where each of its seven verses has a little sketch to illustrate it. Sometimes Hovey also quotes from Dick or Kinsley, or historical accounts, to give factual context to a song's creation, as he does in amongst the many bits and pieces of information given for "Auld lang syne." And sometimes, as with "Jamie come try me," Hovey will make decisions to aid performance. These melodies are notoriously technically difficult for singers, because many of them, as Jo Miller points out, were associated with the fiddle and not the voice.[30] Here Hovey adapts the melody, the wide range of which makes it impossible for many singers, to ensure that the second, higher-set, part of the melody remains at the same tessitura as the opening strain of the tune. In this case, the melody certainly loses some of its evocative quality, but more folk will be able to sing it.

Even though neither Johnson nor Thomson gave such annotations, there are clearly many musical similarities between Hovey's "Song Book" and the settings for Johnson's *Scots Musical Museum* (1787–1803) or, more particularly, with Thomson's *Select Collection of Original Scotish [sic] Airs* (1793–1846). Hovey's arrangements follow similar formulaic structures, most often with introductory and concluding sections on either side of the song proper. In this way he mirrors Thomson's collections which Hovey greatly admired, undoubtedly because Thomson was commissioning highly skilled composers, including Haydn and Beethoven. Like Thomson's collections, Hovey's final arrangements, used for the recordings, also include other instrumental parts. Hovey likes a perpetual motion in his piano accompaniment, often simple in style, and which relies heavily on arpeggios over which the melody flows. This constant rhythmic motion can cause difficulties for the singer, who frequently has little time for breath. But, again akin to Thomson, Hovey is always keen to stress his interest in how the songs might best be performed. His "Retrieval and Performance" volume illustrates that he felt live performance was essential to "revive the songs and get them before the public in an authentic yet exciting form."[31] His major recording project began in 1979 and is the outlet through which Hovey's work is best known to this day. Loved by

---

[30] See Jo Miller, "Burns Songs: A Singer's View," in Kenneth Simpson (ed.), *Burns Now* (Edinburgh, 1994), pp. 193–207 (p. 194). Miller notes that Burns's songs are technically challenging for singers because they have wide ranges and intervallic leaps. Many of these tunes, she states, were easier to play than to sing.

[31] See Hovey, "The Retrieval and Performance of The Songs of Robert Burns," pp. 23–4.

many, hated by some, these recordings have become a cultural curiosity, because they bring together an American composer and his new realizations of Burns's songs with a traditional Scottish folk singer who does not read a note of music.

Jean Redpath explains that it was Hamish Henderson, her "guru" at the School of Scottish Studies in Edinburgh, who introduced her to Hovey during the 1970s and that this was when she "found herself embarking on a truly mammoth project" to record Burns's songs.[32] Hovey describes the meeting with Redpath as a moment of "good fortune,"[33] but it is worth noting that it was Henderson who put these two artists together. Henderson, hugely knowledgeable about Scots song tradition and surely the most important figure of the later twentieth century in terms of Scottish ethnomusicology, saw something special in Hovey's project. He had felt for some time the necessity for Scottish culture to recognize Burns's role as disseminator of tradition, but was unable to find a way to liberate Burns from the myths that surrounded him. From this perspective, regardless of the fact that Hovey and Henderson were men from very different cultural and musical backgrounds, they were at one. Henderson's suggestion that Hovey make contact with Redpath, who had made her place in the American folk music scene by this time, was a stroke of genius. The recordings which they undertook, while controversial for some, had the desired effect of opening up the minds of traditional musicians to Burns and his songs.

Timothy Neat's documentary entitled "The Tree of Liberty—A Tribute to Serge Hovey"[34] was shown for the first time in 1987 and followed the process of Redpath, Hovey, and a group of musicians recording the songs. By the time of the recording project, Hovey was already suffering from Lou Gehrig's disease, with which he had been diagnosed around 1970. A form of motor neurone disease, Hovey became increasingly debilitated from this time until his death. By 1982 he had lost all use of his hands and legs and required a respirator. He was unable to communicate verbally, and so he was able to discuss the songs with Redpath only through a translator who interpreted the tiniest of physical movements with the use of a letterboard. Clearly those who worked with him, and lived with him, loved him very much—as Neat captures so beautifully in his film. This is a moving depiction of how art triumphs almost over life itself. But neither Hovey's powerful spirit nor the clear respect between singer and composer meant that there were no artistic disagreements. And Redpath is forthright about these, stating that she and Hovey had "a couple of run-ins to begin with, but they were always amiable because of the mutual respect for each other." Redpath had no formal musical training,

---

[32]   See David Skipper, "Jean Redpath Champions Burns and Traditional Scottish Music," *Burns Chronicle and Club Directory*, 99 (1990): 75–8 (76).

[33]   Letter to Joseph A. Diana, p. 5.

[34]   This documentary film was produced by Everallin films and created with the help of The Scottish Film Production Fund and in association with Channel 4. Neat's personal recollection of making the film is entitled "Serge Hovey Remembrances," in the *Edinburgh Review* pp. 141–5.

and it took some time for them to establish a system of clear communication which involved, as Redpath notes, quite a bit of compromise on both sides. As she explained to David Skipper:

> Every song has to be approached with the idea of either "I like that setting" or "I don't think I could go out there and tell a story where you have to go out and sing it before the denouement." Serge has a trick of putting long pauses in the setting. If you sing unaccompanied, you can't walk around the stage and read a book for three bars before you hit the punch line. He may compromise musically if he believes the point you are making is valid, but he won't compromise on any other level.[35]

Redpath explains that she did not choose the songs for recording herself, but that she was sent a cassette with the melodies played on piano, which she then learned by ear, before meeting to record the songs. Hovey polished the settings he chose for recording and made the relevant instrumental scores. Redpath notes that the songs were "at very different stages of completion and we worked with those that were 'ready'." She continues:

> I didn't always like them, either. Although I'm glad those 7 LPs were made so that I have somewhere to go back and learn the songs again—there are a few I'll never sing again. One shouldn't ask me which ones, because if I did the job right, it doesn't show! I do wonder if there aren't quite a few of his songs that have never been sung to the tunes he intended ... the ranges are pretty demanding and the breath required for some would benefit from an independent source of oxygen.[36]

While Redpath believes that the most powerful song "needs only a tune and a set of words," she also explains that "not everyone will either sing or listen for long to that combination."[37] Her impressive work on this project, and another with Donald Low to record the tunes in the *Scots Musical Museum* for Douglas Gray's company Scottish Records, has forever associated her with the songs of Burns, and has, indeed, let the public hear many of the more obscure Burns songs and tunes which could otherwise have been entirely lost. But her work also, almost single-handedly, brought Burns back to the attention of traditional singers who had, until then and through the 1960s Folk Song Revival, largely ignored him. Redpath comments that she had learnt hardly any Burns songs during her childhood. Some, she suspects she "had from my mother, because as a Fifer of my particular vintage,

---

[35] Skipper, "Jean Redpath Champions Burns and Traditional Scottish Music," pp. 76–7.

[36] Email from Jean Redpath to Kirsteen McCue, 3 April 2009. And my warm thanks to Jean Redpath for sharing her thoughts with me and talking so openly of the project with Hovey.

[37] Ibid.

I don't think I learned much, if anything about Burns in a formal setting."[38] She notes that working with Hovey was thus "almost baptism by total immersion" and that she was inspired by the work he had undertaken: "had I not been caught up in his unfailing enthusiasm and optimism about the project, it would have been completely daunting."[39] The awe-inspiring quality of Hovey's research-based approach has also been acknowledged by other Scottish traditional singers including Sheila Douglas and Sheena Wellington, both of whom greatly respect Hovey's achievement and express their pride in the fact that Hovey devoted so much of his time and energy to bettering knowledge of Scotland's national poet and songster.[40]

Sheila Douglas's article on "Burns and the Folksinger" gives a clear account of the reasons for folk singers' avoidance of Burns's songs until the very last decades of the twentieth century. Firstly, she states that most Scottish children are introduced to Burns in a formal setting at school where the songs are most often taught as poetry in a foreign language. Moreover, if songs are heard, they are performed in what she describes as "a classical style in the music class."[41] Folk singers simply did not associate Burns with "the folk" because the renditions they most often heard were those of "the stuffed shirt Burns Supper scene and the clasped hand delivery that was exactly what the Revival was aiming to get away from."[42] And as Hovey himself argues in his "Retrieval and Performance" volume, the nineteenth-century hijacking of Burns's songs as "art songs" (regardless of the fact that the first publications of Burns's songs were also in this style) certainly contributed to this set of affairs. Not all traditional singers, nor those with classical training, necessarily liked Hovey's settings—Redpath explains that she has only two responses to the Hovey recordings: "Best thing you've ever done" and "What did you do THAT for?"[43] But these recordings did inspire knowledge and understanding of Burns's songs more widely. And the new generation of folk singers, including Dick Gaughan, Dougie McLean, and the McCalmans, for example, began to perform some of Burns's songs. More and more, as Douglas states, singers realized that Burns's songs did have strong connections with other traditional songs or tunes that they already knew or had learned from other singers

---

[38]   Ibid. Here Redpath is noting that in Fife there is not such a strong tradition of teaching Burns in schools. In other areas south of Fife, particularly Ayrshire, Dumfries, and Galloway, the opposite would probably be true.

[39]   Email from Redpath to McCue, 3 April 2009.

[40]   Sheila Douglas wrote to Hovey on 25 February 1987 praising him for his work. Sheena Wellington presented a radio program celebrating Hovey's achievement shortly after his death. She also engaged in discussion with me by email in July 2009, referring to her "pleased pride" in Hovey's project.

[41]   See Sheila Douglas, "Burns and the Folksinger," in Kenneth Simpson (ed.), *Love and Liberty: Robert Burns, A Bicentenary Celebration* (Edinburgh, 1997), pp. 299–307 (p. 303).

[42]   Ibid.

[43]   Email from Redpath to McCue, 3 April 2009.

or family members. And, as the bicentenary of Burns's death loomed in 1996, folk singers began to see how important Burns was as a vehicle for disseminating the tradition of Scots song more generally. In the early 1990s, Fred Freeman's undertaking with Linn Records to provide 12 CDs of *The Complete Songs of Robert Burns*, based closely on Donald A. Low's new 1993 edition of *The Songs of Robert Burns*, brought together a wide group of contemporary folk performers to record the songs. While this may well have happened anyway, it is arguably the case that the Hovey/Redpath recordings played a crucially important role in attracting such performers to the importance of Burns's songs.

What Hovey discovered in his research and consequently displayed in his settings is that "Burns's songs may be viewed in a double light":

> On the one hand, they were the embodiment of a spontaneous personal emotion, often humorous, generous and radiantly human. On the other hand, all his songs were a conduit for the flow of tradition, perpetuating and developing the culture of his nation. In all his hundreds of songs, the personal, local and national are perfectly integrated. We see the general in the particular; his Ayrshire is a microcosm for the entire human condition.[44]

As his widow Esther has explained, Hovey was indeed drawn to Burns's lyrics because he identified with "Burns's political and humanist outlook regarding poverty and oppressive rulers."[45] But, as Hovey himself stated in his autobiographical letter to Joseph Diana, the cold war and McCarthyism constituted a hammer-blow to the rising "democratic upsurge of the 1940s" with which Hovey so closely allied himself. "Disappointed with world-wide political and cultural retrogressions," he writes that he "felt a great desire for personal expression in my own music."[46] Thus in Burns's work he found a great deal of similarity in artistic outlook and principle—a fellow artist who had his eye on wider experience yet was able to capture this best, most especially in his songs, through the personal.

Above all else, it was those Scottish melodies of Burns's songs and their connections with popular music across the Atlantic that still proved the "magnetic attraction" for Hovey. He explains to Henderson that when he hears a fine slow melody by Ives or Copland, he *"think[s]* they are echoing old Gaelic airs."[47] He notes that many hymns and Negro spirituals have a "haunting association" for him and that he is acutely aware of the strength of the Scottish musical connection with the Appalachians. Hovey believes he has built up a "Scottish American approach" in a musical sense, which he describes as "an interesting hybrid plant that may yield colorful fruits." This passion for the Scottish links to the roots of American

---

[44] Taken from the sleeve notes on vols 3 and 4 of *The Songs of Robert Burns* Greentrax (cdtrax 115), 1996.

[45] Email from Esther Hovey to McCue, 3 June 2009.

[46] Letter to Joseph Diana, p. 4.

[47] All quotations in this paragraph are from Hovey's Letter to Hamish Henderson, "A Robert Burns Rhapsody," p. 122.

music is the major element of his compositional output for well over thirty years. His "Burns Rhapsody" and his "Robert Burns Song Book" are not the only fruits. It is notable that his last major composition from 1983 was a "Little Dance Suite" in three movements for Chamber Ensemble and computer music system called "Scottish-Americana." His death made no difference to the Burns recording project, which carried on almost without a break.[48]

With his Burns project Hovey created his planned musical hybrid. And his work with Redpath also embodied a physical transatlantic thoroughfare, enhancing knowledge of these songs in America while, at the same time, sending them back into a Scottish living tradition. But, Hovey was aware that his settings came from a different musical culture which offered simply a new perspective. With his characteristic respect of Burns's national musical tradition, he stated to Hamish Henderson:

> I am reflecting light back on the Scots music so that it may, perhaps, see itself more clearly, but there is a vast difference between motely Scottish-Americana (full of hybrid forms, odd combinations and mixtures) and the unadorned but vital, pure melody that you seem to wish to define as the quintessence of the national Scots musical idiom. And this distinction must be kept straight.[49]

---

[48] See Timothy Neat, "Serge Hovey Remembrances January 1996," p. 144. Neat quotes from a letter from Esther Hovey written only three weeks after Hovey's death, and refers to the recording session which is going on as she writes.

[49] Hovey's letter to Hamish Henderson, "A Robert Burns Rhapsody," p. 122.

Chapter 14
Transatlanticism and Beyond:
Robert Burns and the World Wide Web

Sharon Alker and Holly Faith Nelson

The goal must not be to do old work more efficiently,
but to do new work differently.[1]

To consider the presence and reception of Robert Burns in cyberspace is to move, strictly speaking, beyond the subject of transatlantic Burns, though as this chapter suggests many of the in-depth sites on Burns originate in Britain and the Americas and involve ongoing transatlantic collaboration. While the previous chapters in the collection highlight the aesthetic, cultural, historical, and political significance of repositioning Burns, and Scottish diasporic studies more generally, in relation to the Americas, we wish to conclude the volume by gesturing toward the global culture in which Burns is now most commonly transmitted and transformed by virtue of new digital technologies. In the process, we will navigate both within and around transatlantic boundaries in charting the afterlife of Burns in the Digital Age.[2]

While many eighteenth-century scholars have been hesitant to abandon the materiality of print culture for the seemingly insubstantial state of virtual reality, it is essential for those working on historical literature to engage with the subject of cyberspace even when this new medium seems radically distinct and distant from the literature of the period under study. The research of Michel Foucault, Walter Ong, and Alan Liu suggests that such engagement is critical in the field. In Foucauldian terms, any significant shift in the dominant episteme will radically alter the way in which texts, literary or otherwise, are interpreted or understood. That is, if "the accepted mode of acquiring and arranging knowledge in a given period" is markedly modified—which is a natural and unavoidable consequence of rapidly evolving digital technologies—then the ways in which we understand or search for meaning in a text will fundamentally change.[3]

---

[1]   Martin K. Foys, *Virtually Anglo-Saxon: Old Media, New Media, and Early Medieval Studies in the Late Age of Print* (Gainesville, 2007), p. 193.

[2]   We would like to thank our research assistants, Aakanksha Veenapani (Whitman College) and Lise van der Eyk (Trinity Western University) for their invaluable assistance in compiling and assessing much of the data for this project.

[3]   "Episteme," in Chris Baldick, *The Oxford Dictionary of Literary Terms* (Oxford, 2008), Oxford Reference Online, http://www.oxfordreference.com/, accessed 25 May 2009. See Michel Foucault, *The Order of Things: An Archaeology of the Human Sciences* (New York, 1994).

In a related vein, Walter Ong in his seminal work, *Orality and Literacy: The Technologizing of the Word*, looks more precisely at the role that different modes of communication play in profoundly altering our conceptual frameworks. In theorizing the "shift from orality to literacy and on to electronic processing," Ong notes that advances in the communication technologies that produce culture and manage knowledge restructure the way the mind encounters and interacts with language in the process of discovering or producing meaning.[4] While we currently inhabit a transitional stage—moving freely between print and cyber culture—eighteenth-century literature will increasingly be viewed, and its academic and popular reception more frequently take place, in cyberspatial contexts. So too, the cognitive processes and reading practices of many twenty-first century readers have been largely shaped by and through cyberspatial encounters given ready access to this increasingly popular medium of information delivery.

Alan Liu maps out in *The Laws of Cool: Knowledge Work and the Culture of Information* and elsewhere the role of the academy in this age of new media. Differentiating between "humanistic" and "professional-managerial-technical" knowledge, he argues that those trained in the humanities are perfectly poised to create depth in cyberspace which is otherwise often lacking.[5] Examining "the role of the arts in the age of knowledge work," he contends that "the hybridization of past and present is the unique contribution the humanities can make." This is necessary because powerful "professional-managerial-technical" ways of knowing have created a society in which the present is privileged and in which the past is caricatured, stereotyped, or excluded, and subordinated wholly to the superficial needs of the present.[6] Depth, in particular, is at risk. Liu's fear of the loss of depth in cyberspace is shared by numerous cyber-theorists, who warn that the Internet creates what Roland Barthes identifies as the reader as an "insatiable consumer" of superficial "information" rather than the reader as the producer, or co-producer, of meaningful knowledge.[7]

Liu's account of "the hybridization of past and present" as the kind of depth that scholars in the humanities can generate in cyberspace may not at first seem to encapsulate what English faculty traditionally view as significant or profound in the discipline. We tend to think of depth as that which is produced by a close reading of literary works that are carefully situated in their historical and cultural contexts by a trained interpreter of imaginative texts written in a particular period. However, this interpretive and analytical process in very broad terms depends on a coming together or fusion, in the terms of Hans-Georg Gadamer,

---

[4]   Walter J. Ong, *Orality and Literacy: The Technologizing of the Word* (London and New York, 1982), p. 1.

[5]   Alan Liu, "The Future Literary: Literature and the Culture of Information," in Karen Newman, Jay Clayton, and Marianne Hirsch (eds), *Time and the Literary* (London and New York, 2002), p. 67.

[6]   Alan Liu, *The Laws of Cool: Knowledge Work and the Culture of Information* (Chicago and London, 2004), p. 301.

[7]   Zahi Zalloua, "Foucault as Educator: The Question of Technology and Learning How to Read Differently," *Symplokē*, 12/1–2 (2004): 232–47 (236–7).

of past and present "horizons of understanding."[8] That is to say, it is not enough to provide representations of the past—for example, letters, portraits, journals— and images of the sites of their origin or current location, alongside concepts and theories of the present. Scholars have to undertake a precise sort of knowledge work to integrate the two. In this chapter, we wish to establish whether such depth can be found at the current time in representations of Robert Burns on the Internet and, if not, how depth in cyberspace can be created and encouraged by those working in the field.

The principal obstacle to fostering intellectual depth in cyberspace may be the search process itself. The cyber-search seems to lead to the exploration of the superficial (or style) rather than depth (or substance). The web confronts us with a discordant global array of visual, auditory, interactive, and hypertextual spaces. This juxtapositioning of random objects is, of course, not a wholly new phenomenon, as the early modern cabinet of curiosities suggests.[9] The curiosity cabinet and the museum into which it would eventually develop seem suitable figures through which to analyze cyber-material. After all, alongside texts on the Internet are web pages that seem more like cultural objects or virtual things. In relation to Robert Burns, board games, paintings, podcasts, iTunes, song collections, cartoons, clothing, and more—on sites that contain far more than written text—effortlessly co-exist in cyberspace.[10]

---

[8]   Hans-Georg Gadamer, *Truth and Method*, trans. Joel Weinsheimer and Donald G. Marshall, 2nd rev. edn (New York, 1994), p. 307.

[9]   Liu, *The Laws of Cool*, p. 302. For a brief account of the history of the curiosity cabinet, see A.J. Lustig, "Cabinets and Collections," in J.L. Heilbron (ed.), *The Oxford Companion to the History of Modern Science* (Oxford, 2003), Oxford Reference Online, http: //www.oxfordreference.com, accessed 25 May 2009.

[10]   The idea of an author or literary text becoming a thing or generating things is nothing new. Novels from the eighteenth century onwards have inspired the production of a multitude of paraphernalia, from hats and posters to fashionable white dresses. While the virtual thing seems to lack the materiality or tangibility of "thingness," Mark Blackwell defends the possible immateriality of the thing by reference to the *Commentaries on the Laws of England* (1765–1769) by William Blackstone. He notes that Blackstone "enumerate[s] multiple and complex categories of thing[s]," for example, "a class that mingles moveable and immoveable species of properties and includes both 'corporeal' and 'incorporeal' things" (see his introduction to *The Secret Life of Things: Animals, Objects, and It-Narratives in Eighteenth-Century England*, Mark Blackwell (ed.) [Lewisburg, 2007], pp. 9–14 [p. 10]). Of course, there is a difference between the (relatively speaking) straightforward relation of authors, literary texts, and related things pre-Internet and the proliferation of objects related to authors and their works in cyberspace because of the instantaneous accessibility of an embarrassing abundance of objects that are often organized in a haphazard, somewhat jarring fashion, with academic sites alongside popular sites and commodities (e.g., pub advertisements) alongside historical chronologies. However, like the collection of curiosities in the early modern period, the organization of things remains fairly idiosyncratic and "perpetually" resists "state attempts to regulate it as a disciplined methodology" (Barbara M. Benedict, *Curiosity: A Cultural History of Early Modern Inquiry* [Chicago, 2002], p. 13).

In *Cabinets for the Curious: Looking Back at Early English Museums*, Ken Arnold theorizes how early curiosity collections shaped the role of the spectator: "Museum-science was…characterised by the rhythm of passing from one particular to the next, by what William Eamon has called the 'epistemology of the hunt,' forming a type of knowledge that ultimately remained bonded to individual instances, rather than leaving them behind in the ascent to loftier abstractions."[11] In encounters with the curiosity collection or the early museum, there is a tendency toward breadth and multiple encounters, rather than depth. To transfer this metaphor of the hunt to cyberspace, though at times we encounter an object in depth—entering a website and examining it in detail—we are constantly compelled to return to the search. The hunt or the cursory encounter is privileged, and the very abundance of objects (and the apparent conflation of style and substance) renders the hunt the more desirable act.

How should we respond to an epistemology that works to diminish the depth that is so crucial to the knowledge work of the academy? Neither despair nor nostalgia is the answer. Liu has undertaken a collaborative project, *Transliteracies*, at the University of California to determine "what kinds of new, untapped intelligences lurk in" what appears to be "shallow, broad, casual, quick, or lateral browsing / searching," so that educated online readers can "gain knowledge" through the surfing process; and gaining knowledge, for Liu, has "self-reflexive," analytical, and evaluative qualities—depth, in other words.[12] We should consider the search process itself, then, as it participates in the shaping of Burns and in turn the shaping of our reading of Burns—feeling reassured (after all) that responses to objects in the early modern curiosity cabinet ultimately led to richer branches of study—perhaps in the way that Google Scholar is starting to do now by narrowing down searches to specific sorts of texts.

It is certainly conceivable, as Liu and others speculate, that the breadth covered during the search process or "hunt" for a cultural object in cyberspace may bring about a measure of depth—just by virtue of making connections between a series of individual objects/things. However, students of Burns and his contemporaries would, generally speaking, find such a suggestion inadequate unless there was something about the assortment of websites examined during the search that would produce in-depth knowledge or that would assist the reader in reaching a deeper understanding of his work. A random scanning of, for example, a series of images of Burns or sites with Burns's poems would not, in and of itself, constitute depth. This leads us to ask, what exists on the web on Burns and which sites produce a measure of depth?

---

[11]   Ken Arnold, *Cabinets for the Curious: Looking Back at Early English Museums* (Aldershot, 2006), p. 2.

[12]   Geert Lovink, "'I work here, but I am cool': Interview with Alan Liu," *Nettime-l list* (23 February 2006), http://www.nettime.org/Lists-Archives/nettime-l-0602/msg00075.html, accessed 22 October 2009; see also http:// networkcultures.org/wpmu/geert/interview-with-alan-liu/, accessed 22 October 2009.

In appraising and cataloguing Burns's afterlife in cyberspace, it is useful to note the distinction between the role of Web 1.0 and Web 2.0 in Burns studies, a distinction that reminds us of the considerable changes over the last decade in representations of the Bard on the Internet. As Heyward Ehrlich explains, Web 2.0 is "characterized as the interactive, read-write, community-based Web—the opposite of the traditional authoritarian, one-way, read only, top-down Web." Its "components"—"social networks...blogs, wikis, and mashups" are "already accounting for the most rapidly expanding areas of Internet traffic."[13] On Web 1.0, print-culture versions of Burns's biography or writings tended to be simply replicated on the Internet. That is, the poetry and prose of Burns appeared on a site in much the same way that they would materialize on a printed page. Greater access to Burns may have increased the possibility that his work would be the subject of close reading, but it offered no more or less depth than printed versions of his works, whose scholarly quality might be measured by careful attention to accuracy and the degree of useful annotation provided. With the development of Web 2.0, scholars, students, and others have made far greater use of the revolutionary potential of this digital mode of communication, thereby increasing the possibility of generating a more in-depth knowledge of Burns's life and work.

While the sites on Burns in cyberspace resist a straightforward taxonomy, for the sake of clarity, we identify below four types of Burns sites currently on the Internet and classify them according to the body or agent with whom they are most frequently associated:

Educational Bodies / Cultural Repositories and Institutions

It is perhaps not surprising that sites established and operated by educational bodies and cultural repositories and institutions often seem the most promising in terms of producing rich contexts for engaging the life and works of Robert Burns. At the present time, the National Library of Scotland Burns site and the University of South Carolina Robert Burns Bicentenary Exhibition may be the most likely to inspire an in-depth textual, visual, or auditory encounter with Burns. The National Library of Scotland Burns site supplements excellent biographical and bibliographical information with digitized visual and oral material: for example, reproductions of paintings, illustrations, handwritten poems, and maps, as well as downloadable modern renditions of Burns's songs.[14] So too, the Robert Burns Bicentenary Exhibition site reproduces an outstanding range of materials that include images from and descriptions of early editions, translations of his poetry,

---

[13] Heyward Ehrlich, "Poe in Cyberspace: Machines, Humans, and Web 2.0," *Edgar Allan Poe Review*, 8/2 (Fall 2007): 99–106 (101).

[14] *Robert Burns 1759–1796*, National Library of Scotland, http://www.nls.uk/burns/, accessed 22 October 2009.

and extracts from his letters.[15] The ample supplementary material supplied would allow informed readers to complicate their readings of Burns's texts, thereby offering a more sophisticated understanding of the Bard's writings to readers who can apply such information to the original poems with nuance and subtlety. For the most part, educational and library sites still currently tend to be text-based although they frequently include selected illustrations from Burns's poetry and portraits of the poet and related figures. There is also little information provided for readers who access the site by chance and are unsure of how to deploy historical and cultural materials to illuminate the substance, style, and structure of Burns's poetry and epistolary prose. A new Robert Burns project by scholars at the Universities of Glasgow and Dundee—*Robert Burns: Inventing Tradition and Securing Memory, 1796–1909*—seeks to change this model by providing "a comprehensive web-based catalogue of public monuments to Robert Burns worldwide erected by 1909, with a selection of images from the same period, combined with a web-based classification of the different kinds of Burns-related material culture available commercially or for domestic use." This new project is designed not merely to provide cultural materials related to Burns, but also to proffer theoretical models that can be used to analyze the material.[16]

Media Outlets

Burns sites created by media institutions—both new media and old—are less common, and their content often less substantial than those designed and managed by educational or cultural bodies. Nevertheless, one media outlet, the BBC, has produced podcasts of nearly 200 performances of Burns's poems read by a variety of celebrities; these are accompanied by texts of those poems which can be accessed according to reader, theme, or date. Interested parties can "subscribe to the Robert Burns podcast for two downloadable readings each week."[17] On the same page, browsers can find recipes for a Burns Night supper, watch a slide show of Burns's cottage in Alloway, click on links to a related television program on Burns, and more. This site takes particular advantage of what Ong has identified as the "secondary orality" of the "electronic age," which has "striking resemblances to the old [orality] in its participatory mystique, its fostering of communal sense, its concentration on the present moment, and even its use of formulas," while at

---

[15]   *Robert Burns 1759–1796: A Bicentenary Exhibition from the G. Ross Roy Collection, originally exhibited March–May 1996*, curated by G. Ross Roy, with assistance from Jamie S. Hansen, hypertext development by Jason A. Pierce, http://www.sc.edu/library/spcoll/britlit/burns/burns.html, accessed 22 October 2009.

[16]   For details of this project, funded by The UK Arts and Humanities Research Council, and information on the research team behind it, see http://projects.beyondtext. ac.uk/sg-murray-pittock/index.php, accessed 15 April 2011.

[17]   *Robert Burns*, BBC Scotland, http://bbc.co.uk/robertburns/, accessed 22 October 2009.

the same time clearly depending on "writing...for its existence" by juxtaposing the oral performances and Burns's written word on the website.[18] This in itself creates a kind of depth because it re-enacts what Burns himself sought to accomplish as a "brilliant re-mediator of oral tradition."[19]

Having celebrities read Burns's poetry also calls our attention not only to the poet's own experience at the advent of celebrity culture, but also to an area that has not always been of interest to literary scholars: the marketing and promotion of imaginative literature.[20] A reader looking for something else entirely—such as the political background of Alex Salmond or the films of Robbie Coltrane or Robert Carlyle—might come across this site and come into contact with the work of Burns. While such a discovery in itself is not likely to produce in the searcher an intellectual awakening, it does create opportunities to influence the general public to pursue literary studies or biographical research—to motivate them to engage in the pursuit of scholarly depth. Unfortunately, legal and financial issues limit access to the materials on the BBC site, and we may want to be alert to the way in which copyright can complicate even a transatlantic exchange of knowledge.

Commercial Enterprises

The third category of Burns websites are those in which commerce and tourism are the focus, a category with countless pages which promote a product that is often related in some way to Scotland, or to Scotland itself. The VisitScotland.com Burns site is representative. It includes images, maps, biographical information, a detailed description of a Burns supper, information on the Homecoming Festival, and one or two Burns poems. Such sites are often well-funded multi-media affairs, intent on selling the product being promoted, but they are not particularly interested in educating their visitors about Robert Burns and his poetry except as it advances their specific marketing agenda. Rather, they continue the long-standing association between Burns and tourism that has tended to diminish the complexity of the poet and his work.[21] Depth cannot exist here because the life

---

[18]   Ong, *Orality and Literacy*, pp. 3, 136.

[19]   Leith Davis and Maureen McLane, "Orality and Public Poetry," in Susan Manning, Ian Brown, Thomas Owen Clancy, and Murray Pittock (eds), *The Edinburgh History of Scottish Literature, Volume 2: Enlightenment, Britain and Empire, 1707–1918* (Edinburgh, 2007), pp. 125–32 (p. 129).

[20]   For a discussion of the rise of celebrity culture in the late eighteenth-century and early nineteenth-century, see Tom Mole, *Byron's Romantic Celebrity: Industrial Culture and the Hermeneutic of Intimacy* (Houndmills and New York, 2007); Tom Mole (ed.), *Romanticism and Celebrity Culture, 1750–1850* (Cambridge, 2009); and David Minden Higgins, *Romantic Genius and the Literary Magazine: Biography, Celebrity and Politics* (London and New York, 2005).

[21]   For the history of the relationship between tourism and Burns, see Katherine Haldan Grenier, *Tourism and Identity in Scotland, 1770–1914* (Aldershot, 2005); John

and writings of Burns have to be emptied of all complex meaning so that they can signify something else, a commercial product, whether that is a box of oatmeal or the Scottish nation.

Private Individuals and Social Networking Sites

The World Wide Web has also made it possible for individuals to transmit to all and sundry their personal responses to Burns—responses that involve the performance or interpretation of Burns's work in cyberspace. Individuals like Lionel McClelland, for example, feel motivated to perform such poems as "Ode to a Haggis" on YouTube, which was viewed over 34,000 times between December 2007 and March 2010.[22] Such widely circulated acts in the public sphere are rapidly becoming cultural artifacts in their own right, worthy of study as they demonstrate the ways in which Burns is read and received in the Digital Age. Public displays of personal responses to Burns are hardly new. However, in the past, only responses that were culturally sanctioned were circulated in the public sphere (for example, in critical review magazines). Now any private creative or interpretive acts that materialize in response to encounters with Burns can be disseminated in moments to a global audience. YouTube, in particular, has a thriving response to Burns with a wide range of performances. Amateur artistic responses to Burns are also evident on, for example, Facebook, where a search for "Robert Burns" recently received over 500 hits.

On these sites *en masse* what we find is a fairly simplistic (though partially accurate) representation of Burns as a sentimental lover and friend, an egalitarian and democratizing force, and a humorous resister of dogma. This is demonstrated in part by the works of Burns that are currently most popular in cyberspace: "O my Luve's like a red, red Rose," "Is there for honest Poverty," "Address to the Deil," "To a Mouse" and "Auld lang syne." However, some of the individuals who circulate readings of these and other poems create sophisticated events that are pedagogical as well as entertaining. Kevin Thompson, for example, who is a Board Member of the World Burns Federation, has created a blog that hosts

---

Glendening, *The High Road: Romantic Tourism, Scotland and Literature* (New York, 1997); and Andrew Nash, "The Cotter's Kailyard," in Robert Crawford (ed.), *Robert Burns and Cultural Authority* (Iowa City, 1997), pp. 180–197. As Nash notes, "when the tourist industry began to gather pace in mid-century, it was the land of Scott and the land of Burns that the guidebooks highlighted and to which the visitors flocked" (pp. 183–4).

[22] Lionel McClelland, "ode to a haggis-robert burns for traditional burns supper," 13 December 2007, *YouTube*, http://www.youtube.com/watch?v=3kzYaIphbzU, accessed 27 February 2010. McClelland identifies himself on *YouTube* as a "Scottish traditional musician, singer, song writer and story teller." His success with "Ode to a Haggis" likely inspired his recent (February 2010) two-part reading of "Tam O' Shanter: A Tale" on *YouTube*, the first and second parts of which were viewed just over 140 and 110 times respectively in their first week.

a series of podcasts on Robert Burns.[23] These podcasts bring together readings and musical performances of Burns's poetry and songs with biographical background, information on the poetic tradition Burns inherited and on Burns's writing practices. Thomson has also posted performances of Burns's poetry to both YouTube and Teachertube.

Burns has long inspired social interaction in real life, hence the countless Burns clubs around the world. However, there is now a new global reach through online social networking sites. More traditional sites of this nature include the Forum on the Global Burns Network at the University of Glasgow and the discussion board on Facebook which facilitates conversations among Burns enthusiasts across the world. In the case of blogs dedicated to Burns, not only can interested parties view these sites, but RSS feeds to which individuals subscribe give users immediate information about new additions to the sites. Most recently, the web phenomenon Twitter, which provides brief snippets of information to subscribers, has been used to send out lines from Burns's poetry daily. Such social networking tools create in the virtual Burns community a sense of immediacy and vitality.

One of the most recent social networks to surface is the 3D virtual world *Second Life*, introduced to the web by Linden Lab in 2003.[24] Based on game technology, it is an immersive, virtual, participatory site which allows users, through the avatars they create, to build landscapes and cultural spaces. Academics, particularly scientists and social scientists, have been quick to recognize the significance of *Second Life* (*SL*) as a pedagogical tool, and many universities have islands in the virtual world. One website that specializes in explaining *Second Life's* educational uses lists, for example, the training of medical students who treat virtual patients in a *SL* hospital; virtual reenactments of historical events; and the formation of immersive virtual exhibits that recreate certain human experiences.[25] In terms of reproducing the realities of specific psychiatric conditions, for instance, the University of California, Davis has designed a site that "give[s] visitors a better understanding of schizophrenia by simulating the experience of visual and aural hallucinations associated with schizophrenia based on interviews with... schizophrenics."[26] Humanities scholars have also found uses for *SL*, constructing virtual libraries and building displays that help readers to better understand the intricate details of spaces described in literary texts. There is a Dante's *Inferno* site that replicates the levels of hell and promotes visitor interaction as well as

---

[23] Kevin Thompson, "About Robert Burns," http://www.aboutrobertburns.co.uk, accessed 22 October 2009.

[24] *Second Life*, Linden Lab, http://secondlife.com/?v=1.1, accessed 22 October 2009.

[25] "Educational Uses of Second Life," *Jokaydia Virtual Worlds Wiki*, http://wiki. jokaydia.com/page/Edu_SL, accessed 22 October 2009.

[26] "Educational Tour Landmarks," *Islands of Jokaydia Wiki*, http://jokaydia.wikispaces. com/Edusquarelandmarks. The University of California, Davis, Second Life site (*Virtual Hallucinations*) can be found at http://slurl.com/secondlife/Sedig/27/44/22/?img=http%, accessed 22 October 2009.

a Tintern Abbey site that supplies "not only an environment to support the text, but also a range of well researched source materials and historical documents including writings and letters from Wordsworth about the experiences which led to the writing of the poem."[27] A Globe Theatre has also been erected, in which virtual avatars can perform plays. Conference spaces, in which workshops or symposiums are held, allow research to be readily shared internationally.

Second Life already has a number of sites focused on Scotland, one of which has a Robert Burns statue. Its virtual capabilities hold future possibilities for Burns conferences, Burns classes, and even Burnsean performances. One could, for example, dramatize Burns's "Tam o' Shanter" or "Cotter's Saturday Night," or even a scene based on Burns's life in one of the theatrical spaces. The richness of a complex virtual world, which contains media sites, educational sites, and libraries and commercial enterprises, not only enables the promotion of Burns to a new audience, but also allows for significant depth as scholars can give lectures to virtual classes with students attending from around the world, and individuals who have never met in real life can create a performative project together virtually. The possibilities for Burns on such a site are only just beginning, but it, perhaps more than any of the others described, may prompt scholars to take advantage of aspects of emergent and evolving "codes and modes of cyberspace" while still retaining critical elements of traditional research and teaching methods in the field.[28]

At the present time, however, very few of the millions of existing pages on, or related to, Robert Burns have the capability of producing what English scholars would call depth or meaningful insight. Almost none as standalone sites provide close readings of Burns's texts as well as accurate and detailed accounts of the contexts of his life and work. Yet, in combination, select educational, archival, and media sites offer the on-line reader valuable contextual information and exposure to nuanced performances of Burns's poems and songs. If provided with guidance on how to synthesize the content of a series of such sites, a wider audience might acquire literary reading skills that could lead to historically and culturally informed close readings of the poetry and prose of Robert Burns.

In order to achieve this end, scholars working in the field must intervene to organize and explicate the most effective uses of the material that is already there and to provide additional information on the life, works, and reception of Burns that is currently unavailable online. It is precisely this synthesis that is at the center of the *Robert Burns: Inventing Tradition and Securing Memory, 1796–1909* project.

---

[27] "Literature, Composition, and Creative Writing," *Jokaydia Virtual Worlds Wiki*, http://wiki.jokaydia.com/page/LiteratureCompositionCreative_Writing. The Dante Inferno and Tintern Abbey sites are located at http://slurl.com/secondlife/Dante%27s%20 Inferno/225/9/58 and http://slurl.com/secondlife/Eduisland%203/195/69/23 respectively, accessed 22 October 2009.

[28] Camille Paglia, "Dispatches from the New Frontier: Writing for the Internet," in Lance Strate, Ron L. Jacobson, and Stephanie B. Gibson (eds), *Communication and Cyberspace: Social Interaction in an Electronic Environment*, 2nd edn (Cresskill, NJ, 2003), pp. 265–75 (p. 272).

This form of scholarly intervention involves a series of steps. First, scholars need to harness the centripetal and centrifugal forces of the web and to do so in a way that involves as many media as possible. This requires devising a filtering system to sort, catalogue, and rank materials on Burns as well as establishing a regularly updated web portal page to assist searchers access materials organized in a range of categories such as academic articles, portraits, news articles, social events, blogs, wikis, private performances of Burns, and so on. Such a centralizing mechanism would allow us to move from a cabinet of curiosities to a museum as it were—at one and the same time drawing visitors into a transitional space before thrusting them outwards in different directions (and back again) into new spaces of knowledge in a radial rather than linear fashion.

The web portal would assist in the acquisition of depth by encouraging access to a select "series of self-contained units" on Burns in cyberspace.[29] These units would undergo periodic review to ensure accuracy (where relevant) and quality, although a peer-review method to evaluate different genres would need to be crafted to accommodate the features of each cyber-form. The portal would take advantage of a "vastly more elastic system of information delivery" while privileging sites that are more likely to create meaningful knowledge about Burns based on the expertise of scholars.[30] Although the portal would primarily be a filtering and organizing site, it would also contain its own original content which might be focused on a series of articles or brief lecture podcasts that give a basic overview of ways to synthesize most effectively the variety of materials recommended to gain a better understanding of Burns's writings.

Second, the wide spectrum of materials on Burns in cyberspace should encourage scholars to err toward inclusion. It is possible to present peer-reviewed scholarly articles on, and podcasts of, Burns songs or poems alongside letters, questions, and essays from members of the general public who simply enjoy the poet. A willingness to appreciate both personal sentiment for Burns and scholarly rigor in the field would likely strengthen Burns's presence in critical studies of Romanticism and provide the everyday lover of Burns with access to more meaningful resources on the Bard. The traditional role of scholar would be reshaped into that of public intellectual and a new sort of public scholarship which reflects Burns's own democratic, egalitarian, and subversive vision and appeal, would be reasserted. In the process, the relevance of the humanities to the public would become more evident.

Third, we propose that humanities scholars embrace collaboration and cooperation, a model that is commonplace in the hard and social sciences, but is still relatively new to literary scholarship. The fundamental nature of Web 2.0 is collaborative on multiple levels—for example, between teacher and student and between scholars from different disciplines. Jaron Lanier explains: "[t]he whole thing with Virtual Reality is that you're breeding reality with other people. You're

---

29   Jay David Bolter, *Writing Space*, qtd. in Foys, *Virtually Anglo-Saxon*, p. 51.
30   Ibid.

making shared cooperative dreams all the time....Eventually, you make your imagination external and it blends with other people's."[31] Interaction on the web involves complex cyber-forms (textual, visual, oral) that demand the cooperation of technology experts, specialists in art and design, musicians, historians, and the like. This collaborative model would help us to reveal the complexity of cultural work on Burns and to explore and demonstrate his relevance to Romanticism, postmodernity, and popular culture. Increased interdisciplinarity may actually lead us to reconsider the way we measure depth in our own discipline.

We might find, for example, that we begin to collapse the border between creative and scholarly work, validating the placement of imaginative exercises alongside analytical articles. A useful case in point might be a video posted to YouTube of the singer Laura McGhee who, in a New York performance of her work, sings the first four lines of Burns's "Tam O' Shanter" at the beginning of her rendition of the Beatles Song, "I've Just Seen A Face."[32] The generative hybrid form created by McGhee invites an in-depth gendered and transnational critique in light of this female singer's appropriation of songs from two hyper-masculine sources (Burns and the Beatles) that also happen to cross domestic (Anglo-Scottish) and transatlantic borders. Placing such a video alongside, say, a scholarly article on Burns and gender or Burns and transatlanticism would stimulate reciprocity between creative responses to Burns's work and the analytical acts we conventionally associate with depth. It would also provide scholars with the opportunity to study contemporary reading practices of Burns in distinct subcultures. Whereas private reading became increasingly common in the nineteenth and twentieth centuries, making reading experiences public is now increasingly popular, whether it is through an oral or dramatic performance of a Burns poem or a detailed textual account of a reader's reception of it.

Finally, eighteenth-century scholars must be responsive to the benefits of immediacy and immersion in the multimedia and multimodal interfaces of Web 2.0, which are especially conducive to creating depth in the online reception of literature of the period. In Daniel Defoe studies, Christopher Flynn has launched an intriguing project that profits from aspects of the interactive, immersive, and up-to-the-moment qualities of cyberspace. He is publishing Defoe's periodical, *The Review*, online, but is updating it day by day in an effort to recreate the reading experience of the eighteenth-century newspaper audience. A reader who follows *The Review* entries as they are added daily is granted the opportunity to acquire depth through a series of momentary reading encounters as the entries accumulate. Readers are also encouraged to add accurate material to the annotations through wiki technology, encouraging them to become personally immersed and

---

[31]   Jaron Lanier, qtd. in Mark Poster, *The Information Subject*, commentary by Stanley Aronowitz (London and New York, 2001), p. 118.

[32]   Laura McGhee, "Rabbie Beatles Laura McGhee @ Knitting Factory New York 07," 21 May 2007, *YouTube*, http://www.youtube.com/watch?v=_bJVD-3iUZU, accessed 27 February 2010.

invested in the language and valid meaning(s) of passages of *The Review*.[33] A similar project has been undertaken with Robert Burns's correspondence in which letters are delivered to readers through RSS feeds on the same day of the month as they were written centuries earlier, though readers are not currently co-creators of the paratextual matter that frames these epistolary texts.[34]

As noted above, at this historical moment, *Second Life* has the most potential to operate as a vehicle for immediacy and immersion in Burns studies; knowledge can be most easily exchanged in that medium since it mimics many features of, and traditional approaches in, the real world classroom while, at the same time, making use of the innovative ways consequential knowledge can be acquired in cyberspace. Such immediacy and immersion may initially appear to work against scholarly depth. Immediacy seems intimately connected to the epistemology of the hunt, encouraging readers to seek out only new momentary experiences, while immersion appears to detract from scholarly objectivity; yet, each might also add something to our understanding of depth. In some cases, such as cyber-editions of Defoe's *Review* or Burns's letters, immediacy recreates, to some extent, the readerly experience of receiving letters or periodical entries at the time of their original creation. Time and temporal shifts acquire greater relevance and complicate readerly understanding of the text. In other cases, such as interactive blogs on Burns, readers can obtain relatively quick responses from literary scholars and students in response to queries and ideas. In regards to immersion, participation in a virtual reenactment of a Burns poem, for example, may provoke an even more sustained critical understanding of a work than a scholarly reading alone. Particularly under the guidance of a knowledgeable tutor, immersive moments that attempt to bring together aspects of the past and present may create hitherto unseen nuances in Burns's poetry and song.

No doubt, there are obstacles to taking advantage of all of the possibilities for producing depth of knowledge on Burns in cyberspace—problems securing financial support and permanent qualified staff are the first that come to mind. However, it is important that we acquire sufficient resources for eighteenth-century literary specialists to help create a cyberspatial afterlife for Burns that will generate more depth in the field. As Alan Liu argues, humanities scholars and artists must transport what students view as cool "into some fuller, more humane spectrum of experience"; we must talk about the "new-media platform of humanistic instruction" and adopt the role of "ethical hacker" inasmuch as we can resist and redesign the sterile and surface-obsessed "New Economy" of

---

[33] The *Review* is located at http://www.defoereview.org/. In a multi-media presentation, Christopher Flynn discusses in detail the motives behind, and the methods used in, producing and editing this online edition of the *Review*: "Defoe's *Review*: Textual Editing and New Media," *Digital Defoe: Studies in Defoe & His Contemporaries*, 1.1 (2009), http://english.illinoisstate.edu/digitaldefoe/, accessed 17 June 2009.

[34] *Robert Burns Letters: The Letters of Burns on the Days They Were Written*, http://burnsletters.wordpress.com/, accessed 22 October 2009.

knowledge work in order to "help launch the future literary."[35] Given that the works of Burns were distinctly multi-media in his own time and that they have generated a substantial public, communal, interactive, and immersive response from the eighteenth century onwards, the time is ripe for deploying new digital technology to deepen in imaginative and innovative ways the knowledge and understanding of the life and works of Burns. We are hopeful, with Liu, that it is possible to educate "the cool...in their singing so that the song of culture they raise will be adequate to an age of knowledge work that is neither prehistorical nor (even more mythical) 'posthistorical,' but in the last instance truly historical." The online transatlantic work in the field that has already begun to take place—some of which has been briefly outlined above—suggests that Burns scholars are indeed "up to the task."[36]

---

[35]   Alan Liu, "Understanding Knowledge Work," *Criticism*, 47/2 (2005): 249–60 (250); Liu, *The Laws of Cool*, p. 8.

[36]   Liu, *The Laws of Cool*, p. 288.

Bibliography

Manuscript Sources

Archives of Ontario
    Fraser Papers, F1015 Mu 1063
    Burns Monument Committee Fonds, 1897–1906, F1150–Mu 449 and 450
City of Toronto Archives
    Burns Statue Rededication, Series 1327, File 67
    City Council Minutes (1909), Appendix A, 1507
Esther Hovey and Daniel Hovey
    Personal Hovey Archive
Halifax Public Library
    City Council Minutes (1915)
National Archives of Canada
    David Martin Fonds, R7612–0–8–E and CVA 518
National Library of Scotland
    Acc. 11416: Kerr Family Correspondence
Nova Scotia Archives
    MG 100, Vol. 172, No. 5d, "Kidston Family—Genealogy," Family Tree with Notes

Primary Printed Sources

The Annals of the North British Society of Halifax, 1904–1923 (Halifax: Imperial Publishing, 1943).

Ballantine, James (ed.), *The Chronicle of the Hundredth Birthday of Robert Burns* (Edinburgh and London: A. Fullarton, 1859).

Barr, Amelia E., *A Daughter of Fife* (Toronto: William Briggs; Montreal: C.W. Coates; Halifax: S.F. Huestis, 1886).

Bartlett, John (comp.), *Familiar Quotations: A Collection of Passages, Phrases, and Proverbs. Traced to their Sources in Ancient and Modern Literature*, 9th edn (Boston: Little Brown, 1891).

Beattie, William, *Odes of Appreciation of Robert Burns* (Toronto, n.d.), The Canadian Institute for Historical Microreproductions (CIHM) 66549.

Bello, Andrés. *Obras Completas* (15 vols, Caracas: Ministerio de Educación, 1951–1956).

Blair, Hugh, *Lectures on Rhetoric and Belles Lettres* (2 vols, London and Edinburgh, 1783).

Brown, Raymond Lamont, *Robert Burns's Tours of the Highlands and Stirlingshire, 1787* (Ipswich: Boydell, 1973).

Brown, Robert, *Paisley Burns Clubs, 1805–1893* (Paisley: Gardner, 1893).

Bryant, William Cullen, *Letters of a Traveller* (London: Bentley, 1850).

Buchan, Peter, *Ancient Ballads and Songs of the North of Scotland* (2 vols, Edinburgh: Laing and Stevenson, 1878).

Burns, Robert, *50 Poemas de Robert Burns*, seleccionados e traduzidos por Luiza Loba, edição bilingüe, Seleção e Colaboração de G. Ross Roy (Rio de Janeiro: Relume-Dumará, 1994).

———, *The Best Laid Schemes: Selected Poetry and Prose of Robert Burns*, Robert Crawford and Christopher MacLachlan (eds) (Edinburgh: Polygon; Princeton, NJ: Princeton University Press, 2009).

———, *The Canongate Burns*, Patrick Scott Hogg and Andrew Noble (eds) (2001; Edinburgh: Canongate, 2003).

———, *The Letters of Robert Burns*, J. De Lancey Ferguson (ed.), 2nd edn, G. Ross Roy (ed.) (2 vols, Oxford: Clarendon, 1985).

———, *The Poems and Songs of Robert Burns*, James Kinsley (ed.) (3 vols, Oxford: Clarendon, 1968).

———, *Reliques of Robert Burns*, R.H. Cromek (ed.) (London: Cadell and Davies, 1803).

———, *Robert Burns: Selected Poems,* Carol McGuirk (ed.) (London: Penguin, 1993).

The Burns Chronicle and Club Directory, 2/10 (1935).

"The Burns' Festival," *Blackwood's Edinburgh Magazine*, 56 (September 1844): 370–399.

"The Burns' Festival," *Daily Illinois State Journal*, 27 January 1859.

"The Burns Statue Number," *The New Albany*, 1/2 (July 1891): 40.

Campbell, J., *The Land of Robt. Burns, and Other Pen and Ink Portraits* (Seaforth, ON: Printed at the Office of the *Seaforth Sun*, 1884).

———, "The Nature of Robert Burns," *Canadian Magazine*, 6 (March 1896): 395–402.

Canada Bookseller (March 1865): 8.

Canada Bookseller (December 1867): 2.

"Canadian Standards of Literary Tastes," *Globe* (Toronto), 5 September 1908.

Carman, Bliss, "The Two Bobbies," in Bliss Carman and Richard Hovey (eds), *Songs from Vagabondia* (Boston: Copeland and Day, 1894).

Celebration of Burns' Centenary, Halifax, Nova Scotia (Halifax: James Bowes and Sons, 1859) (CIHM 14108).

Celebration of the Hundredth Anniversary of the Birth of Robert Burns, by the Boston Burns Club (Boston: H.W. Dutton, 1859).

Census of Canada (1901).

Census of Canada (1911).

"A City of Memories," *Vancouver Sun*, 13 March 1928.

Cleland, William. *A Collection of Several Poems and Verses, Composed upon Several Occasions* (1697).

Cobbett, William, *Detection of a Conspiracy Formed by the United Irishmen* (Philadelphia: William Cobbett, 1798).

Coleridge, H[enry] N[elson] (ed.), *Specimens of the Table Talk of the Late Samuel Taylor Coleridge*, 2nd edn (London: Murray, 1836).

Colombo, John Robert, *Canadian Literary Landmarks* (Willowdale, ON: Hounslow Press, 1984).

The Colonist (Victoria, BC), 11 November 1900.

"Cornwallis Statue Hurtful," *Metro Halifax*, 30 May–1 June 2008.

Cunningham, Allan, *Life and Land of Burns* (New York: J. and H. G. Langley, 1841).

——— (ed.), "The Garb of Old Gaul," *The Songs of Scotland, Ancient and Modern* (4 vols, London: John Taylor, 1825).

Cunningham, J. (ed.), *The Centennial Birth-day of Robert Burns as Celebrated by the Burns Club of the City of New York* (New York: Lang and Laing, 1860).

Currie, James, *The Works of Robert Burns; with an Account of his Life and a Criticism on his Writings* (4 vols, London: Cadell and Davies, 1800).

"The Declaration of Independence," *The Debate on the Constitution: Federalist and Antifederalist Speeches, Articles, and Letters During the Struggle over Ratification, Part One: September 1787 to February 1788*, Bernard Bailyn (ed.) (New York: Library of America, 1993).

Dodds, Joseph, *Records of the Scottish Settlers in the River Plate and their Churches* (Buenos Aires: Grant and Sylvester, 1897).

Dow, John G., "Burns in America," in Donald A. Low (ed.), *Robert Burns: The Critical Heritage* (London and Boston: Routledge and Kegan Paul, 1974).

Drummond, M.V., Letters to the Editor, *Toronto Star*, 29 August and 7 September 1962.

Duncan, Sara Jeannette, "My Washerwoman's Story," *The Week* (Toronto), 5/13 (23 February 1888): 203.

Edinburgh Advertiser, 13–17 and 17–20 April 1787.

Edinburgh Review, 13 (January 1809): 333–53.

Emerson, Ralph Waldo, "Speech at Burns Centenary Dinner in Boston, January 1859," in Donald A. Low (ed.), *Robert Burns: The Critical Heritage* (London and Boston: Routledge and Kegan Paul, 1974).

Erskine, David Stewart, Earl of Buchan, *Address to the Americans at Edinburgh, on Washington's birth-day, February 22nd, 1811* (Edinburgh, 1811), Glasgow University Library, Special Collections, d.9.8.

Erskine, Henry, "The Emigrant," *Poetry; Original and Selected* (4 vols, Glasgow: Brash and Reid, 1796–1798).

Evening Telegram, 20 July 1962.

Evening Telegram, 31 May 1963.

Fagg, Jane B., Biographical Introduction, *The Correspondence of Adam Ferguson*, Vincenzo Merolle (ed.) (2 vols, London: William Pickering, 1995).

Featherstonehaugh, G.W., *The Centennial Anniversary of the Birthday of Robert Burns, As Commemorated by his Countrymen in the City of Milwaukee, Wisconsin, January 25, 1859* (Milwaukee: Daily News Book and Job Steam Printing Establishment, 1859).

Fergusson, Robert, *Poems on Various Subjects By Robert Fergusson, Part II.* 3rd edn (Edinburgh: T. Ruddiman and Co., 1785).

Field, Henry Martyn, *History of the Atlantic Telegraph* (New York: C. Scribner, 1869).

"First Day's Sale," *Sales Catalogue for Puttock and Simpson*, May 1861.

Fraser, Alexander, *The Mission of the Scot in Canada* (Toronto: R.G. McLean, 1903).

Fraser, Thomas, *Prize Poem, Written for the Baltimore Burns Club Centennial Celebration of the Birthday of Burns* (Baltimore: Samuel Mills, 1859).

Freeman's Journal, or the North American Intelligencer, 23 July 1788.

Frost, Robert, *Selected Letters of Robert Frost*, Lawrence Thompson (ed.) (London: Jonathan Cape, 1965).

Gerson, Carole and Gwendolyn Davies (eds), *Canadian Poetry: From the Beginnings Through the First World War* (Toronto: McClelland and Stewart, 1994).

The Globe (Toronto), 22 July 1902.

Globe and Mail, 21 December 1946.

Globe and Mail, 12 and 14 January, 23, 27 and 30 July, and 3 August 1962.

Globe and Mail, 1 and 29 June 1963.

Globe and Mail, 10 August 1999.

Goldsmith, Oliver, "The Deserted Village," *Poems and Plays* (Dublin, 1785).

Grant, Rev. Robert, *Robert Burns, Scotia's Immortal Bard: His Life and Labours* (Halifax: Nova Scotia Print Company, 1884).

Halifax Journal, 2 May 1799.

Harvey, M., "Burns's Natal Day," *Stewart's Literary Quarterly Magazine*, 3/4 (January 1870): 425–42.

Henry, William, *A Philippic Oration, against the Pretender's Son, and his Adherents. Addressed to the Protestants of the North of Ireland* (Dublin, 1745).

Heywood, John, *The Proverbs of John Heywood*, Julian Sharman (ed.) (London: George Bell and Sons, 1874).

History of Simple Simon (York: J. Kendrew, *c.* 1820).

A History of the Celebration of Robert Burns's 110th Natal Day, at the Metropolitan Hotel, New York (Jersey City: J. H. Lyon, 1869).

Hogg, Patrick Scott, *Robert Burns: The Patriot Bard* (Edinburgh: Mainstream, 2009).

Holmes, Oliver Wendell, "Some Aspects of Robert Burns," *Cornhill Magazine* (October 1879): 408–9.

Hovey, Serge, "Bobby Burns Songs," *Music Journal*, 33/10 (December 1975): 14–15, cont. 25 and 39.

———, Letter to Hamish Henderson, 14 September 1972, in "A Robert Burns Rhapsody," *Edinburgh Review*, 96 (Autumn 1996): 121–31.

———, "The Retrieval and Performance of the Songs of Robert Burns," unpublished paper.

———, *The Robert Burns Song Book* (Pacific MO: Mel Bay, 2001).

————, "The Songs of Robert Burns," *Burns Chronicle and Club Directory*, 4/4 (1979): 19–23.

Illustrated London News, 29 January, 5 February, 1859.

The Imperial Dictionary of the English Language: A Complete Encyclopedic Lexicon, Literary, Scientific, Technological, John Ogilvie and Charles Annandale (eds), new edn (4 vols, London: Blackie and Son, 1883).

Independent Journal, 7 July 1787.

Irving, David, ed. *The Poetical Works of Robert Fergusson, with the Life of the Author* (Glasgow: Chapman and Lang, 1800).

Jefferson, Thomas, *Thomas Jefferson: Writings*, Merrill D. Peterson (ed.) (New York: Library of America, 1984).

Joussaye, Marie, "Two Poets," in Carole Gerson and Gwendolyn Davies (eds), *Canadian Poetry: From the Beginnings through the First World War* (Toronto: McClelland and Stewart, 1994).

King, Martin Luther, *The Autobiography of Martin Luther King, Jr.*, Clayborne Carson (ed.) (New York: Warner, 1998).

The Knickerbocker, 2 (August 1833): 148–9.

The Knickerbocker, 24 (October 1844): 386.

Lincoln, Abraham, "Memoranda on Robert Burns, [January 25 1865]," in Roy P. Basler (ed.), *The Collected Works of Abraham Lincoln* (9 vols, New Brunswick, NJ: Rutgers University Press, 1953–1955).

Longfellow, Henry Wadsworth, "Robert Burns," *The Complete Poetical Works of Henry Wadsworth Longfellow* (Boston and New York, 1894).

————, "Robert Burns," *The Poetical Works of Henry Wadsworth Longfellow*, Walter Jerrold (ed.) (London: Collins, n.d.).

Low, Donald A. (ed.), *Robert Burns: The Critical Heritage* (London and Boston: Routledge and Kegan Paul, 1974).

MacColl, Evan, "Beannachd Dheireannach An Eilthirich Ghaelich/The Last Farewell of a Gaelic Emmigrant," in *Selections from Scottish-Canadian Poets, Being a Collection of the Best Poetry Written by Scotsmen and their Descendants in the Dominion of Canada*, Daniel Clark, Rev. William Clark, and George Kennedy (eds) (Toronto: Imrie, Graham and Co., 1900).

Machar, Agnes Maule, "An Evening with Burns," *Century Illustrated Magazine*, 27/3 (January 1884): 479.

————, *Roland Graeme: Knight: A Novel of our Time* (1892) (Ottawa: Tecumseh, 1996).

Mackay, James, *RB: A Biography of Robert Burns* (Edinburgh: Mainstream, 1992).

MacKenzie, Henry, *"Surprising effects of Original Genius, exemplified in the Poetical Productions of* Robert Burns*, an Ayrshire Ploughman,"* in Donald A. Low (ed.), *Robert Burns: The Critical Heritage* (London and Boston: Routledge and Kegan Paul, 1974).

MacKeracher, W.M., "To a Copy of Burns' Poems," in *Selections from Scottish-Canadian Poets, Being a Collection of the Best Poetry Written by Scotsmen and their Descendants in the Dominion of Canada*, Daniel Clark, Rev. William Clark, and George Kennedy (eds) (Toronto: Imrie, Graham and Co., 1900).

Mac Mhannian, Calum Ban, "Imrich nan Eileanach/Emigration of the Islanders," *The Emigrant Experience: Songs of the Highland Emigrants in North America*, Margaret MacDonell (ed.) (Toronto: University of Toronto Press, 1982).

The Mail and Empire, 22 July 1902.

Manojo de Poesías Inglesas, puestos en verso castellano por Salvador de Madariaga, proluguillo de R.B. Cunningham Graham (Cardiff: William Lewis, 1919).

McFarlane, E., "A Suggestive Lesson Plan. The Cotter's Saturday Night," *Educational Journal of Western Canada*, 4/4 (June/July 1902): 114–16.

McKenzie, Rev. W., *Centenary of Robert Burns: A Lecture* (Montreal: Becket, 1859).

McLachlan, Alexander, *The Emigrant*, D.M.R. Bentley (ed.) (London, ON: Canadian Poetry Press, 1991).

———, "The Old Settler, or, The Trials and Troubles of Paisley John," *Poems* (Toronto: Geikie, 1856).

———, *Poems and Songs* (Toronto: Hunter, Rose and Company, 1874).

———, *The Poetical Works of Alexander McLachlan* (Toronto: W. Briggs, 1900).

McLeod, D.D., "Sermon Preached on the Occasion of Burns's Anniversary, January 23, 1885" (Barrie, ON?, 1885?), The Canadian Institute for Historical Microreproductions (CIHM) 24578.

The Metropolitan Fifth Reader ... Arranged Expressly for the Catholic Schools in Canada (Montreal: J. Sadlier, 1891).

Moir, David Macbeth (Delta), "Stanzas for the Burns' Festival," *Blackwood's Edinburgh Magazine*, 56 (September 1844): 399–400.

Montgomery, L.M., "Letter from L.M. Montgomery to G.B. MacMillan, 23 Aug. 1905," in Francis W. Bolger and Elizabeth R. Epperly (eds), *My Dear Mr. M: Letters to G.B. MacMillan from L.M. Montgomery* (Toronto: Oxford University Press, 1992).

The Monthly Review, 85 (December 1786): 439–48.

"Monumental Mistakes," *Halifax Daily News*, 31 July 2002.

Moore, Thomas, *Memoirs of Captain Rock* (London: Longmans, 1824).

Morning Chronicle, 15 September 1919.

Morning Star, 26 August 1928.

Morrison, Toni, *Beloved* (London: Chatto and Windus, 1987).

Mortimer, John, "After a Hundred Years," in *Selections from Scottish-Canadian Poets, Being a Collection of the Best Poetry Written by Scotsmen and their Descendants in the Dominion of Canada*, Daniel Clark, Rev. William Clark, and George Kennedy (eds) (Toronto: Imrie, Graham and Co., 1900).

Muir, Edwin, "Burns and Holy Willie," in Andrew Noble (ed.), *Edwin Muir: Uncollected Scottish Criticism* (London: Vision, 1982).

Muir, John, *John of the Mountains: The Unpublished Journals of John Muir*, Linnie Marsh Wolfe (ed.) (Boston: Houghton, 1938).

Muir, Thomas, "Letter & Memorandum—Muir to Talleyrand," Appendix C in Hector MacMillan (ed.) *Handful of Rogues: Thomas Muir's Enemies of the People* (Glendaruel: Argyll, 2005).

Mulligan, Hugh, *Poems Chiefly on Slavery and Oppression* (London: W. Lowndes, 1788).

New York Monthly Magazine, 24 October 1844.

Northern Star, 58 (18–21 July 1792): 3.

The Oxford Dictionary of Nursery Rhymes, Iona Opie and Peter Opie (eds) (1951; Oxford: Oxford University Press, 1997).

Paine, Thomas, "Liberty Tree," *The Thomas Paine Reader,* Michael Foot and Isaac Kramnick (eds) (London: Penguin, 1987).

Pennsylvania Packet, 10 January 1788.

Pennsylvania Packet, 16 July 1788.

Pennsylvania Packet, 24 July 1787.

Poetas Líricos Ingleses, selección de Ricardo Baeza; estudio preliminar por Silvina Ocampo; traducciones de Ricardo Baeza, Silvina Ocampo, J.R.Wilcock, R.B. Hopenhaym, Jorge Borges, Alcala Galiano, Diez-Canedo y Salvador de Madariaga; noticias biobibliográficas de Ricardo Baeza y José Manuel Conde (Buenos Aires: W.M. Jackson, 1949).

Poetry; Original and Selected (4 vols, Glasgow: Brash and Reid, 1796–1798).

Pope, Alexander, "Third Epistle," in John Butt (ed.), *The Poems of Alexander Pope* (London: Methuen, 1965).

"The Portraits of Burns," *Burns Chronicle and Club Directory*, 1 (25 January 1892): 79–95.

Pound, Ezra, *Collected Early Poems of Ezra Pound*, Michael L. King (ed.) (London: Faber and Faber, 1977).

Price, Richard, "A Discourse on the Love of Our Country," *Richard Price: Political Writings*, D.O. Thomas (ed.) (Cambridge: Cambridge University Press, 1991).

Quebec Gazette, 18 June 1789.

Ramsay, Allan (comp.), *A Collection of Scots Proverbs* (1737), *The Works of Allan Ramsay*, Alexander M. Kinghorn and Alexander Law (eds) (6 vols, Edinburgh, 1944–1974).

Ramsay, Allan. *A Succinct Review of the American Contest, Addressed to Those Whom it May Concern. By Zero* (London: Printed for R. Faulder, R. Blaimire, and B. Law, 1782).

Reid, A. Fraser, "Scots Won Site for Burns' Statue," *Vancouver Sun*, 24 January 1948.

Robert Burns 1759–1796: A Collection of Original Manuscripts, Autograph Letters, First Editions and Association Copies (Philadelphia and New York: Rosenbach Company, 1948).

Roxburghe Ballads, W. Chappell and J.W. Ebsworth (eds) (9 vols, Hertford: Ballad Society, 1871–1899).

Ruddiman, Thomas, Preface, *Poems on Various Subjects by Robert Fergusson, Part II* (Edinburgh: Printed for Walter and Thomas Ruddiman, 1779).

Scott, Walter, *Redgauntlet*, G.A.M. Wood and David Hewitt (eds) (New York: Penguin, 2000).

Scottish American Journal, 9 October 1873.

Selections from Scottish-Canadian Poets, Being a Collection of the Best Poetry Written by Scotsmen and their Descendants in the Dominion of Canada, Daniel Clark, Rev. William Clark, and George Kennedy (eds), published under the Auspices of The Caledonian Society of Toronto (Toronto: Imrie, Graham and Co., 1900).

Shakespeare, William, *Julius Caesar*, in G. Blakemore Evans et al. (eds), *The Riverside Shakespeare*, 2nd edn (Boston: Houghton Mifflin, 1997).

Sheridan, Richard Brinsley, *The Speeches of the Right Honourable Richard Brinsley Sheridan*, Edited by A Constitutional Friend (3 vols, New York: Russell and Russell, 1969).

Shiels, Andrew, *The Witch of Westcot; A Tale of Nova Scotia, in Three Cantos* (Halifax: Joseph Howe, 1831).

Smith, William Wye, *The Poems of William Wye Smith* (Toronto: Dudley and Burns, 1888).

Spedon, Andrew Learmont, *The Woodland Warbler; A Volume of English and Scottish Poems and Songs* (Montreal: J.C. Becket, 1857).

Steinbeck, John, *Of Mice and Men* (New York: Modern Library, 1937).

Sunday Province, 26 August 1928.

Swift, Jonathan, *A Complete Collection of Genteel and Ingenious Conversation, According to the Most Polite Mode and Method Now Used at Court, and in the Best Companies of England. In Three Dialogues. By Simon Wagstaff, Esq.* (London: Motte, 1738).

———, *A Letter to a Young Gentleman*, vol. 9 of *The Prose Works of Jonathan Swift*, Herbert Davis et al. (eds) (14 vols, Oxford, 1939–1968).

Taylor, J. Bayard, *Views A-Foot or Europe Seen with Knapsack and Staff* (New York: Wiley and Putnam, 1847).

Thomson, George, *A Select Collection of Original Scotish Airs* (London: Preston and Son, 1799).

Toronto Daily Star, 22 July 1902.

Toronto Star, 9, 16, 17, 21, 23, 28, 30 July, 31 August, and 14 September 1962.

Upper Canada Gazette and American Oracle, 2 November 1796.

Vallancey, Charles, *An Essay on the Antiquity of the Irish Language*, 3rd edn (London: Richard Ryan, 1818).

Vancouver Daily Province, 25 August 1928.

Vancouver Sun, 27 August 1928.

Vancouver's Tribute to Burns, published to commemorate the unveiling of a statue to Scotland's immortal bard in Stanley Park (Vancouver: Vancouver Burns Fellowship, 1928).

Vere, Aubrey Thomas de, "Irish Colonization," in Seamus Deane (gen. ed.), *The Field Day Anthology of Irish Writing* (3 vols, Derry: Field Day, 1991).

Whiting, Charles E., *New Public School Music Course*, fifth reader (Toronto: Gage, 1912).

Whitman, Walt, "*Walt Whitman: Complete Poetry and Collected Prose*, Justin Kaplan (ed.) (New York: Library of America, 1982).

Whittier, John Greenleaf, "Burns. On receiving a sprig of heather in blossom," in Donald A. Low (ed.), *Robert Burns: The Critical Heritage* (London and Boston: Routledge and Kegan Paul, 1974).

———, "The Drunkard to his Bottle," in *The Poetical Works of John Greenleaf Whittier* (London: Henry Frowde, 1904).

———, *The Poetical Works of John Greenleaf Whittier* (London: Macmillan and Co., 1874).

Wilder, Laura Ingalls, *By the Shores of Silver Lake* (New York: Harper Trophy, 1971).

———, *Little Town on the Prairie* (New York: Harper Trophy, 1971).

———, *These Happy Golden Years* (New York: Harper Trophy, 1971).

Wilson, James Grant, *American Editions of Robert Burns's Poems* (New York, 1900).

Wodehouse, P[elham] G[renville], *How Right You Are, Jeeves* (New York: Simon, 2000).

Wordsworth, William, "Preface to *Lyrical Ballads, with Pastoral and Other Poems* (1802)," in Stephen Gill (ed.), *The Oxford Authors: William Wordsworth* (Oxford: Oxford University Press, 1984).

Secondary Printed Sources

Adams, Ian, and Meredyth Somerville, *Cargoes of Despair and Hope: Scottish Emigration to North America 1603–1803* (Edinburgh: John Donald, 1993).

Alberich, Jose, "English Attitudes Towards the Hispanic World in the Time of Bello as Reflected by the *Edinburgh Review* and *Quarterly Review*," in John Lynch (ed.), *Andrés Bello: The London Years* (Richmond, Surrey: Richmond Publishing, 1982).

Allan, Hervey, *Israfel: The Life and Times of Edgar Allan Poe* (2 vols, London: Brentano's, 1927).

Alston, Sandra, "Canada's First Bookseller's Catalogue," *Papers of the Bibliographical Society of Canada*, 30/1 (1992): 7–26.

Appiah, Kwame Anthony, "Cosmopolitan Patriots," in Bruce Robbins and Pheng Cheah (eds), *Cosmopolitics: Thinking and Feeling Beyond the Nation* (Minneapolis: University of Minnesota Press, 1998).

Aravamudan, Srinivas, *Tropicopolitans: Colonialism and Agency, 1688–1804* (Durham: Duke University Press, 1999).

Armitage, David, *The Declaration of Independence: A Global History* (Harvard: Harvard University Press, 2007).

Arnold, Ken, *Cabinets for the Curious: Looking Back at Early English Museums* (Aldershot: Ashgate, 2006).

Ashworth, M.W., and G.A. Carroll, *George Washington: First in Peace* (7 vols, London: Scribner, 1957).

Auerbach, Jeffrey, *The Great Exhibition of 1851: A Nation on Display* (New Haven: Yale University Press, 1999).

Ballaster, Ros, *Fabulous Orients: Fictions of the East in England 1660–1785* (Oxford: Oxford University Press, 2005).

Barman, Jean, "Erasing Indigenous Indigeneity in Vancouver," *BC Studies*, 155 (Autumn 2007): 3–30.

———, *Stanley Park's Secret: The Forgotten Families of Whoi Whoi, Kanaka Ranch and Brockton Point* (Vancouver: Harbour, 2005).

Barrell, John, "Rus in Urbe," in Philip Connell and Nigel Leask (eds), *Romanticism and Popular Culture in Britain and Ireland* (Cambridge: Cambridge University Press, 2009).

Bartlett, Thomas, Kevin Dawson, and Dáire Keogh, *The 1798 Rebellion: An Illustrated History* (Boulder, CO: Roberts Runchart, 1998).

Bauer, Karl, and Robert W. Johannsen, *The Mexican War: 1846–1848* (Lincoln: University of Nebraska Press, 1992).

Bell, Bill, "The Scottish Book Trade at Home and Abroad, 1707–1918," in Susan Manning, Ian Brown, Thomas Owen Clancy, and Murray Pittock (eds), *The Edinburgh History of Scottish Literature Volume Two: Enlightenment, Britain and Empire, 1707–1918* (Edinburgh: Edinburgh University Press, 2007).

Benedict, Barbara M., *Curiosity: A Cultural History of Early Modern Inquiry* (Chicago and London: University of Chicago Press, 2002).

Beveridge, Albert J., *Abraham Lincoln* (2 vols, Boston: Houghton Mifflin, 1928).

Bewley, Christina, *Muir of Huntershill* (Oxford: Oxford University Press, 1981).

Bhabha, Homi, "Of Mimicry and Man: The Ambivalence of Colonial Discourse," in Gaurar Desai and Supriya Nair (eds), *Postcolonialisms: An Anthology of Cultural Theory and Criticism* (Oxford: Berg, 2005).

Bialystok, Franklin, "Neo-Nazis in Toronto: The Allan Gardens Riot," *Canadian Jewish Studies*, 4–5 (1996–1997): 1–38.

Black, Fiona A., "'Advent'rous Merchants and Atlantic Waves': A Preliminary Study of the Scottish Contribution to Book Availability in Halifax, 1752–1810," in Marjorie Harper and Michael E. Vance (eds), *Myth, Migration and the Making of Memory: Scotia and Nova Scotia c.1700–1990* (Halifax: Fernwood; Edinburgh: John Donald, 1999).

———, "Book Availability in Canada, 1752–1820, and the Scottish Contribution" (unpublished PhD diss., Loughborough University, 1999).

———, "Book Distribution to the Scottish and Canadian Provinces, 1750–1820: Examples of Methods and Availability," in Peter Isaac and Barry McKay (eds), *The Reach of Print: Making, Selling and Using Books* (Winchester: St. Paul's Bibliographies; New Castle, DE: Oak Knoll, 1998).

———, "Importation and Book Availability," in Patricia Lockhart Fleming, Gilles Gallichan and Yvan Lamonde (eds), *History of the Book in Canada, Volume I, Beginnings to 1840* (Toronto: University of Toronto Press, 2004).

———, "Newspapers as Primary Sources in Canadian-Scottish Book Trade History: The Example of Halifax, Nova Scotia, 1752–1820," *Épilogue*, 10/1–2 (1995): 43–51.

————, "North America," in Bill Bell (ed.), *The Edinburgh History of the Book in Scotland, Volume 3, Ambition and Industry, 1800–1880* (Edinburgh: Edinburgh University Press, 2007), 442–53.

————, "Searching for the 'Vanguard of an Army of Scots' in the Early Canadian Book Trade," *Papers of the Bibliographical Society of Canada*, 38/2 (2000): 65–100.

————, "Supplying the Retail Trade," in Yvan Lamonde, Patricia Lockhart Fleming, and Fiona A. Black (eds), *History of the Book in Canada, Volume II, 1840–1918* (Toronto: University of Toronto Press, 2005).

Blackwell, Mark, Introduction, *The Secret Life of Things: Animals, Objects, and It-Narratives in Eighteenth-Century England*, Mark Blackwell (ed.) (Lewisburg: Bucknell University Press, 2007), pp. 9–14.

Brown, Hilton, *There Was a Lad: An Essay on Robert Burns* (London: Hamish Hamilton, 1949).

Brown, Michael, "Alexander Carlyle and the Shadows of the Enlightenment," in Bob Harris (ed.), *Scotland in the Age of the French Revolution* (Edinburgh: John Donald, 2005).

Bryce, George, *The Scotsman in Canada* (2 vols, Toronto: Musson, 1911).

Bumsted, J.M., *The Scots in Canada* (Ottawa: Canadian Historical Association, 1982).

————, "Scottishness and Britishness in Canada, 1790–1914," in Marjory Harper and Michael Vance (eds), *Myth, Migration and the Making of Memory: Scotia and Nova Scotia, c. 1700–1900* (Halifax: Fernwood; Edinburgh: John Donald, 1999).

Burke, Peter, "Co-Memorations: Performing the Past," in Karin Tilmans, Frank Van Vree, and Jay M. Winter (eds), *Performing the Past: Memory, History, and Identity in Modern Europe* (Amsterdam: Amsterdam University Press, 2010).

Burness, Edwina, "The Influence of Burns and Fergusson on the War Poetry of Robert Service," *Studies in Scottish Literature*, 21 (1986): 135–46.

Butler, Marilyn, "Burns and Politics," in Robert Crawford (ed.), *Robert Burns and Cultural Authority* (Iowa City: University of Iowa Press, 1997).

C., Fort Rouge, *Robert Burns as Thinker, Seer, Poet* (Winnipeg: Winnipeg Printing Co., 1913).

Caldera, Rafael, "Bello in London: The Incomprehensible Sojourn," in John Lynch (ed.), *Andrés Bello: The London Years* (Richmond, Surrey: Richmond Publishing, 1982).

Cambron, Micheline, and Carole Gerson, "Authors and Literary Culture," in Yvan Lamonde, Patricia Lockhart Fleming, and Fiona A. Black (eds), *History of the Book in Canada, Volume Two: 1840–1914* (Toronto: University of Toronto Press, 2005).

Carruthers, Gerard (ed.), *The Edinburgh Companion to Robert Burns* (Edinburgh: Edinburgh University Press, 2009).

————, *Robert Burns* (Tavistock: Northcote, 2006).

————, "Robert Burns and Slavery," *Drouth*, 26 (Winter 2008): 21–6.

Casanova, Pascale, *The World Republic of Letters*, trans. M.B. De Bevoise (Cambridge, MA: Harvard University Press, 2004).

Cavell, Stanley, *Emerson's Transcendental Etudes*, David Justin Hodge (ed.) (Stanford: Stanford University Press, 2003).

Clark, Daniel, Introduction, *Selections from Scottish-Canadian Poets, Being a Collection of the Best Poetry Written by Scotsmen and their Descendants in the Dominion of Canada*, Daniel Clark, Rev. William Clark, and George Kennedy (eds) (Toronto: Imrie, Graham and Co., 1900).

Coleman, Daniel, *White Civility: The Literary Project of English Canada* (Toronto: University of Toronto Press, 2006).

Colley, Linda, *Captives: The Story of Britain's Pursuit of Empire and How Its Soldiers and Civilians Were Held Captive by the Dream of Global Supremacy* (New York: Pantheon, 2002).

Corbett, John, "Burns in Brazil," unpublished paper.

Covi, Giovanni et al., *Caribbean-Scottish Relations: Colonial and Contemporary Inscriptions in History, Language and Literature* (London: Mango, 2007).

Crawford, Robert, *The Bard: Robert Burns, A Biography* (London: Jonathan Cape; Princeton: Princeton University Press, 2009).

————, *Devolving English Literature*, 2nd edn (Edinburgh: Edinburgh University Press, 2000).

———— (ed.), *Robert Burns and Cultural Authority* (Iowa City: University of Iowa Press, 1997).

————, "Robert Fergusson's Robert Burns," in Robert Crawford (ed.), *Robert Burns and Cultural Authority* (Iowa City: University of Iowa Press, 1977).

————, "Robert Frosts," *Identifying Poets: Self and Territory in Twentieth-Century Poetry* (Edinburgh: Edinburgh University Press, 1993).

Crawford, Thomas, *Burns: A Study of the Poems and Songs* (1960; Stanford: Stanford University Press, 1965).

Creeley, Robert, Introduction, *The Essential Burns*, Robert Creeley (ed.) (New York: Ecco, 1989).

Curran, Stuart, *Poetic Form and British Romanticism* (Oxford: Oxford University Press, 1987).

Curtin, Nancy J., *The United Irishmen: Popular Politics in Ulster and Dublin, 1791–1798* (Oxford: Clarendon, 1994).

Curtis, Perry, *Apes and Angels: The Irishman in Victorian Caricature*, 2nd edn (Washington, DC: Smithsonian Institution Press, 1997).

Darnton, Robert, "What is the History of Books?" *Daedalus*, 111 (Summer 1982): 65–83.

Davis, Leith, "Burns and Transnational Culture," in Gerard Carruthers (ed.), *The Edinburgh Companion to Robert Burns* (Edinburgh: Edinburgh University Press, 2009).

————, "Negotiating Cultural Memory: James Currie's *Works of Robert Burns*," *International Journal of Scottish Literature*, 6 (2010), http://www.ijsl.stir. ac.uk/ issue6/davis.htm.

Davis, Leith, and Maureen McLane, "Orality and Public Poetry," in Susan Manning, Ian Brown, Thomas Owen Clancy, and Murray Pittock (eds), *The Edinburgh History of Scottish Literature, Volume 2: Enlightenment, Britain and Empire, 1707–1918* (Edinburgh: Edinburgh University Press, 2007).

Deleuze, Gilles, and Félix Guattari, "Introduction: Rhizome," in Susan Manning and Andrew Taylor (eds), *Transatlantic Literary Studies: A Reader* (Edinburgh: Edinburgh University Press; Baltimore: Johns Hopkins University Press, 2007).

———, *A Thousand Plateaus: Capitalism and Schizophrenia,* trans. Brian Massumi (1987; London: Continuum, 2004).

Dembling, Jonathan, "You Play It as You Would Sing It: Cape Breton, Scottishness, and the Means of Cultural Production," in Celeste Ray (ed.), *Transatlantic Scots* (Tuscaloosa: University of Alabama Press, 2005).

Derrida, Jacques, "Aphorism Countertime," in Derek Attridge (ed.), *Acts of Literature*, trans. Nicholas Royle (London and New York: Routledge, 1992).

———, "Ulysses Gramophone: Hear Say Yes in Joyce," in Derek Attridge (ed.) *Acts of Literature* (London and New York: Routledge, 1992).

Dewalt, Bryan, "Printing Technology," in Yvan Lamonde, Patricia Lockhart Fleming, and Fiona A. Black (eds), *History of the Book in Canada, Volume II, 1840–1918* (Toronto: University of Toronto Press, 2005).

Dobson, David, *Scottish Emigration to Colonial America, 1607–1785* (Athens: University of Georgia Press, 1994).

Douglas, Sheila, "Burns and the Folksinger," in Kenneth Simpson (ed.), *Love and Liberty* (Edinburgh: Tuckwell, 1997).

Durey, Michael, *Transatlantic Radicals and the Early American Republic* (Lawrence: University Press of Kansas, 1997).

Ehrlich, Heyward, "Poe in Cyberspace: Machines, Humans, and Web 2.0," *Edgar Allan Poe Review*, 8/2 (Fall 2007): 99–106.

Evans, William R. (ed.), *Robert Frost and Sidney Cox, Forty Years of Friendship* (Hanover, NH: University Press of New England, 1981).

Fechner, Roger J, "Burns and American Liberty," in Kenneth Simpson (ed.), *Love and Liberty* (Edinburgh: Tuckwell, 1997).

Ferguson, Frank, and Andrew R. Holmes (eds), *Revising Robert Burns and Ulster: Literature, Religion and Politics, c. 1770–1920* (Dublin, 2009).

Filler, Louis, *The Muckrakers* (Stanford: Stanford University Press, 1994).

Fleming, Patricia Lockhart, and Sandra Alston, *Early Canadian Printing* (Toronto: University of Toronto Press, 1999).

Ford, John, "Rudolph Ackermann: Culture and Commerce in Latin America, 1822–1828," in John Lynch (ed.), *Andrés Bello: The London Years* (Richmond, Surrey: Richmond Publishing, 1982).

Foucault, Michel, *The Order of Things: An Archaeology of the Human Sciences* (New York: Vintage, 1994).

Foys, Martin K., *Virtually Anglo-Saxon: Old Media, New Media, and Early Medieval Studies in the Late Age of Print* (Gainesville: University Press of Florida, 2007).

Freeman, Kirrily, *Bronzes to Bullets: Vichy and the Destruction of French Public Statuary, 1941–1944* (Stanford: Stanford University Press, 2009).

Gadamer, Hans-Georg, *Truth and Method*, trans. Joel Weinsheimer and Donald G. Marshall, 2nd rev. edn. (New York: Continuum, 1994).

Gerson, Carole, and Victoria Strong-Boag, *Paddling Her Own Canoe: The Times and Texts of E. Pauline Johnson (Tekahionwake)* (Toronto: University of Toronto Press, 2000).

Gibbons, Luke, *Edmund Burke and Ireland: Aesthetics, Politics and the Colonial Sublime* (Cambridge: Cambridge University Press, 2003).

Giles, Paul, *Transatlantic Insurrections: British Culture and the Formation of American Literature, 1730–1860* (Philadelphia: University of Pennsylvania Press, 2001).

———, "Transnationalism and Classic American Literature," in Susan Manning and Andrew Taylor (eds), *Transatlantic Literary Studies: A Reader* (Edinburgh: Edinburgh University Press; Baltimore: Johns Hopkins University Press, 2007).

———, *Virtual Americas: Transnational Fictions and the Transatlantic Imaginary* (Durham, NC: Duke University Press, 2002).

Gilroy, Paul, *The Black Atlantic: Modernity and Double Consciousness* (1993; London: Verso, 2002).

———, *There Ain't No Black in the Union Jack: The Cultural Politics of Race and Nation* (London and New York: Routledge, 1987).

Glendening, John, *The High Road: Romantic Tourism, Scotland and Literature* (New York: St. Martin's, 1997).

Glissant, Édouard, *Poetics of Relation*, trans. Betsy Wing (Ann Arbor: University of Michigan Press, 1997).

Goodwillie, Edward, *The World's Memorials of Robert Burns* (Detroit: Waverley, 1911).

Gordon, Charles W., *Postscript to Adventure: The Autobiography of Ralph Connor* (Toronto: McClelland and Stewart, 1975).

Gordon, George, Lord Byron, "Extracts from Byron's Journal," in Donald A. Low (ed.), *Robert Burns: The Critical Heritage* (London and Boston: Routledge and Kegan Paul, 1974).

Goslee, Nancy Moore "Contesting Liberty: The Figure of William Wallace in Poems by Hemans, Hogg, and Baillie," *Keats-Shelley Journal*, 50 (2001): 35–63.

Gould, Eliga H., *The Persistence of Empire: British Political Culture in the Age of the American Revolution* (Chapel Hill, NC: University of North Carolina Press, 2000).

Graham, Eric J. *Burns and the Sugar Plantocracy of Ayrshire*. Ayrshire Monographs 36 (Ayr: Ayr Archaeological and Natural History Society, 2009).

Gray, John, "Burns and his Visitors from Ulster: From Adulation to Disaccord," *Studies in Scottish Literature*, 33/34 (2004): 320–334.

Grenier, Katherine Haldan, *Tourism and Identity in Scotland, 1770–1914* (Aldershot: Ashgate, 2005).

Grosart, Alexander B., *The Works of Robert Fergusson,* Famous Scots Series (Edinburgh: Oliphant, Anderson and Ferrier, 1898).

Harvey, David, *The Condition of Postmodernity* (Oxford: Oxford University Press, 1990).

Herod, Andrew, *Geographies of Globalization: A Critical Introduction* (Malden, MA: Blackwell, 2009).

Higgins, David Minden, *Romantic Genius and the Literary Magazine: Biography, Celebrity and Politics* (London and New York: Routledge, 2005).

Hook, Andrew, "Philadelphia, Edinburgh and the Scottish Enlightenment," in Richard B. Sher and Jeffrey R. Smitten (eds), *Scotland and America in the Age of Enlightenment* (Edinburgh: Edinburgh University Press, 1990).

Hopkins, Paul, *Glencoe and the End of the Highland War* (1986; Edinburgh: John Donald, 1998).

Horn, James, "British Diaspora: Emigration from Britain, 1680–1815," in P.J. Marshall (ed.), *The Oxford History of the British Empire: The Eighteenth Century* (Oxford: Oxford University Press, 1998).

Hovey, Esther, "The Genesis of Serge Hovey's *The Robert Burns Song Book*," *Studies in Scottish Literature*, 30 (1994): 287–9.

Howes, Marjorie, Plenary Address: "The Irish in Nineteenth-Century Atlantic Culture," *Global Nations? Irish and Scottish Expansion Since the 16th Century*, University of Aberdeen, 31 October 2009.

Hudson, Nicholas, "'Britons Never Will be Slaves': National Myth, Conservatism and the Beginnings of British Antislavery," *Eighteenth Century Studies*, 34/4 (2001): 559–76.

Innis, Harold, *Empire and Communications* (Toronto: University of Toronto Press, 1950).

Iriye, Akira, "Internationalizing International History," in Thomas Bender (ed.), *Rethinking American History in a Global Age* (Berkeley: University of California Press, 2002).

Jackson, Joseph Henry, Introduction, *Of Mice and Men*, by John Steinbeck (New York: Modern Library, 1937).

Jacques, Martin, review of *Dangerous Nation: America and the World, 1600–1898*, by Robert Kagan, *Guardian Review* (17 October, 2009).

Kaplan, Fred, *Lincoln: The Biography of a Writer* (New York: HarperCollins, 2008).

Kee, Robert, *The Most Distressful Country* (London: Penguin, 1972).

Kelly, Stuart, "The Browser," *Scotland on Sunday*, 25 January 2009.

Kennedy, Deborah, *Helen Maria Williams and the Age of Revolution* (Lewisburg: Bucknell University Press, 2002).

Kheraj, Sean, "Improving Nature: Remaking Stanley Park's Forest, 1888–1931," *BC Studies*, 158 (Summer 2008): 63–90.

Klinck, Carl F., "Literary Activity in Canada East and West, 1841–1880," in Carl F. Klinck (ed.), *Literary History of Canada* (Toronto: University of Toronto Press, 1965).

Landivar, Rafael, *Rusticatio Mexicana: Por los Campos de México*, Prólogo, Versión y Notas de Octaviano Valdés (México: Editorial Jus, 1965).

Leask, Nigel, "Burns and the Poetics of Abolition," in Gerard Carruthers (ed.), *The Edinburgh Companion to Robert Burns* (Edinburgh: Edinburgh University Press, 2009).

———, *Curiosity and the Aesthetics of Travel Writing, 1770–1840: "From an Antique Land"* (Oxford: Oxford University Press, 2002).

———, *Robert Burns and Pastoral: Poetry and Improvement in Late Eighteenth-Century Scotland* (Oxford: Oxford University Press, 2010).

———, "Salons, Alps and Cordilleras: Helen Maria Williams, Alexander von Humboldt, and the Discourse of Romantic Travel," in E. Eger, C. Grant, C. O'Gallchoir, and P. Warburton (eds), *Women, Writing and the Public Sphere 1700–1830* (Cambridge: Cambridge University Press, 2001).

Lenman, Bruce, "Aristocratic 'Country' Whiggery in Scotland and the American Revolution," in Richard Sher and Jeffrey Smitten (eds), *Scotland and America in the Age of Enlightenment* (Edinburgh: Edinburgh University Press; Princeton: Princeton University Press, 1990).

———, "Scotland and the American Revolution 1775–1784," in Bruce Lenman (ed.), *Enlightenment and Change: Scotland 1746–1832*, 2nd rev. edn (Edinburgh: Edinburgh University Press, 2009).

Lennon, Joseph. *Irish Orientalism: A Literary and Intellectual History* (Syracuse: Syracuse University Press, 2004).

Levy, Pierre, *Becoming Virtual: Reality in the Digital Age*, trans. Robert Bononno (New York and London: Plenum, 1998).

Linebaugh, Peter, and Marcus Rediker, *The Many-Headed Hydra: Sailors, Slaves, Commoners, and the Hidden History of the Revolutionary Atlantic* (London: Verso, 2000).

Liu, Alan, "The Future Literary: Literature and the Culture of Information," in Karen Newman, Jay Clayton, and Marianne Hirsch (eds), *Time and the Literary* (London and New York: Routledge, 2002).

———, *The Laws of Cool: Knowledge Work and the Culture of Information* (Chicago and London: University of Chicago Press, 2004).

———, "Understanding Knowledge Work," *Criticism*, 47/2 (2005): 249–60.

Lobo, Luiza, "The Reception in Brazil of the First Portuguese Translation of Robert Burns," *Studies in Scottish Literature*, 30 (1998): 249–60.

Lotz, Patricia A., "Scots in Groups: The Origin and History of Scottish Societies with Particular Reference to Those Established in Nova Scotia" (unpublished MA thesis, St Francis Xavier University, 1975).

Low, Donald A. Introduction, *Robert Burns: The Critical Heritage*, Donald A. Low (ed.) (London and Boston: Routledge and Kegan Paul, 1974).

Lynch, John (ed.), *Andrés Bello: The London Years* (Richmond, Surrey: Richmond Publishing, 1982).

Mack, Douglas S., "Introduction: Can the Subaltern Speak?" *Scottish Fiction and the British Empire* (Edinburgh: Edinburgh University Press, 2006).

Mackay, James A., *The Burns Federation, 1885–1985* (Kilmarnock: Burns Federation, 1985).

———, *Burnsiana* (Alloway: Alloway Publishing, 1988).

Mackenzie, Niall, "Some British Writers and Gustavus Vasa," *Studia Neophilologica*, 78 (2006): 63–80.

MacLean, Kenneth, *Agrarian Age: A Background for Wordsworth* (New Haven: Yale University Press, 1950).

MacMillan, Hector, *Handful of Rogues: Thomas Muir's Enemies of the People* (Glendaruel: Argyll, 2005).

Magnusson, Magnus (ed.), *Chambers Biographical Dictionary* (Edinburgh: Chambers, 1990).

Manley, John, "'Starve, Be Damned!' Communists and Canada's Urban Unemployed, 1929–39," *Canadian Historical Review*, 79/3 (1998): 466–91.

Manning, Susan, "Burns and God," in Robert Crawford (ed.), *Robert Burns and Cultural Authority* (Iowa City: University of Iowa Press, 1997).

———, *Fragments of Union: Making Connections in Scottish and American Writing* (Basingstoke: Palgrave, 2002).

———, "'Ae spark o' Nature's Fire': Was Robert Burns a Transcendental Philosopher?" unpublished paper delivered at Robert Burns 1759–2009 Conference, University of Glasgow, 15–17 January 2009.

Manning, Susan, and Andrew Taylor, Introduction, in Susan Manning and Andrew Taylor (eds), *Transatlantic Literary Studies: A Reader* (Edinburgh: Edinburgh University Press; Baltimore: Johns Hopkins University Press, 2007).

Manning, Susan, and Francis D. Cogliano (eds), *The Atlantic Enlightenment* (Aldershot: Ashgate, 2008).

Mathison, Hamish, "Robert Burns and National Song," in David Duff and Catherine Jones (eds), *Scotland, Ireland, and the Romantic Aesthetic* (Lewisburg, PA: Bucknell University Press, 2007).

McArthur, Colin, "Transatlantic Scots and the Scottish Discursive Unconscious," in Celeste Ray (ed.), *Transatlantic Scots* (Tuscaloosa: University of Alabama Press, 2005).

McDougall, Warren, "James Robertson," in Patricia Lockhart Fleming, Gilles Gallichan, and Yvan Lamonde (eds), *History of the Book in Canada, Volume I, Beginnings to 1840* (Toronto: University of Toronto Press, 2004).

———, "Scottish Books for America in the Mid-18th Century," in Robin Myers and Michael Harris (eds), *Spreading the Word: The Distribution Networks of Print, 1550–1850* (Winchester: St. Paul's Bibliographies; Detroit: Omnigraphics, 1990), 21–46.

McFarland, E.W., *Ireland and Scotland in The Age of Revolution: Planting the Green Bough* (Edinburgh: Edinburgh University Press, 1994).

McGoogan, Ken, *How the Scots Invented Canada* (Toronto: Harpercollins, 2010).

McGuirk, Carol, "Burns and Nostalgia," in Kenneth Simpson (ed.), *Burns Now* (Edinburgh: Canongate Academic, 1994).

———, "Haunted by Authority: Nineteenth-Century American Constructions of Robert Burns and Scotland," in Robert Crawford (ed.), *Robert Burns and Cultural Authority* (Iowa City: University of Iowa Press, 1997).

———, *Robert Burns and the Sentimental Era* (1985; East Linton: Tuckwell, 1997).

———, "Writing Scotland: Robert Burns," in Susan Manning, Ian Brown, Thomas Owen Clancy, and Murray Pittock (eds), *The Edinburgh History of Scottish Literature Volume Two: Enlightenment, Britain and Empire, 1707–1918* (Edinburgh: Edinburgh University Press, 2007).

McIlvanney, Liam, *Burns the Radical: Poetry and Politics in Late Eighteenth-Century Scotland* (East Linton: Tuckwell, 2002).

McLane, Maureen, *Balladeering, Minstrelsy, and the Making of British Romantic Poetry* (Cambridge: Cambridge University Press, 2008).

McLean, Scott A., and Michael Vance (eds), *William Wye Smith: Recollections of a Nineteenth-Century Scottish Canadian* (Toronto: Natural Heritage, 2008).

Message, Kylie, *New Museums and the Making of Culture* (Oxford: Berg, 2006).

Miller, Jo, "Burns Songs: A Singer's View," in Kenneth Simpson (ed.), *Burns Now* (Edinburgh: Canongate Academic, 1994).

Mole, Tom, *Byron's Romantic Celebrity: Industrial Culture and the Hermeneutic of Intimacy* (Houndmills and New York: Palgrave Macmillan, 2007).

———, (ed.), *Romanticism and Celebrity Culture, 1750–1850* (Cambridge: Cambridge University Press, 2009).

Monnickendam, Andrew, "Burns in Spain," paper presented at the Robert Burns in European Culture Conference, Charles University, Prague, 6–8 March, 2009.

Montgomery, James M, "How Robert Burns Captured America," *Studies in Scottish Literature*, 30 (1998): 235–48.

Morgan, Cecilia, *"A Happy Holiday": English-Canadians and Transatlantic Tourism, 1870–1930* (Toronto: University of Toronto Press, 2008), 71–5.

Morley, Vincent, *Irish Opinion and the American Revolution, 1760–1783* (Cambridge: Cambridge University Press, 2002).

Murray, Heather, "Readers and Society," in Patricia Lockhart Fleming, Gilles Gallichan, and Yvan Lamonde (eds), *History of the Book in Canada, Volume I, Beginnings to 1840* (Toronto: University of Toronto Press, 2004).

Nash, Andrew, "The Cotter's Kailyard," in Robert Crawford (ed.), *Robert Burns and Cultural Authority* (Iowa City: University of Iowa Press, 1997).

Neat, Timothy, "Serge Hovey Remembrances January 1996," *Edinburgh Review*, 96 (Autumn 1996): 141–5.

Newman, Steve, *Ballad Collection, Lyric and the Canon: The Call of the Popular from the Restoration to the New Criticism* (Philadelphia: University of Pennsylvania Press, 2007).

Nussbaum, Felicity A. (ed.), *The Global Eighteenth Century* (Baltimore: Johns Hopkins University Press, 2003).

O'Brien, Conor Cruise, *The Great Melody: A Thematic Biography and Commented Anthology of Edmund Burke* (1992; London: Minerva, 1993).

O'Grady, Jane, Review of Susan Neiman's *Moral Clarity: A Guide for Grown-up Idealists*, *Guardian Review*, 25 July 2009.

O'Hagan, Andrew, *The Atlantic Ocean: Essays on Britain and America* (London: Faber and Faber, 2008).

O'Halloran, Clare, *Golden Ages and Barbarous Nations: Antiquarian Debate and Cultural Politics in Ireland, c. 1750–1800* (Cork: Cork University Press, 2004).

Ong, Walter J., *Orality and Literacy: The Technologizing of the Word* (London and New York: Routledge, 1982).

Orr, Jennifer, "1798, Before, and Beyond: Samuel Thomson and the Poetics of Ulster-Scots Identity," in Frank Ferguson and Andrew R. Holmes (eds), *Revising Robert Burns and Ulster: Literature, Religion and Politics, c.1770–1920* (Dublin: Four Courts, 2009).

O'Toole, Fintan, *A Traitor's Kiss: The Life of Richard Brinsley Sheridan* (1997; New York: Farrar, Strauss and Giroux, 1998).

Pace, Joel, "Towards a Taxonomy of Transatlantic Romanticism(s)," *Literature Compass*, 5/2 (2008): 228–91.

Pace, Joel, and Matthew Scott (eds), *Wordsworth in American Literary Culture* (New York: Palgrave Macmillan 2005).

Paglia, Camille, "Dispatches from the New Frontier: Writing for the Internet," in Lance Strate, Ronald L. Jacobson and Stephanie B. Gibson (eds), *Communication and Cyberspace: Social Interaction in an Electronic Environment* (Cresskill, NJ: Hampton, 1996).

Painter, Anna M., "American Editions of the Poems of Burns Before 1800," *The Library*, 4th series, 12 (1932): 434–56.

Pardo, Aristobulo, Review of *El Repertorio Americano*, *Thesaurus*, *BICC*, 30 (1975), 176–9.

Paton, Norman R., *Song O' Liberty: The Politics of Robert Burns* (Fareham: Sea-Green Ribbon, 1994).

Peers, Douglas, "Britain and Empire," in Chris Williams (ed.), *A Companion to Nineteenth-Century Britain* (Malden, MA: Blackwell, 2004).

Petrone, Penny (ed.), *First People, First Voices* (Toronto: University of Toronto Press, 1985).

Pittock, Murray, "Historiography," in Alexander Broadie (ed.), *The Cambridge Companion to the Scottish Enlightenment* (Cambridge: Cambridge University Press, 2003), 258–79.

———, (ed.), *Robert Burns in Global Culture* (Lewisburg, PA: Bucknell University Press, 2011).

———, *Scottish and Irish Romanticism* (Oxford: Oxford University Press, 2008).

Poster, Mark, *The Information Subject,* commentary by Stanley Aronowitz (London and New York: Routledge, 2001).

Pratt, Mary Louise, *Imperial Eyes: Travel Writing and Transculturation* (London and New York: Routledge, 1992).

Prunier, Clotilde, *Anti-Catholic Strategies in Eighteenth-Century Scotland* (Frankfurt: Peter Lang, 2004).

Ray, Celeste (ed.), *Transatlantic Scots* (Tuscaloosa: University of Alabama Press, 2005).

Reyes, Alfonso, *The Position of America, and Other Essays*, trans. Harriet de Onis (New York: Alfred A. Knopf, 1950).

Rheinhamer, Hans P., *Topo: The Story of a Scottish Colony near Caracas, 1825–27* (Edinburgh: Scottish Academic Press, 1988).

Richardson, Joseph, "Political Anglicanism in Ireland 1691–1801: From the Language of Liberty to the Language of Union," in Michael Brown, Patrick M. Geoghegan, and James Kelly (eds), *The Irish Act of Union, 1800: Bicentennial Essays* (Dublin: Irish Academic Press, 2003), 58–67.

Ricks, Christopher, *Allusion to the Poets* (New York: Oxford University Press, 2002).

Rigney, Ann, "Embodied Communities: Commemorating Robert Burns, 1859," *Representations*, 115/1 (2011): 71–101.

———, "Plenitude, Scarcity and the Circulation of Cultural Memory," *Journal of European Studies*, 35/1 (2005): 11–28.

Robert Burns: The Poet's Progress, Exhibition Catalogue (Philadelphia: Rosenbach Museum and Library, 1995).

Ross, John D., *Scottish Poets in America* (New York, 1889).

Roy, Ross G. (ed.), *Robert Burns and America: A Symposium* (Columbia, SC, and Kircaldy: University of South Carolina Press, 2001).

Rubio, Mary Henley, *Lucy Maud Montgomery: The Gift of Wings* (Toronto: Doubleday Canada, 2008).

Salcedo-Bastardo, José Lus, "Bello and The "Symposium" of Grafton Street," in John Lynch (ed.), *Andrés Bello: The London Years* (Richmond, Surrey: Richmond Publishing, 1982).

Sandburg, Carl, *Abraham Lincoln: The Prairie Years* (2 vols, New York: Harcourt Brace, 1926).

Saul, John Ralston, *Voltaire's Bastards: The Dictatorship of Reason in the West* (New York: Vintage, 1993).

Scharnhorst, Gary, "Whitman on Robert Burns: An Early Essay Recovered," *Walt Whitman Quarterly Review*, 13 (Spring 1996): 217–20.

Scobie, Stephen, "Double Voicing—a View of Canadian Poetry," in Jorn Carlson (ed.), *O Canada: Essays on Canadian Literature and Culture* (Aarhus, Denmark: University of Aarhus Press, 1995), 38–49.

"Serge Hovey: The Strongest Possible Roots," *Edinburgh Review*, 96 (Autumn 1996): 134–9.

Sharman, Julian, Introduction, *The Proverbs of John Heywood*, Julian Sharman (ed.) (London: George Bell and Sons, 1874).

Shaw, Matthew, *Great Scots! How the Scots Created Canada* (Winnipeg: Heartland Associates, 2003).

Sheps, Arthur, "The Edinburgh Reform Convention of 1793 and The American Revolution," *Scottish Tradition*, 5 (1975): 23–37.

Sher, Richard B., *The Enlightenment and the Book: Scottish Authors and Their Publishers in Eighteenth-Century Britain, Ireland and America* (Chicago and London: University of Chicago Press, 2006).

Simpson, Kenneth (ed.), *Burns Now* (Edinburgh: Canongate Academic, 1994).

———— (ed.), *Love and Liberty: Robert Burns, A Bicentenary Celebration* (Edinburgh: Tuckwell, 1997).

————, *The Protean Scot: The Crisis of Identity in Eighteenth Century Scottish Literature* (Aberdeen: Aberdeen University Press, 1988).

Skipper, David, "Jean Redpath Champions Burns and Traditional Scottish Music," *Burns Chronicle and Club Directory*, 99 (1990): 75–8.

Stafford, Fiona, "Scottish Poetry and Regional Literary Expression," in John Richetti (ed.), *The Cambridge History of English Literature, 1660–1780* (Cambridge: Cambridge University Press, 2005), 340–62.

————, *Starting Lines in Scottish, Irish, and English Poetry: From Burns to Heaney* (Oxford: Oxford University Press, 2000).

St Clair, William, *The Reading Nation in the Romantic Period* (Cambridge: Cambridge University Press, 2004).

Stevens, Harry Robert, "Folk Music on the Midwestern Frontier 1788–1825," *Ohio State Archaeological and Historical Quarterly*, 57 (April 1948): 126–46.

Stevens, Laura M., "Transatlanticism Now," *American Literary History*, 16/1 (Spring 2004): 93–102.

Stocker, Mark, "'The head o' the Bard sweeps the Southern Sky!' Sir John Steell's Statues of Robert Burns: From Dundee to Dunedin," *Journal of the Scottish Society for Art History*, 11 (2006): 18–25.

Strong-Boag, Veronica, "'A People Akin to Mine': Indians and Highlanders within the British Empire," *Native Studies Review*, 14/1 (2001): 27–53.

Sullivan, Rosemary, *Shadowmaker: The Life of Gwendolyn MacEwen* (Toronto: HarperCollins, 1995).

Szasz, Ferenc Morton, *Abraham Lincoln and Robert Burns: Connected Lives and Legends* (Carbondale: Southern Illinois University Press, 2008).

Taylor, James, *Robert Burns: Patriot and Internationalist* (Vancouver: Vancouver Burns Statue Fund, 1926).

Tennyson, Hallam, *Alfred Lord Tennyson: A Memoir by His Son* (2 vols, London: Macmillan, 1897).

Thomas, D.O., Introduction, *Richard Price: Political Writings*, D.O. Thomas (ed.) (Cambridge: Cambridge University Press, 1991).

Thorning, Joseph F., *Miranda: World Citizen* (Gainesville: University of Florida Press, 1952).

Thornton, Robert D., "Serge Hovey and the Others," *Studies in Scottish Literature*, 30 (1994): 277–85.

Thuente, Mary Helen, *The Harp Re-strung: The United Irishmen and the Rise of Irish Literary Nationalism* (New York: Syracuse University Press, 1994).

Todd, J.E., "The Apprenticeship of a Professor of History, 1903–1919," *History*, 44/151 (June 1959): 115–98.

Tremaine, Marie, *A Bibliography of Canadian Imprints 1751–1800* (1952; Toronto: University of Toronto Press, 1999).

Tyrrell, Alex, "Paternalism, Public Memory and National Identity in Early Victorian Scotland: The Robert Burns Festival at Ayr in 1844," *Historical Association*, 90/297 (2005): 42–61.

Usborne, Richard, *Plum Sauce*: *A P. G. Wodehouse Companion* (London: Ebury, 2002).

Vail, Jeffery, "Thomas Moore in Ireland and America: The Growth of a Poet's Mind," *Romanticism*, 10/1 (2004): 41–62.

Vance, Michael, "A Brief History of Organized Scottishness in Canada," in Celeste Ray (ed.), *Transatlantic Scots* (Tuscaloosa: University of Alabama Press, 2005).

Washington, Booker T., *Up from Slavery* (Oxford: Oxford University Press, 1965).

Waterston, Elizabeth, "The Lowland Tradition in Canadian Literature," in W. Stanford Reid (ed.), *The Scottish Tradition in Canada* (Toronto: McClelland and Stewart, 1976).

———, *Rapt in Plaid: Canadian Literature and the Scottish Tradition* (Toronto: University of Toronto Press, 2001).

Watkins, Larissa P. (ed.), *Burnsiana: A Bibliography of the William R. Smith Collection in the Library of the Supreme Council, 33°, S.J.* (New Castle, DE: Oak Knoll and the Library of the Supreme Council, 33°, S.J., 2008).

Weisbuch, Robert, *Atlantic Double-Cross: American Literature and British Influence in the Age of Emerson* (Chicago: University of Chicago Press, 1986).

Whatley, Christopher A., "Robert Burns, Memorialization, and the 'Heart-beatings' of Victorian Scotland," in Murray Pittock (ed.), *Robert Burns in Global Culture* (Lewisburg, PA: Bucknell University Press, 2011).

Wheeler, Michael, *The Old Enemies: Catholic and Protestant in Nineteenth-Century English Culture* (Cambridge: Cambridge University Press, 2006).

Whelan, Kevin, *Fellowship of Freedom: The United Irishmen and the 1798 Rebellion* (Cork: Cork University Press, 1998).

Whyte, Iain, *Scotland and the Abolition of Black Slavery, 1756–1838* (Edinburgh: Edinburgh University Press, 2006).

Wilmshurst, Rea, "L.M. Montgomery's Use of Quotations and Allusions in the 'Anne' Books," *Canadian Childrens' Literature*, 56 (1989): 15–45.

———, "Quotations and Allusions in L.M. Montgomery's Other Novels," ts. Toronto, November 1990.

Wilson, Rob, and Wimal Dissanayake, Introduction, *Global/Local: Cultural Production and the Transnational Imaginary*, Rob Wilson and Wimal Dissanayake (eds) (Durham: Duke University Press, 1996).

Woodham-Smith, Cecil, *The Great Hunger: Ireland 1845–1849* (1962; London: Penguin, 1991).

Wright, Julia M. *Ireland, India, and Nationalism in Nineteenth-Century Literature* (Cambridge: Cambridge University Press, 2007).

Zalloua, Zahi, "Foucault as Educator: The Question of Technology and Learning How to Read Differently," *Symploke*, 12/1–2 (2004): 232–47.
Zamoyski, Adam, *Holy Madness: Romantics, Patriots and Revolutionaries* (New York, 2000).

Electronic Sources

Am I not a Man and a Brother? An Exhibition to Commemorate the 200th Anniversary of the Abolition of the Slave Trade, The Bodleian Library of Commonwealth and African Studies at Rhodes House, University of Oxford, 23 April–4 May 2007, http://www.bodley.ox.ac.uk/dept/scwmss/projects/abolition/, accessed 25 March 2009.
Angelou, Maya, "Angelou on Burns," BBC TV Documentary, directed by Elly M. Taylor, 1996, accessed 15 June 2009.
Annan, Kofi, "The Brotherhood of Man," Inaugural Robert Burns Memorial Lecture, 13 January 2004, http://www.unis.unvienna.org/unis/pressrels/2004/sgsm9112.html, accessed 23 March 2009.
Baldick, Chris, "Episteme," *The Oxford Dictionary of Literary Terms* (Oxford: Oxford University Press, 2008), Oxford Reference Online, http://www.oxfordreference.com/, accessed 25 May 2009.
Banda de Gaitas del Batallón de San Patricio, http://www.bandadegaitas.com.mx/historiaEng.html, accessed 27 March 2009.
Cahill, J.B., "Brymer, Alexander," in *Dictionary of Canadian Biography Online* (http://www.biographi.ca/), accessed 9 February 2010.
Craig, Barbara L., "Clark, Daniel," *Dictionary of Canadian Biography Online*, http://www.biographi.ca/, accessed 25 October 2009.
Dalry Burns Club, http://www.dalryburnsclub.org.uk/founders/founders.html, accessed 8 May 2009.
Defoe, Daniel, *Defoe's "Review": An Interactive Version of one of the Earliest English Periodicals, 1704–1713*, http://www.defoereview.org/, accessed 22 October 2009.
Douglass, Frederick, "A Fugitive Slave Visiting the Birth-place of Robert Burns," *New York Weekly Tribune*, 18 July 1846, http://library.sc.edu/spcoll/douglass/fugitive.pdf, accessed 2 April 2010.
———, "Speech at a Burns Supper, January 1849," http://www.bulldozia.com/projects/index.php?id=256, accessed 12 June 2009.
"Educational Tour Landmarks," *Islands of Jokaydia Wiki*, http://jokaydia.wikispaces.com/Edusquarelandmarks, accessed 22 October 2009.
"Educational Uses of Second Life," *Jokaydia: Virtual Worlds Wiki*, http://wiki.jokaydia.com/page/Edu_SL, accessed 22 October 2009.
Edwards, Mary Jane, "Drummond, William Henry," in the *Dictionary of Canadian Biography Online*, http://www.biographi.ca/, accessed 1 May 2009.
English Short Title Catalogue, The British Library, http://estc.bl.uk/, accessed 9 February 2010.

Eva Cassidy: "Fields of Gold," http://www.evacassidy.org/eva/fog.htm, accessed 8 June 2009.

Flynn, Christopher, "Defoe's *Review*: Textual Editing and New Media," *Digital Defoe: Studies in Defoe and His Contemporaries*, 1.1 (2009), http://english. illinoisstate.edu/digitaldefoe/multimedia/review/defoe_final.html, accessed 17 June 2009.

"Gringo," *Wikipedia*, http://en.wikipedia.org/wiki/Gringo, accessed 25 March 2009.

Homecoming Scotland, http://www.homecomingscotland2009.com/default.html, accessed 9 February 2010.

Hovey, Esther, "Burns's Songs: An American Connection," Exhibition by G. Ross Roy, *2001 Robert Burns World Federation Annual Conference*, Atlanta, Georgia, 20–22 July, 2001, http://www.worldburnsclub.com/expert/burns_ songs_an_american_ connection.htm, accessed 15 June 2009.

———, email to Kirsteen McCue, 3 June 2009.

Hovey, Serge, "Arnold Schoenberg filmed by Serge Hovey," 12 August 2008, *YouTube,* http://www.youtube.com/watch?v=v7QbWP1rpIg, accessed 15 June 2009.

"Literature, Composition, and Creative Writing," *Jokaydia Virtual Worlds Wiki*, http://wiki.jokaydia.com/page/LiteratureCompositionCreative_Writing, accessed 22 October 2009.

Lovink, Geert, "'I work here, but I am cool': Interview with Alan Liu," *Nettime-l list*, 23 February 2006, http://www.nettime.org/Lists-Archives/nettime-l-0602/ msg00075.html, accessed 22 October 2009; see also http://networkcultures. org/wpmu/geert/interview-with-alan-liu/, accessed 22 October, 2009.

Lustig, A. J., "Cabinets and Collections," in J. L. Heilbron (ed.), *The Oxford Companion to the History of Modern Science* (Oxford: Oxford University Press, 2003), Oxford Reference Online, http://www.oxfordreference.com/, accessed 25 May 2009.

Marquand, David, "MacDonald, (James) Ramsay (1866–1937)," *Oxford Dictionary of National Biography Online* (Oxford: Oxford University Press, 2004), http://www.oxforddnb.com/, accessed 25 October 2009.

McClelland, Lionel, "ode to a haggis-robert burns for traditional burns supper," 13 December 2007, *YouTube*, http://www.youtube.com/watch?v=3kzYaIphbzU, accessed 27 February 2010.

McGhee, Laura, "Rabbie Beatles Laura McGhee @ Knitting Factory New York 07," 21 May 2007, *YouTube*, http://www.youtube.com/watch?v=_bJVD-3iUZU, accessed 27 February 2010.

McSmith, Andy, "Robert Burns: Socialist Hero or Just a Scottish Social Climber?" *The Independent UK*, 24 January 2008, http://www.independent.co.uk/ news/uk/this-britain/robert-burns-socialist-hero-or-just-a-scottish-social-climber-773594.html, accessed 13 May 2010.

Newman, Lance, Introduction, *Sullen Fires Across the Atlantic: Essays in Transatlantic Romanticism*, special edition of the *Romantic Circles' Praxis*

Series (November 2006), http://www.rc.umd.edu/praxis/sullenfires/intro/intro. html, accessed 1 January 2010.

"The Obituary Record," *The New York Times,* 14 May 1894, *New York Times* Article Archive: 1851–1980, http://www.nytimes.com/ref/membercenter/ nytarchive.html, *accessed* 8 May 2009.

Proud to Live in America, http://www.proudtoliveinamerica.com/, accessed 27 March 2009.

"The Queen's Own Rifles of Canada: A Brief History," *The Rifleman Online—The QOR of C*, http://www.qor.com/history/history.html, accessed 1 May 2009.

Redpath, Jean, email to Kirsteen McCue, 3 April 2009.

Redpath, Jean, and Serge Hovey, vol. 3 and 4 of "The Songs of Robert Burns," Greentrax (cdtrax 115), 1996.

Richthammer, John, "Ralph Connor/The Rev. Dr. Charles W. Gordon: The Role of Archives in the Memorialization of a Canadian Literary and Theological Giant," *Miscellanea Manitobiana* 4 (Winnipeg: University of Winnipeg Press, 2004), online edn, 1 January 2005, http://cybrary.uwinnipeg.ca/people/dobson/ manitobiana/isses/004.cfm, accessed 29 April 2009.

Robert Burns, BBC Scotland, http://www.bbc.co.uk/robertburns/, accessed 22 October 2009.

Robert Burns 1759–1796: A Bicentenary Exhibition from the G. Ross Roy Collection, originally exhibited March–May 1996, curated by G. Ross Roy, with assistance from Jamie S. Hansen, hypertext development by Jason A. Pierce, http://www.sc.edu/library/spcoll/britlit/burns/burns.html, accessed 22 October 2009.

Robert Burns 1759–1796, National Library of Scotland, http://www.nls.uk/burns/, accessed 22 October 2009.

Robert Burns: Inventing Tradition and Securing Memory, 1796–1909, http:// projects.beyondtext.ac.uk/sg-murray-pittock/index.php, accessed 15 April 2011.

Robert Burns' Letters: The Letters of Burns on the Days they were Written, http:// burnsletters.wordpress.com/about/, accessed 22 October 2009.

Scottish Book Trade Index, National Library of Scotland, www.nls.uk/catalogues/ resources/sbti/, accessed 9 February 2010.

Second Life, Linden Lab, http://secondlife.com/?v=1.1, accessed 22 October 2009.

Siempre Scout Cancionero, http://www.siemprescout.org/pdf/cancionero.pdf, accessed 27 March 2009.

Smith, William Wye, *The Poems of William Wye Smith* (Toronto: Dudley and Burns, 1888), http://www.archive.org/details/wyesmithpoems00smitrich, accessed 8 May 2009.

"The Song of the Emigrant," *The Word on the Street,* Broadsides at the National Library of Scotland, http://www.nls.uk/broadsides/broadside.cfm/id/14940/, accessed 8 May 2009.

St Andrews Society of Mexico, http://standrewsmexico.synthasite.com/, accessed 25 March 2009.

Sumner, Gordon (Sting), "Fields of Gold," http://www.elyrics.net/read/s/sting-lyrics/fields-of-gold-lyrics.html, accessed 8 June 2009.

Thompson, Kevin, *About Robert Burns*, http://www.aboutrobertburns.co.uk/, accessed 5 March 2009.

The Tree of Liberty—A Tribute to Serge Hovey, Everallin Films (with the assistance of The Scottish Film Production Fund and in association with Channel 4), directed by Timothy Neat, 1987.

Virtual Hallucinations (University of California, Davis), http://slurl.com/secondlife/Sedig/27/44/22/?img=http%, accessed 22 October 2009.

Voss, Christoph, "James Inglis Reid, Ltd. Fonds," *City of Vancouver Archives Newsletter*, 3 (October 2006): 1–2, http://vancouver.ca/ctyclerk/archives/about/NewsNo3.pdf, accessed 25 October 2009.

"The Word on the Street," National Library of Scotland, http://www.nls.uk/broadsides/broadside.cfm/id/14940, accessed 8 May, 2009.

The World Famous Burns Supper, http://www.burnssupper2009.com/this-year/default.aspx, accessed 9 February 2010.

Index

For Product Safety Concerns and Information please contact our EU
representative GPSR@taylorandfrancis.com
Taylor & Francis Verlag GmbH, Kaufingerstraße 24, 80331 München, Germany

www.ingramcontent.com/pod-product-compliance
Ingram Content Group UK Ltd.
Pitfield, Milton Keynes, MK11 3LW, UK
UKHW021621240425
457818UK00018B/667